*Oracle Press*™

PeopleSoft People Tools: Mobile Applications Development

About the Authors

Jim J. Marion is an AICPA certified information technology professional who currently works as a principal sales consultant at Oracle. He is the author of the Oracle Press book *PeopleSoft PeopleTools Tips & Techniques* and co-author of *PeopleSoft PeopleTools Data Management and Upgrade Handbook*. Jim is an international presenter of PeopleTools development topics at conferences such as Oracle OpenWorld, UKOUG events, HEUG's Alliance, Quest's IOUG, and OAUG's Collaborate.

Sarah K. Marion is an English major with more than 20 years of experience working in education and 12+ years of professional experience in technology and publishing. She has a background in curriculum development and public speaking. Sarah received the Outstanding Graduate Award, graduating as a member of the honor society. She previously acted as the Developmental Editor for *Peoplesoft PeopleTools Data Management and Upgrade Handbook*. Sarah is a writer, wife, and mother of four.

About the Technical Editors

Dave Bain joined PeopleSoft as a developer in the spring of 1996. After spending 4 years in a research group, Dave became a development manager in the PeopleTools organization that is responsible for App Designer, AppClass PeopleCode, AppEngine, and other core technologies. Dave transitioned into a role of Product Manager where he worked on defining requirements for PeopleTools releases. After PeopleSoft was acquired by Oracle, Dave spent a year working on Fusion Applications, assisting the application teams with adoption of Fusion Technology. Dave transitioned back to PeopleTools product management where he covers Integration Technology, Mobile Technology, and Lifecycle Management. Dave is a regular at major PeopleSoft conferences and can be contacted at david.bain@oracle.com.

Hakan Biroglu is a PeopleTools 8 Application Developer Certified Expert, Oracle WebCenter Content 11*g* Certified Implementation Specialist, Oracle SOA Suite 11*g* Certified Implementation Specialist, and Oracle Application Development Framework 11*g* Certified Implementation Specialist. He has over 15 years of experience as a software architect on Oracle Applications, working on all technical areas of PeopleSoft, E-Business Suite, and Fusion Applications. In 2013, Hakan was named Oracle ACE for Oracle Applications Technology. He is a frequent speaker at regional and international conferences, regularly publishes articles on his blog, and is an active member of the OTN forum. Hakan lives in the Netherlands with his wife Öznur and their three children Murat, Lara, and Elisa.

 Oracle Press™

PeopleSoft People Tools: Mobile Applications Development

Jim J. Marion
Sarah K. Marion

New York   Chicago   San Francisco
Athens   London   Madrid   Mexico City
Milan   New Delhi   Singapore   Sydney   Toronto

Cataloging-in-Publication Data is on file with the Library of Congress

McGraw-Hill Education books are available at special quantity discounts to use as premiums and sales promotions, or for use in corporate training programs. To contact a representative, please visit the Contact Us pages at www.mhprofessional.com.

PeopleSoft People Tools: Mobile Applications Development

1234567890   DOC/DOC   1098765

ISBN   978-0-07-183652-4
MHID   0-07-183652-7

Sponsoring Editor	**Technical Editors**	**Production Supervisor**
Wendy Rinaldi	David Bain, Hakan Biroglu	Pamela Pelton
Editorial Supervisor	**Copy Editor**	**Composition**
Donna Martone	Cenveo Publisher Services	Cenveo Publisher Services
Project Manager	**Proofreader**	**Illustration**
Namita Gahtori,	Cenveo Publisher Services	Cenveo Publisher Services
Cenveo® Publisher Services	**Indexer**	**Art Director, Cover**
Acquisitions Coordinator	Jack Lewis	Jeff Weeks
Amanda Russell		

In loving memory of Kathleen Rae Corrick Hendrickson.
"Many women do noble things, but you surpass them all."
Proverbs 31:29

In loving memory of Kathleen Rae Corrick Hendrickson.
"Many women do noble things, but you surpass them all."
Proverbs 31:29

Contents at a Glance

Contents

PART I
PeopleSoft Mobile Tools

PART II
Building Mobile Applications with HTML5

Contents

PART I
PeopleSoft Mobile Tools

PART II
Building Mobile Applications with HTML5

PART III
Constructing Native Applications

Acknowledgments

Thank you to our children for allowing us to write a third book. Chris Couture, thank you for the great ideas and inspiration, Graham Smith (and Jeffrey) for the encouragement and words of wisdom, Keith Collins for the Mobile Application Platform lessons.

Dave Bain and Hakan Biroglu spent months of their lives reading, testing, fixing, and debugging the code samples included with this book. Donna and Öznur, thank you so much for allowing your husbands to help us write this book.

Thank you to Karl Eberhardt, Michael Boucher, and Michael Rosser for approving this book and supporting us while writing this text. Paco Aubrejuan, Binu Mathew, and Willie Suh for approving the content and providing access to your knowledgeable staff.

To Mike and Rose, for your loving support of our literary endeavors; Marshall and Peggy for encouraging us to keep writing; and Donnie, Wally, and Jan for your constant love. Thanks to CAB and MJB. Jody, for keeping us grounded. Thank you to Pastor Mike and Shelly and Pastor Joe and Yadi for praying for us. Rich and Jill, Taylor and Anne for your interest in our writing. WEGM and the LPM staff for cheering us on.

Thanks to McGraw-Hill, Paul Carlstroem, Amanda Russell, Wendy Rinaldi, Bettina Faltermeier, and Namita Gahtori.

Thanks to all the PeopleSoft customers, consultants, and technical presales consultants who visit my blog, ask me questions at user groups, and communicate with me on a daily basis.

Most importantly, thank you to our personal Lord and Savior, Jesus Christ, without whom none of this would be possible. You are our peace during the storms of life.

Introduction

Once upon a time, in a not too distant past, knowledge workers entered information into large stationary computers connected to even larger super computers. As time passed, computing power increased while physical size of computers decreased. Computers are now so small they fit inside your shirt pocket, or even in your eyewear. If you are holding this book, then chances are pretty high that you carry an Internet-connected computer in your pocket. In fact, you may even be reading this introduction on a smartphone (if you are, I hope you have an excellent vision health plan).

We live in an always-on, connected world and we expect our enterprise systems to be a part of our connected ecosystem. If your organization has implemented PeopleSoft 9.2 applications along with PeopleTools 8.54, then you already have mobile-ready transactions just waiting for a smartphone or tablet connection. On the other hand, if your company hasn't upgraded and you need to make the most of what you already have, then you may be investigating ways to mobile-enable your PeopleSoft applications. Whether your organization uses the latest PeopleTools toolset or struggles to maintain a much older 8.4x release, this book will help you free your PeopleSoft Enterprise system from the confines of a desk, making important features available to your mobile workforce.

What's Inside

The content of this book is divided into three parts:

- PeopleSoft Mobile Tools

- Building Mobile Applications with HTML5

- Constructing Native Applications

PeopleTools Mobile Tools

PeopleTools 8.54 represents a dramatic shift in the PeopleSoft user experience. Prior to 8.54, Oracle focused on delivering a world-class desktop environment. With PeopleTools 8.54, the PeopleSoft user experience strategy shifted to mobile-first, which means, "First develop for mobile, and then progressively enhance pages as the form-factor and device capabilities increase." To deliver this mobile-first user experience, PeopleTools added two very important development features:

- Fluid pages

- Mobile Application Platform

In Chapter 1, you will learn how to configure your desktop development for maximum mobile development productivity. Chapter 2 will teach you how to build responsive and adaptive mobile-first PeopleSoft transaction pages using PeopleTools new fluid page definitions. Chapter 3 finishes up this first section of the book by showing you how to use a PeopleTools online mobile application designer called Mobile Application Framework.

Building Mobile Applications with HTML5

HTML5 is the latest iteration of the HTML specification. This new specification contains a significant number of features designed to improve the mobile user experience. In this section of the book, you will learn how to build HTML5 applications using standard web development tools such as NetBeans, git, and npm. You will combine well-known development libraries, such as jQuery Mobile (Chapter 5) and AngularJS (Chapter 6), with PeopleTools integration technologies, such as iScripts (Chapter 7) and REST services (Chapter 8). This section of the book is very critical because it introduces PeopleTools developers to common web development practices. Chapters 5 and 6 stand in contrast to each other in that Chapter 5 attempts to show the simplest way to build mobile applications: let the library do the work. Chapter 6 demonstrates flexibility and control through the libraries AngularJS, Topcoat, and FontAwesome. The point of these two chapters is to show that development can be as simple or as complex as you desire. Chapters 7 and 8 complete this section by demonstrating two different data-delivery mechanisms: iScripts (Chapter 7) and REST (Chapter 8). If you are using PeopleTools 8.51 or an earlier version of PeopleTools, which doesn't support REST, then you will find Chapter 7 valuable because it offers an alternative to REST.

Constructing Native Applications

The first two segments of this book describe methods for mobile-enabling the PeopleSoft web application. The third part, Constructing Native Applications, shows you how to build native applications. In Chapter 9, you will learn how to build a native Android application using the Android SDK and PeopleSoft REST services. Chapter 10 will show you how to convert the AngularJS application from Chapter 6 into a hybrid on-device application that can access native device features. The final chapter, Chapter 11, demonstrates how to build Oracle Mobile Application Framework hybrid applications using JDeveloper and PeopleTools REST services.

PeopleTools Versions and Naming Conventions

The examples in this book were built using PeopleTools 8.54.05, the latest version available. All examples were compiled and tested against a PeopleSoft HCM 9.2 Update Manager image. The examples in this book reference employee tables that exist in PeopleSoft HCM.

Each custom object described in this book is prefixed with the letters BMA to help you distinguish your organization's custom objects from the custom objects in this book (unless, of course, your organization also uses the prefix BMA). This prefix is an abbreviation for *Building Mobile Applications*.

PART
I

PeopleSoft Mobile Tools

PART
I

PeopleSoft Mobile Tools

CHAPTER
1

Configuring your
Development Workstation

I n Part I of this book, you will learn how to build mobile solutions using the PeopleTools development framework. You will use Application Designer and online configuration pages to construct and configure web-based applications. No other tools are required except what you installed when you implemented PeopleTools. There are, however, a few client-side development tools that help you build better solutions quicker. In this chapter, you will learn how to install and configure these development tools. Before installing new software, let's review the various types of mobile applications.

Mobile Application Types

In this book, we will discuss three different types of mobile applications:

■ HTML5 web applications

■ Native applications

■ Hybrid applications

When running one of these applications on a mobile device, it may be quite difficult to distinguish between the various types. From a development perspective, however, the application type can have a significant impact on deployment, maintenance, and functionality.

HTML5 Web Applications

HTML5 is very closely aligned with mobile. Support for LocalStorage, offline applications, and responsive layouts fit well with the ever-changing, sometimes-disconnected nature of mobile devices.

The three key differences between HTML5 applications and the other two types of mobile applications are

■ Delivery mechanism

■ Device feature accessibility

■ Portability

In simplest terms, HTML5 applications are just plain web pages accessed through a web browser. These applications are deployed and "installed" through a device's web browser, not an app store. They do not have locally installed binary files. I use the term "installed" loosely because the installation of an HTML5 application involves creating an icon that either points to a local web cache or a remote web site.

One of the primary limitations of HTML5 applications is feature accessibility. It would not be wise to allow all web pages access to your camera, contacts, installed application data, etc. Applications that require access to these device capabilities must ask for your permission. With that said, we are seeing an interesting shift in device accessibility: newer devices are making more of these features accessible to HTML5 applications in a secure manner.

A primary motivation for building HTML5 applications is portability. Through web standards and browser support, HTML5 makes it possible to write an application using a single technology and deploy it to a variety of different mobile operating systems.

Native Applications

Native applications are built using a device-specific toolkit and are written using vendor-specific languages. A developer targeting multiple devices would need to maintain multiple code lines, one for each operating system. These applications are usually delivered through a tightly controlled app store. A key reason for choosing native applications over HTML5 is to gain access to device capabilities that are not available to HTML5 applications.

Case Study: Facebook and HTML5

Several news stories of 2012 quote Mark Zuckerberg as saying, "I think the biggest mistake we made as a company is betting too much on HTML5 as opposed to native." That is a pretty strong statement. Why would Mark say this? Here is the story: In an attempt to streamline development, Facebook merged its iOS and Android applications into a single HTML5 app distributed in a hybrid model. Plagued with performance problems, however, Facebook abandoned HTML5 in favor of native applications. What went wrong? Is HTML5 really slow compared to native applications? There are lots of rumors as to why Facebook experienced poor performance with HTML5. Some point to a flawed architecture and design, due to which, perhaps significant amounts of extraneous data in page updates caused performance problems. Others state the poor performance of JavaScript on mobile hardware. For every blog stating that HTML5 is slow, you can find another saying it is just as fast as native. It is hard to say who is correct. One thing is certain—a well-performing HTML5 app requires good engineering.

It is hard to say which technology will ultimately win the performance war. As you begin your mobile development project, be sure to evaluate your deployment options: HTML5, native, or hybrid. Performance is just one metric. Consider all of the benefits of each and choose the model that is right for your organization.

Hybrid Applications

Hybrid applications are standard HTML5 web applications that run in a native container. They are often distributed through a web store in a manner similar to native applications. Hybrid applications share the pros and cons of each of the other two types of applications. Similar to HTML5 applications, hybrid applications share a common code base across multiple operating systems. Since these applications are web applications, they also share the real time, always current nature of HTML5 applications. Through their native containers, hybrid applications gain trusted access to device capabilities in a manner similar to native mobile applications. PhoneGap, a popular hybrid container, makes device capabilities accessible through a plugin architecture exposed through a JavaScript Application Programming Interface (API).

 NOTE
We will cover PhoneGap (and Apache Cordova)
in Part III of this book.

HTML5 Defined

PeopleSoft Fluid and Mobile Application Platform (MAP) applications are considered HTML5 applications. What is HTML5? Simply put, HTML5 is the fifth revision of the HTML specification. It includes a few new semantic elements: header, nav, section, article, but the real magic of HTML5 is in its API and related specifications. These APIs include support for multimedia, SVG, Canvas, web storage, offline web applications, drag-and-drop, and many others. When a person or organization identifies a web application as an HTML5 application, they often also

Adobe Flash

Through the Internet's history, we have seen many attempts at a rich user experience. Until Apple's announcement that it would not support Flash, Adobe Flash player was the Internet's favorite rich user experience. While certainly offering a compelling user interface, Flash left developers wanting. They desired something that was closer to a pure internet that wasn't dependent on vendor-specific plugins. Hardware vendors expressed concern as well. Apple went as far as banning flash from iOS devices. Steve Jobs had very unkind words to say about Adobe Flash player.

What makes HTML5 so attractive? It delivers a rich, hardware-accelerated user experience without performance problems. HTML5 includes many of the features that users love about Flash, but without vendor-specific plugins.

include the following related specifications: CSS3, geolocation, Web Workers, Web Sockets, WebGL, etc. Here is the definition we will use: If you can find an article about it on the HTML5 Rocks website (http://www.html5rocks.com/), we will call it HTML5.

Development Tools

Through the remainder of this chapter you will learn how to install various development tools that help you build mobile applications.

Browsers

To effectively test HTML5 applications, access to a browser that supports HTML5 is critical. All modern browsers support HTML5: Chrome, Firefox, Internet Explorer 10, Safari, and Opera. You can view your favorite browser's scorecard at http://html5test .com/ or see scores for all modern desktop browsers at http://html5test.com/results/ desktop.html.

If we are building *mobile* web applications, why do we care about a *desktop* browser? Modern desktop browsers include a lot of developer tools and extensions that are not available on mobile devices. Testing and debugging mobile web applications is easier on a desktop browser.

WebKit

WebKit is the rendering engine used by a significant number of modern web browsers, including Android, Amazon's Kindle e-reader, Safari, iOS, BlackBerry 10, and many other lesser-known web browsers. Until recently, even the Google Chrome web browser used WebKit. So what is WebKit exactly? It is an open-source web parsing and layout engine, NOT a web browser. WebKit determines where to place elements and the WebKit "port," or browser, draws those elements. Since most mobile devices share this same rendering and layout engine, Cascading Style Sheet (CSS) and Document Object Model (DOM) support are similar across mobile devices. As web developers, we don't need to concern ourselves with the intricacies of WebKit. Nevertheless, knowing about WebKit is important.

You can learn more about WebKit from these online resources:

- http://www.webkit.org/
- http://en.wikipedia.org/wiki/WebKit
- http://www.paulirish.com/2013/webkit-for-developers/

If your organization maintains tight control over your desktop browser and you discover that your organization's standard browser does not support HTML5, all is not lost. Take heart. You have the following options:

- Lobby for special treatment so you can use a modern browser.

- Use a mobile emulator with its modern browser.

- Use a modern browser in VirtualBox.

Using a mobile emulator will give you a modern browser, but will not include the robust developer tools found in desktop browsers. Using VirtualBox, however, you can easily spin up a virtualized desktop using Windows or Linux that contains the latest Chrome, Firefox, or Internet Explorer browser. I am a big fan of virtualization. I am actually writing this book in a VirtualBox VM. I am a hardcore Linux user (Oracle Enterprise Linux, of course), but I am required to use Microsoft Word for my manuscripts. To cooperate with the publication process, I spin up a Windows 7 VM with Microsoft Word and type away.

Virtual Development Environment

Many organizations only allow Windows desktops with Internet Explorer 8. Some still use Windows XP with Internet Explorer 6 or 7. These browsers are far too old to support HTML5 development. If you find yourself in this situation, you may be able to build a virtualized development environment. If you have experience with Linux, or are willing to learn, you can build your development environment without paying for software licenses. To get started, download and install Oracle VirtualBox desktop virtualization software from http://www.virtualbox.org/. Do NOT download the Extension Pack unless you satisfy the licensing requirements. Next, create a Virtual Machine (VM). You can find many written and video tutorials online for creating VMs. I recommend starting with Chapter 1 of the VirtualBox manual: https://www .virtualbox.org/manual/ch01.html. Alternatively, you can download prebuilt VMs from various providers, such as http://virtualboxes.org/. If you choose to download a prebuilt VM, I recommend choosing one of the light-weight Ubuntu derivatives such as Xubuntu or Lubuntu. These distributions require less memory and hard disk than other distributions.

Once you have a working VM, download browsers and test, test, test.

Text Editors

HTML5 applications consist of plain text files. This means your computer already has all of the software you need to construct HTML5 applications. If your operating system is Windows, you have Notepad. If you are using Linux, your operating system has gedit, kate, vim, vi, emacs, and many other text editors. Let's create a quick HTML5 web page to get a feel for constructing HTML5 apps with a plain text editor. Type the following into a text editor, save, and then load it into your favorite HTML5 browser.

```
<!DOCTYPE html>
<html>
    <head>
        <script>
            window.addEventListener("load", function() {
                    var canvas = document.getElementById("greeting"),
                        context = canvas.getContext("2d"),
                        x = 20,
                        y = 20;

                    context.fillText("Hello World!", x, y);
            }, false);
        </script>
    </head>
    <body>
        <canvas id="greeting" width="100" height="20"></canvas>
    </body>
</html>
```

After loading this into your web browser, you should see something similar to Figure 1-1.

When it comes to text editors, Linux users definitely have an advantage over Windows users because all of the common Linux text editors support syntax highlighting. Unfortunately, Windows Notepad users are left wanting. If you find

FIGURE 1-1. *Screenshot of "Hello World!" HTML5 canvas page*

yourself in this category, then you may want to try out some of the advanced syntax highlighting text editors available for Windows. Here is a list of some common text editors:

- Notepad++
- jEdit
- vim
- Sublime
- UltraEdit
- TextPad
- EditPlus

Notepad++ is probably the most popular free text editor among PeopleSoft developers. jEdit is my personal favorite free text editor because of its flexible plugin architecture. But for those willing to pay for a good text editor, Sublime wins hands down.

NOTE
You can download SQR and PeopleCode syntax files for Notepad++ from http://greyheller.com/Blog/ editing-enhancements-for-sqr-and-peoplecode.

Debuggers and Browser Tools

As we saw in our "Hello World!" HTML5 example, the code we write represents instructions that the browser will interpret. I find it quite convenient to see how the browser will interpret my instructions in real time. Here are some tools I use for online prototyping and debugging:

- Built-in browser tools
- Firebug
- Fiddler
- Weinre

Browser Tools

Internet Explorer, Safari, Chrome, and Firefox all contain developer tools that let you inspect, debug, and execute scripts against the currently loaded page. In Chrome, IE, and Firefox, you display the developer tools by pressing the F12 key on your keyboard. Safari is a little different. If you are using Safari, I suggest reviewing the following articles to see how to turn on developer tools:

- http://macs.about.com/od/usingyourmac/qt/safaridevelop.htm

- http://www.jonhartmann.com/index.cfm/2011/4/28/Enabling-Safari-Developer-Tools

Figure 1-2 is a screenshot of our "Hello World!" HTML5 page in Chrome developer tools.

Firebug

With Chrome and Safari's Elements, Network, Sources, Timeline, Profiles, Resources, Audits, and Console tabs, you can learn just about anything about the page you are

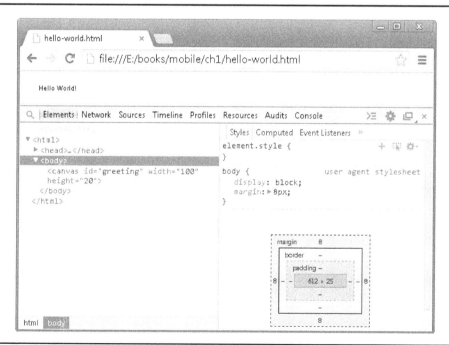

FIGURE 1-2. *Chrome developer tools*

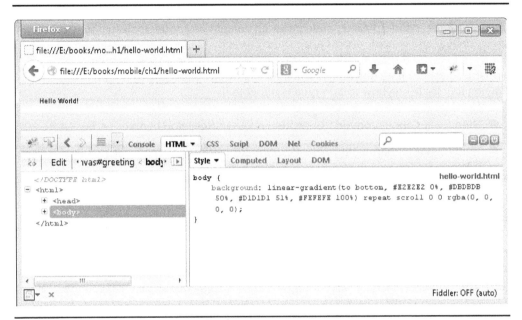

FIGURE 1-3. *CSS prototyping in Firebug*

viewing. But when it comes to prototyping and stepping through JavaScript, I prefer a Firefox plugin named Firebug. Firebug allows me to easily test JavaScript fragments and prototype CSS changes. Figure 1-3 is a screenshot of me prototyping some CSS in Firebug.

Fiddler

Fiddler is a network debugging proxy. It allows its user to eavesdrop on the back-end communication happening between the browser and an HTTP(S) server. This is extremely valuable when debugging Ajax requests and HTTP redirects. You can download Fiddler from http://www.telerik.com/fiddler. Figure 1-4 is a screenshot of Fiddler.

Weinre

Weinre is a remote web inspector. It gives you tools similar to Firebug or WebKit (Chrome and Safari), but for remote browsers. This is especially convenient when debugging applications running on mobile devices. When this book was written, you could find information about Weinre at http://people.apache.org/~pmuellr/weinre/docs/latest/.

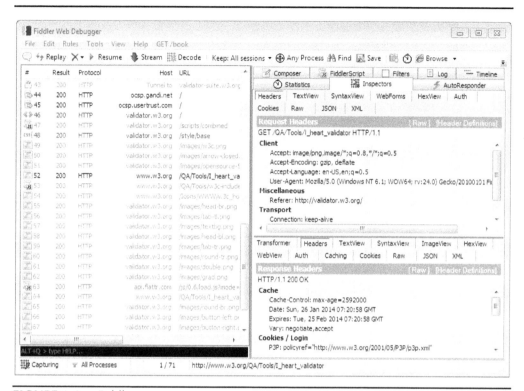

FIGURE 1-4.   *Fiddler*

Weinre runs through Node.js. To use it, first visit http://nodejs.org/download/ and install the Node.js binaries appropriate for your operating system. After installing node, open a command prompt and type the following command:

```
sudo npm -g install weinre
```

After installation, start the Weinre server by executing the command `weinre` at the command prompt. View the Weinre graphical user interface through Google Chrome web browser by navigating to http://localhost:8080/. A Weinre page should appear with instructions and links to demos. From the Weinre page, open the debug client user interface link in a new tab. You will find the URL for the debug client under the Access Points heading. The URL should point to something like http://localhost:8080/client/#anonymous. Next, launch one of the target demos in a new tab. The demo should connect to the debug client allowing you to inspect elements, view resources, see downloaded files, and type commands into the console. To test the console, type `window.location` and press ENTER. After a brief moment, you

FIGURE 1-5. *Weinre web inspector*

will see an object appear in the Web Inspector Console output. Figure 1-5 is a screenshot of the Weinre web inspector.

Integrated Development Environments

When making minor changes to files or prototyping something new, I like the lightweight, unstructured benefits of a syntax highlighting text editor. But when building applications, I prefer the robust features of an Integrated Development Environment (IDE). My two favorite web development IDEs are Eclipse and NetBeans. Personally, I find that Eclipse offers a prettier user experience, whereas NetBeans offers tighter HTML5 integration. Even though I can configure Eclipse to accomplish many of the tasks I require, such as JSLint integration, NetBeans 7.4 offers these features right out of the box. The examples in this book are based on NetBeans 7.4.

NetBeans IDE 7.4 Download

7.3.1   7.4   8.0 Beta   Development   Archive

Email address (optional): [_____]

Subscribe to newsletters: ☑ Monthly ☐ Weekly
☑ NetBeans can contact me at this address

IDE Language: [English ▼]   Platform: [Windows ▼]

Note: Greyed out technologies are not supported for this platform.

NetBeans IDE Download Bundles

Supported technologies ▲	Java SE	Java EE	C/C++	HTML5 & PHP	All
NetBeans Platform SDK	•	•			•
Java SE	•	•			•
Java FX	•	•			•
Java EE		•			•
Java ME					•
HTML5		•		•	•
Java Card™ 3 Connected					•
C/C++			•		•
Groovy					•
PHP				•	•
Bundled servers					
GlassFish Server Open Source Edition 4.0		•			•
Apache Tomcat 7.0.41		•			•
	Download	Download	Download	Download	Download
	Free, 84 MB	Free, 185 MB	Free, 59 MB	Free, 60 MB	Free, 204 MB

FIGURE 1-6.   *NetBeans download options*

To download NetBeans navigate to http://www.netbeans.org/downloads/ and select the HTML5 & PHP Download. This is the smallest download and will give you just what you need to build HTML5 applications. Figure 1-6 is a screenshot of the NetBeans download options.

NOTE
The NetBeans installer will check your system for the latest version of the Java JDK. If not found, it will take you to the download site, so you can download and install it.

NetBeans Test Application

Let's create an HTML5 application in NetBeans just to confirm that our IDE is properly installed. Launch NetBeans from your operating system's applications menu or from your new desktop icon. When NetBeans appears, select File | New Project. Figure 1-7 is a screenshot of the New Project dialog.

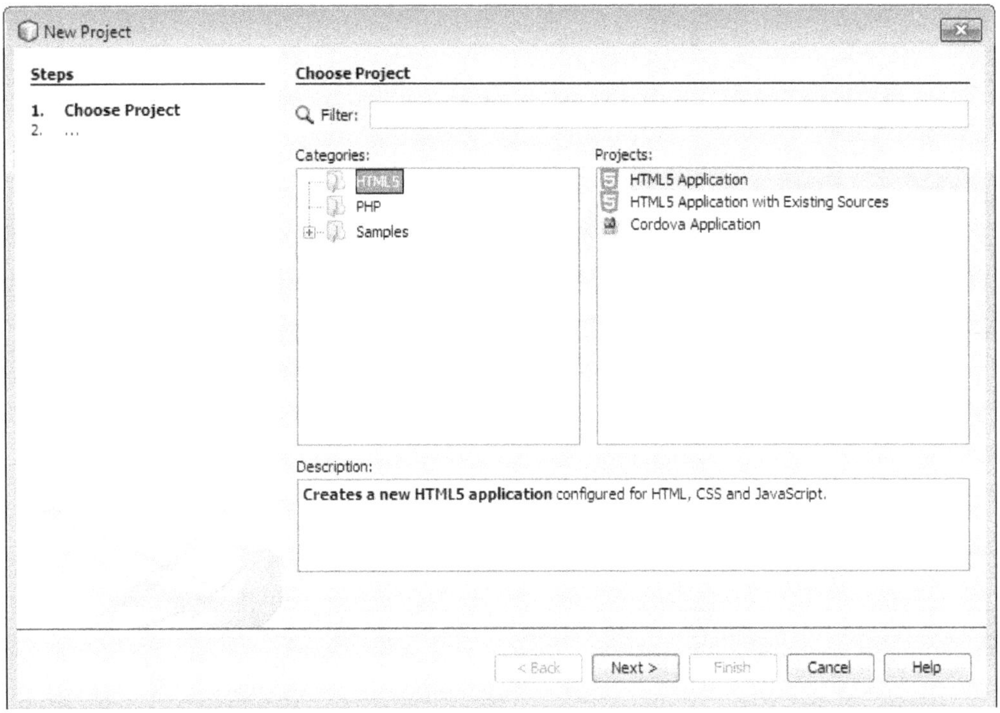

FIGURE 1-7. *NetBeans New Project dialog*

From the Categories list, select HTML5, and then from the Projects list, select HTML5 Application. Name your project ch01_nbtest. Take note of the project location and project folder. We will use these later to create web server mappings. My project folder is C:\Users\jmarion\Documents\NetBeansProjects\ch01_nbtest. Figure 1-8 is a screenshot of the new project's file system properties.

NetBeans has built-in support for several HTML5 templating systems and gives you the option to select one from a list. When you choose a site template, your projects files, libraries, and structure are determined by the template. Templates usually give you an HTML structure, CSS formatting, and responsive layout.

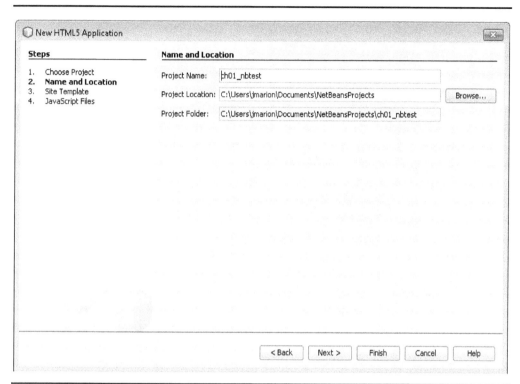

FIGURE 1-8. *NetBeans project file system properties*

You don't have to select one, but templating systems are rather convenient. Templates provide a lot of user experience features, allowing the developer to focus on structure and content. For this test application, choose the Download Online Template option and select the Twitter Bootstrap template. Figure 1-9 is a screenshot of NetBeans template options.

Step 4 of the New Project dialog allows you to select from a predefined list of JavaScript libraries. We aren't actually going to use any of these libraries in the project, but feel free to scroll through the list and look for your favorite JavaScript libraries. Notice that you can select different versions of each library from the

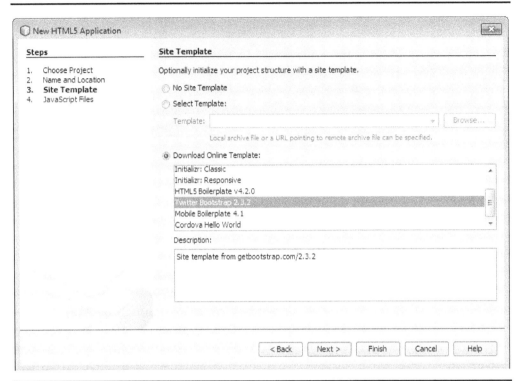

FIGURE 1-9. *NetBeans template options*

Versions column. Click the Finish button to create the new project. Your project should look similar to the project in Figure 1-10.

NOTE
You may see an "Updated: Never" link just below the list of libraries. If that is the case, I recommend you click the link to update your list of libraries.

You can view the prebuilt index.html page in a web browser by right-clicking the source file in the project browser or right-clicking the text in the editor window and selecting Run File from the context menu. If you have Google Chrome installed, NetBeans will open the index.html file in Chrome using the NetBeans connector. The NetBeans connector allows you to step through JavaScript code and debug HTML5 applications inside of NetBeans instead of through Chrome's developer tools. Figure 1-11 is a screenshot of the index.html file in the Chrome browser.

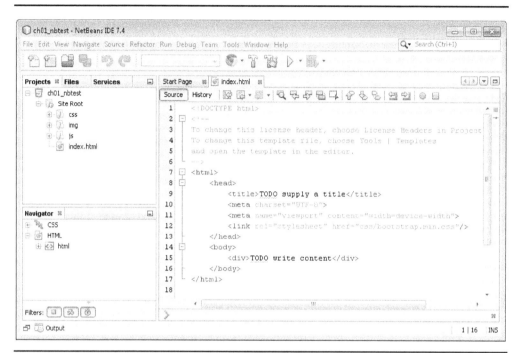

FIGURE 1-10.   *New project in NetBeans IDE*

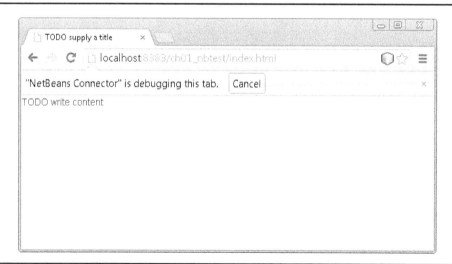

FIGURE 1-11.   *The application's index file in Google Chrome*

A Bootstrap page should be a visually attractive page. Notice that ours isn't very pretty. This is because it doesn't contain a reference to the bootstrap CSS file. Add a reference by inserting the following just below the last `meta` tag in the `head` section as shown below:

```
<link rel="stylesheet" href="css/bootstrap.min.css"/>
```

NOTE
The type attribute is optional in HTML5. I left it out
to save bandwidth. Every byte counts.

When entering text into NetBeans HTML editor, notice how it intelligently suggests elements, attributes, and values based on the editor's context. Another great feature of an IDE like NetBeans or Eclipse is auto formatting. Press the combination ALT-SHIFT-F to format the editor's contents according to the standard HTML formatting template.

Web Server

Some of our code will include Ajax requests. Ajax is a data-transfer mechanism that allows us to transparently communicate between our mobile web pages and a back-end web server. These requests must run from a web server and can only communicate with the domain of origin. If we want to test local web pages that use Ajax, we need to have a local web server. There are many web servers to choose from. I am most familiar with Apache httpd (plus it is free). Later, we will reverse proxy PeopleSoft content into an Apache httpd domain for Ajax requests. The instructions I provide at that time will pertain to Apache httpd.

Cross-origin Resource Sharing

There was a time when browsers required developers to proxy all content into the same domain to abide by the "Domain of Origin" security policy. The purpose of the "Domain of Origin" policy is to eliminate cross-site scripting vulnerabilities. Modern browsers now support a cross-domain mechanism called cross-origin resource sharing (CORS). You can read more about CORS at http://en.wikipedia.org/wiki/Cross-origin_resource_sharing. Since PeopleSoft Integration Broker does not support CORS, our alternatives are to

- Proxy Integration Broker content into another domain.
- Enable CORS through a reverse proxy server.

The Apache Software Foundation does not distribute binaries for the latest version of httpd. Therefore, you will need to find a binary distribution of Apache httpd. I prefer the one from https://www.apachelounge.com/download/. Installing Apache Lounge is usually just a matter of expanding a zip file into c:\. You can find the complete installation instructions in the ReadMe.txt file included in the downloaded zip file. The Apache directives used by the examples in this book relate to Apache version 2.4 (with alternate 2.2 syntax in comments).

Configure a Virtual Directory

Your NetBeans project exists in one folder, but your web server is configured to serve content out of a different folder. Let's assign a web server virtual directory to our NetBeans project's web root. First, find your NetBeans project's web root folder. You can identify the root folder by right-clicking on the Site Root folder in your NetBeans project explorer (the outline in the upper left) and selecting Properties from the context menu. This displays your Project Folder and Site Root Folder. Your web root is the concatenation of these two properties. Based on Figure 1-12, you

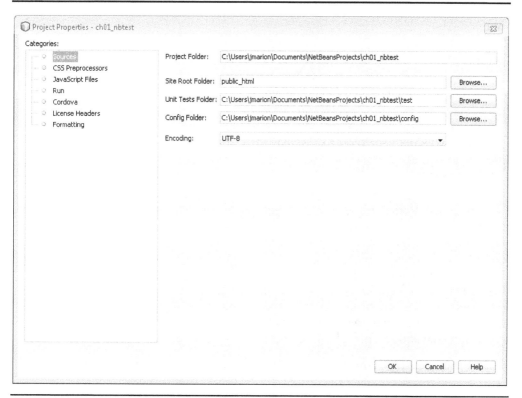

FIGURE 1-12. *Project Properties dialog*

can see that my web root folder is C:\Users\jmarion\Documents\NetBeansProjects\ ch01_nbtest\public_html.

Next, create a new configuration file in your Apache web server's conf directory. My configuration file is located in the directory c:\Apache24\conf, but yours may be in a different location. Name your new file ch01_nbtest.conf. To this new file, add the contents:

```
# ch01 NetBeans Test configuration

Alias /ch01_nbtest "C:/Users/jmarion/Documents/NetBeansProjects/\
ch01_nbtest/public_html"
<Directory "C:/Users/jmarion/Documents/NetBeansProjects/ch01_nbtest/\
public_html">
    Options Indexes FollowSymLinks
    AllowOverride None
    # Apache 2.2 directives
    # Order allow,deny
    # Allow from all

    # Apache 2.4 directives
    Require all granted
</Directory>
```

NOTE
The code fragment's paths were too long for the printed page. I intentionally placed line breaks in the path and used the Apache conf file line continuation character "\" at the end of each line. If you place your entire path on a single line then you do not need to add this special character to your configuration file.

When creating your configuration file, replace the path to my NetBeans project with the path to your NetBeans project. I included my path for reference purposes. Be sure to use a slash in your file paths instead of the standard Windows file path backslash.

Now we need to tell Apache to use our configuration. Rather than clutter the delivered httpd.conf file with all of our development configurations, we can store them in separate files and *Include* them in Apache's main configuration file. Open the file httpd.conf from the Apache configuration directory (conf directory). Scroll to the end of the file and add the following line:

```
Include conf/ch01_nbtest.conf
```

After making these changes, start Apache from a cmd prompt by executing the following command (assuming Apache 2.4 is installed at c:\Apache24):

```
c:\Apache24\bin\httpd.exe
```

Test your Virtual Directory configuration by using a web browser to navigate to http://localhost/ch01_nbtest. If you see the test index.html page, then your configuration is correct.

Installing Emulators

We can do a pretty good job of testing HTML5 mobile applications with a modern HTML5 web browser. Nevertheless, just to confirm that your sites work properly with your target devices, it is a good idea to test your web pages on real devices and potentially in device emulators.

Android

Android has a complete development environment that runs on multiple operating systems. We won't need the full Android Development Toolset until Chapter 9. We could just install Android SDK Tools only. But if you plan to build native Android applications, then it will be good to download the full bundle. Begin by navigating to https://developer.android.com/sdk/index.html. Search for the *Download the SDK ADT bundle* button. Figure 1-13 is a screenshot of this button's appearance when writing this chapter.

FIGURE 1-13.   *SDK ADT bundle download button*

Using Android SDK Tools Only

The example in this chapter shows you how to install the Eclipse and Android tools bundle. If you don't plan to build native Android apps, or if you already have an instance of Eclipse, you can get the emulators by installing just the Android SDK. On the Android SDK download page, instead of selecting the large, obvious download button, search for the heading **DOWNLOAD FOR OTHER PLATFORMS**. Clicking this link will expose the *ADT Bundle and SDK Tools Only* sections. Scroll down to the *SDK Tools Only* section and select the download that matches your Operating System. Since this book is written in Windows, I chose `adt-bundle-windows-x86-20131030.zip`. When the download completes, either unzip the file or run the installation (depending on the download you chose).

The ADT SDK is delivered as a zip file. To install the tools, extract the zip file someplace convenient on your computer. It is customary to place programs like these in your program files directory. Inside your Android installation directory, you will find a program named SDK Manager.exe. Run this program to download a platform for our emulator. The SDK Manager will automatically select several downloads the first time you run it. I recommend you also download the platform version that matches your target devices. The samples in this book use the Android 4.2.2 platform. Figure 1-14 is a screenshot of the SDK Manager with several downloads selected. Use the Install button to download and install the required files. Be advised that this download may take several minutes.

 NOTE
The quickest way to launch an emulator is through the command line. Rather than typing the full path to your Android SDK tools and platform-tools directories, I recommend adding these directories to your operating system's PATH environment variable.

When the download completes, select Tools | Manage AVDs from the Android SDK Manager menu bar. AVD is an acronym for Android Virtual Device. Basically, we are creating a profile that identifies the type of device we intend to emulate. When the *Android Device Manager* dialog appears, select the New button to create a new virtual device profile. Give the new device profile a name and set its parameters to match your target device. Be sure to stay within the confines of your development computer's hardware limits. Some of the newer, larger devices can

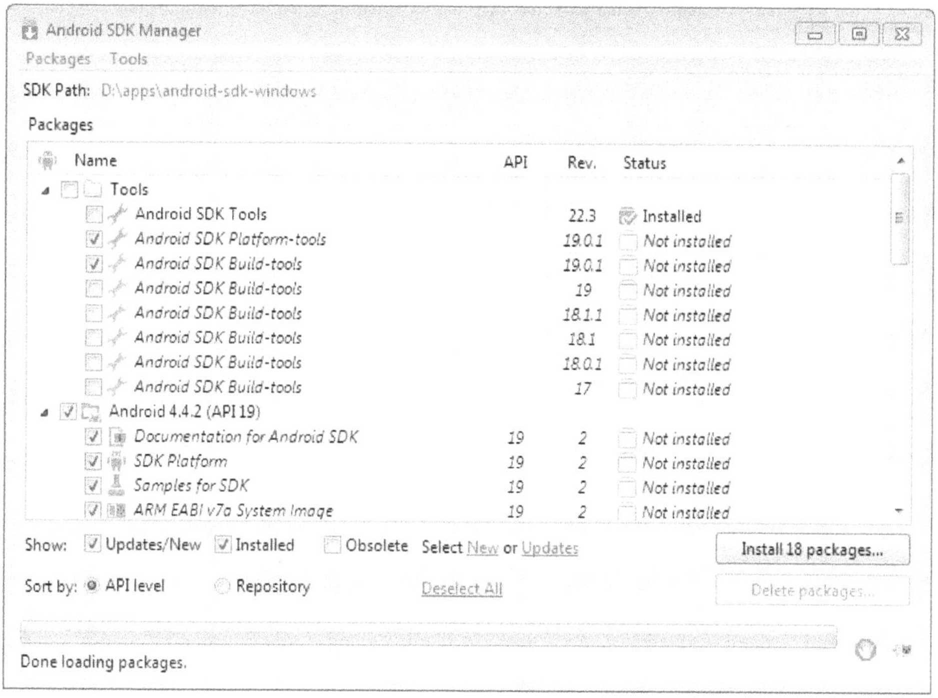

FIGURE 1-14. *SDK Manager with downloads selected*

have too much RAM for the standard development laptop. Figure 1-15 is a screenshot of the Create New Virtual Device dialog.

You can launch your new AVD from the Android Device Manager or from the command line. To launch from the command line, type `emulator -avd NameOfAVD`. The following is the command I use to launch my AVD named `NexusOne`:

```
emulator -avd NexusOne
```

Test your emulator by opening its web browser and navigating to a mobile page. http://maps.google.com/ and http://m.google.com/ are both examples of well-known mobile pages. While you are testing, make sure your Android emulator can access your local development workstation. From your emulator's web browser, try connecting to http://10.0.2.2/. From the emulator's perspective, this is your development workstation's IP address.

Faster Android Emulators

One of the frustrations of Android development is the slow Android emulator. Intel offers a hardware-accelerated Android CPU emulator called HAXM that uses Intel VT to speed up Android emulation on host machines that support Intel VT. Another alternative is the Android-x86 project. Android-x86 builds ISO disk images that allow you to install Android operating systems on an x86 architecture. A great use case for Android-x86 is running a version of Android in a VirtualBox VM. You can learn how to run Android-x86 in VirtualBox at http://www.android-x86.org/documents/virtualboxhowto/.

the left of the label Allow remote computers to connect. Restart Fiddler after changing this setting. Figure 1-16 is a screenshot of the Fiddler Options dialog box.

With Fiddler ready to accept remote connections, launch your emulator using the following command. This instructs the emulator to send all HTTP(S) requests through Fiddler.

```
emulator -avd NexusOne -partition-size 256 -http-proxy 127.0.0.1:8888
```

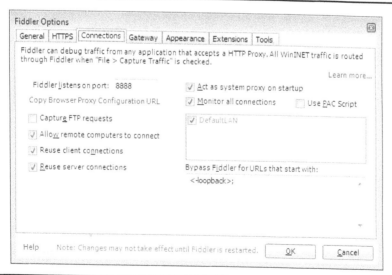

FIGURE 1-16.   *Fiddler options*

Alternatively, configure the emulator's proxy settings by opening the Settings app and then navigating to Wireless & Networks | More | Mobile Networks | Access Point Names | T-Mobile US. Set the Proxy value to match the IP address of the machine running Fiddler (likely your laptop or desktop) and the Port to 8888. When using this method, be sure to clear the emulator's proxy settings before closing Fiddler. Otherwise the emulator will not be able to connect to external resources.

NOTE
The command line uses a transparent proxy that may or may not work as expected. I sometimes find that it drops important headers such as the host header.

DNS Resolution   You may also want to reference your development workstation by host name rather than IP address. If you type your workstation's host name into your emulator's web browser and see a "Webpage not found" error, then open a command prompt on your workstation and execute the following sequence of commands. This will add an IP address/host name mapping to your emulator's hosts file. Unfortunately, you will need to execute this sequence every time you restart your emulator:

```
adb remount
adb shell
root@android:/ # echo '10.0.2.2 dev.example.com' >> /etc/hosts
echo '10.0.2.2 dev.example.com' >> /etc/hosts
```

NOTE
If you receive an error message telling you the system is a read-only file system, then make sure you execute adb remount.

Confirm your hosts file setting changes with the following:

```
root@android:/ # cat /etc/hosts
cat /etc/hosts
127.0.0.1                      localhost
10.0.2.2 dev.example.com
root@android:/ # ping dev.example.com
ping dev.example.com
PING dev.example.com (10.0.2.2) 56(84) bytes of data.
64 bytes from dev.example.com (10.0.2.2): icmp_seq=1 ttl=255 time=2.69 ms
64 bytes from dev.example.com (10.0.2.2): icmp_seq=2 ttl=255 time=1.13 ms
```

Finally, confirm your settings by attempting to load your local web server in your emulator's web browser. In my case, my local development workstation's host name is dev.example.com. Be sure to update the commands above with your host's name.

BlackBerry

If you intend to deliver applications for BlackBerry devices, then you may want to download a BlackBerry simulator. BlackBerry makes several versions available for download. Most of them are self-contained downloads. The BlackBerry 10 simulators are actually VMWare VMs. You will need to download and install VMWare Player to run these VMs. The BlackBerry 10 simulator is available at https://developer.blackberry.com/develop/simulator/. Follow the instructions to download the simulator installation program (search for the "Install the Simulator" link and then the "Get the Simulator" link), and then run the installer.

Windows Mobile

At the time I wrote this chapter, the Windows Mobile Developer Tool Kit version 6.5.3 was available at http://www.microsoft.com/en-us/download/details.aspx?id=5389. You need only the standard tool kit, not the professional bundle.

iOS

To run an iOS (iPad and iPhone) simulator, you must have a Mac. If you plan to build solutions for iPads or iPhones, then it is critical that you properly outfit yourself with a Mac development machine. When I wrote this chapter, the Xcode IDE was available at https://developer.apple.com/xcode/.

Conclusion

Near the beginning of this chapter, I described HTML5 application source files as plain text files. I also said the only tool you need is a text editor. I then proceeded to explain how to install full IDEs, debuggers, and emulators. Why? Even though these tools are not necessary, they certainly make your development efforts more productive.

Your desktop is now configured for testing and building HTML5 applications. In the remaining chapters of Part I, we will use these tools to test and debug Fluid and MAP applications. In Parts II and III, we will dig further into the development aspects of these tools.

CHAPTER
2

PeopleTools Mobile Design (Fluid)

In this chapter, you will use standard PeopleTools to construct touch-first PeopleSoft components that render on a variety of device form factors, including mobile and desktop devices. If you know how to create records, pages, and components, then you already know most of what is required to create this mobile PeopleSoft user experience. In this chapter, we will focus specifically on what makes fluid unique.

While working through this chapter, you will create several new fluid pages. You will learn how to combine delivered CSS classes with delivered layouts to construct intuitive user interfaces. You will learn how to compose search pages and configure search metadata. This chapter is not intended to provide a complete fluid reference but as a "Getting Started" guide. For a complete reference, see *PeopleTools 8.54: Fluid User Interface Developer's Guide*.

About PeopleTools Fluid Pages

Users no longer enter transactions into information systems using just a keyboard and a mouse. Today's users employ mobile devices, such as phones and tablets, as well as desktops, laptops, touch screens, and netbooks. *Fluid* is the term Oracle uses to describe PeopleSoft's mobile-first, touch-first, but yet desktop-friendly application pages. Fluid pages are constructed in Application Designer using a drag-and-drop approach that is similar to classic PeopleTools pages. Both page types benefit from PeopleSoft's data binding and persistence, they support the same events, and they support nested subpages. Here are a few features that are unique to fluid pages:

- Responsive design

- Adaptive design

- CSS3 layout

- HTML5 runtime controls

Responsive and Adaptive Design

Mobile devices come in various shapes and sizes, ranging from small smartphones to large tablets. The variety in screen sizes presents a problem: How does a developer (or designer) display the right amount of information for each device size? Here are a few common solutions:

- Create a separate website for each supported device classification.

- Use CSS3 media queries to change the layout of information on a page (responsive).

■ Employ adaptive design which involves choosing what and how to display information based on device capabilities.

The "separate website" approach was common in the early days of the mobile web. CSS3 didn't exist yet, so responsive design was not practical. Adaptive design didn't make sense because some devices didn't support HTML, but rather WAP/WML. Content displayed on mobile devices was different enough to warrant two separate code lines. Often this approach resulted in two or three websites: desktop, phone, and (occasionally) tablet. Developers who take this approach have to maintain multiple versions of the same application.

Responsive design uses CSS3 media query *break points* to apply layout rules. These rules include placement of information on a page, the size and location of graphics, and even whether to show or hide various page elements. A page constructed using responsive design will contain data, but very few layout instructions. This approach differs from the multisite approach in that all devices browse the same website. It is similar in that it still requires two code lines: separate CSS definitions for each form factor. Responsive design is very common. To see it in action, go to almost any consumer website (Amazon, Wal-Mart, and so on) and resize the browser window: At some predetermined screen width, you will see the header region change. One problem with responsive design is how to optimize content for low-bandwidth browsing. It doesn't make sense, for example, to send a high-resolution photo to a small device where the image will be displayed as a thumbnail—too small to see any significant detail.

Adaptive design uses progressive enhancement to determine what content to display and how to display it. Developers applying adaptive design may either use client-side JavaScript or server-side programs to investigate device capabilities and render appropriate content. This approach ensures that each device receives tailor-made content. Adaptive design may employ concepts similar to responsive design, but with the key differentiator being that adaptive design won't send content a device can't reasonably consume.

PeopleTools fluid pages use both responsive and adaptive design. Through CSS3 media queries, preconfigured PeopleTools CSS3 stylesheets change a page's layout at various breakpoints. Data entry and display elements contain adaptive properties, ensuring that we only send critical, important, and relevant information to various devices. For example, a grid displayed on a desktop may contain more fields than the same grid displayed on a mobile device.

CSS3 Layout

The PeopleTools classic page designer is a What You See Is What You Get (WYSIWYG) drag-and-drop designer. If you don't like the placement of an item on a page, then you can drag it somewhere else. While it is convenient to visually see the runtime appearance of a page, the layout process is a bit tedious. I don't know how many times I registered a classic component just so I could iteratively modify the layout while viewing that component in a web browser. Fluid pages, on the other hand, use CSS3 layouts. A developer just places fields on a page in the desired order and a fluid layout takes care of placement. Fluid chooses the position of an element through the layout, CSS, or class name.

HTML5 Runtime Controls

As long as PeopleSoft applications have been internet facing, we have had data input formats and date-specific input controls. Those classic data-entry fields require a significant amount of JavaScript and CSS. HTML5 specifies a whole set of data-entry field types, including date, time, number, numeric range, e-mail, search, and URL. The device, not PeopleSoft, determines how to display these special types of data entry fields.

Fluid Mode Setup

Before we build some cool, responsive fluid pages, let's make sure your PeopleSoft application is configured for fluid mode. Log into your PeopleSoft server and navigate to PeopleTools | Web Profile | Web Profile. Scroll to the bottom and ensure that neither of the "Disable fluid…" checkboxes is selected. Restart your web server after changing your web profile. After making this change, mobile browsers will automatically see the fluid home page. Desktop browsers, however, will continue to default to the classic home page. On a per-user basis you can make desktop browsers default to the fluid home page by navigating to My Personalizations and then selecting the Personalize General Options category. Override the PC Homepage row by setting the Override Value to Fluid, as shown in Figure 2-1.

Skillset

So, with all of this information about web technologies such as CSS3, JavaScript, and HTML5, you may be wondering if you need to become a web developer as well as a PeopleTools expert. Let me calm your fears right now and say, "No, you do not need to learn all of that fancy web stuff if you don't want." It is amazing what you can create if you choose to learn about web design, but the only hard knowledge requirement is core PeopleTools. With a working knowledge of Application Designer, including standard pages, components, and PeopleCode, you can create all the fluid pages you desire. I have to warn you though, if you stick with just core PeopleTools, your fluid mileage will vary. It really is in your best interest to learn CSS3 at the minimum.

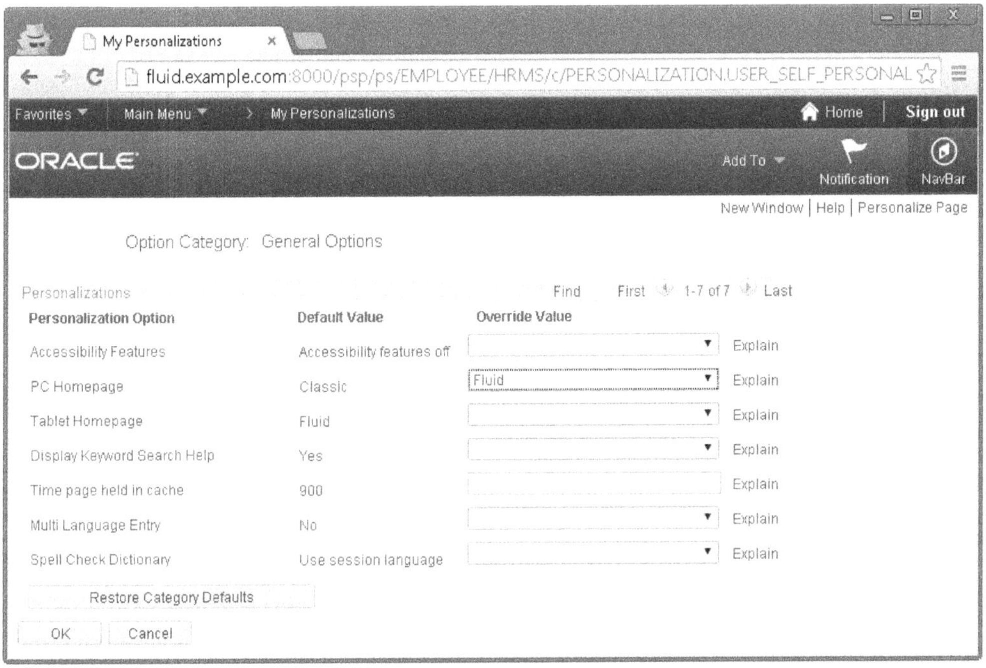

FIGURE 2-1. *Personalize General Options page*

My First Fluid Page

Creating an application module in PeopleTools involves describing data with record
definitions and then exposing that data through pages and components. In this
chapter, I want to focus specifically on fluid page development. To avoid all those
other data definition tasks, we will build fluid pages against mock PeopleTools
record definitions. Specifically, we will create a fluid version of the Translate Values
component that uses a clone of PSXLATITEM, the translate values detail table.

The Fluid Page's Data Model

Let's start by cloning the delivered PeopleTools table. Log into Application Designer
and open the PSXLATITEM record definition. From the Application Designer menu
bar, select File | Save As. Name the new record definition BMA_XLATITEM. Select
No when prompted to copy the base record's PeopleCode. Build the record

definition before continuing. Be sure to select Create Table and the appropriate execution option (I prefer execute and build script).

NOTE
Developers often ask whether or not to copy PeopleCode when copying a record. Of course, the answer depends. If the source record has PeopleCode that should exist in the target, then yes, absolutely, choose to copy the PeopleCode. But don't click that button if you don't really intend to copy the source record's PeopleCode. Even worse, don't click Yes if the source record has no PeopleCode. The copy feature doesn't know this, so it will loop through all the events for each field attempting to copy PeopleCode events that don't exist. These are moments lost that you will never regain.

The PSXLATITEM record definition is effective dated. The component processor has a special way of treating effective-dated rows. The Translate Values component, however, doesn't use the component processor's special effective-date handling. The way we work around this is to cleverly disguise the PSXLATITEM.EFFDT field by wrapping the whole PSXLATITEM record definition in a view. Rather than create our own, we can copy the existing one and just update the SQL to point to our source table. Open PSXITMMNT_VW and save it as BMA_XITMMNT_VW. Switch to the Record Type tab and verify that the Non-Standard SQL Table Name field is blank. Open the SQL Editor and change the source table from PSXLATITEM to PS_BMA_XLATITEM. Save and build this definition.

NOTE
Instead of PS_BMA_XLATITEM, you could use Meta-SQL %Table(BMA_XLATITEM) equivalent.

Constructing a Fluid Page

Within Application Designer, choose File | New from the menu bar. When the New Definition dialog appears, select Page (Fluid). Figure 2-2 is a screenshot of the New Definition dialog with Page (Fluid) selected.

As soon as you click the OK button on the New Definition dialog, you experience your first difference between fluid and classic pages. Fluid pages require layouts.

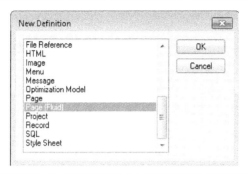

FIGURE 2-2. *New Definition dialog*

A layout helps position page elements for responsive design. Basically, a layout is a series of group boxes placed on a page to group content within a responsive grid. Common PeopleTools fluid page layouts include PSL_APPS_CONTENT, PSL_TWOPANEL, and PSL_2COLUMN_FLOAT. The layout you choose determines the position of the page's starting group boxes (I say "starting" because you can always add more group boxes and/or rearrange content). For example, using the PSL_2COLUMN_FLOAT layout will create a page with a series of nested group boxes. The innermost boxes of the PSL_2COLUMN_FLOAT layout contain left and right boxes for a two-column grid layout. The point of the two columns is to allow the content to change in some manner depending on device orientation and screen size. For example, a tablet may show both columns whereas a mobile phone might show one column at a time. Figure 2-3 is a screenshot of the layout selection dialog.

NOTE
A layout is just a PeopleSoft page, with the page type set to Layout Page. You can create your own layouts that contain any valid page content including subpages.

Select the PSL_APPS_CONTENT layout. When prompted, name the page BMA_XLAT_FL and choose to copy the PeopleCode associated with the layout. Application Designer will present you with a new page containing a single group box that stretches the width and height of the page. Regardless of the layout chosen, the first element is a group box. All other content resides within this outer group box.

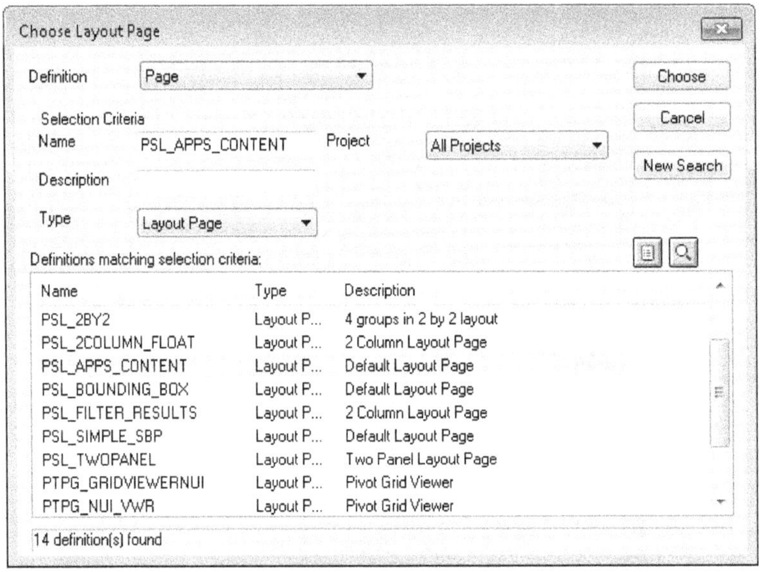

FIGURE 2-3. *Layout selection dialog*

Double-click the group box to inspect its properties. The first four tabs (Record, Label, Use, and General) are pretty standard. PeopleTools 8.54 adds a new tab to group boxes called Fluid. Switch to this tab and review the properties of the Fluid tab. Notice that the Default Style Name property is `ps_apps_content`. This is the most common style for the outermost group box on primary and secondary fluid pages. Figure 2-4 is a screenshot of the Fluid properties available to group boxes. The Form Factor Override section allows you to specify an alternate class name depending on device size, and the Suppress On Form Factor section allows a developer to hide the group box on various device sizes. These two segments differ in that the latter section will not send content to a device if it fits a category with suppression enabled. This saves valuable bandwidth on devices where the content is not relevant.

Inside the group box of this new page, add the `BMA_XLATDEFN.FIELDNAME` field. Set the field's Display Only and Display Control Field properties. Next, add the `PSDBFLD_XLAT.LENGTH` field and mark it as a related field that is related to the `Field Name` field. Placement of these fields within the group box doesn't matter too much. CSS class names and layout determine placement, not location within the designer. Unlike classic, fluid design is not WYSIWYG. Application Designer does, however, maintain parental hierarchies, so make sure the fields are within the page's

FIGURE 2-4.   *Fluid group box properties*

one and only group box. Likewise, PeopleTools uses placement to determine field order. Figure 2-5 is a screenshot of the page thus far.

We will develop this page further, but let's stop here and create the metadata required to test this page. Create a new component and add our new page to the component. Application Designer requires us to specify a search record before we can save the component. The search record for the original PSXLATMAINT component, which we are sort of copying, is PSDBFLD_XLAT. Therefore, set the search record for this component to the same: PSDBFLD_XLAT. While you are at it, disable the Add action. The level 0 record represents field definitions, which we don't add online, so the Add action is irrelevant. The point of this component is to

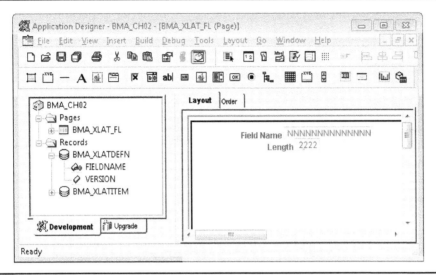

FIGURE 2-5. *BMA_XLAT_FL page in development*

update field metadata, not create new fields. While still viewing the component's properties, switch to the Fluid tab and select the Fluid Mode checkbox. This checkbox is the sole differentiator between a classic component and a fluid component. Save the component and name it BMA_XLAT_FL, the same name as the page.

As with any component, we need to attach it to a menu. Create a new standard menu named BMA_FLUID. Double-click the empty space in the menu. The empty space is between the Language and Help items. When the pop-up dialog appears, set its label to Custom. Double-click on the new drop-down item that appeared under the Custom menu item and change its type to Separator. We don't actually need a separator, but this menu can't be empty. PeopleTools requires a menu to contain content before you can save the menu. Adding a separator is enough to satisfy Application Designer.

We are just about to register our new fluid component. The component registration wizard is going to ask us the folder that will hold this new component. All fluid components in the Portal Registry belong in a subfolder of Fluid Structure and Content | Fluid Pages. Log into your PeopleSoft application online and navigate to PeopleTools | Portal | Structure and Content. Next, navigate through the Portal Registry to Fluid Structure and Content | Fluid Pages. Create a new folder named BMA_PEOPLETOOLS and label it BMA PeopleTools.

Use the Component Registration Wizard in Application Designer to register the component. Select the options to add the component to a menu, portal registry, and permission list (all three options on the first page of the wizard). When prompted for a menu, select BMA_FLUID and bar MENUITEM1. On the third page of the wizard, where it asks you for information about the content reference, change the folder to BMA_PEOPLETOOLS and the Content Reference Label to BMA Translate Values. Before clicking Next, set the Node Name to the local portal node name. Since I am using an HRMS database, I chose the HRMS portal node. Figure 2-6 is a screenshot of this step in the registration wizard. On the next step, the permission list step, select the PTPT1200 permission list.

Finish the wizard to create the content reference. The last step of the registration wizard asks if you would like to add the permission list to your project. While this may be convenient, many organizations discourage (or don't allow) transferring

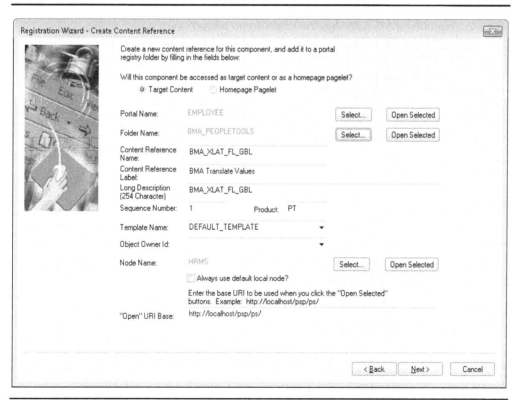

FIGURE 2-6. *Component Registration Wizard Create Content Reference step*

Demystifying Nodes

The Component Registration Wizard asks for a node name. There are a lot of values a developer could choose. Knowing the proper node can be confusing. One of the options, for example, is the node localnode. This node name tells PeopleSoft to always use the local portal node. It is a great generic node name for components that will exist in various applications. Using this node, however, is rarely acceptable. This specific node begins to cause problems when a system administrator pairs applications together through the Interaction Hub. The node localnode really means the local node. From Interaction Hub, it is likely that the target node is really a remote node, not a local node.

Another point of confusion is the types of nodes. There are multiple types of nodes, but only two that really matter: portal and integration nodes. Portal nodes host portal registry content. Components should be registered against portal nodes. Portal nodes differ by application, not by application instance. For example, the HRMS node has the same name regardless of whether you are viewing that node in development, test, or a production system. An integration node, on the other hand, varies by application and instance. An example of an integration node is the delivered PSFT_HR node (which should be renamed immediately upon install).

As a general rule, when registering a component, pick the node that matches your application. If it is an HCM application, then pick HRMS. If it is Interaction Hub, then pick the EMPL node. If you use the same PeopleTools instance to access multiple applications, such as both FSCM and HCM, then make sure you update the registration wizard node name when registering components.

security definitions such as permission lists. Furthermore, comparing projects that contain permission lists can take a significant amount of time. As a general rule, I do not add permission lists to development projects.

Fluid Search Pages

As a developer, one of my favorite features of PeopleTools is the metadata-driven component search page. It is not a real page, but is constructed at runtime using attributes of the search record. Every other development environment requires you to create your own search page. As a functional user, on the other hand, I am not fond of the classic component search page. It is too generic.

Fluid components take a hybrid approach, allowing us to choose between a configured, metadata-driven, and generic search page or a custom search definition. Fluid forces us to rethink component search. Here are a few alternatives:

- Use the default fluid search.

- Create and register Pivot Grids.

- Keyword search.

- Construct fluid search components that collect transaction search parameters and then transfer to a target fluid page (also known as "custom search pages").

- Add a search header or sidebar to a fluid page.

 NOTE
Group boxes have a special layout type called
Custom Header Search that is designed for header
search.

Fluid Default Search
Configuring the default search for a fluid component is as simple as checking a box and adding a page. Let's configure our component to use this default search. Step 1 is to enable search, so open the component's properties and switch to the Fluid tab. Find and select the Enable Search Page option. Figure 2-7 is a screenshot of the Enable Search Page option of the component attributes collection.

Step 2 is to add PT_SEARCHPAGE to the component. This isn't a page you want someone to select from a list of page tabs within a component, so mark the page as hidden. Save your component.

Pivot Grid Search
Pivot Grid search is a very powerful search feature that uses multidimensional transaction data to identify transactions. Because it is multidimensional, it requires facts and dimensions. The transaction itself is the fact and foundation tables, such as ChartFields, location, and position information, represent dimensions. Multidimensional search doesn't work as well for foundation data because each foundation component, such as the location table, represents one dimension. Using Pivot Grid search involves creating a query and Pivot Grid. The search page for Pivot Grid search is PTS_NUI_SEARCH.

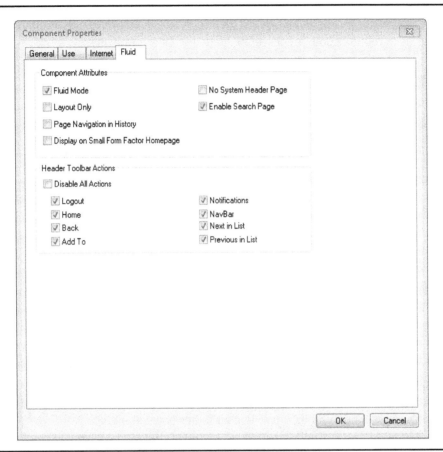

FIGURE 2-7. *Enable Search Page option*

Keyword Search

Keyword search uses SES indexes to populate a search page. Keyword search configuration requires the following steps:

1. Open the component's properties and switch to the internet tab. Select the Keyword search option.

2. On the Fluid tab of the component's properties, select the Enable Search Page option.

3. While still viewing the Fluid tab of the component's properties, select the Next in List and Previous in List options.

4. The final step is to log into the PeopleSoft application online and create and configure an SES index to map to the new component.

NOTE
Creating SES indexes is beyond the scope of this chapter.

Custom Search Components

A developer taking this approach would create a component that exists specifically to gather requirements to locate a transaction. The component would contain data entry fields as well as some type of selection list. This approach is not very common because the PT_SEARCHPAGE and PTS_NUI_SEARCH pages can serve as a foundation for creating your own custom search pages within a component.

Search Headers and Sidebars

The search header and sidebar approaches are very common. We will create a page with a sidebar search later in this chapter.

Fluid Page Navigation

We have a great start on a fluid page and component. Now is a good time to review our progress, but we have one problem: How do you access a fluid component? You won't see fluid components in the standard PeopleTools menu or navigator. One way to access the component is to open its portal registry content reference and click the Test Content Reference hyperlink. Try that now by navigating to PeopleTools | Portal | Structure and Content. Within the portal registry, navigate to Fluid Structure and Content | Fluid Pages | BMA PeopleTools. Click the Edit hyperlink to the right of the BMA Translate Values item and then click the Test Content Reference hyperlink. PeopleSoft should present you with the basic search page we added to the component. Figure 2-8 is a screenshot of the component search page.

Figure 2-9 is a screenshot of the small-form-factor version of the Translate Values page. Notice how the fields and labels are vertically stacked and horizontally aligned around a midpoint in spite of the fact that I randomly placed these fields on a page in Application Designer. Horizontally resize your browser window and notice how the header buttons change. Take note of the fact that the component doesn't contain the classic page bar (help link, new window link, and so on) or the footer toolbar (save, return to list, and so on). Later we will use the new PeopleTools save action to add a save button.

FIGURE 2-8.   *Fluid default search page*

FIGURE 2-9.   *Screenshot of Translate Values page*

Since fluid pages don't appear in the menu, we need another mechanism to access them. While viewing the component, click the three-bar hamburger button in the upper right corner. A pop-up menu will appear with three navigation options:

- Add to Homepage
- Add to NavBar
- Add to Favorites

Choosing Add to Homepage displays a list of home pages as well as a shortcut for creating an entirely new home page. Since the current URL for this transaction is a fully qualified URL that includes search key values, choosing Add to Homepage will create a home page button directly to the transaction page. This is good enough for now. A better alternative would have been to bookmark the search page. Figure 2-10 is a screenshot of the fluid home page containing the newly created *grouplet* that points to the BMA Translate Values component.

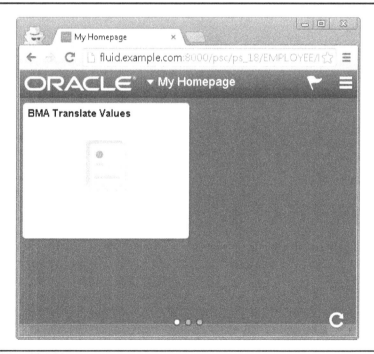

FIGURE 2-10.   *Fluid home page*

NOTE
A grouplet is a home page artifact that represents some type of relevant information or transaction page. A lot of people call them tiles rather than grouplets. The grouplet term comes from the fact that the content for these tiles can come from group boxes contained in a fluid PeopleSoft page. You configure individual grouplets through the Fluid Attributes tab of fluid content references. Later in this chapter you will learn how to change a grouplet's icon and content type.

Optimizing the Component for Fluid

Our component is a single page component, so open the component properties and disable Display Folder Tabs. You can find this option in the Multi-Page Navigation section of the Internet tab. While editing the component, change the page's Item Label to "Translate Values." The Item Label is what PeopleSoft displays in the page's header.

Fluid Grids

Add a grid to the fluid page. To this grid, add the following BMA_XITMMNT_VW fields:

FIELD_VALUE

DATE_FROM

EFF_STATUS

XLATLONGNAME

XLATSHORTNAME

Change the label for EFF_STATUS, XLATLONGNAME, and XLATSHORTNAME to RFT Short. Save your page, and then refresh your online view of the page. You should now see a grid positioned underneath the Length field. The grid includes lots of padding, similar to other fluid elements, but the appearance just isn't very pretty. What we are seeing is a Classic Grid on a fluid page. We can transform this grid into a responsive grid by changing one attribute in Application Designer. Return to Application Designer and double-click the grid to reveal its property window. On the General tab, select the Unlimited Occurs Count attribute. Switch to the Use tab

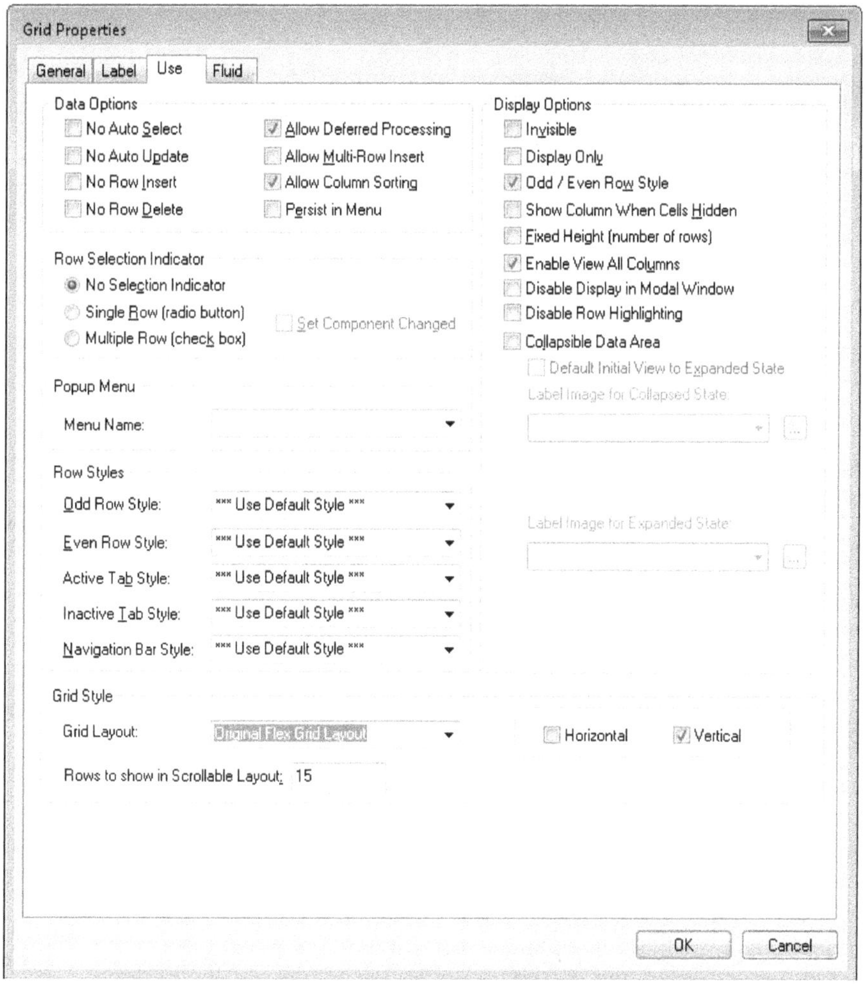

FIGURE 2-11. *Grid Use properties*

of the grid properties dialog and change the Grid Layout from Original Grid Layout to Original Flex Grid Layout, as shown in Figure 2-11.

Save the page in Application Designer and refresh the online view. You should now see a much narrower responsive grid. Figure 2-12 is a screenshot of a responsive fluid component containing data entry fields and a flex grid.

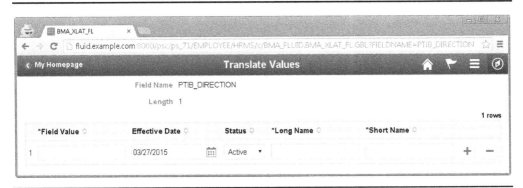

FIGURE 2-12. *Fluid page with a flex grid*

NOTE
Even though we haven't added a save button to this component, you can still save using the classic UI shortcut keyboard combination ALT-1 (ALT with number one key). If you enter data into the grid and press the ALT-1 combination, then the component processor will save the child record but not the parent.

HTML5 Data-Entry Fields

There was a time when web browsers could gather feedback only through input text fields and buttons (including radio buttons, checkboxes, and push buttons). Developers used to write a lot of JavaScript to create date entry fields, numeric spinners, e-mail address fields, and so on. Web browsers are a lot smarter now than they used to be. HTML5, the latest HTML specification, includes special elements for date, telephone, e-mail, number, and so on. The specification doesn't define how to display these special elements. Rather, each device determines the best input method. A desktop computer's web browser, for example, displays a date entry field using a combination of a calendar and numeric spinners designed for easy use with a mouse and keyboard. A smartphone, on the other hand, may display a date input field as a large selection wheel suitable for gestures.

Our Translate Values page contains a date field: DATE_FROM. PeopleTools is displaying the date field using the old method: lots of JavaScript. Let's bring this page into the modern era by enabling HTML5 data-entry types. Return to Application Designer and open the BMA_XLAT_FL page definition. Locate and double-click the DATE_FROM field. It is the grid field with the label Effective Date. When the Edit Box Properties dialog appears, locate the Input Type property at the bottom of the fluid tab. Change the Input Type to Date. Figure 2-13 is a screenshot of the Fluid tab with the date input type selected.

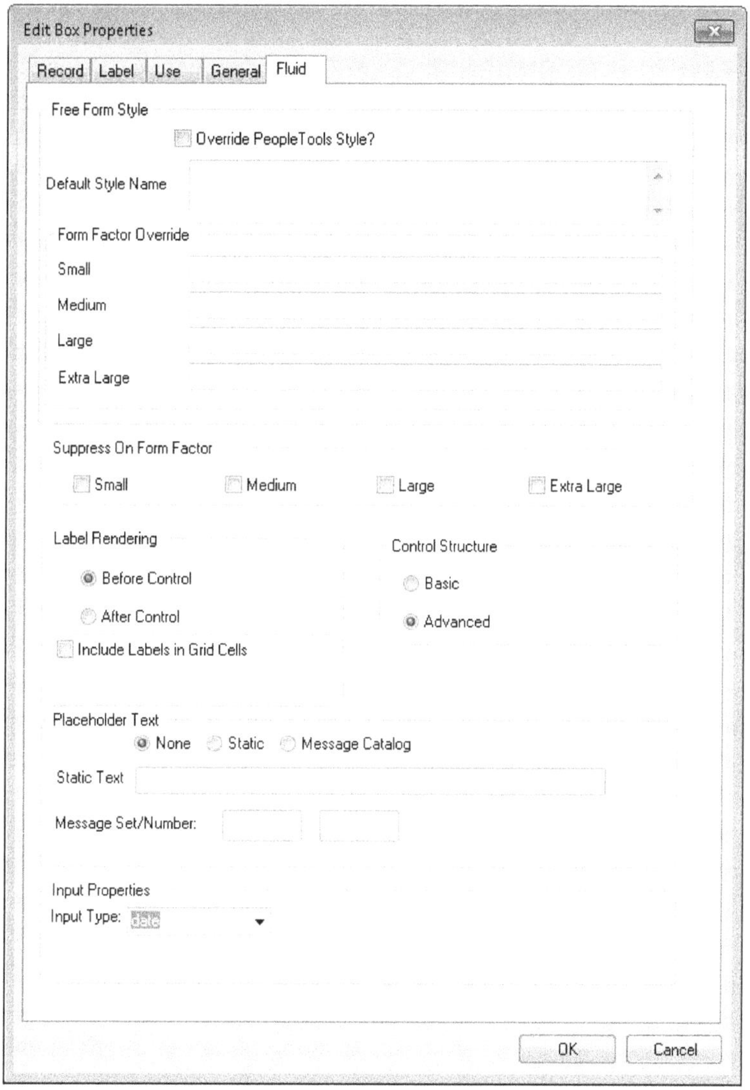

FIGURE 2-13. *HTML5 input types*

Reload the online page and notice that it no longer displays a calendar icon inside the Effective Date field. Depending on your device and browser, however, you will see calendar-specific controls as you interact with the field. Using the Chrome web browser, for example, I receive a desktop-friendly calendar drop-down as well as a numerical spinner for manipulating the field's date.

Adding Transaction Buttons

Those in the know can save this transaction page using the ALT-1 keyboard combination, but that isn't very intuitive for the rest of the population. We need a better way. Fluid pages can use a special pushbutton destination called Toolbar Action. You can then specify the action to invoke when the button is selected. Add a button to the top left corner of the BMA_XLAT_FL page. Open the button's properties and change the Destination to Toolbar Action. A few lines below the Destination field you will see the Action Type field. Set the Action Type to Save. Figure 2-14 is a screenshot of the button's type properties.

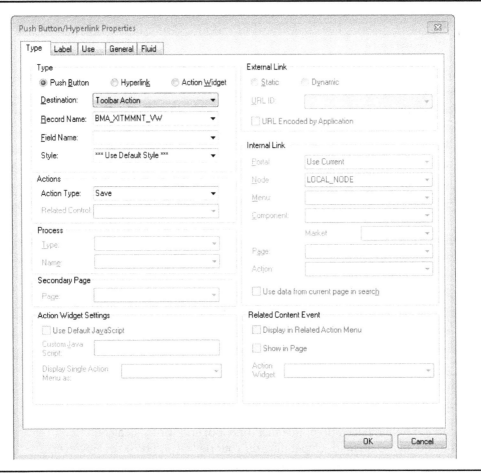

FIGURE 2-14. *Pushbutton type properties*

Switch to the Label tab of the properties dialog and set the type to Text and the Text to Save. Now switch to the Fluid tab and set the Default Style Name to `psc_float-right psc_primary`. The first class, `psc_float-right`, places the button in the upper right corner of the transaction page. The `psc_primary` class changes the buttons color to make it evident that it is the primary button for this page. Figure 2-15 is a screenshot of the page in Application Designer and Figure 2-16 is a screenshot of the live page viewed through a web browser. Notice that the alignment of fields within Application Designer differs greatly from the online appearance. This is the nature of fluid. Fluid lets the device (with a little help from CSS3) determine where to place items.

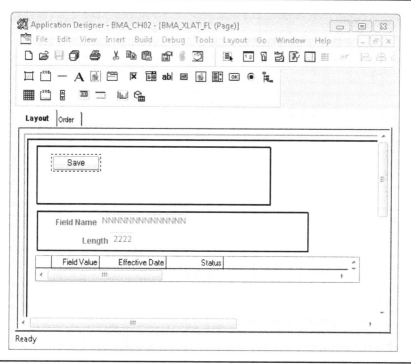

FIGURE 2-15. *Page in Application Designer*

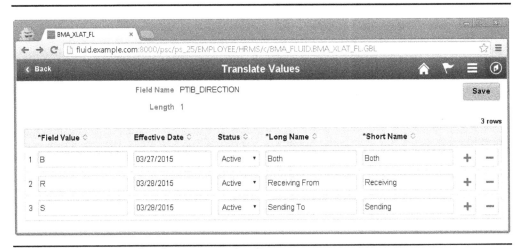

FIGURE 2-16. *Completed page viewed online*

NOTE
Figure 2-15 contains a few extra group boxes that weren't included in the text of this chapter. Specifically, the level 0 fields are surrounded by a group box and the save button is contained within its own group box. These group boxes are not necessary, but are recommended. PeopleTools recommends that you surround related items with a group box. When in doubt, group it. When grouping items, be sure to change the group box's type to Layout Only.

Create some test data and confirm that the save button works as expected. One of the features I miss from classic is the notification message in the upper right corner that confirms the transaction saved successfully. Fluid contains no such notifications. It does, however, contain a not-so-secret, but undocumented FUNCLIB function that will display a notification message. We can use this function to add a notification with the SavePostChange event. Open the BMA_XLAT_FL component's PeopleCode editor and add the following PeopleCode to the SavePostChange event:

```
Declare Function SetConfirmationMessage PeopleCode
     PT_WORK.PT_CONFIRM_MSG FieldFormula;

SetConfirmationMessage("Translate value saved");
```

NOTE
Best practice recommends using the message catalog over hard-coded text.

After adding a few new values and pressing the save button, you will see a message appear just below the header. Figure 2-17 is a screenshot of the Translate Values component showing the save confirmation message.

In the next section, you will learn how to use the two-column (or two-panel) layout. Before moving onto that section, use this page to add a few rows of translate values to various fields. I chose the fields PTIB_DIRECTION, PTCACHEABLE, and PTCOMPARABLE. The more test data you enter, the better your next page will look.

Those are the basics of fluid. You now have a responsive transaction page. Except for a few attribute differences, we used the same development procedures as other classic PeopleTools pages. There is a lot more to fluid, but as you experienced, you do not need to learn anything new to create fluid pages. Now let's investigate some of its more features.

Fluid Design Patterns

Beyond the obvious visual differences between fluid and classic pages, fluid is about transaction redesign. Fluid desires to be mobile-first. It is no secret that traditional data entry is difficult on touch-oriented mobile devices. Screen resolution, input method, and network bandwidth are all constrained on a mobile device.

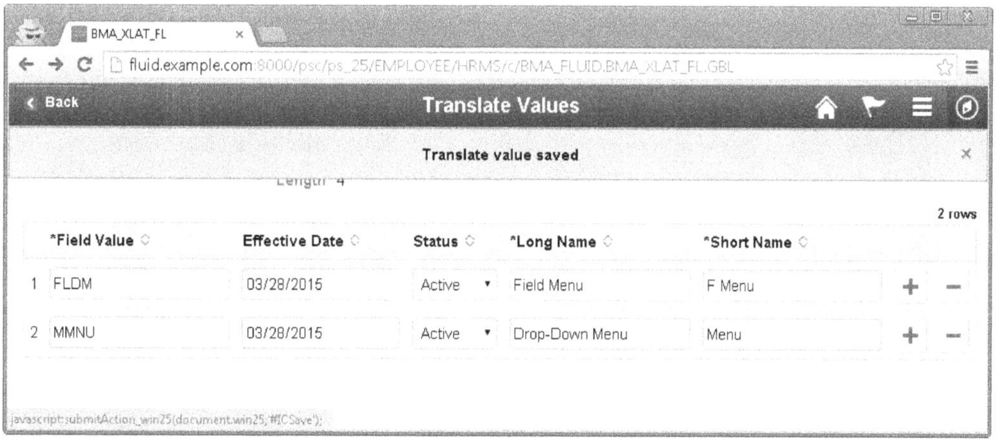

	BMA_XLAT_FL	×		
← → C	fluid.example.com:8000/psc/ps_25/EMPLOYEE/HRMS/c/BMA_FLUID.BMA_XLAT_FL.GBL			☆ ≡

‹ Back	Translate Values	🏠 🏴 ≡ ⊙

Translate value saved ×

Length 4

2 rows

	*Field Value ⬦	Effective Date ⬦	Status ⬦	*Long Name ⬦	*Short Name ⬦		
1	FLDM	03/28/2015	Active ▾	Field Menu	F Menu	+	−
2	MMNU	03/28/2015	Active ▾	Drop-Down Menu	Menu	+	−

javascript:submitAction_win25(document.win25,'#ICSave');

FIGURE 2-17. *Save confirmation message*

Fluid forces us to think differently about how we enter and process data. It forces us to ask questions such as:

- Can we reduce the number of user interactions (touch, type, and so on)?

- What data must be visible to process a particular transaction?

- How many pages does the user need to visit to complete the transaction?

The traditional PeopleSoft design pattern starts with a home page. Let's count the number of interactions required to reach a classic business process. From the home page (1) a user interacts with a menu (2) to navigate to a transaction search page. On the search page (3), the user enters criteria (4) and searches for a specific transaction (5). The user selects a transaction (6) and then begins processing information. I count six interactions required just to reach a transaction processing page. Many of us are so comfortable with this traditional paradigm that we don't even think about the process required to reach a transaction page. For years, PeopleSoft classic has provided usability enhancements, such as Pagelets and WorkCenters, to simplify transaction access. Fluid forces a change upon us by breaking the standard development paradigm. You already saw that Fluid navigation is different. Fluid navigates through home pages, favorites, and recent places. Likewise, transaction search is no longer free (which is good, because every transaction is different).

A New Paradigm

Let's rethink our transaction-access strategy (navigation and search). What if the search results were always present, sort of like a part of the transaction? In our case, the search result is a list of fields. Let's put that list in a sidebar on the left.

Search Record

The list on the left side of the component is our search page. In this case it is a summary list of fields. Create a new record definition with two fields: FIELDNAME and COUNT1. Change the record type to SQL View and save it as BMA_XLAT_FLD_VW. We are going to seriously cheat here. Our level 0 record is a delivered PeopleTools table with real data. Level 0 is read only, so this is not a problem. Level 1 however is read/write. We are relating it to a mock record so that we don't accidentally corrupt delivered metadata. The following SQL selects from our mock level 1 record rather than the delivered PeopleTools table. Enter the following into the view's SQL editor and then build the view.

```
SELECT FIELDNAME
     , COUNT(*)
  FROM PS_BMA_XLATITEM
 GROUP BY FIELDNAME
```

Before continuing, be sure to build the record definition, selecting the Create Views option.

A Two-Panel Layout

Create a new fluid page that uses the PSL_TWOPANEL layout. Name the new page BMA_XLAT_2PNL_FL. Application Designer should present you with a fluid page containing a series of nested group boxes. The innermost collection should contain two group boxes, a narrow one on the left and a wider one on the right. We will be using the group boxes labeled `panel action - interior` and `apps content`. Delete the empty group box inside the apps content group box. We won't be using that small inner group box. Figure 2-18 is a screenshot of the Application Designer's two-panel layout.

The apps content group box is supposed to contain the same grid as the BMA_XLAT_FL page. The easiest way to recreate the grid is to copy it from the BMA_XLAT_FL page definition and paste it into the apps content group box. After pasting (or recreating) the grid, open the grid's properties dialog and switch to the Use tab. Check the No Auto Select option. Unlike BMA_XLAT_FL, this transaction page has no level 0 to tell the component processor which rows to select. Instead we will use PeopleCode to populate the Translate Values grid.

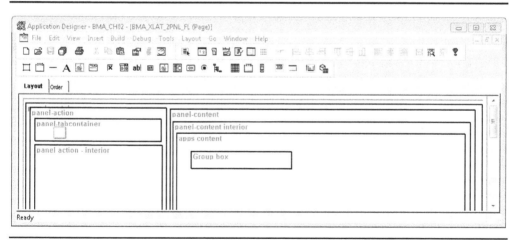

FIGURE 2-18. *PSL_TWOPANEL layout*

NOTE
If you review the PeopleSoft delivered fluid content, you will see lots of fluid pages that contain subpages rather than standard page content. Instead of adding content directly to layouts, some developers create subpages with content and add those subpages to layouts. This is purely a matter of preference and convenience. One added benefit to the subpage approach is that you can embed the same subpage in both classic and fluid pages.

The left side of our layout will also contain a grid, but we don't want it to look like a grid. Rather, we want the left side of the screen to look like an iPhone or Android list view. We will use PeopleSoft's predefined CSS3 classes to obtain the desired appearance. Drag a new grid into the panel action-interior group box. Open the grid's properties and make the following changes to the general tab:

- Set the main record and page field name to BMA_XLAT_FLD_VW.

- Select Unlimited Occurs Count.

We need to disable a lot of the label options, so switch to the Label tab. For example, to turn off the row counter, click the Properties button for the navigation bar and then switch to the Row Cntr tab. Select the Invisible checkbox to turn off the row counter. Now disable the navigation bar by deselecting the Display Navigation Bar checkbox. Move down the properties dialog to the Body area and deselect Show Row Headings. Likewise, deselect Show Column Headings.

On the Use tab, select the following items:

- No Row Insert

- No Row Delete

- Display Only

At the bottom of the Use tab, change the grid layout to List Grid Layout. Switch to the Fluid tab and set the Default Style Name to `psc_list-linkmenu`.

To this left-hand grid, add a pushbutton/hyperlink field. Open the button's properties to mark it as a hyperlink and then set its Field Name property to FIELDNAME. Switch to the Label field and change the Label Type to Text. When a user invokes this hyperlink, PeopleCode will filter the grid on the right to show just translate values for the selected field. Since we want that PeopleCode to execute when a user clicks (or touches) a row, switch to the Use tab and select the

Execute PC on Row/Group Click option. While still viewing the Use tab, select the Enable When Page is Display Only option.

Add the BMA_XLAT_FLD_VW.COUNT1 field to the grid. We want the translate value count to show in a little circle on the right side of the list, similar to the way approvals and exceptions appear in employee self-service fluid pages. Open the field's properties and switch to the Fluid tab. Add the `psc_list_count` style class to the Default Style Name property.

A Smart Component

Unlike the first example, where we created a page with all of the necessary data-binding metadata, this page just contains a lot of structure and references. The hyperlinks on the left, for example, won't display field names without some PeopleCode intervention. Likewise, the grid on the right won't display data without some PeopleCode to select the correct values. Let's create a component and write some PeopleCode.

Create a new component named BMA_XLAT_2PNL_FL. Open the component's properties and make the following changes:

- Set the search record to INSTALLATION.

- Disable the Add action (Use tab to the right of the search record).

- In the Internet tab, uncheck Display Folder Tabs.

- Switch to the Fluid tab and mark the Fluid Mode checkbox.

Add the BMA_XLAT_2PNL_FL page and set its Item Label to Maintain Translate Values. Open the component's PeopleCode editor by choosing View | View PeopleCode from the Application Designer menu bar. Scroll through the list of objects in the upper left to find the BMA_XLAT_FLD_VW record and then locate the RowInit event on the right. Add the following to the PeopleCode editor. Figure 2-19 is a screenshot of the component PeopleCode editor.

```
BMA_XLAT_FLD_VW.FIELDNAME.Label = BMA_XLAT_FLD_VW.FIELDNAME
```

Register this component using values similar to the prior component. Add it to a menu, portal registry, and permission list. Choose the BMA_FLUID menu. Set the content reference label and description to BMA Maintain Translate Values. Use the PTPT1200 permission list and complete the wizard.

After registration, test the component by visiting its Content Reference in the Portal Registry and then clicking Test Content Reference. You can find the Portal Registry online using the navigation PeopleTools | Portal | Structure and Content. The new component is registered at Fluid Structure and Content | Fluid Pages | BMA PeopleTools. Figure 2-20 is a screenshot of the new component with its sidebar exposed.

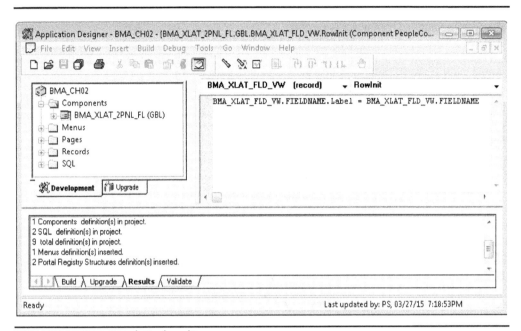

FIGURE 2-19. *PeopleCode editor*

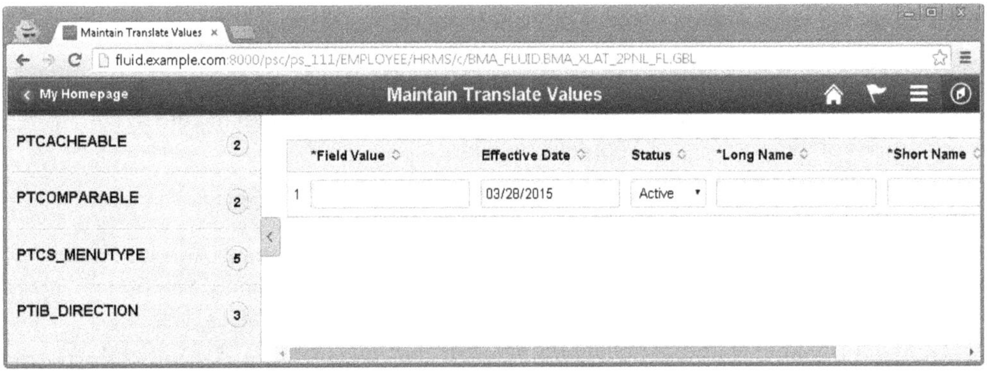

FIGURE 2-20. *Responsive Translate Values page with a sidebar*

NOTE

If the component looks like a classic component instead of a fluid component, then verify that you selected Fluid Mode on the Fluid tab of the component properties.

Return to Application Designer and enter the following PeopleCode into the BMA_XLAT_FLD_VW.FIELDNAME FieldChange event. The component processor will invoke this PeopleCode when a user selects a row in the left panel.

```
REM ** Row selection container;
Component Row &selectedRow;

Local Row &r0 = GetLevel0().GetRow(1);
Local Rowset &xlatRs = &r0.GetRowset(Scroll.BMA_XITMMNT_VW);
Local string &fieldName = GetField().Value;

&xlatRs.Flush();
&xlatRs.Select(Record.BMA_XITMMNT_VW, "WHERE FIELDNAME = :1",
        &fieldName);

If (All(&selectedRow)) Then
    &selectedRow.Style = "";
End-If;

REM ** Update the selected row style class;
&selectedRow = GetRow();
&selectedRow.Style = "psc_selected";
```

Save and then reload the page in your web browser. Select an item from the list on the left and notice that the grid now contains data.

We have a minor problem with this page. No rows are selected when the page first appears. Let's resolve this with some component PostBuild PeopleCode. Add the following to the component's PostBuild event:

```
REM ** Row selection container;
Component Row &selectedRow;

Local Row &r0 = GetLevel0().GetRow(1);
Local Rowset &xlatRs = &r0.GetRowset(Scroll.BMA_XITMMNT_VW);
Local string &fieldName;

&selectedRow = &r0.GetRowset(Scroll.BMA_XLAT_FLD_VW).GetRow(1);
&fieldName = &selectedRow.GetRecord(Record.BMA_XLAT_FLD_VW).GetField(
        Field.FIELDNAME).Value;
```

```
&xlatRs.Select(Record.BMA_XITMMNT_VW, "WHERE FIELDNAME = :1",
    &fieldName);


REM ** Update the selected row style class;
&selectedRow.Style = "psc_selected";
```

NOTE
*Are you tired of seeing cryptic text such as BMA_*
XLAT_2PNL_FL in the browser tab or page title? I am.
You can change this by changing the item's label in
the menu definition.

If the device screen width is wide enough, I would like to see the sidebar on the left default to an expanded, rather than collapsed state. We can force the sidebar to default to the expanded state by adding the following PeopleCode to the Page Activate event:

```
Declare Function initializeTwoPanel PeopleCode
PT_TWOPNL_WORK.BUTTON FieldFormula;

initializeTwoPanel(1, False, Null, 0);
```

Figure 2-21 is a screenshot of the final two-panel Maintain Translate Values component.

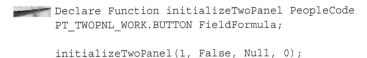

FIGURE 2-21. *Two-panel Maintain Translate Values component*

Application Class Controllers

Did you see the duplicate code shared by the FieldChange and PostBuild events? Both events update the selected row and populate the Translate Values grid. One strategy PeopleCode developers employ for DRY (Don't Repeat Yourself) code is to write business logic in Application Classes. Some developers write all of their business logic in Application Classes, treating them like component controllers. The PeopleTools platform already has the component processor, so I'm not fond of the Application Class controller pattern. Nevertheless, Application Classes have a lot to offer. For example, Application Designer does not allow a developer to save an Application Class that contains undeclared variables. I don't know how many hours I have lost trying to resolve an issue caused by a misspelled variable. Another great reason to use Application Classes is to facilitate test-driven development. We can't write tests for component event-based PeopleCode, but we can use PSUnit to test Application Classes. While the trend shows more business logic moving away from event-based PeopleCode and into Application Classes, my intention is to stay with event-based PeopleCode and only create Application Classes when it makes sense. In the preceding example, encapsulating the common code in an Application Class would make sense. Conversely, one of our PeopleCode events required only one line of PeopleCode. Moving that one line into an Application Class would have resulted in a tenfold increase in the number of lines of code.

NOTE
In this chapter, we used several delivered CSS classes. As you build fluid components, you may need to create your CSS definitions. You can include custom CSS stylesheets into fluid components using the new `AddStylesheet` *PeopleCode function.*

Grouplets

Grouplets are group boxes displayed on home pages. Most people refer to them as tiles but we will stick with the official name of grouplet. Grouplets are normally small in stature, but can span multiple columns. You can see the grouplet attributes and grouplet types from the Fluid tab of any content reference. The HRMS Team Time grouplet is a great example. The Team Time grouplet is actually a group box within a standard fluid page. Other grouplet types include images and iScripts.

Most grouplets are image links that point to transaction pages. These are the easiest to configure because they just require an image reference in the fluid tab of a content reference. In fact, any page, including classic pages, can be added as a grouplet to a fluid home page. One thing to keep in mind when using images is caching. Once you add a grouplet to a home page, the image that was specified on the content reference before adding the grouplet is the image that will be visible until someone clears the PeopleSoft application's cache. This is mainly significant when a person navigates to a transaction and then uses the "Add To" header item to add a transaction page to a home page. Many times, I have added a grouplet to a home page only to see the default icon appear. My greatest desire at that point is to update the icon. Even after adding an icon to the content reference, I won't see that new icon until someone clears the cache.

Conclusion

Beauty is in the eye of the beholder. There are many people who believe fluid pages are prettier than classic pages. Although just a matter of opinion, it is an opinion shared by many (including me). At this time, however, it does not make sense to convert every page to Fluid. Fluid excels at displaying low-density information and collecting information using touch devices. Some transactions, however, require high information density and dexterity.

In this chapter, we experienced a few drops from the PeopleTools fluid reservoir. We built a couple of fluid pages, learned about fluid search, fluid layouts, and fluid design patterns. There is a lot more to fluid than what we covered in the few pages between the start and end of this chapter. For example, the PeopleTools team has added new PeopleCode functions specifically for fluid. You can read more about them, and other fluid concepts, in the PeopleTools Fluid User Interface Developer's Guide located at http://docs.oracle.com/cd/E55243_01/pt854pbr0/eng/pt/tflu/index.html.

CHAPTER
3

Building Applications
with the Mobile
Application Platform

P eopleSoft Mobile Application Platform (MAP) is the second of two mobile development tools in the PeopleTools chest (Fluid is the first). Although both produce similar mobile results, they take a very different approach. As you learned in the last chapter, Fluid uses Application Designer and core PeopleTools development concepts. Fluid serves content through the PeopleSoft Pure Internet Architecture (PIA), just like classic pages. MAP is very different. MAP uses an online configuration tool and serves content through Integration Broker's REST listening connector. About the only part of MAP that is familiar to PeopleSoft developers is the PeopleCode editor. MAP uses PeopleCode Application Classes to respond to events.

Since PeopleSoft includes two mobile development tools, it is very reasonable to ask the question, "Which mobile tool should I use?" Oracle recommends that customers use fluid whenever possible because it uses standard PeopleTools development patterns. Since MAP serves content through Integration Broker, Oracle recommends that customers use MAP when building mobile applications that span multiple PeopleSoft databases. You might also choose to use MAP when creating a responsive, mobile version of a complex component. In this scenario, you would create a component interface for the complex component and then use that component interface in a MAP application.

MAP combines online design and modeling tools with PeopleCode to create mobile applications. The online designer is functional enough to share with subject matter experts, allowing them to make mobile user interface changes that would normally require a PeopleSoft developer.

MAP produces MV* applications. I hesitate to identify the * because there is a lot of gray area surrounding that last element. Is it a ViewModel? A Controller? A Presenter? How about just "glue" (MVG). The Model (or ViewModel) is described through a PeopleSoft Document. The View is configurable through a Layout Designer. In this chapter, we will first create Documents to represent the data required by Layouts. Second, we will create Layouts to display information. As a final step, we will connect the model to the view using PeopleCode.

Hello MAP

Let's build the simplest MAP application possible... how about `"Hello "` | `%OperatorID`?

Creating a Document

Since PeopleSoft moved to the PIA, Integration Broker Message definitions have described data going into and out of Integration Broker. The problem with Message definitions is that they only describe hierarchical Record structures. Another shortcoming of Message definitions is that they only support XML. Considering the popularity of JSON, PeopleTools needed a new way to represent data in other formats. PeopleTools added the Documents module to PeopleTools 8.51 as a structured abstraction, abstracting the structure of a data set from the representation of that data. We can use PeopleCode to populate a Document and then render that Document in a variety of formats including XML and JSON.

In MAP, Documents represent the ViewModel. Each Layout (View) is attached to a Document (Model), and that Document contains all of the data rendered by the Layout.

Log into your PeopleSoft online application and navigate to PeopleTools | Documents | Document Builder. Create a new document that has the package BMA_HELLO, document HELLO_USER, and version V1. I used upper case words to define this document, but you can use any mixture of upper and lower case characters. Figure 3-1 is a screenshot of the Add New Document page.

When the new document appears, select the HELLO_USER node in the tree on the left and add a new primitive child. Primitive values represent basic data types, such as binary, number, string, and so on. Name the new primitive element GREETING and select the Text type. Documents can contain primitive, collection, and compound types. You can think of a collection as an array. The child of a

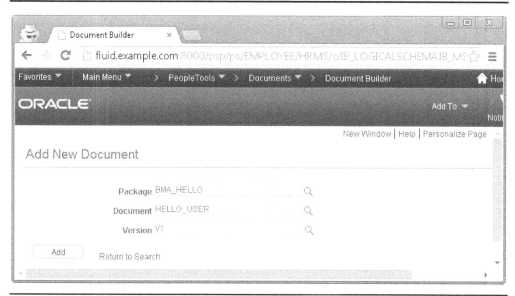

FIGURE 3-1. *Add New Document page*

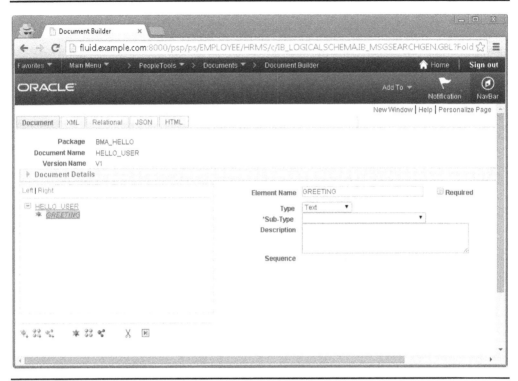

FIGURE 3-2. *New Document definition*

collection is either a primitive or a compound. A compound is a reference to another Document. Figure 3-2 is a screenshot of the Document.

Configuring a Layout

With our ViewModel defined, we can move onto the layout. Navigate to PeopleTools | Mobile Application Platform | Layout Designer. Switch to Add mode and create a new layout named BMA_HELLO_USER. The first step in creating a new layout is to specify the Layout Document (also known as the ViewModel). Figure 3-3 is a screenshot of the Layout document selection. After selecting a document, select the PT_TEMPLATE_ONE template. Layout templates allow for reuse by moving commonly used items into templates. MAP Layout templates are the MAP synonym for Fluid layouts.

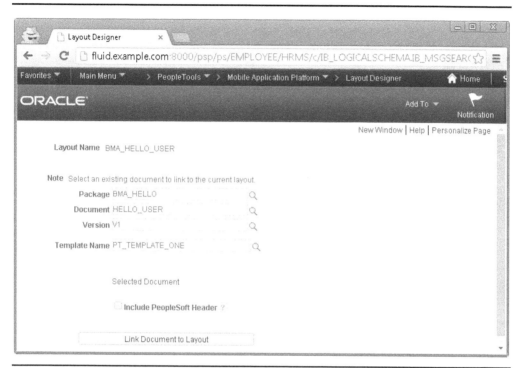

FIGURE 3-3.   *Specify a document for a layout*

Figure 3-4 is a screenshot of the Layout Designer. Notice that the left side contains a representation of the Document we created specifically for this layout. Just above and to the right of that you see a template name. Below the template name is a toolbar. This toolbar contains buttons that insert input and output controls into the layout. Below the toolbar you find a list of items that are part of this layout. Container elements contain a start and end item. For example, mapheader_1 is immediately followed by mapheader_end. Anything you add between these items is displayed within the header. Nearly everything you add to a page will exist in some sort of container. While viewing the Layout grid, set the Label Text for mapheader_1 to `Hello World`.

The arrow in the left column of the Layout grid determines the new item insertion point. Move the arrow to mapheader_end by clicking on that row's bar in the left column. Now click the 'A' icon in the toolbar to insert a static text element. MAP will respond by asking you what you want to put in the static text element.

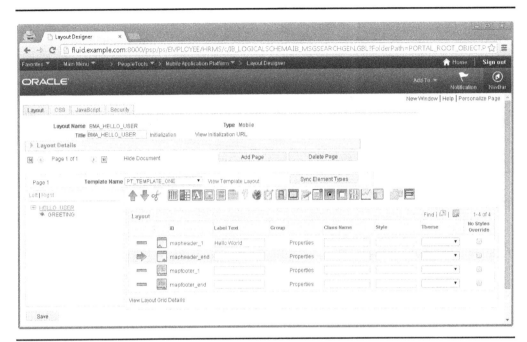

FIGURE 3-4.   *Layout Designer*

Choose the Primitive radio button and then check the box for the GREETING row. Figure 3-5 is a screenshot of the text element properties. The Layout Designer grid will now contain a mapstatictxt_1 element that has the label text GREETING.

NOTE
If you add an element in the wrong place, then ensure that row has an arrow in the left column and then use the up and down arrows in the toolbar to move the row up or down within the grid. If you want to completely delete a row, then select the row and then use the scissors icon to delete the row.

Layout Security
Switch to the security tab in the Layout Designer and change Req Verification from none to Basic Authentication and SSL. Next, click the Layout Permissions link and add a Permission List. I chose PTPT1000, which is the permission list common to all users.

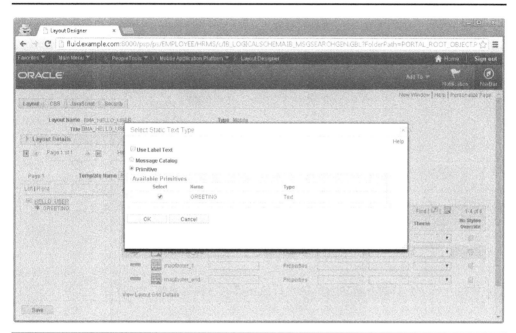

FIGURE 3-5. *Adding a text element to a layout.*

NOTE
Never authenticate without SSL. SSL is the encryption layer that ensures your username and password are protected as they travel across the network.

At some point we need to populate the ViewModel. Let's first view our layout without data. Switch back to the Layout tab and click the View Initialization URL link. This will display a dialog containing the MAP application's URL. Paste this URL into a web browser to load the application. Figure 3-6 is a screenshot of the layout as viewed at runtime.

Data Initialization

When Integration Broker receives a request for a layout, it runs the Layout's initialization routine. The initialization routine is responsible for populating the Layout's Document. These initialization routines are Application Classes. Let's create the initialization routine for this layout. Log into Application Designer and create a new Application Package. Name the new package BMA_HELLO_MAP. To this

FIGURE 3-6.   *Hello User layout without data*

Application Package, add the class HelloUser. Open the HelloUser PeopleCode editor and add the following PeopleCode:

```
import PS_PT:Integration:IDocLayoutHandler;

class HelloUser implements PS_PT:Integration:IDocLayoutHandler
   method OnInitEvent(&Map As Map) Returns Map;
end-class;

method OnInitEvent
   /+ &Map as Map +/
   /+ Returns Map +/

   Local Compound &COM = &Map.GetDocument().DocumentElement;

   &COM.GetPropertyByName("GREETING").Value = "Hello " | %OperatorId;

   Return &Map;
end-method;
```

This PeopleCode first asks MAP for a reference to the ViewModel and then it updates the GREETING property to a relevant greeting.

NOTE
There is a great book named PeopleSoft PeopleTools
Tips and Techniques *published by Oracle Press that
contains a chapter on creating Application Classes.*

Return to the online application and find the Initialization link. Select this link and then expand the Base Event Method group box. Enter the application package and class we just created. Figure 3-7 is a screenshot of the Base Event Method properties.

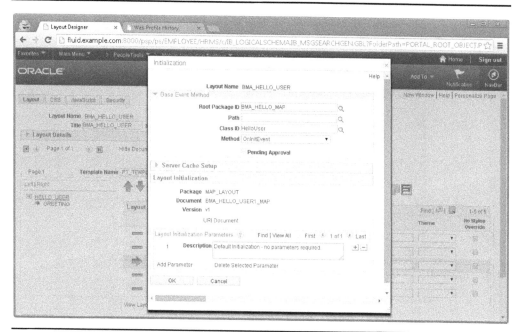

FIGURE 3-7. *Base Event Method properties*

Save your layout and then reload the runtime version of the layout. It should now contain the text GREETINGHello PS (or whomever you logged in as). A greeting doesn't need a label, so return to the layout and delete the mapstatictxt_1 Label Text, which currently has a value of GREETING. Save the layout. Reload your runtime MAP application and confirm your changes are successful. Figure 3-8 is a

FIGURE 3-8. *Final Hello User MAP application*

FIGURE 3-9. *mLayoutDocument*

screenshot of the final Hello User MAP application. Congratulations! You have now created your first MAP application.

One more thing before we move onto the next concept... at the top of the Layout Designer there is a collapsed group box labeled Layout Details. Expand this group box and locate the Document Dump checkbox. This checkbox adds the `mLayoutDocument` JavaScript variable to the layout page at runtime. I find this immensely valuable. When I create a layout and don't see the data I expect, I can review the contents of the `mLayoutDocument` variable to determine whether the problem is with the initialization PeopleCode or a property within the Layout. After enabling Document Dump, reload your online MAP application and open the JavaScript console. At the prompt, enter `mLayoutDocument`. Figure 3-9 is a screenshot of the `mLayoutDocument` output.

The Role of jQuery

Our Hello User layout contained a header, text area, and footer. When we viewed the MAP application at runtime, we saw that the header consisted of a very dark color with centered, contrasting text. Likewise, the body had a lighter color with contrasting text, the text having an outline. The styling present in this MAP application is standard jQuery Mobile styling. You can change an element's appearance by selecting a different theme letter from the Layout grid. For example, to change the header's background color from black to blue, change the value in the theme drop-down to "b." As you interact with the Layout Designer, you will notice quite a few allowances for jQuery Mobile configuration data. For example, the JavaScript tab contains a section dedicated to jQuery Mobile Document Events.

A PeopleTools Cross-Pillar Mobile Process Monitor

Every PeopleSoft application has a process monitor. It would be convenient to be able to access all of the monitors from one location. Since this functionality requires web services, it is a great candidate for MAP. Our process monitor will consist of an initial page containing a list of processes. Each item in the list will be a link to a details page. Considering that the process scheduler has the potential to generate a significant amount of data, we will limit results to just the logged in user, and then further restrict the rows to only the most recent 30.

Data Model

As we saw from our Hello MAP example, there are multiple layers to the MAP data model. At the lowest level we have the database logical model and at the highest level we have the MAP view model document structure. There is a fair amount of overlap between the database model and the view model. The Documents module includes a great tool that generates a Document from a Record definition. First, however, we need a record definition. Let's create a Record definition that matches our process monitor data structure and then use it to create a portion of our view model. Open Application Designer and create a new Record definition. To this new record definition, add the following fields:

    PRCSINSTANCE

    PRCSTYPE

    PRCSNAME

    RUNDTTM

    OPRID

    PT_AESTATUS

Switch to the Record Type tab and change the Record Type to SQL View. Open the view's SQL editor and insert the following effective dated SQL:

```
SELECT RQST.PRCSINSTANCE
  , RQST.PRCSTYPE
  , RQST.PRCSNAME
  , RQST.RUNDTTM
```

```
, RQST.OPRID
, XLAT.XLATSHORTNAME
 FROM PSPRCSRQST RQST
 , PSXLATITEM XLAT
WHERE RQST.RUNSTATUS = XLAT.FIELDVALUE
  AND XLAT.FIELDNAME = 'RUNSTATUS'
  AND XLAT.EFF_STATUS = 'A'
  AND XLAT.EFFDT = (
SELECT MAX(XLAT_ED.EFFDT)
 FROM PSXLATITEM XLAT_ED
WHERE XLAT.FIELDNAME = XLAT_ED.FIELDNAME
  AND XLAT.FIELDVALUE = XLAT_ED.FIELDVALUE
  AND XLAT_ED.EFFDT <= RQST.RUNDTTM )
 ORDER BY RUNDTTM DESC
```

Save the Record and name it BMA_PRCSRQST_VW. Build the record by choosing Build | Current Definition from the Application Designer menu bar. Figure 3-10 is a screenshot of this new record definition.

NOTE
I chose to relate the process status translate value to the run date. If a translate value changes, then older processes will show the prior value, whereas newer processes will show the current value. Alternatively, I could have chosen the current date so that all processes would show the most current status label.

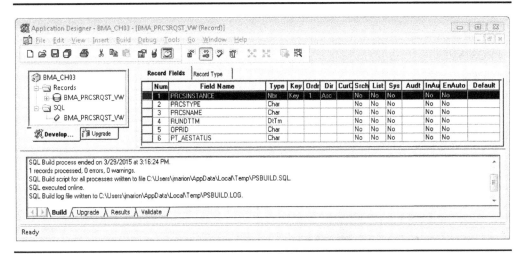

FIGURE 3-10. *BMA_PRCSRQST_VW Record definition*

With our data record in place, let's log into PeopleSoft online and create a Document that matches this record's definition. After authenticating, navigate to PeopleTools | Documents | Document Utilities | Create Document from Record. When prompted, choose the BMA_PRCSRQST_VW Record definition. The utility will inspect the selected record and give you the opportunity to select which fields to include in the target Document. Set the Package Name to BMA_PROCESS_ MONITOR_MOBILE. Accept the defaults, and click the OK button. Figure 3-11 is a screenshot of the utility.

After clicking OK, the Create Document from Record utility displays a Build Result. You want that Build Result column to contain the text, "Document created successfully." If it does, then click that text because it is a hyperlink to the newly created Document. If the Build Result column contains a different message, then you may need to build the Document manually.

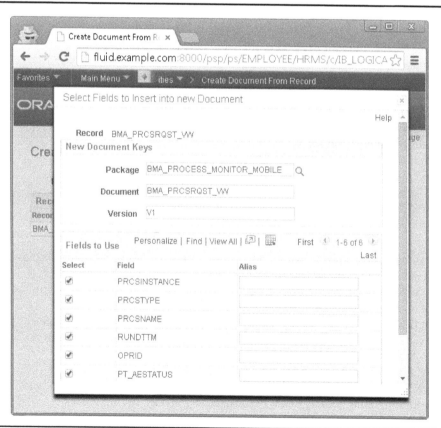

FIGURE 3-11. *Create Document from Record utility*

The Create Document from Record utility is a convenience tool that saves some typing and clicking. While great for a back-end data model, the generated document contains some primitive configurations that won't display well. For example, the RUNDTTM primitive contains a highly specific date format that is designed for integration, not display purposes. As currently defined, the RUNDTTM will be a little difficult to comprehend in the view layer. Let's change the RUNDTTM from a DateTime type to a Text type (Don't try to save yet because changing the type will make the document invalid). Later we will use PeopleCode to format the RUNDTTM into something meaningful. After changing the RUNDTTM, switch to the Relational tab and expand the Relational Details section. Clear the record name from the record prompt (Now you can save because the document is now valid). The Documents module maintains the record/document relational mapping for the `Document.GetRowset` and `Document.UpdateFromRowset` methods. The relationship however is quite strict, requiring the Document's and Record's fields to have the same types.

NOTE
The Create Document from Record utility created a Document representation of a Record definition. If a Document and Record share the same structure, then having them share the same name, BMA_ PRCSRQST_VW, also makes sense. However, we changed the structure of the Document, so that it no longer matches the source record definition. With that in mind, it seems misleading to have the Document and Record sharing the same name. Perhaps a better name would have been BMA_PRCSRQST_VM, the suffix VM representing ViewModel.

We now have a Document that contains a field for each item we plan to display in the Process Monitor mobile list. This Document represents just one row. Our Layout ViewModel requires multiple rows. To accomplish this, we must wrap this Document in a container Document. Navigate to PeopleTools | Documents | Document Builder and create a new document in the package BMA_PROCESS_ MONITOR_MOBILE. Name the new document BMA_PROCESS_LIST_VM and set the version to V1. When the Document structure appears, click on the BMA_ PROCESS_LIST_VM node and then add a Collection child node. Name the collection ROWS. To the ROWS collection, add a Compound child node. The basis for the compound child node is BMA_PROCESS_MONITOR_MOBILE.BMA_ PRCSRQST_VM.V1. Figure 3-12 is a screenshot of the compound child node

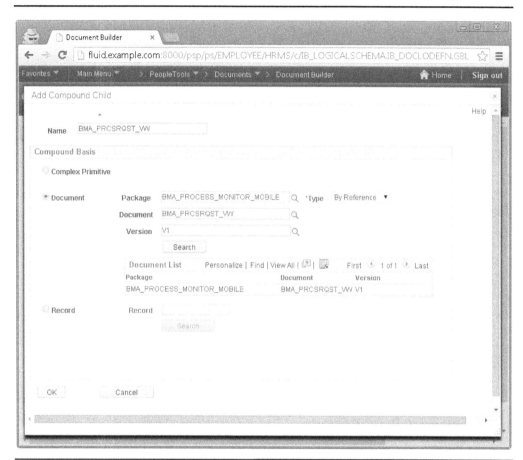

FIGURE 3-12.   *Adding a Compound Child node*

selection dialog. Select a basis Document and then save this new compound Document.

NOTE
Don't click the OK button in the compound child node selection dialog. Instead, search for a basis document and then select it from the list. This will populate the Document's metadata and close the dialog.

We are just a few pages away from creating a layout. The list in our first layout will link to a details layout. That target layout MUST exist before we create our list. As you saw with the Hello MAP example, we have to create a Document before we can create a layout. We can modify both later, but we need to create something for placeholders. Return to the BMA_PROCESS_MONITOR_MOBILE.BMA_PRCSRQST_VW.V1 Document and click the Copy button. BMA_PRCSRQST_VW contains the base fields we will display on a details page. Later we will want to add more fields to the details Document without changing the initial process list Layout and Document. Place the new Document in the same package: BMA_PROCESS_MONITOR_MOBILE and name the new Document BMA_PROCESS_DETAILS_VM. Set the version to V1.

Layout

Our application consists of two layouts: A list layout and a details layout. We need to create the details layout first because the list layout will link to the details layout. The target (details) layout must exist before we can create that link.

Details Layout

Navigate to PeopleTools | Mobile Application Platform | Layout Designer. Create a new Layout named BMA_PMON_DETAILS. The Document for this layout is the Document we just created: BMA_PROCESS_MONITOR_MOBILE.BMA_PROCESS_DETAILS_VM.V1. Choose the template PT_TEMPLATE_ONE and then click the Link Document to Layout button.

When the new Layout appears, set the mapheader_1 label text to `Process Details`. Select the mapheader_end item and use the toolbar button to add a container. Inside the container, add a static text element. MAP will ask how to populate the static text element. Select Primitive and then choose the PRCSINSTANCE field.

The first Layout exists to help a user select a process instance. This second layout displays details about the process instance. Since this Layout represents the second page within our application, it needs a parameter. Click the Layout Initialization link near the top of the Layout. When the Initialization dialog appears, identify the Layout Initialization Parameters section. Add a new row by clicking the "plus" signed button. When the Parameter List appears, use the Select Primitive link to select the PRCSINSTANCE field. Figure 3-13 is a screenshot of the Layout parameters.

Switch to the Security tab and configure security for the Layout. Set the Req Verification to Basic Authentication and SSL and then use the Layout Permissions to assign this Layout to a permission list. I chose PTPT1000 so all users can access the mobile process monitor. We could view this layout now by handcrafting a URL with the appropriate parameters, but we will wait and let the list Layout create one for us.

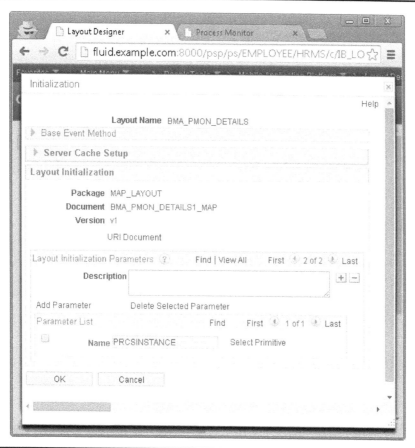

FIGURE 3-13.   *Layout parameters*

List Overview Layout

Create a new Layout named BMA_PMON_LIST. Select the Document BMA_
PROCESS_MONITOR_MOBILE.BMA_PROCESS_LIST_VM.V1 and set the template
name to PT_TEMPLATE_ONE. Click the Link Document to Layout button to
continue. Locate mapheader_1 and set the label to Process Monitor. Select the
mapheader_end element and add a Listview element. When prompted if you want
to create a group, click "No." The Listview configuration dialog will appear. Check
the Add URL and Dynamic Flag attributes. Add URL will allow us to associate a
target link with each item in the list. The Dynamic Flag will let us select elements
from a collection. In the Listview Composition grid, set values for Title, Description,
and Aside. For the title, choose the primitive PRCSNAME. Set the description to

PRCSTYPE and the aside to RUNDTTM. Just above the grid is a link titled Add Field. Use this link to add one additional field. For this new field, set the primitive to PT_ AESTATUS. Figure 3-14 is a screenshot of the Listview configuration dialog.

Since we specified Add URL, MAP will prompt us for URL details. Select the Call Layout option and then select the Layout BMA_PMON_DETAILS. The details Layout has two URLs:

■ A default initialization URL with no parameters.

■ The URL we created that expects a process instance.

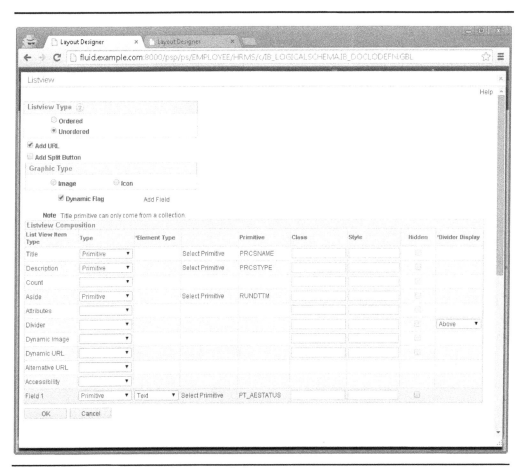

FIGURE 3-14. *Listview configuration dialog*

Select the second URL (the one with no description). The URI Parameters grid will appear, allowing us to map the PRCSINSTANCE parameter to a primitive from our ViewModel. Select the PRCSINSTANCE primitive. Figure 3-15 is a screenshot of the URL mapping.

After assigning security to the Layout (Basic Authentication with SSL and permission list PTPT1000) return to the Layout tab and click the View Initialization URL link. A dialog will appear that contains the URL for launching the Layout. On my VirtualBox image, the URL is http://fluid.example.com:8000/PSIGW/RESTListeningConnector/PSFT_HR/BMA_PMON_LIST1_MAP.v1/INIT/-1. If you are interested, you can paste your Layout's URL into a browser and view the current state of the Layout. Since we haven't populated the Layout's Document, all you will see is the header.

Initialization

Our Layouts need some data. Log into Application Designer and create a new Application Package named BMA_PMON_MOBILE.

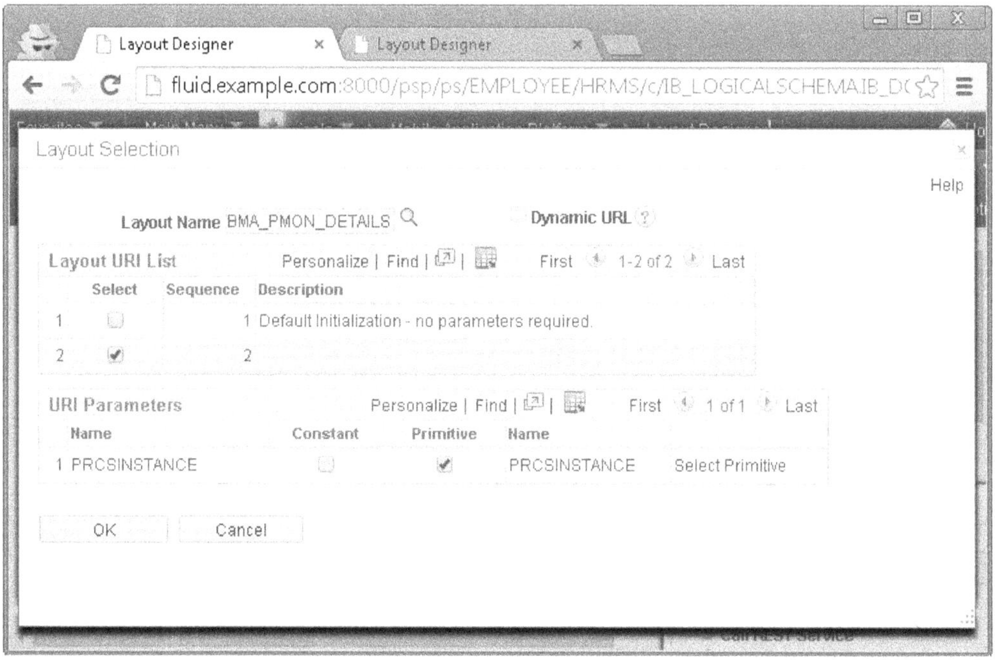

FIGURE 3-15. *URL mapping*

List Overview Initialization

Add a new Application Class to the BMA_PMON_MOBILE Application Package and name the new class `ProcessOverviewList`. Add the following PeopleCode:

```
import PS_PT:Integration:IDocLayoutHandler;

class ProcessOverviewList implements
        PS_PT:Integration:IDocLayoutHandler
   method OnInitEvent(&Map As Map) Returns Map;
end-class;

method OnInitEvent
   /+ &Map as Map +/
   /+ Returns Map +/

   Local Rowset &rs = CreateRowset(Record.BMA_PRCSRQST_VW);
   &rs.Fill("WHERE OPRID = :1 AND ROWNUM < 31", %OperatorId);

   Local Document &doc = &Map.GetDocument();
   Local Compound &COM = &doc.DocumentElement;
   Local Collection &items = &COM.GetPropertyByName("ROWS");
   Local Compound &resultItem;
   Local number &rowIdx = 1;
   Local Row &row;

   For &rowIdx = 1 To &rs.RowCount
      &row = &rs.GetRow(&rowIdx);
      &resultItem = &items.CreateItem();
      &resultItem.GetPropertyByName("PRCSINSTANCE").Value =
            &row.GetRecord(Record.BMA_PRCSRQST_VW).GetField(
            Field.PRCSINSTANCE).Value;
      &resultItem.GetPropertyByName("PRCSTYPE").Value =
            &row.GetRecord(Record.BMA_PRCSRQST_VW).GetField(
            Field.PRCSTYPE).Value;
      &resultItem.GetPropertyByName("PRCSNAME").Value =
            &row.GetRecord(Record.BMA_PRCSRQST_VW).GetField(
            Field.PRCSNAME).Value;
      &resultItem.GetPropertyByName("RUNDTTM").Value =
            DateTimeToLocalizedString(&row.GetRecord(
            Record.BMA_PRCSRQST_VW).GetField(Field.RUNDTTM).Value ,
            "MM/dd/yyyy 'at' hh:mm:ss a");
      &resultItem.GetPropertyByName("OPRID").Value =
            &row.GetRecord(Record.BMA_PRCSRQST_VW).GetField(
            Field.OPRID).Value;
```

```
    &resultItem.GetPropertyByName("PT_AESTATUS").Value =
        &row.GetRecord(Record.BMA_PRCSRQST_VW).GetField(
        Field.PT_AESTATUS).Value;
    Local boolean &ret = &items.AppendItem(&resultItem);
  End-For;

  Return &Map;
end-method;
```

The PeopleCode initialization routine is very similar to the Hello MAP example, but with a few lines of code to copy a rowset into the Layout Document's collection. I wrote the WHERE clause of the `Rowset.Fill` method to specifically limit the returned results to no more than 30 rows. The process scheduler can generate a significant amount of data. It is important to restrict how much information you send over a wireless network.

Return to the online Layout Designer for the BMA_PMON_LIST Layout and click the Initialization link. Expand the Base Event section and enter the Application Class `BMA_PMON_MOBILE:ProcessOverviewList`. Select the method `OnInitEvent`. Figure 3-16 is a screenshot of the Base Event Application Class properties. Save the Layout and then attempt to access the Layout through the initialization URL. Figure 3-17 is a screenshot of the Overview list. It isn't very pretty yet, but it contains data. After implementing the details initialization routine we will return to the layout and adjust properties for an optimal viewing experience.

Details Initialization

Inside Application Designer, add a new Application Class to the BMA_PMON_ MOBILE Application Package. Name the new class `ProcessInstanceDetails` and add the following PeopleCode:

```
import PS_PT:Integration:IDocLayoutHandler;

class ProcessInstanceDetails implements
       PS_PT:Integration:IDocLayoutHandler
  method OnInitEvent(&Map As Map) Returns Map;
end-class;

method OnInitEvent
  /+ &Map as Map +/
  /+ Returns Map +/

  REM ** access the URL parameters, specifically the
      process instance;
  Local Compound &reqDocElement =
      &Map.GetURIDocument().DocumentElement;
```

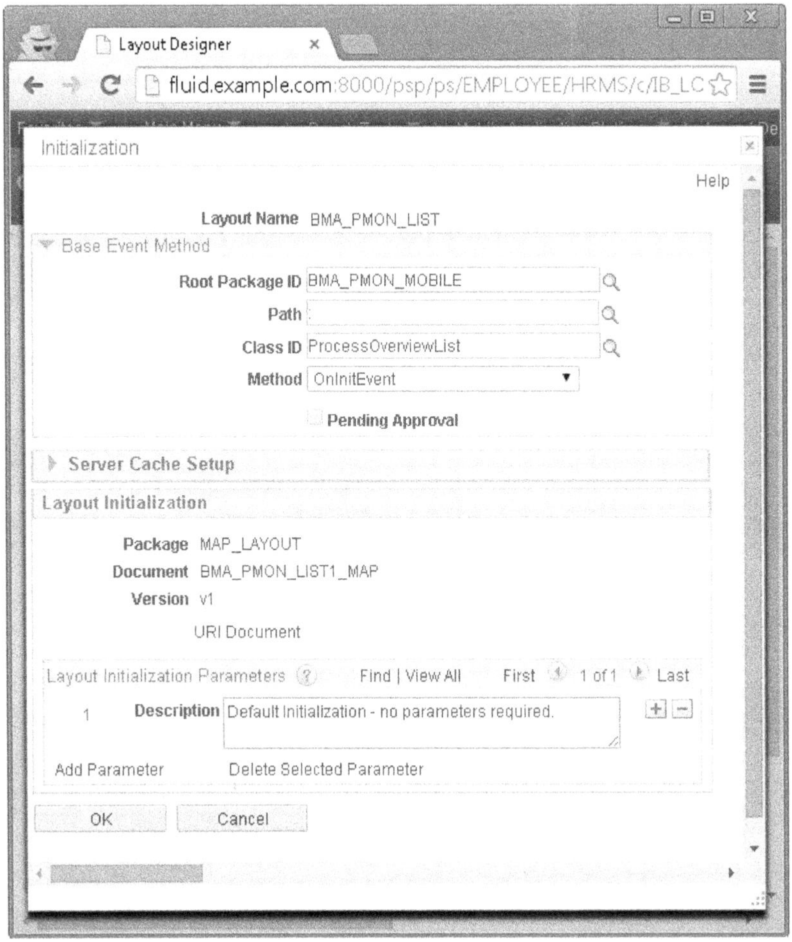

FIGURE 3-16. *Base Event properties*

```
Local number &prcsInstance = &reqDocElement.GetPropertyByName(
     "PRCSINSTANCE").Value;

REM ** select the process details from the database;
Local Record &rec = CreateRecord(Record.BMA_PRCSRQST_VW);
&rec.GetField(Field.PRCSINSTANCE).Value = &prcsInstance;
&rec.SelectByKey();

Local Compound &COM = &Map.GetDocument().DocumentElement;
```

FIGURE 3-17. *Process Monitor overview with data*

```
&COM.GetPropertyByName("PRCSINSTANCE").Value = &prcsInstance;
&COM.GetPropertyByName("PRCSTYPE").Value =
      &rec.GetField(Field.PRCSTYPE).Value;
&COM.GetPropertyByName("PRCSNAME").Value =
      &rec.GetField(Field.PRCSNAME).Value;
&COM.GetPropertyByName("RUNDTTM").Value =
      DateTimeToLocalizedString(&rec.GetField(
      Field.RUNDTTM).Value, "MM/dd/yyyy 'at' hh:mm:ss a");
&COM.GetPropertyByName("OPRID").Value = &rec.GetField(
      Field.OPRID).Value;
&COM.GetPropertyByName("PT_AESTATUS").Value =
      &rec.GetField(Field.PT_AESTATUS).Value;


  Return &Map;
end-method;
```

Return to the online Layout Designer for the BMA_PMON_DETAILS Layout and click the Initialization link. Expand the Base Event section and enter the Application Class BMA_PMON_MOBILE:ProcessInstanceDetails. Select the method OnInitEvent. Save the Layout and then attempt to access the Layout by clicking through the Process Overview Layout list. Figure 3-18 is a screenshot of the Details page. This page is not very pretty, either. Right now, we are just testing the initialization routine.

FIGURE 3-18. *Unformatted Details page with data*

Final Layout Adjustments

Our Layouts are now functional. Let's make some configuration changes to enhance the user experience.

List Overview Layout

Open the BMA_PMON_LIST Layout in the Layout Designer. Identify the maplist_view1 element in the Layout grid and click the element's Properties link. Scroll half way down the Listview Properties dialog to find the Dialog checkbox and check the box to select it. The default MAP behavior is to open links in a new window. Using the dialog option will keep the list active while loading the details Layout in the same window. Scroll the rest of the way through the dialog and find the Listview Properties group. Select the Inset and Filter options. Figure 3-19 is a screenshot of the Listview Properties.

Reload the Process Monitor mobile page, and notice that the list now has a filter at the top and the list is inset rather than filling the entire screen. Enter some text into the filter box to see the results list filtered to show only matching items. For example, enter SQR to see only SQR reports.

The list still has a few visual idiosyncrasies. For example, the process type is not aligned quite right and the run status seems to be oddly placed. Let's move the run status to the right so that it appears under the run date. I am also not fond of the overwhelming blue background within the list. Let's use the jQuery Mobile theme support to select a different color scheme for the list. Return to the Layout Designer and locate the Theme column. Change the theme for maplistview_1 to the "c" theme.

We can solve the remainder of the layout issues with CSS. There are two ways to apply CSS. The first is to add CSS attributes to the style property of each element we want to change. The second method is to define CSS style classes in the Layout's CSS

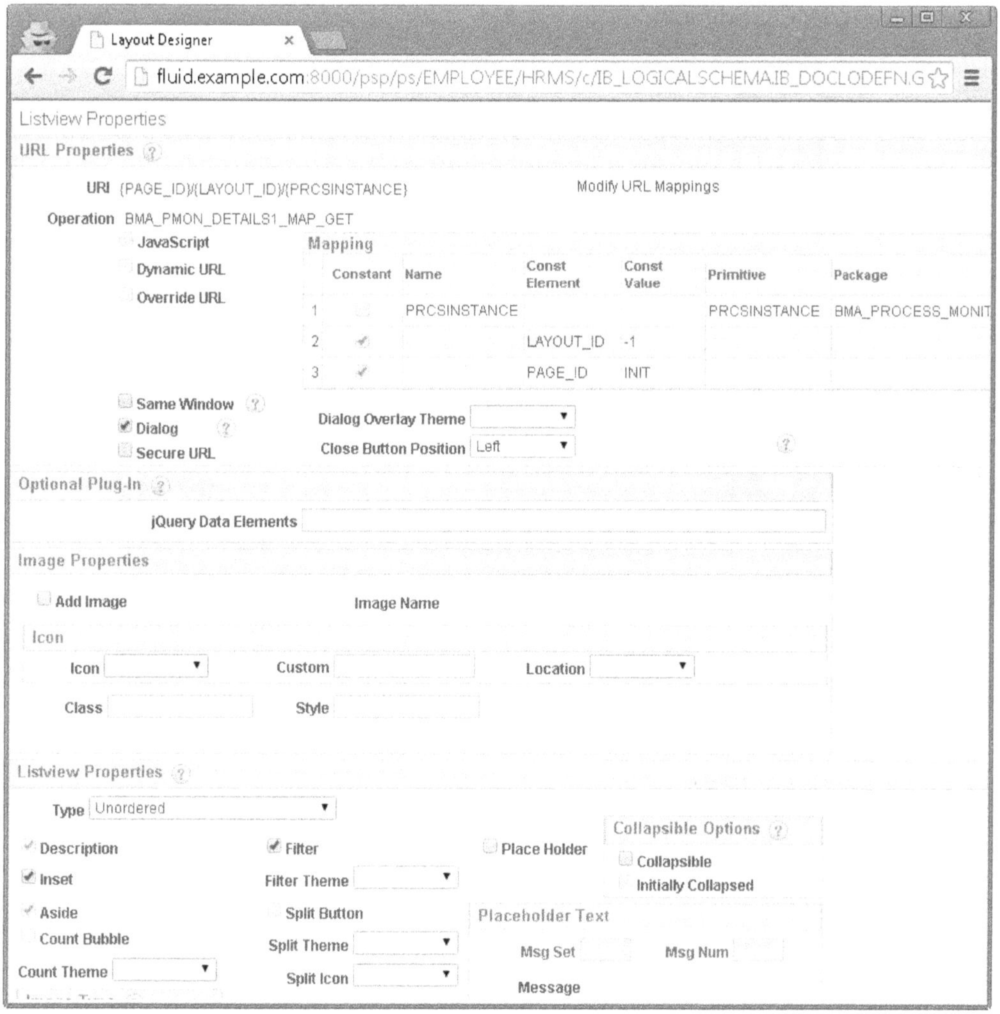

FIGURE 3-19. *Listview Properties*

tab and then assign those classes to each element. We will use this second approach. Return to the Layout Designer and switch to the CSS tab. About the middle of the page, click the button labeled Add Stylesheet. This will add a row to the Stylesheets grid. Enter a name in the CSS Name field. The name is not that important. It just needs to end with .css. I named the file list-layout.css. Enter the following into the text field below the CSS Name field. Figure 3-20 is a screenshot of the Layout Designer CSS editor.

```css
.prcsType {
    margin: .2em 0;
}

.prcsStatus {
    position: absolute;
    top: 36px;
    right:
```

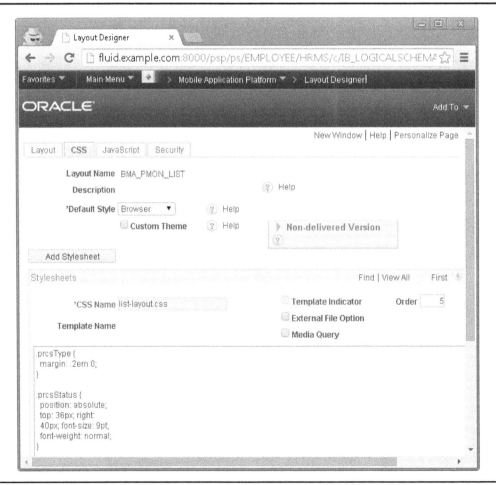

FIGURE 3-20. *Layout Designer CSS editor*

```
40px;
font-size: 9pt;
font-weight: normal;
}
```

NOTE
We can solve a lot of problems with CSS. For example, MAP does not have a mechanism to concatenate fields. Fields added to a page are stacked vertically. We can align them horizontally by adding the css `display: inline-block`. *We can also add delimiters with CSS using the* `:after` *and* `:before` *pseudo-classes.*

Return to the Layout tab and then select the Properties link of the maplistview_1 element. Locate the Field and Description items at the bottom of the properties dialog. Set the class name for the Description item to `prcsType` and the class name for the Field item to `prcsStatus`. Figure 3-21 is a screenshot of the field and class properties. Refresh the Process Monitor application and confirm that the layout changed as expected. Select one of the process links and verify that it opens the

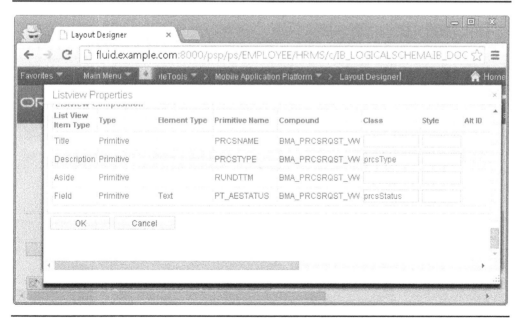

FIGURE 3-21. *Field and class properties*

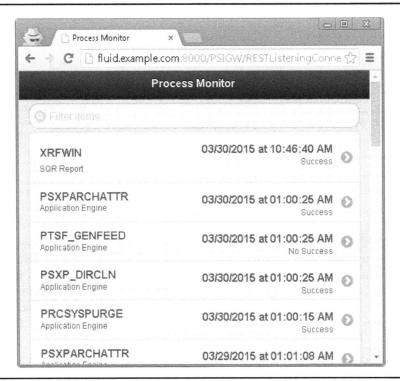

FIGURE 3-22. *Updated Process Monitor*

details page in a dialog box. Figure 3-22 is a screenshot of the Process Monitor list after applying styling adjustments.

The Process Monitor Overview is complete. Let's return to the details layout and make a few adjustments. Specifically, let's add a grid for layout purposes and then add a few primitives from our ViewModel.

Open the BMA_PMON_DETAILS Layout in the Layout Designer. Delete the mapcont_start_1, mapstatictxt_1, and mapcont_end_1 fields by selecting them and then clicking the "scissor" toolbar button. With mapheader_end selected, click the Add Mobile Grid toolbar button. This will add mapmobl_start_1 to the Layout. Ensure mapmobl_start_1 is selected and add two containers. Do not nest the containers. These containers need to be siblings. Inside the new first container within the grid, add PRCSINSTANCE and PRCSNAME as static text fields. Add PRCSTYPE and OPRID as static text fields to the second container. The grid now contains content, but the grid needs some internal metadata. Click the grid's properties link and a message will appear stating, "Defaulting mobile grid counts.

Column count defaults to 2 and row count to 1." This is perfect. We want a two-column grid with a single row. Click OK to dismiss the properties dialog and then save the layout. Adding the grid element created a nonresponsive two-column grid within the details dialog. The fields we added to each container are vertically stacked. Open the Mobile Process Monitor Overview list in a new window and click a row to see the changes we made to the details layout.

The fields within the details grid have labels, but the labels run right into the detail values as if they were all one word. The containers also run together as if they represented one single container. Let's apply CSS to improve the appearance of the dialog. As we saw with the Overview list, the Layout Designer has provisions for CSS files. We just have one problem: jQuery doesn't load external stylesheets into dialogs. We have a couple of options:

1. Convert the dialog into a standard link that opens either in the current window or a new window.

2. Use the style property instead of CSS files and class names.

3. Add the CSS to the parent Layout.

Option 1 is a great option, but would require the overview list to refresh each time we return to the list. Option 2 will let us apply some styling, but won't allow us to style nested elements that are hidden from the Layout table. We will choose option 3 because it avoids refreshing the list and lets us apply as much styling as we desire. Open the BMA_PMON_LIST Layout in the Layout Designer, switch to the CSS tab, and locate the list-layout.css file. Append the following to the end of the file:

```css
.bma-text {
  font-weight: bold;
  margin: .4em 0;
}

.bma-text span {
  font-weight: normal;
}

.bma-text span:before {
  content: ": ";
}

.bma-grid-container {
  margin: 0 .4em;
}
```

```
/* stack all grids below 40em (640px) */
@media all and (max-width: 35em) {
  .bma-responsive-grid .ui-block-a,
  .bma-responsive-grid .ui-block-b,
  .bma-responsive-grid .ui-block-c,
  .bma-responsive-grid .ui-block-d,
  .bma-responsive-grid .ui-block-e {
     width: 100%;
     float: none;
   }
}
```

Save the Layout and open the BMA_PMON_DETAILS Layout in the Layout Designer. In this Layout, we want to change the labels and add some CSS class names. First, use the values from Table 3-1 to update the CSS class names. The first column of the table contains the element type. The second column contains the CSS class name. For container elements (elements with a start and end element), only update the start element, not the end element.

Update the labels to something meaningful. Figure 3-23 is a screenshot of the Layout grid within the Layout Designer. Reload the Mobile Process Monitor Overview list and select an item. Figure 3-24 is a screenshot of the updated dialog. Make the browser window width smaller (resize the window) and notice that the containers within the grid stack vertically. Figure 3-25 shows the responsive grid.

Multipage Layouts

In this scenario, we created a separate Layout for each view within the Process Monitor mobile application. Alternatively, we could have created multiple pages within the same Layout. All pages within the same Layout must share the same Document ViewModel. Each page can use different fields (primitives, compounds, and collections), but they all share the same Document. Using the multipage approach would have required us to add the details view Compound to the same Document used by the process overview list. This is acceptable because a Layout Document structure exists specifically for the Layout, not for the underlying data

Element Type	CSS Class Name
Mobile Grid	bma-responsive-grid
Container	bma-grid-container
Static Text	bma-text

TABLE 3-1. *Element/Class mappings*

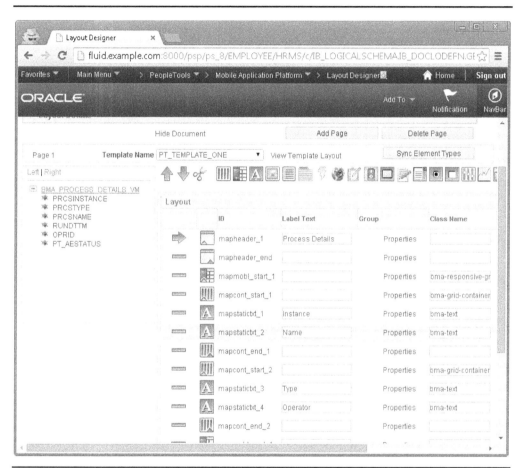

FIGURE 3-23. *Layout grid showing labels class properties*

model. Personally, however, I do not like to clutter my Layout Documents. I would rather create multiple Layouts with comprehensible Documents.

The multipage approach shares the same initialization Application Class between pages. If all of the pages within the Layout use the same Document fields (primitives), then initialization follows the same approach demonstrated in this chapter. If each page uses different fields (primitives), then you can determine the selected page from the `GetURIDocument()` method of the `&Map` variable that is passed to the initialization routine. You only need to initialize the primitives that are used by the page identified by the request parameters.

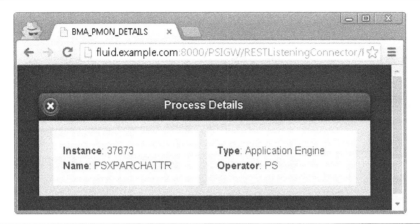

FIGURE 3-24. *Details dialog after applying CSS changes*

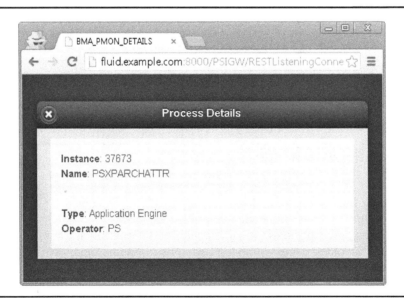

FIGURE 3-25. *Responsive layout*

Conclusion

In this chapter, you learned how to use PeopleSoft Mobile Application Platform configuration tool to build mobile applications. We created Document ViewModels and related Layouts. We worked with collection items and used CSS to change the layout and appearance. In the next section of this book, you will learn how to use HTML5 frameworks to create mobile applications.

PART II

Building Mobile
Applications with HTML5

CHAPTER
4

Creating a Data Model

In the early days of web applications, a primary frustration for developers was the intermingling of data (the model) with presentation logic (the view). As developers, we often wrote Active Server Pages and Java Server Pages applications with data and presentation logic weaved tightly together. It was not practical to hand the view layer over to a designer because the data and presentation logic were inseparable. Developers and architects began looking for a better way. For most, the solution came in the form of a well-known user interface pattern called the Model-View-Controller (MVC) pattern. Although very popular, many find it confusing because so many people interpret the concept differently. And, if differing interpretations isn't confusing enough, web applications can further apply MVC on both the server and the client tiers. Java Server Faces, Struts, Spring, Ruby on Rails, and ASP.NET are a few of the many common server-side MVC frameworks. More recently, developers are using client-side JavaScript MVC frameworks including Backbone.js, AngularJS, Ember.js, and Kendo UI. Regardless of interpretation or location, the heart of MVC remains constant: *Separation of Concerns*.

In Chapter 2 of this book, we built responsive mobile applications using PeopleTools page definitions and PeopleCode. We built record definitions for the Model layer and page definitions for the View layer. PeopleTools transparently handled the Controller layer. In Part II, we will continue using PeopleTools for the Model but will transfer the View layer to common HTML mobile frameworks, such as jQuery Mobile, and we will take responsibility for the Controller layer.

In this chapter, we will build the Model layer for our MVC application using SQL, Component Interfaces, and Documents. SQL and Component Interfaces will provide low-level data access. Documents will act as an abstract representation of the data Model and will be used by the Controller to transfer data in and out of the View layer. In Chapters 5 and 6, we will build HTML5 View layers to display and update data from the Model. In Chapters 7 and 8, we will build iScript and REST service controllers to communicate between the Model and View layers. For those of you familiar with both iScripts and/or REST, you may be asking questions such as:

- Aren't iScripts usually used to build the View layer?

- Isn't REST for transferring data (the model)?

- Why did you use the plural form for iScript and Controller? Doesn't MVC specify one controller?

However, we choose to interpret MVC, the key tenet remains: *Separation of Concerns*. MVC is a very flexible term packed with meaning. For this section of the book, we define MVC as:

■ Model: data structures implemented as PeopleTools Documents.

■ View: presentation layer built in HTML5.

■ Controller: bridge between the Model and View. The controller executes SQL and Component Interface commands to update the Model, and transfers data to the View layer.

Scenario

There are a lot of great mobile scenarios: time entry, asset management, project portfolio management, recruiter interview details, etc. Many of these examples are quite complex and application database specific. My intention in this book is to teach the fundamentals of mobile development for PeopleSoft. With that in mind, I want to keep the scenario simple. For our example, we will build a basic personnel directory using the PeopleSoft PERSONAL_DATA record as our foundation. Most PeopleSoft applications include the PERSONAL_DATA record so this scenario will apply across multiple applications. In the next few chapters, we will build the same personnel directory using multiple layouts, HTML5 frameworks, and PeopleSoft strategies. This will allow us to compare and contrast differences between these technologies.

Our mobile personnel directory will contain three pages:

■ Search

■ Search results

■ Person details

The Data Model

Whether we use iScripts or Service Operations, HTML5 or Hybrid applications, our examples will use the same data model based on PeopleTools Documents.

SQL Definitions

PeopleSoft development best practices discourage direct SQL access in favor of Component Interfaces because direct SQL access bypasses component-specific business logic. SQL, however, offers the best performance. A reasonable compromise is to use SQL for read operations and Component Interfaces for create, update, and delete operations. With this in mind, we will create some SQL definitions to support our read operations. Open Application Designer and create a new project definition.

Search and Search Results Page SQL

Our search page will allow us to search by the following fields:

- Employee ID
- Name
- Last Name

The search results page will contain the same fields. In Application Designer, add a new SQL definition. Name the new SQL definition BMA_PERSON_SRCH. Inside this new SQL definition, add the following SQL:

```
SELECT EMPLID
    , NAME
    , LAST_NAME_SRCH
    FROM PS_PERS_SRCH_ALL
```

NOTE
The PERS_SRCH_ALL record definition used in this SQL definition is the search view used by the online Personal Data Component. It handles name resolution (for people with multiple names), effective dating, and other relational constructs (sounds like this handles relationships even better than Zoosk or eHarmony).

Details Page SQL

The details page will contain the following information:

- Employee ID
- Name

- Address fields

- Phone number

In Application Designer, create a new SQL definition named `BMA_PERSON_DETAILS`. Inside this new SQL definition, add the following SQL:

```
SELECT EMPLID
 , NAME
 , ADDRESS1
 , CITY
 , STATE
 , POSTAL
 , COUNTRY
 , COUNTRY_CODE
 , PHONE
  FROM PS_PERSONAL_DATA
 EMPLID = :1
```

Documents

With our data access objects (SQL definitions) defined, we can model our data structures using the Documents module. In Chapter 3, we used Documents as a foundation for MAP development. In the remainder of this book, we will use Documents to model service-oriented data structures. As you learned in Chapter 3, Documents provide an abstract data model that can be rendered in several different formats including JSON and XML.

NOTE
If you skipped Chapter 3 because your version of PeopleTools does not include MAP, then I recommend returning to Chapter 3 to read the segment describing the PeopleTools Documents module.

Besides describing REST responses, PeopleTools REST services use Documents to describe URL input parameters. You will learn more about this in Chapter 8 when we create Service Operations. We will need Documents for the following data transmissions:

- Search parameters received by the controller from the search page (request)

- Search results sent from the controller (response)

- Employee ID for the details view (request)

- Employee details (response)

Defining the Search Parameters Document

The initial page of our application is a search page. Users will enter search criteria into a parameter form and submit this form. The code that responds to this request will access the search criteria through a Document structure. When creating an input Document (also known as the Template Document) for a REST service, it is important to think about your URL design and the expected REST request type (GET, POST, etc.). If the URL target points to a specific item, such as an employee, then the URL parameter will be an employee identifier, or as we call it in PeopleSoft: EMPLID. The URL for accessing the employee with the ID KU0010 would look something like: .../employees/KU0010. From this URL, we see a natural hierarchy: employees → EMPLID. For our search page, however, the REST service URL will point to a collection of items so we shouldn't use a specific identifier-type URL. It also isn't possible to apply a hierarchical structure to our parameters of emplid, name, or last name. Instead, we will use a query-string-style URL pattern. In Chapter 8, we will see how to construct URLs using input documents. For now, we have made enough decisions to create our input Document.

Create the search Document by logging into your PeopleSoft online application and navigating to PeopleTools | Documents | Document Builder. Click the Add a New Value link and enter the values found in Table 4-1:

Figure 4-1 is a screenshot of the Add New Document data-entry page. Click the Add button to create the document.

To this new Document, add three Primitives: EMPLID, NAME, LAST_NAME_ SRCH and set their properties according to the values in Table 4-2. As you learned in Chapter 3, Primitive values represent basic data types, such as binary, number, string, etc.

Field Name	Field Value
Package	BMA_PERSONNEL_DIRECTORY
Document	SEARCH_FIELDS
Version	v1

TABLE 4-1. *New Document metadata*

FIGURE 4-1. *Add New Document*

NOTE
The primitives I added share the same names as the fields they represent. This is not required. I use the same names to simplify my designs. This may or may not be desirable. For example, the LAST_NAME_SRCH field name is quite long. A shorter name would reduce the resultant Document size.

Figure 4-2 is a screenshot of the new Document structure. We will use this Document for our search parameters and as the base for the search results compound Document. Be sure to save your Document before continuing.

Defining the Search Results Document

The second page of our mobile web application is a search results page. The results page contains a list having the same fields as our parameter form. We can model the relationship between the search parameters and search results by creating a new Document that has a collection compound child consisting of the same Document

Element Name	Type	Length
EMPLID	String	11
NAME	String	50
LAST_NAME_SRCH	String	30

TABLE 4-2. *Document Primitives with their property types and lengths*

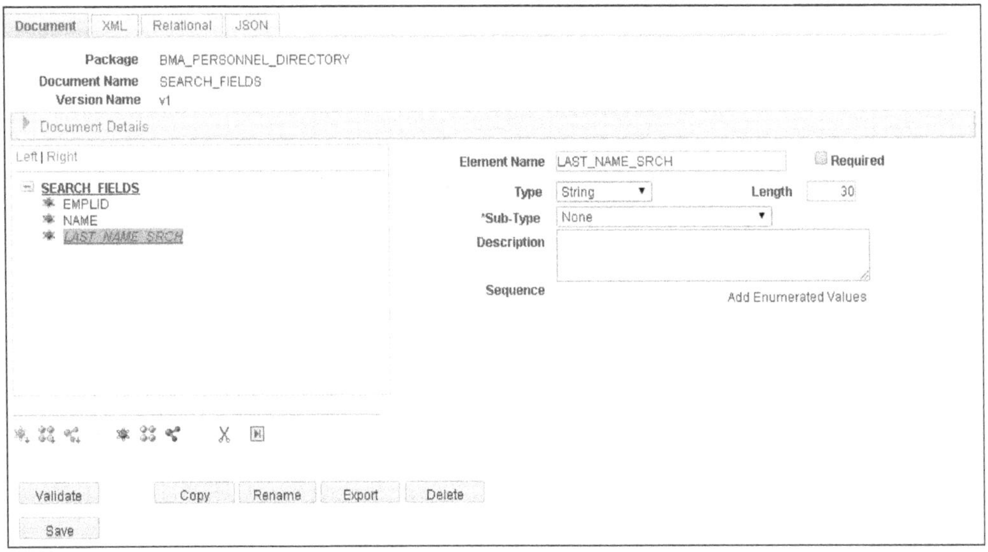

FIGURE 4-2.   *BMA_PERSONNEL_DIRECTORY.SEARCH_FIELDS.v1 Document structure*

as the search parameters: `BMA_PERSONNEL_DIRECTORY.SEARCH_FIELDS.v1`. Create a new Document in package `BMA_PERSONNEL_DIRECTORY` named `SEARCH_RESULTS` with a version of `v1` as shown in Table 4-3.

Click the Add button to create the document. To this new Document, add a Collection child named `RESULTS`. To the `RESULTS` Collection, add a Compound child referencing `BMA_PERSONNEL_DIRECTORY.SEARCH_FIELDS.v1`. Figure 4-3 is a screenshot of the Compound child search results. Select the matching row to

Field Name	Field Value
Package	BMA_PERSONNEL_DIRECTORY
Document	SEARCH_RESULTS
Version	v1

TABLE 4-3.   *SEARCH_RESULTS Document metadata*

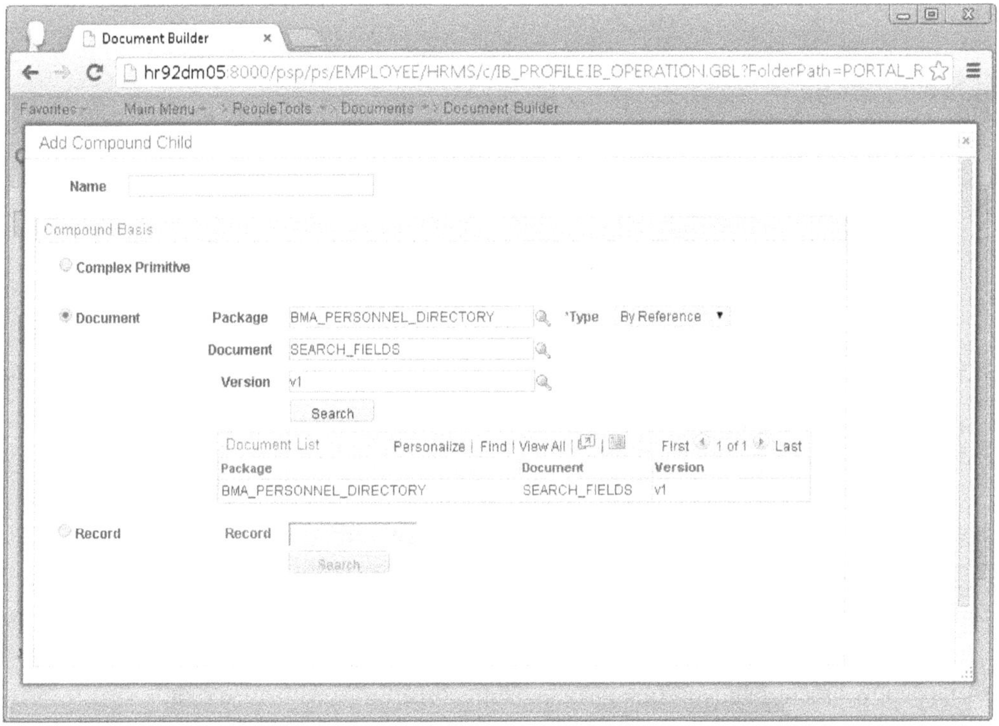

FIGURE 4-3. *Compound child search results*

add the `SEARCH_FIELDS` Document as the child compound. Figure 4-4 is a screenshot of the entire Document structure.

Defining the Details Input Document

From the search page, a user will select an employee and expect to see the employee's details. Since we know exactly which `EMPLID` to update, we can use a specific resource-based URL pattern—something similar to `.../employees/KU0010`. Our input Document, therefore, will contain an `EMPLID` property. In Chapter 8, we will associate this document with a Service Operation URL pattern.

Create a new Document in package `BMA_PERSONNEL_DIRECTORY` named `EMPLID` with a version of `v1` as shown in Table 4-4.

FIGURE 4-4. *BMA_PERSONNEL_DIRECTORY.SEARCH_RESULTS.v1 Document*

To this new Document, add one primitive named `EMPLID` with a Type of `String` and a Length of `11`. Figure 4-5 is a screenshot of this new Document.

Defining the Details Document

The final page of the application displays information about an employee. Create a new Document similar to the other two, but having a package name of `BMA_PERSONNEL_DIRECTORY`, a Document name of `DETAILS`, and a version of `v1`. Table 4-5 contains a listing of each Primitive to add to this new Document.

Figure 4-6 is a screenshot of this new Document.

Field Name	Field Value
Package	BMA_PERSONNEL_DIRECTORY
Document	EMPLID
Version	v1

TABLE 4-4. *EMPLID Document metadata*

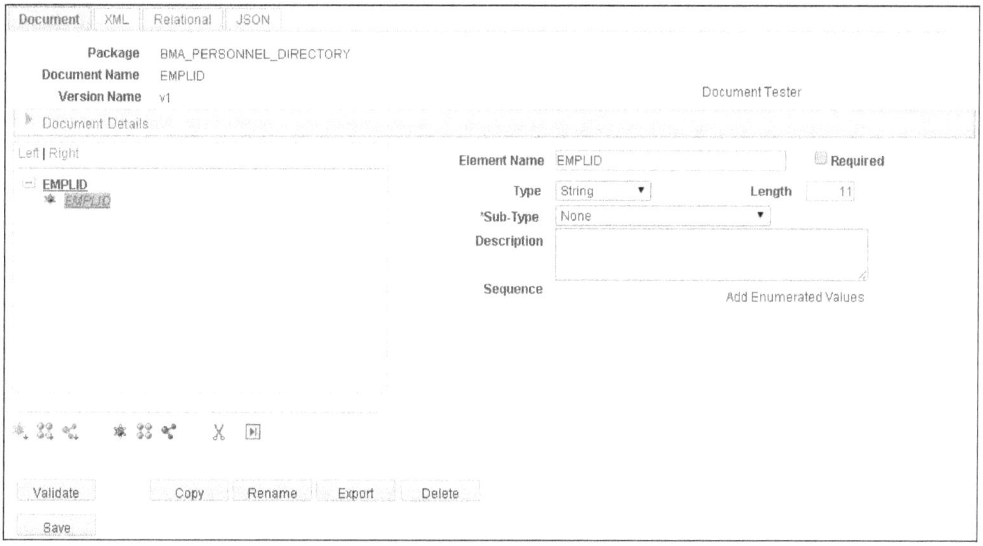

FIGURE 4-5. *EMPLID Document*

Element Name	Type	Length
EMPLID	String	11
NAME	String	50
ADDRESS1	String	55
CITY	String	30
STATE	String	6
POSTAL	String	12
COUNTRY	String	3
COUNTRY_CODE	String	3
PHONE	String	24

TABLE 4-5. *Details Document primitives*

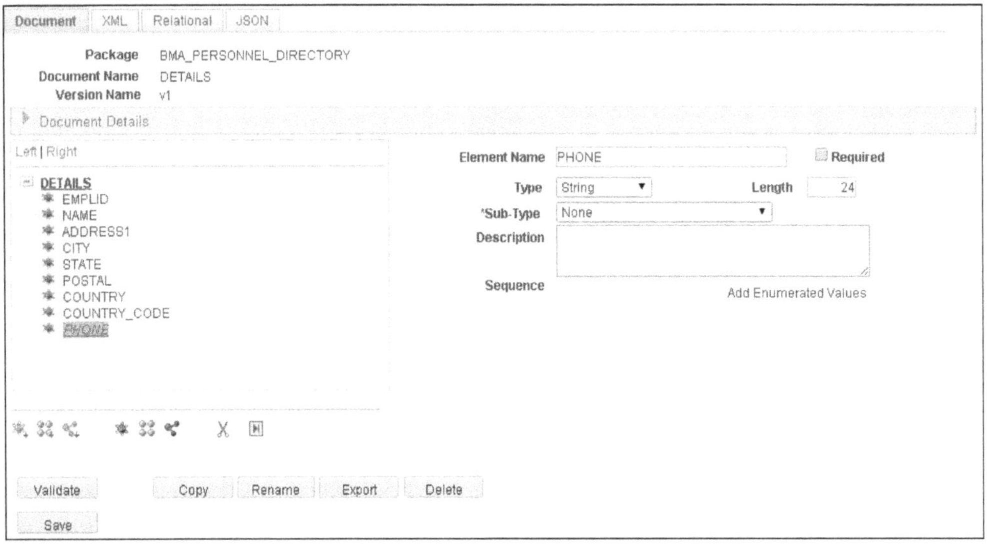

FIGURE 4-6. *Screenshot of BMA_PERSONNEL_DIRECTORY.DETAILS.v1*

Updating Your Own Profile

Besides basic, read-only functionality, let's also make it possible for employees to update certain details about their profiles. This, of course, will require authentication, which will give us a great opportunity to highlight a key difference between iScripts and REST services: the security model.

For the *update* scenario, we will let users change their primary phone number. At the beginning of this chapter, I said we would use Component Interfaces for update operations. Rather than build our own, we can use the delivered CI_ PERSONAL_DATA Component Interface. In Chapter 8, we will build a REST service to call the Component Interface. In this chapter, we will define the Document required for receiving the HTTP request.

Create another Document in package BMA_PERSONNEL_DIRECTORY and name it PRIMARY_PHONE. Set the version to v1. Table 4-6 contains a listing of each Primitive to add to this new Document.

Element Name	Type	Length
COUNTRY_CODE	String	3
PHONE	String	24

TABLE 4-6.   *PRIMARY_PHONE Document primitives*

Demo Data

In the next two chapters, we will create several Views for the Model layer we designed in this chapter. Let's use the Document Tester to create demo data files to use with these View layer prototypes.

Access the online Document Tester by navigating to PeopleTools | Documents | Document Utilities | Document Tester. Search for the Document BMA_ PERSONNEL_DIRECTORY.SEARCH_RESULTS.v1. When the page opens, you will see the Document structure on the left. The green icon next to the word *RESULTS* identifies RESULTS as a collection. The following red icon identifies the next element, the *SEARCH_FIELDS* element, as a compound structure. The RESULTS collection already contains one SEARCH_FIELDS element. For each field: EMPLID, NAME, and LAST_NAME_SRCH, click the field name to enter a value. Figure 4-7 is a screenshot of me setting the EMPLID field in the Document Tester.

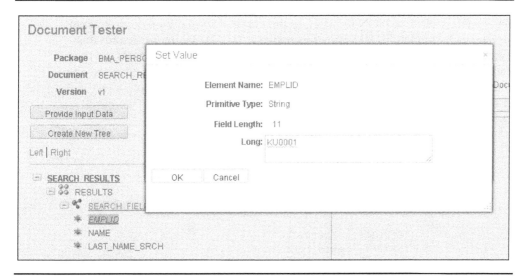

FIGURE 4-7.   *Setting values in the Document Tester*

After adding data to each of the three fields, click on the RESULTS element. A dialog will appear that gives you the option to append a new item or delete the last item. Choose Append Collection Item and click the OK button. This will copy the prior SEARCH_FIELDS node into a new node. Update the values to make each row unique. Repeat these steps to add one more row.

We can use the Document Tester to generate a PeopleCode stub for populating this Document. In Chapter 8, we will write similar PeopleCode to populate this Document. From the Physical Format Type drop-down located in the upper right portion of the Document Tester, select the PeopleCode format and then click the Generate button. I don't recommend copying the PeopleCode directly out of the Document Tester. The variables are too cryptic to be valuable. This PeopleCode does, however, show you exactly how to populate a Document from PeopleCode:

1. Create an instance of a Document.

2. Access the DocumentElement property.

3. Search for the collection element using the GetPropertyByName method.

4. Create a child node within the collection by calling the CreateItem method of the collection element.

5. Populate the properties of the new child node.

6. Repeat until you have added the necessary elements to the collection.

With this chapter we want to generate some test data. The Document Tester will generate data in XML or JSON format. Use the Physical Format Type drop-down to select the JSON format. HTML5 browsers natively parse JSON into structures that are easy to manipulate from JavaScript. Although possible, XML structures are more complicated to consume in JavaScript. Click the Generate button again to view the Document structure in JSON format. Copy and paste the JSON data into a text file and save it so we can reference it when we prototype the view layer. Figure 4-8 shows JSON formatted data in the Document Tester.

The following listing contains a pretty-printed version of the JSON displayed in Figure 4-8:

```
{
    "SEARCH_RESULTS": {
        "SEARCH_FIELDS": [
            {
                "EMPLID": "KU0001",
                "NAME": "Lewis,Douglas",
```

```
                            "LAST_NAME_SRCH": "LEWIS"
                },
                {
                            "EMPLID": "KU0002",
                            "NAME": "Baran,Charles",
                            "LAST_NAME_SRCH": "BARAN"
                },
                {
                            "EMPLID": "KU0003",
                            "NAME": "Parsons,Jean",
                            "LAST_NAME_SRCH": "PARSONS"
                }
            ]
        }
}
```

Repeat these steps with the DETAILS Document. Figure 4-9 is a screenshot of the
DETAILS Document viewed through the Document Tester.

The following code listing contains the pretty-printed JSON results of the
DETAILS document as viewed in the Document Tester. Save these results for use in
the next two chapters.

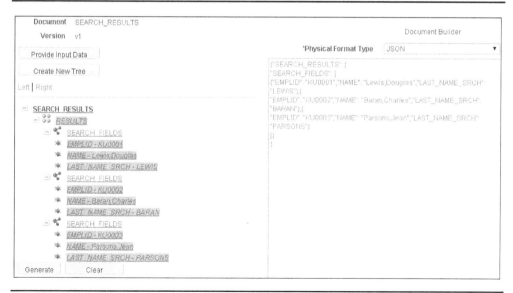

FIGURE 4-8. *JSON formatted SEARCH_RESULTS*

FIGURE 4-9. *DETAILS Document in the Document Tester*

```
{
    "DETAILS": {
        "EMPLID": "KU0001",
        "NAME": "Lewis,Douglas",
        "ADDRESS1": "3569 Malta Ave",
        "CITY": "Newark",
        "STATE": "NJ",
        "POSTAL": "07112",
        "COUNTRY": "USA",
        "COUNTRY_CODE": "1",
        "PHONE": "973/622-1234"
    }
}
```

Conclusion

In this chapter, we built the data structures required to support three read-only pages of an HTML5 web application. We also laid the foundation for updating a user's personal information. We call this the Model layer of the MVC architecture. In the next two chapters, we will prototype the View layer using static data derived from the Model layer. Chapters 7 and 8 will each tie the Model and View together but using different Controller technologies.

CHAPTER
5

Prototyping the HTML5 "View" Layer with jQuery Mobile

I n this chapter, we will use jQuery Mobile to prototype the *View* layer of our MVC application. In Chapters 7 and 8, we will connect the View layer to the Model layer of Chapter 4 using iScripts and REST services.

Wireframes

Figure 5-1 contains wireframes describing each of the personnel directory's three views. The first view is a search page and will be used to gather search parameters. The second view contains a list of search results. When a user selects a result from the list of search results, the personnel directory will display the details view (View 3).

The upper right corner of View 2 and View 3 contains a search button. Touching this button will navigate to the first view (the search view) allowing the user to enter new search criteria. It probably goes without saying, but we don't need the search button on View 1 because the purpose of the search button is to take the user to View 1.

I placed a three-lined icon in the upper left corner of each view to facilitate navigation. On a small form factor device, such as a mobile phone, touching this icon will reveal a panel with the last search results. The panel should be visible all the time on wider devices. Figure 5-2 is a wireframe describing the appearance of the panel view.

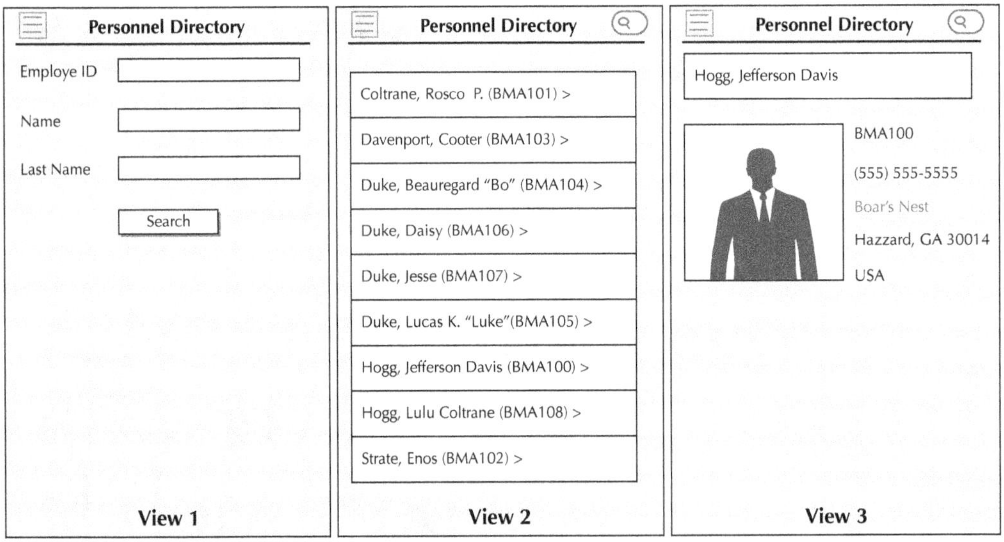

FIGURE 5-1. *The three views of the mobile application*

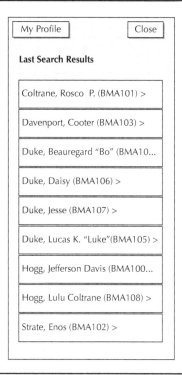

FIGURE 5-2.   *The panel view*

Prototyping with jQuery Mobile

As we all know, each browser is unique, with varying levels of CSS and JavaScript support. Wouldn't we be so much more productive if we could build good sites without regard for a browser's vendor or version? Actually, we can. For example, we could build to the lowest common denominator: create sites that *only* use JavaScript, CSS, and HTML features that are common to all devices we plan to support. This approach would require us to research each device and build a capability matrix showing commonalities and eliminating differences. Besides being a rather difficult and tedious exercise, the resultant site would be rather boring, not something that our users would want to use (WAP and WML anyone?).

Two other cross-browser development strategies include graceful degradation and progressive enhancement. The intent of these two strategies is the same, but the approach is different. Graceful degradation starts with a rich user experience, and then provides alternatives for browsers that do not support a rich feature set. Progressive enhancement is the opposite. Progressive enhancement starts with baseline functionality and *progressively enhances* a page's content according to browser capabilities.

jQuery Mobile employs progressive enhancement. Progressive enhancement allows developers to write very simple, semantic HTML, leaving the rich content portion of the user experience to the progressive framework. I am a *huge* fan of jQuery Mobile, because it allows me to rapidly build compelling mobile user experiences.

We used jQuery Mobile in Chapter 3 when we built mobile applications using the PeopleTools Mobile Application Platform (MAP). In that chapter, we were more focused on learning MAP and less on jQuery Mobile. In fact, to successfully use MAP, we didn't even have to know jQuery Mobile exists. This chapter is quite a bit different. In this chapter, we will cover a significant amount of jQuery Mobile features.

A word about jQuery versus jQuery Mobile.... jQuery is cross-browser JavaScript library with no visual appearance. Familiarity with the jQuery JavaScript library is helpful, but not necessary. jQuery Mobile, on the other hand, is a mobile user interface on top of the jQuery library. In other words, jQuery Mobile uses the jQuery JavaScript library so you don't have to.

Creating the Netbeans Source Project

Launch NetBeans (or your favorite text editor or development environment). Select File | New Project from the NetBeans menu bar. In the New Project dialog, select HTML5 from the Categories list and HTML5 Application from the Projects list. Figure 5-3 is a screenshot of the New Project dialog. Click the Next button to continue.

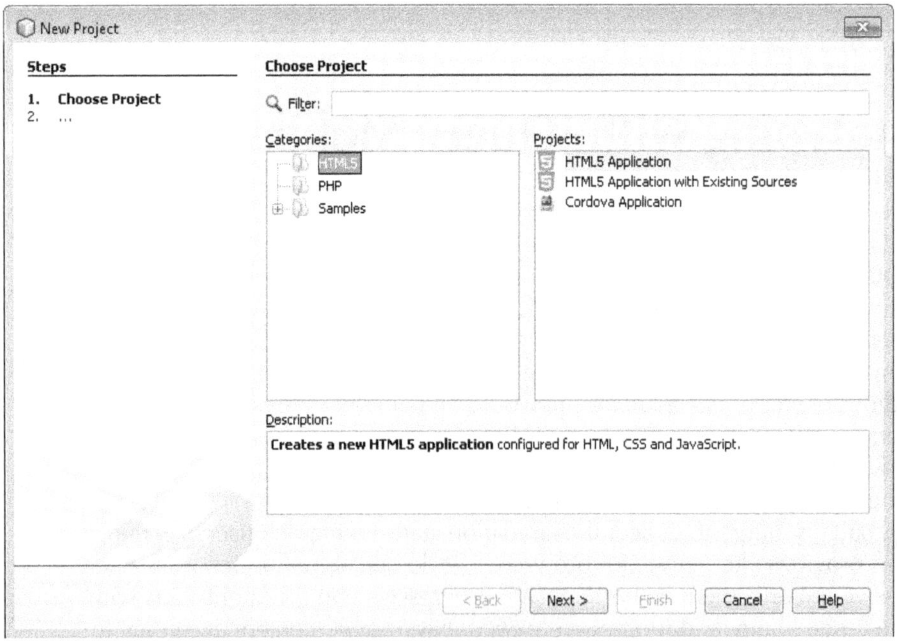

FIGURE 5-3. *New Project dialog with HTML5 Application selected*

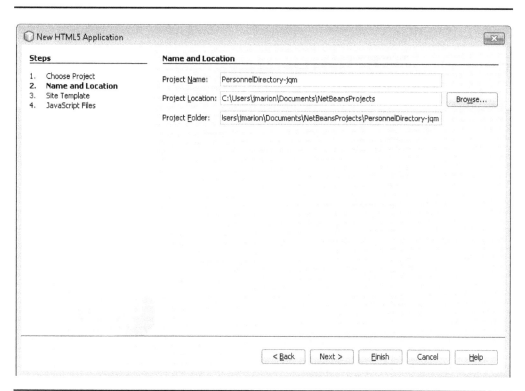

FIGURE 5-4. *Step 2 of the New Project dialog*

In step 2 of the New Project wizard, name the new project
`PersonnelDirectory-jqm` (jqm is an abbreviation for jQuery Mobile).
Figure 5-4 is a screenshot of step 2. In step 3, choose No Site Template and
click Next to move to step 4.

Step 4 allows us to add JavaScript libraries to the project. Before selecting JavaScript
libraries, look for the blue hyperlink underneath the list of libraries. That hyperlink
identifies when the list of libraries was last updated. If it has been a few weeks since
you updated your list or if know there are newer versions of your favorite JavaScript
libraries available, click this link to download a new list. If your list is up to date, then
select jQuery and jQuery mobile. Figure 5-5 is a screenshot of step 4 of the New
Project dialog. Click Finish to create the new project.

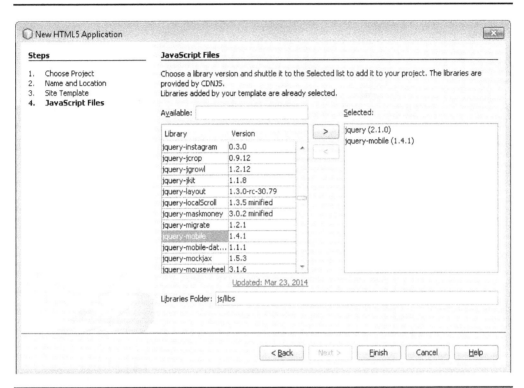

FIGURE 5-5. *Step 4 of the New Project dialog*

NOTE
The jQuery Mobile JavaScript library was added to PeopleTools in version 8.53 to support the 9.1 and early 9.2 iScript-based mobile applications. The PeopleTools team configured the jQuery Mobile JavaScript and stylesheet definitions to use Meta-HTML for loading external references from PeopleTools. Having these JavaScript libraries preconfigured in this manner is very helpful. Unfortunately, however, the included version is 1.0.1—a good, but old release. This chapter was built with version 1.4 and leverages features that were not available in version 1.0.1.

Manually Downloading jQuery and jQuery Mobile

The NetBeans project wizard automatically downloads the latest stable, uncompressed version of JavaScript libraries from http://cdnjs.com. Here are a few reasons why you might want to download the jQuery libraries yourself:

- You want to use a newer version of jQuery than what is available on cdnjs.

- You are satisfied with the features available in an older release, such as 1.01.

- You prefer the compressed version of jQuery Mobile (as I do).

- You have to support legacy versions of Internet Explorer, which require one of the 1.x jQuery versions.

The compressed version of jQuery is nearly 70% smaller than the one downloaded by NetBeans, so that by itself is reason enough to manually download these files. The NetBeans downloaded version is good enough for development purposes, but I recommend downloading the minified "production" version before deploying your mobile applications in a production environment.

If you prefer to retain tighter control over your JavaScript files, point your desktop web browser at http://jquerymobile.com/ and download the appropriate version of jQuery Mobile. Note the range of jQuery versions required for your chosen version of jQuery Mobile. From the jQuery website (http://jquery .com), download the version that falls within the range required for your version of jQuery Mobile. For example, jQuery Mobile 1.4.2 requires jQuery versions 1.8–1.10 or version 2.0. If you don't need the legacy features of the 1.x branch, choose 2.0 (because the 2.x version file size is smaller).

Creating the Search Page

Our project now contains a "boilerplate" index page and the jQuery JavaScript libraries. Ignore the index page for now and create a new search page. From the NetBeans menu bar, select File | New File. In step 1, select HTML File from the HTML5 Category. Figure 5-6 is a screenshot of the New File dialog. Click Next to move onto step 2 and name the new file `search`. Notice that the Created File text box at the bottom of the New HTML File wizard will show the file path, name, and extension. When naming your file, don't include the .html extension. NetBeans adds that automatically. Click Finish to create the file.

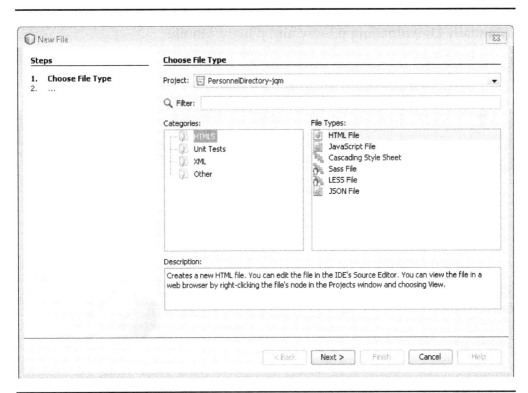

FIGURE 5-6. *New File dialog*

The newly created file will contain the following HTML:

```
<!DOCTYPE html>
<!--
To change this license header, choose License Headers in Project
Properties.
To change this template file, choose Tools | Templates
and open the template in the editor.
-->
<html>
    <head>
        <title>TODO supply a title</title>
        <meta charset="UTF-8">
        <meta name="viewport" content="width=device-width">
    </head>
    <body>
        <div>TODO write content</div>
    </body>
</html>
```

It is hard to believe this is HTML5. It looks just like regular HTML. What makes this code HTML5 is the DOCTYPE statement at the very top.

The file does not yet contain jQuery Mobile content; not even references to the jQuery JavaScript libraries. Add references by inserting the following link and script tags into the head section of the new file:

```
<link rel="stylesheet" href="js/libs/jquery-mobile/jquery.mobile.css">
<script src="js/libs/jquery/jquery.js"></script>
<script src="js/libs/jquery-mobile/jquery.mobile.js"></script>
```

While you are updating the head section, change the contents of the title tag to Search.

CDNs

Rather than hosting popular JavaScript libraries on your servers, best practices recommend using a Content Delivery Network (CDN) whenever possible. A CDN hosts popular, static content, such as JavaScript, CSS, and images and shares that content with an unlimited number of sites. As previously mentioned NetBeans uses the cdnjs CDN. The benefits of using a CDN include caching, proximity, and connection availability. Many of the popular JavaScript libraries (jQuery, AngularJS, Ext, etc.) are available on CDNs.

The concern I have with a CDN is access: CDN hosted JavaScript files have complete access to the contents of a page. A malicious script could deface a site, install spyware on an unsuspecting visitor's computer, or steal information from your secure pages. By using a CDN, you relinquish physical control over the JavaScript files hosted by the CDN. You have no way of confirming that those files are safe.

Another problem with CDNs is trust. Let me define trust in two ways:

- You keep confidential information confidential.
- You do what you say you will do (integrity).

If your site runs over SSL, your users see a visual indicator that they are communicating with the real you, not an imposter. When you include JavaScript from a CDN in that SSL conversation, the CDN also has access to the information on your pages. It is no longer just a conversation between you and the user. It is now a conversation between you, the user, and the CDN. Even worse, your site users probably don't know the CDN is part of the conversation. This is a violation of the trust principle that you keep confidential information confidential. You can

(Continued)

read a great hypothetical explanation of this trust issue at http://wonko.com/post/javascript-ssl-cdn.

It seems like every website has a (not so) prominently displayed privacy policy describing statistics collected about users and how the site owner intends to use that information. If you bring a CDN into the conversation, then the CDN may be using that information in a manner contrary to your privacy policy.

There are many CDN vendors available; some commercial and some free. As with any cloud service, make sure you understand the details of your hosting arrangement.

Replace the contents of the body section with the following. This will create a jQuery Mobile page definition containing header and footer regions.

```
<div data-role="page" id="search">

    <div data-role="header">
        <h1>Personnel Directory</h1>
    </div><!-- /header -->

    <div data-role="content">
        <p>Search form will go here</p>
    </div><!-- /content -->

    <div data-role="footer" data-position="fixed">
        <h4>
            Copyright &copy; Company 2014, All rights reserved
        </h4>
    </div><!-- /footer -->
</div><!-- /page -->
```

We have entered enough code to see jQuery Mobile progressive enhancement in action. To launch the page in a web browser, right-click within the NetBeans code editor and choose Run File from the context menu. The Google Chrome web browser should appear and show the search.html page. Figure 5-7 is a screenshot of the search page viewed in Google Chrome. Notice that the page has a clear header, content section, and footer.

Take a moment to use Chrome developer tools to inspect the contents of the page. For example, right-click the header section and choose Inspect element from the context menu. Notice that both the header `div` and the corresponding `h1` contain new attributes. This is progressive enhancement. jQuery Mobile identified your browser as supporting additional features and modified the HTML accordingly.

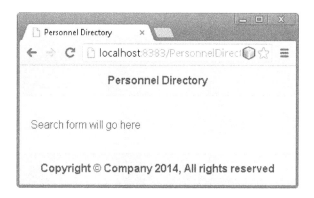

FIGURE 5-7. *Search page viewed through Google Chrome*

NOTE
If you don't like the rather lifeless shades of gray employed by the jQuery mobile default themes, then create your own at http://themeroller .jquerymobile.com/.

A jQuery Mobile HTML document is composed of a series of div elements with varying `data-role` attributes. The `data-role` attribute identifies the purpose of each element. For example, the `data-role` for the page container is `page`. Why create a specific element for a page? Isn't HTML document a synonym for page? jQuery Mobile allows you to include multiple *pages* or *views* in a single HTML document. You can then transfer between "pages" within a single document by linking to other pages by ID.

jQuery Mobile leverages the `data-*` HTML5 custom attribute specification for all jQuery Mobile–specific attributes. As we add more content to this page, you will see additional `data-*` jQuery Mobile attributes such as `data-icon` and `data-theme`.

To add a search form to this page, replace the contents of the div `data-role="content"` element with the following HTML:

```
<form action="results.html" method="GET">
  <div class="ui-field-contain">
    <label for="emplidSearch">Employee ID:</label>
    <input type="text" name="emplidSearch" id="emplidSearch">
  </div>
  <div class="ui-field-contain">
    <label for="nameSearch">Name:</label>
    <input type="text" name="nameSearch" id="nameSearch">
```

```
      </div>
      <div class="ui-field-contain">
        <label for="lastNameSearch">Last Name:</label>
        <input type="text" name="lastNameSearch"
            id="lastNameSearch">
      </div>
      <input type="submit" value="Search" data-icon="search"
            data-theme="b">
    </form>
```

NOTE
The form in the code listing uses the GET method because the web server running with the NetBeans debugger won't POST to the results.html page. We will change the method to POST when we connect this to an iScript.

A form consists of a collection of label/input pairs. The default jQuery Mobile form display behavior is to stack labels on top of their corresponding input fields regardless of page width. Wrapping each pair in a `div class="ui-field-contain"` element causes jQuery Mobile to use a side-by-side horizontal layout when the screen width is over 448 pixels (28 em). The `ui-field-contain` class also adds a nice border between fields when there are two or more fields in a form. Figure 5-8 is a screenshot of the mobile search page.

I styled the Search button using `data-theme="b"` to increase the contrast (and also to demonstrate how to use alternate jQuery Mobile theme swatches). Prior versions of jQuery Mobile included several theme swatches, each identified by a letter of the alphabet. Version 1.4, however, only has two themes: light and dark. You can create your own themes at http://themeroller.jquerymobile.com/. There are also several good themes available from other sources. The site http://www.gajotres. net/top-10-best-looking-free-jquery-mobile-themes/, for example, lists 10 good themes available from various sources on the internet.

The `data-icon` attribute attached to the search button tells jQuery Mobile to display a search icon. jQuery Mobile maintains an icon demo for each major release of jQuery Mobile. The demo page for the 1.4.2 release is at http://demos.jquerymobile .com/1.4.2/icons/. jQuery Mobile includes additional `data-*` attributes to specify positioning, shadow, surrounding disc, and so on.

Mocking up the Results Page

The search results page will contain a list of matching items. In NetBeans, create a new HTML5 page and name it `results.html`. jQuery Mobile uses Ajax to load additional pages into the original DOM. This means we don't actually need to create

FIGURE 5-8. *Personnel Directory search page*

a full HTML page, only a jQuery Mobile page fragment. The following code listing contains the necessary fragment to display a list of results:

```
<div data-role="page" id="results">
  <div data-role="header">
    <h1>Personnel Directory</h1>
  </div><!-- /header -->

  <div data-role="content">
    <ul data-role="listview" data-filter="true"
        data-filter-placeholder="Filter results..." data-inset="true">
      <li><a href="details.html?EMPLID=BMA101">
          Coltrane, Rosco P. (BMA101)</a></li>
      <li><a href="details.html?EMPLID=BMA103">
          Davenport, Cooter (BMA103)</a></li>
      <li><a href="details.html?EMPLID=BMA104">
          Duke, Beauregard "Bo" (BMA104)</a></li>
```

```
        <li><a href="details.html?EMPLID=BMA106">
            Duke, Daisy (BMA106)</a></li>
        <li><a href="details.html?EMPLID=BMA107">
            Duke, Jesse (BMA107)</a></li>
        <li><a href="details.html?EMPLID=BMA105">
            Duke, Lucas K. "Luke" (BMA105)</a></li>
        <li><a href="details.html?EMPLID=BMA100">
            Hogg, Jefferson Davis (BMA100)</a></li>
        <li><a href="details.html?EMPLID=BMA108">
            Hogg, Lulu Coltrane (BMA108)</a></li>
        <li><a href="details.html?EMPLID=BMA102">
            Strate, Enos (BMA102)</a></li>
    </ul>
  </div><!-- /content -->

  <div data-role="footer" data-position="fixed">
    <h4>
      Copyright &copy; Company 2014, All rights reserved
    </h4>
  </div><!-- /footer -->

</div><!-- /page -->
```

Notice that the markup in this listing is very clean, minimal semantic HTML. The only interesting attributes in this code listing are the ones attached to the `ul` element. The `data-role="listview"` identifies this unordered list as a special jQuery Mobile list view. The `data-inset` attribute places a shadowed border around the list. The `data-filter` attribute instructs jQuery Mobile to add a special search box at the top of the list. Typing in this search box limits the results displayed to just list items that match the criteria. The initial display text in the search box comes from the `data-filter-placeholder` attribute.

Since our search results page is a page fragment and doesn't contain references to the jQuery JavaScript and CSS libraries, we can't launch it directly (well, we can, but it won't have the progressive enhancements of a jQuery Mobile page). Therefore, to view the search results page, first run the search page from the NetBeans code editor. When the search page appears, don't enter any criteria, just click the search button. We haven't implemented any logic for handling search requests, so the criteria are irrelevant at this time. Your search results page will appear. Figure 5-9 is a screenshot of the search results page.

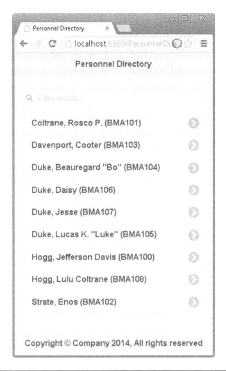

FIGURE 5-9. *Search results page*

NOTE
The reason we launch pages from NetBeans instead of just browsing to them within the file system is because page fragments must be loaded from a web server. jQuery Mobile uses Ajax to load pages, and Ajax requests must follow the domain of origin policy (or use CORS). This requires a web server. Browsers block Ajax requests for files within the local file system. If you are using a code editor other than NetBeans (Notepad, for example), then you will want to run your jQuery Mobile pages from a different development web server, such as the one we configured in Chapter 1.

Fragment or Full HTML Page?

The first page of a jQuery Mobile application is the only full HTML page required to create progressively enhanced mobile applications. This is because jQuery Mobile uses Ajax to handle navigation including form posts and links. If the Ajax response contains a jQuery Mobile page definition (`data-role="page"` attribute), then jQuery Mobile will append that page definition to the DOM. I chose to create the results page as an HTML fragment rather than a full HTML page because the jQuery Mobile framework will discard everything outside of the page definition. When building for mobile devices connecting over low bandwidth networks, it is important to eliminate unnecessary data.

The disadvantage of fragments is that loading the fragment by itself, the results.html page, for example, will render a semi-operational page with none of jQuery Mobile progressive enhancements. This is important to consider when creating pages you expect users to bookmark or pages to which you expect others might want to link. For example, some other mobile application may attempt to post directly to this results page, expecting a fully enhanced results page. If that other mobile app also uses jQuery Mobile and can use Ajax to access the results page (same domain or CORS), then everything will work fine. Otherwise, the results page will display as plain, unenhanced HTML.

If you compare Figure 5-9 to our wireframe in Figure 5-1, you will notice that our search results page is missing a couple of buttons in the header. Specifically, we haven't added a button to return to the search page or a button to display the panel. Let's go ahead and add the search page button now and save the panel button for when we actually create the panel. Implement the search button by adding the following link element to the header. The link element is in bold:

```
<div data-role="header">
  <h1>Personnel Directory</h1>
  <a href="#search" data-icon="search" data-iconpos="notext"
    class="ui-btn-right">Search</a>
</div><!-- /header -->
```

The target for the search button (or link) is #search, which is the ID for the search.html page definition. Since the search page is the application entry point, we know that it will exist in the DOM and can refer to it by ID rather than by URL. It is important to note that the page identified by #search doesn't have to be the same page we created earlier. The only requirement is that the search page definition that loads this results page has an ID of #search. Referring to the search page by ID gives us some flexibility; the #search placeholder could point to a search form defined by an entirely different page than the one we built. Figure 5-10 shows the search results page with the new search button.

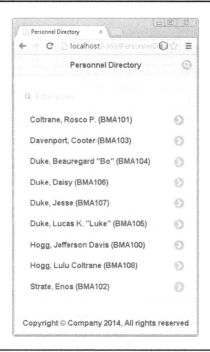

FIGURE 5-10. *Search results with search button*

Bookmarking is an important consideration when choosing to link by ID rather than by URL. By linking to a page that isn't in the results page HTML structure we are assuming the page was loaded into an existing DOM. If this page was loaded by itself, for example, from a bookmark, the search button would not function because the `#search` page definition would not exist. The decision to assume the results page was loaded into an existing DOM, however, is consistent with our previous decision to construct the results page as a page fragment rather than a full HTML document.

Coding the Details Page

After identifying the correct search result, the user will drill into a details page to see information about a particular person within the organization. In NetBeans, create another HTML5 HTML file and name it `details.html`. Replace the contents of the new file with the following page fragment:

```
<div data-role="page" id="details">
  <div data-role="header">
    <h1>Personnel Directory</h1>
    <a href="#search" data-icon="search" data-iconpos="notext"
       class="ui-btn-right">Search</a>
  </div><!-- /header -->
```

```
<div data-role="content">
  <h2>Hogg, Jefferson Davis</h2>
  <div>
    <img src="images/avatar.svg" class="avatar" alt="J.D.'s Photo">
    <p>BMA100</p>
    <p><a href="tel:5555555555">(555) 555-5555</a></p>
    <p>
      <a href="https://maps.google.com/?q=Boars+Nest+Hazzard
+Georgia+30014+USA">Boars Nest</a><br>
      Hazzard, Georgia 30014<br>
      USA
    </p>
  </div>
</div><!-- /content -->

<div data-role="footer" data-position="fixed">
  <h4>
    Copyright &copy; Company 2014, All rights reserved
  </h4>
</div><!-- /footer -->

</div><!-- /page -->
```

NOTE
The avatar included in the screenshots is a derivative of the one found at http://www.openclipart.org/ detail/21409/buddy-icons-by-eguinaldo. It is a Scalable Vector Graphic (SVG), which means it retains its high quality appearance regardless of dimensions. SVG images are great for responsive design. I find http://www.openclipart.org to be a great resource for free graphics. I included the avatar placeholder image with the source download for this chapter. To use this image, create an "images" folder in your project and then copy the `avatar.svg` file into your new folder.

Again we used a page fragment rather than a full HTML page. To view this page in a web browser, you will first have to navigate to it through an existing jQuery Mobile page, such as our search page. As with the search and search results pages, launch the search page first, and then work through the navigation use case to arrive at the details page. Specifically:

- Launch the search page from NetBeans (or view through another web server).

- Click the search button to see the search results.

- Click any one of the search results to see the details page.

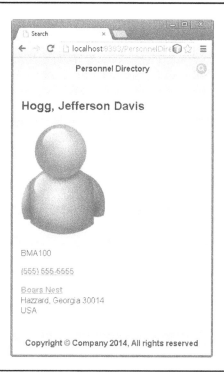

FIGURE 5-11. *Details page*

We haven't implemented any logic, so it doesn't matter which search result you choose. They will all display the same content. Figure 5-11 is a screenshot of the details page.

NOTE
The map link will take you to Google Maps, but won't actually load Hazzard. Hazzard is a fictitious county from the Dukes of Hazzard television series. But if you are looking for Cooter's garage, try 542 Parkway, Gatlinburg, TN 37738.

Notice that the phone number appears as a hyperlink? The phone number uses the tel: protocol so the mobile web browser will identify it as a callable number. Touching the link will launch the mobile phone dialer.

Custom Styling with jQuery Mobile

The details page is now fully functional. It has a photo of the employee, displays the phone number in a hyperlink, and links to a map. The markup is very clean and semantically correct. But visually speaking, the page needs improvement. For example, the employee name and other text are proportionally large when compared to the header. Likewise, the employee photo displays in a block above the personal information rather than beside the personal information. The way to resolve this is through CSS. We can implement CSS in one of three ways:

- Using the inline style attribute of each element

- Linking to external stylesheets

- Embedding an internal stylesheet using the style element

There is no perfect approach to inserting style information into an Ajax-loaded jQuery Mobile page. Let's review the good and the bad of each option.

Inline Styling   Adding style attributes to each element is simple to implement and easy to prototype. We can actually open Chrome Developer Tools and mockup the CSS changes in Chrome. But here is why we won't be using the style attribute:

- The style attribute increases the HTML content in our HTML file. In later chapters, we will convert these HTML files into reusable templates with parameters for content. Polluting the HTML with style information will make these templates harder to maintain.

- The web browser won't cache style information embedded in HTML. Since our HTML is dynamic, inline style information has to be downloaded on each request.

External Stylesheets   An external stylesheet linked into the head of an HTML document has all of the benefits of inline styles but without their unfavorable attributes. External stylesheets will not clutter our HTML templates, and browsers readily cache external stylesheets. There is just one problem—for valid HTML, an external stylesheet must be identified inside the HTML head element. As you may have noticed, our page fragments don't have an HTML head element. We could add a head element, but it wouldn't matter because jQuery Mobile wouldn't use it anyway. Here is why:

When jQuery Mobile loads a page definition through Ajax, it searches the Ajax response for elements with the data-role attribute set to the value page (`data-role="page"`). We refer to this as the *page* definition. Anything inside the page definition is appended to the `body` element of the primary HTML document (the `search.html` page). Anything outside the page definition is ignored. Figure 5-12 is a screenshot of Chrome Developer Tools with the details page (`id="details"`) highlighted.

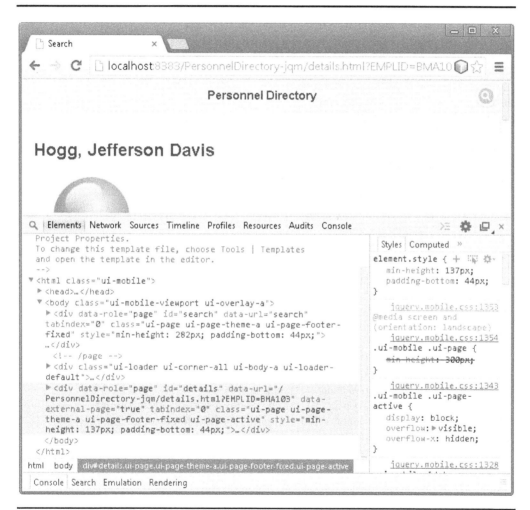

FIGURE 5-12. *Details page HTML structure*

jQuery Mobile Page Caching and the DOM

In Figure 5-12, if you look closely at the screenshot, just two rows above the highlighted row, you can see the search page (id="search"). jQuery Mobile keeps multiple pages in the DOM but only displays the active page. Do you notice anything missing between the search page and the details page? If pages are appended to the current document and jQuery Mobile loaded two pages through Ajax (results and details), then a logical question to ask is, "Where is the results page?" As jQuery Mobile loads additional pages, the DOM (and memory) has the potential to grow large enough to impact performance. jQuery Mobile keeps the in-memory DOM as small as possible by deleting Ajax-loaded pages as soon as they are hidden. Therefore, we don't see the results page in the Chrome structure browser because the results page no longer exists. All DOM nodes associated with the prior Ajax-loaded page (including link and style definitions) are deleted.

> **NOTE**
> *I intentionally distinguish between Ajax-loaded page definitions and those that were defined in the initial HTML document. All page definitions in the primary file remain in the DOM. Only Ajax-loaded pages are deleted after they are hidden.*

This can get interesting if an application has multiple Ajax-loaded pages with style information. As the former page is hidden and the new one is displayed, the former page's style rules are still active. During the page transition, style information from the old page may alter the display of the new page. Once the transition completes, the old page and its DOM nodes are deleted and the new page display will revert to what you expect. Later we will see how we can use *scoped* stylesheets to avoid this problem.

JavaScript content behaves exactly the opposite of external stylesheets. When a web browser encounters a script tag, it creates a corresponding DOM node, but rarely is that important. What is important is how the browser interprets the contents of that script DOM node. The browser's JavaScript engine will parse the node contents, adding new definitions to the global window JavaScript object. Once parsed, the node can be deleted but all JavaScript objects (functions, variables, etc.) will remain for the duration of the HTML document.

jQuery Mobile allows you to control caching through additional attributes. Adding the data-dom-cache="true" attribute to any page definition will keep the page in the DOM rather than deleting it when it is no longer visible. You can also prefetch pages into the DOM by adding the data-prefetch attribute to links (a elements).

Knowing how jQuery Mobile loads pages into the DOM is important when considering strategies for addressing page-specific CSS. HTML nodes that are part of the initial jQuery Mobile page (`search.html`) will remain throughout the duration of the application. Therefore, if we have CSS declarations that are used on multiple pages, then we can link those declarations in the head section of the main jQuery Mobile page (`search.html`). In fact, this is the only valid mechanism for linking to external stylesheets. You want to know something interesting? Browsers don't necessarily follow the rules. Even though it is not valid, you can add an external stylesheet to a page definition (`data-role="page"`) and your web browser will interpret and apply the CSS correctly. Be careful when using this approach. Browsers are not required to honor invalid content. Furthermore, as noted in the sidebar *jQuery Mobile Page Caching and the DOM*, this approach may have side effects.

Internal Stylesheets   An internal stylesheet (the `style` element) has all of the benefits of inline styles plus one additional benefit: It keeps style information out of the HTML details of our templates. Unfortunately, since internal stylesheets are embedded in HTML, browsers will not cache them. Like external stylesheets, traditional, internal stylesheets must be declared in the head section of an HTML document (although browsers don't enforce this requirement).

HTML5 allows us to include *scoped* stylesheets anywhere in a document. Scoping only applies style information to the parent element (our page container). This eliminates the side effects common to the external stylesheet approach. Unfortunately, scoped stylesheets are not well-supported. At this time, recent builds of Chrome and Firefox support scoped stylesheets, but Safari, Opera, and Internet Explorer do not—at least not in the sense of scoping style definitions to the parent container. All browsers will interpret and apply style information even if the style element is used outside the `head` element, they just won't apply the scoping rules. Browsers that don't support scoped stylesheets will exhibit the same side effects as external stylesheets.

An internal scoped stylesheet would look something like this (page element included for context):

```
<div data-role="page" id="details">
  <style type="text/css" scoped>
    div[data-role=content] h2 {
      font-size: inherit;
    }

    img.avatar {
      border: 2px solid #ddd;
      float: left;
      height: auto;
      margin-right: 20px;
      max-width:120px;
      padding: 8px;
      width: 40%;
    }
  </style>
```

As I mentioned, an internal stylesheet is embedded in the HTML. Since our HTML is different for each employee, it isn't possible to cache the embedded stylesheet. It will just be part of the HTML response sent to the browser with each request for the details page...unless we use a CSS `import` at-rule. The `import` at-rule allows us to define the CSS in an external file and import it into the embedded scoped stylesheet. This gives us an HTML5-valid approach to caching stylesheets without cluttering up our HTML templates. Assuming you placed the CSS contents above in a folder and file named `css/details.css`, the scoped CSS would look similar to the following (page element included for context):

```
<div data-role="page" id="details">
  <style type="text/css" scoped>
    @import url("css/details.css");
  </style>
```

NOTE
NetBeans 7.4 marked this @import rule with the error message "Unexpected token IMPORT_SYM found." Don't worry. No scoped stylesheets were harmed during the creation of this mobile website. The HTML and CSS are valid. Hopefully a future version of NetBeans will properly recognize this valid syntax.

The sample download for this chapter uses this scoped/import stylesheet approach. Figure 5-13 is a screenshot of the restyled details page. Notice that the font sizes are now consistent and the avatar floats to the left of the employee details.

Implementing the Responsive Panel

Our wireframes describe a panel that is hidden on small-form-factor devices, such as mobile phones, and visible on larger devices. When a user touches a certain button in the header, the panel is supposed to appear.

Panels in jQuery Mobile are elements (usually `div` elements) defined with the `data-role="panel"` attribute/value combination. If you place a panel inside a page definition as a sibling of the content element, then the jQuery Mobile framework will automatically hide the panel and style it appropriately. Placing the panel outside of a page definition is possible but requires a little bit of JavaScript to initialize the panel. Since this panel will display the same contents on every page within the personnel directory, we will add it to the application's entry point: `search.html` as a sibling of the search page definition (outside of the page definition). This means we will have to add a few lines of JavaScript to initialize the panel. We will also need to add the menu display button to each page and copy the contents of the results into the panel.

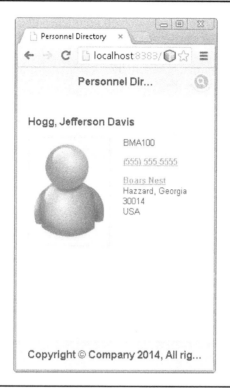

FIGURE 5-13. *Restyled details page*

Panels have many configurable features including themes, positioning, and reveal animations. There are also configurable and scripted mechanisms for opening and closing panels. We will explore some of these while constructing the panel for the personnel directory. You can learn more about panels at http://demos .jquerymobile.com/.

Let's start by revisiting the `search.html` document to add a button to reveal the panel and the markup necessary to create the panel. To the header element (not the HTML `head` element, but the jQuery Mobile header defined as `div data-role="header"`), add the markup from the following code listing. I included the full header HTML for reference. Just add the markup displayed in bold:

```
<div data-role="header">
  <h1>Personnel Directory</h1>
  <a href="#panel" class="show-panel-btn" data-icon="bars"
     data-iconpos="notext">Menu</a>
</div><!-- /header -->
```

The three-bar icon has become the standard icon used to represent a hidden menu (or panel). jQuery Mobile includes an icon with that same three bar design. To use it, we just add a `data-icon="bars"` attribute/value pair to our link. This markup opens the panel by specifying the panel ID in the `href` attribute.

Just after the search page definition, before the closing body tag, insert the following HTML. This HTML fragment defines the panel.

```
<div data-role="panel" id="panel" data-display="push"
    data-theme="b">
  <ul data-role="listview">
    <li data-icon="delete" class="hide-panel-btn">
      <a href="#" data-rel="close">Close menu</a>
    </li>
    <li data-icon="user">
      <a href="profile.html">My Profile</a>
    </li>
  </ul>
</div><!-- /panel -->
```

The `data-role="panel"` attribute/value pair identifies this HTML fragment as a panel. The `data-display` attribute tells jQuery Mobile the type of animation to apply when displaying the panel. Options include overlay, reveal, and push. Overlay causes the panel to appear on top of the page content. Reveal makes the panel look like it is under the page content. Push slides the panel in from the outside, pushing the page content off the screen.

The panel contains a jQuery Mobile list view styled slightly different from the one used in the search results. The first two rows of the list view display a close button and a link to edit the logged-in user's profile. Later we will add JavaScript to copy the search results into the panel.

Since we defined this panel outside of the jQuery Mobile page definition, we need to add some JavaScript to get jQuery Mobile to treat this panel as a jQuery Mobile panel. To the HTML head section, just before the closing `</head>` tag, add the following:

```
<script id="panel-init">
  $(function() {
    $("#panel")
            .panel()
            .enhanceWithin();
  });
</script>
```

If you are familiar with jQuery, then you may recognize this code. The `$(function() {...}` is standard jQuery JavaScript for "run this code when the DOM is ready for manipulation." It is shorthand for `$(document).ready(function() {...}`. The next line (line 3) is a jQuery CSS selector. It tells jQuery to select all elements with the ID `panel`. The remaining two method calls (`.panel()` and `.enhanceWithin()`) are jQuery Mobile–specific methods.

The `.panel()` method tells jQuery Mobile to treat the selected element as a panel. The `.enhanceWithin()` method tells jQuery Mobile to apply the usual progressive enhancement rules to content found within the selected elements.

NOTE
If you have multiple panels that reside outside of page elements, you can initialize all of them by using the jQuery selector `$("body>[data-role='panel']")`. This tells jQuery to select all elements that are direct descendants of the `body` element and have the attribute `data-role` with a value equal to `panel`.

Now is a good time to test this page. From within Netbeans, right-click within the code editor of the search.html page and choose Run File from the context menu. The panel will appear similar to the screenshot in Figure 5-14.

With the panel defined and working properly, let's add the panel/menu button to the other two pages. Open the results.html page and the details.html, and insert the same three-bar icon hyperlink HTML we added to the search page:

```
<div data-role="header">
  <h1>Personnel Directory</h1>
  <a href="#panel" class="show-panel-btn" data-icon="bars"
     data-iconpos="notext">Menu</a>
</div><!-- /header -->
```

Making the Panel Responsive

Concerning panels and sidebars, the typical responsive design pattern is to automatically display panels and sidebars on larger devices (or landscape mode). The jQuery Mobile panel widget has built-in responsive support, but it works a little differently. jQuery Mobile does not automatically display panels. Instead, if the user chooses to display a panel (by touching the three-bar button) and the device width is larger than 55em (880px), then jQuery Mobile will leave the panel open and reflow the page contents so that both fit side by side. In responsive design, the point at which a display changes is known as a breakpoint. We can enable the default 55em breakpoint by adding the `class="ui-responsive-panel"` attribute/value pair to the `body` element. Oh...there is one more requirement: the panel display animation has to be set to either *push* or *reveal*. You can test this on the search page by adding the `ui-responsive-panel` class, touching (or clicking) the three-bar button, and then resizing your browser window (after running search.html from NetBeans, of course). As the window width grows wider you will see the contents reflow to fill the available content space. Likewise, when shrinking the window width, you will see the contents shrink to a certain point (the breakpoint), and then reflow again, pushing extra content off the screen to the right. The following code

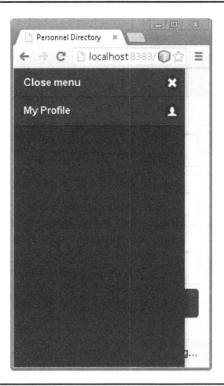

FIGURE 5-14. *jQuery Mobile Panel component*

listing displays the body element change required to activate jQuery Mobile's responsive breakpoint (additions are in bold).

```
<body class="ui-responsive-panel">
```

With the panel's data-display mode set to push and the page containing the class ui-responsive-panel, jQuery Mobile will hide the *dismiss* layer, allowing the user to work with the page contents without dismissing the panel.

Our content is small enough that we can (and should) use a narrower breakpoint. We can override jQuery Mobile's default breakpoint by defining our own CSS media query and stylesheet. To create your own breakpoint, add the following HTML immediately following the jQuery CSS file link in the head element of the search .html document (link element included for context only):

```
<link rel="stylesheet" href="js/libs/jquery-mobile/jquery.mobile.css">
<style>
@media (min-width:42em) {
```

```
.ui-responsive-panel
.ui-panel-page-content-open.ui-panel-page-content-position-left {
  margin-right: 17em;
}
.ui-responsive-panel
.ui-panel-page-content-open.ui-panel-page-content-position-right {
  margin-left: 17em;
}
.ui-responsive-panel .ui-panel-page-content-open {
  width: auto;
}
.ui-responsive-panel .ui-panel-dismiss-display-push,
.ui-responsive-panel.ui-page-active ~
.ui-panel-dismiss-display-push {
  display: none;
}
}
</style>
```

NOTE
The CSS above comes directly from the jQuery Mobile 1.4 jquery.mobile.css file. I searched the file for `ui-responsive-panel`, *copied the contents (including the media query), and changed the* `min-width` *value.*

Earlier in this chapter, we chose to import an external stylesheet into a page definition to take advantage of browser caching. In this example, however, we embedded the CSS directly into the HTML. The key difference is the other page is dynamic: our service will regenerate the contents on each request. This page is static and should reside in the web browser cache along with other CSS and JavaScript files.

Using matchMedia to Show and Hide the Panel   It is a little trickier to make the panel appear when the screen reaches a certain width and then disappear when the screen becomes too narrow. What makes this difficult is that jQuery Mobile uses JavaScript to toggle classes when you open a panel. It is not possible to toggle these same classes from a CSS media query, but we can trigger the panel display state from a JavaScript `MediaQueryList` event.

Remember the `panel-init` script element we created earlier that initializes the panel? We need to add a closure, a few variables, and a few other lines of JavaScript to that script block. The following code listing contains a new version of the `panel-init` script. It uses feature detection for `mediaMatch`. If the `mediaMatch` method is available, then the script uses a MediaQueryList to show or hide the panel depending on the screen width. Code changes are displayed in bold.

```
<script id="panel-init">
  (function() {
    // can't call open/close until panel is created
    var panelCreated = false;

    // function to show/hide panel on media query event
    // called from media query event and panel create event
    var setPanelState = function(mql) {
      if (panelCreated) {
        if (mql.matches) {
          $("#panel").panel("open");
        } else {
          $("#panel").panel("close");
        }
      }
    };
    var query = null;

    // feature detection
    if (window.matchMedia) {
      query = window.matchMedia("(min-width: 42em)");
      query.addListener(setPanelState);
    }

    // jQuery $(document).ready(...)
    $(function() {
      $("#panel")
              .panel({
                create: function() {
                  panelCreated = true;
                  if (!!query) {
                    // call previously defined function on create
                    setPanelState(query);
                  }
                }
              })
              .enhanceWithin();
    });

    // show the panel after page changes
    $(document).on("pagechange", function() {
      if (!!query) {
        // call previously defined function on create
        setPanelState(query);
      }
    });
  }());
</script>
```

Test your code changes by reloading search.html in your web browser. If you are using NetBeans and the NetBeans Chrome connector, then the page will automatically reload. Resize the page and notice how the panel appears and disappears at the responsive breakpoint.

When your screen is wide enough to display both the panel and the search form at the same time, look at the three-bar icon and the close button (first list item). Notice that these buttons are visible all the time. Keeping them visible gives the user the option to hide (and show) the panel even after our media query automatically displays it. If you prefer to hide these buttons on wide-width devices, then add the following CSS to the inline stylesheet of the search.html page:

```css
.show-panel-btn,
.hide-panel-btn {
  display: none !important;
}
```

Figures 5-15 is a screenshot of the details page as viewed on a Droid Incredible 2 by HTC. Notice that the menu button is visible but the panel is hidden.

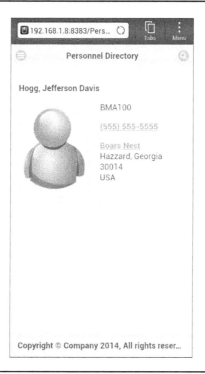

FIGURE 5-15.   *Details page on a Droid Incredible 2*

Copying Search Results into the Panel

When a user clicks the search button on the search page, jQuery Mobile will use Ajax to submit the search parameters to the server and then display the results as a new page definition within the same shell as the search page. We can bind an event handler to the page create event for the results page and clone the contents into the panel. Add the following script to the end of the head element, just below the `panel-init` script:

```
<script id="results-clone">
  $(document).on("pagecreate", "#results", function(event) {
    var $targetList = $("#panel").find("ul");

    // delete all items EXCEPT the top two with icons
    $targetList.children().not("[data-icon]").remove();

    // clone the child list
    $("#resultsList").children().clone().appendTo($targetList);

    // remove the copied first-child class from the first result
    // element
    $targetList.children(".ui-first-child").not("[data-icon]")
            .removeClass("ui-first-child");

    // note: the following may not be necessary. It depends on
    // whether the panel is visible when the new list items are
    // added
    $targetList.trigger("updatelayout");
  });
</script>
```

Test your jQuery Mobile app again by either reloading the search page or running the search page from NetBeans. This time, when you click search, the results will be copied into the panel on the left. Figure 5-16 is a screenshot of the details page with the panel visible and showing the cloned search results.

Figure 5-17 is a screenshot of the same details page viewed on an iPad. Since the iPad is wider, it displays the panel but no menu or close button.

The Profile Update Page

Besides viewing information about people within our organization, let's make it possible for users to update their own contact details. Create a new HTML5 HTML File named profile.html and replace its contents with the following HTML fragment:

```
<div data-role="page" id="profile">
  <style type="text/css" scoped>
    @import url("css/details.css");
```

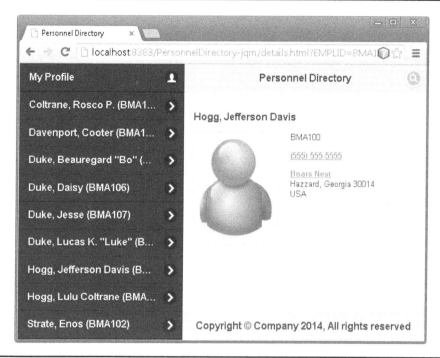

FIGURE 5-16. *Details page with search results visible*

```
    @media (min-width:28em) {
      img.avatar {
        margin-bottom: 20px;
      }
    }
  </style>

  <div data-role="header">
    <h1>Personnel Directory</h1>
    <a href="#panel" class="show-panel-btn" data-icon="bars"
      data-iconpos="notext">Menu</a>
    <a href="#search" data-icon="search" data-iconpos="notext"
      class="ui-btn-right">Search</a>
  </div><!-- /header -->

  <div data-role="content">
    <form action="#" method="POST">
      <img src="images/avatar.svg" class="avatar" alt="J.D.'s Photo">
      <h2>Hogg, Jefferson Davis</h2>
      <div>BMA100</div>
```

```
        <div class="ui-field-contain">
          <label for="phone">Phone:</label>
          <input type="tel" value="(555) 555-5555" name="phone"
                 id="phone">
        </div>
        <div class="ui-field-contain">
          <label for="address">Address:</label>
          <input type="text" value="Boars Nest" name="address"
                 id="address">
        </div>
        <div class="ui-field-contain">
          <label for="city">City:</label>
          <input type="text" value="Hazzard" name="city" id="city">
        </div>
        <div class="ui-field-contain">
          <label for="state">State:</label>
          <input type="text" value="Georgia" name="state" id="state">
        </div>
        <div class="ui-field-contain">
          <label for="postal">Postal Code:</label>
          <input type="text" value="30014" name="postal" id="postal">
        </div>
        <div class="ui-field-contain">
          <label for="country">Country:</label>
          <input type="text" value="USA" name="country" id="country">
        </div>

        <input type="submit" value="Save" data-theme="b">
      </form>
    </div><!-- /content -->

    <div data-role="footer" data-position="fixed">
      <h4>
        Copyright &copy; Company 2014, All rights reserved
      </h4>
    </div><!-- /footer -->

  </div><!-- /page -->
```

This HTML is a combination of the search page and the details page. It contains data-entry fields similar to the ones found in the search page but has a layout resembling the details page.

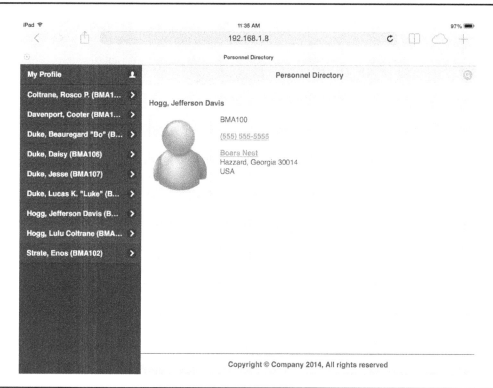

FIGURE 5-17. *Details page on an iPad*

Semantic HTML5

Wow! jQuery Mobile pages sure have a lot of div elements. Many of the structural elements in the Personnel Directory are div elements with special attributes. The meaning (semantics) of each div is determined by the data-role attribute. This is not the way we are supposed to write HTML5 applications. HTML5 is a semantic release that includes elements such as header, article, footer, nav, and aside. It seems that our jQuery Mobile div elements with attributes are trying to emulate many of those HTML5 elements.

jQuery Mobile actually places no restrictions on element types, using semantic attributes rather than element types to apply progressive enhancements. This means you are free to use the new HTML5 semantic elements as long as your target devices support HTML5. The key reason to

(Continued)

stay with div elements is if some of your target devices won't render the newer semantic elements.

Consider our early jQuery Mobile template along with a short panel template. Using semantic HTML5 tags, we could have written it like this:

```
<body>
  <main data-role="page" id="search">

    <header data-role="header">
      <a href="#panel" class="show-panel-btn" data-icon="bars"
         data-iconpos="notext">Menu</a>
      <h1>Personnel Directory</h1>
    </header><!-- /header -->

    <nav data-role="panel" id="panel" data-display="push"
         data-theme="b">
      <ul data-role="listview">
        <li data-icon="delete" class="hide-panel-btn">
          <a href="#" data-rel="close">Close menu</a>
        </li>
        <li data-icon="user">
          <a href="#">My Profile</a>
        </li>
      </ul>
    </nav><!-- /panel -->

    <article data-role="content">
      <p>Search form will go here</p>
    </article><!-- /content -->

    <footer data-role="footer" data-position="fixed">
      <h4>
        Copyright &copy; Company 2014, All rights reserved
      </h4>
    </footer><!-- /footer -->
  </main><!-- /page -->

</body>
```

Wait . . . did I say that this semantic approach only works with HTML5-capable browsers? Actually, that isn't true. HTML5-capable browsers understand HTML5 semantic elements, which means they know how to style them appropriately (`display: block`, etc.), but nearly all web browsers will let you mark up HTML with elements they don't recognize. Taking this a bit further, we could create our own jQuery Mobile elements named `page`, `content`, and `panel` (`header` and `footer` HTML5 elements already exist).

I added a media query to this page definition to provide more space between the avatar and data entry fields. At 28em device width, jQuery Mobile changes the way it displays fields and labels. Below 28em it stacks labels above fields. In this vertically stacked view, jQuery Mobile includes enough space between the avatar and data-entry fields. On wider displays, however, jQuery Mobile uses a horizontal layout. In this horizontal state, the avatar is too close to the first input field. The media query resolves this by adding a bottom margin to the avatar on wider displays. Figure 5-18 contains two screenshots of the profile update page as viewed on a mobile phone. The image on the left shows most of the profile page. The image on the right shows the numeric keypad that is displayed when the telephone field is

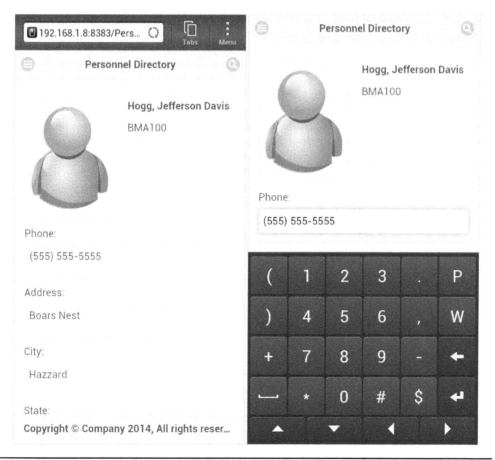

FIGURE 5-18.   *Two views of the profile page*

active. Because the Phone field is defined as an HTML5 `tel` input type, the browser displays keys appropriate for entering a phone number.

A "Safe" URL

Although our jQuery Mobile application contains 4 HTML files, it is really a single page application. Only one of the files contains a full HTML document. The rest are just HTML fragments. When jQuery Mobile loads one of these fragments, it will change the browser's URL. The problem with this behavior is that our application is dependent enough on the initial page to make those other URLs unusable. Here is a list of those dependencies:

- Each page references the search page by ID.

- The panel definition only exists in the search.html file.

- The search.html file contains references to CSS and JavaScript used by all of the pages.

We could eliminate a couple of these dependencies by making minor changes to each file but solving the panel dependency is more complicated.

We could also ignore this URL issue and just expect people to enter our single page application through the front door: search.html. The reason we have to find a resolution, however, is because of what happens when you leave and then return to a mobile browser. For example, imagine that you are searching this new Personnel Directory when your mobile phone rings. You choose to answer the call. After saying goodbye 15 minutes later, you unlock your screen and return to the Personnel Directory. Instead of picking up exactly where you left off, the mobile browser reloads the current page. If you tested loading one of the page fragments earlier, then you know what just happened. The user is now staring at an ungracefully degraded web page with very little, if any, usable features. A simple way to solve this is to tell jQuery Mobile not to change the URL whenever it loads a page. To implement this solution, add the following JavaScript to either of the script tags in the search.html file:

```
$.mobile.hashListeningEnabled = false;
$.mobile.pushStateEnabled = false;
```

Conclusion

In this chapter, you learned how to construct a responsive mobile application using jQuery Mobile. In the next chapter, we will build the same application using AngularJS, Topcoat.io, and Font Awesome, frameworks and libraries that help us build responsive applications without the heaviness of progressive enhancement.

CHAPTER
6

Constructing the HTML
View Without jQuery

As you saw in the last chapter, jQuery Mobile dramatically simplifies mobile development. With jQuery Mobile we are responsible for basic HTML structures (lists, forms, and the like). That is it. Through JavaScript and CSS, jQuery Mobile handles the rest (appearance, page transitions, and so on). Although convenient, those jQuery features come at a price: performance. jQuery Mobile expects page structures containing a combination of HTML elements and application data. That is a lot of information to send over a mobile network. In this chapter, we will learn how to build the same mobile Personnel Directory using a client-side MV* pattern that allows us to cache everything locally *except* data, reducing our network cost to just the data that differs between each page.

Probably the hardest part about writing this chapter was deciding which HTML5 frameworks and libraries to use. There are so many to choose from! For MV*, we can choose from hundreds, with Backbone, Ember, Knockout, Kendo UI, and AngularJS being the most common. Likewise, the Internet is filled with templating and presentation libraries. Common JavaScript template libraries include Mustache, Handlebars, Dust, Underscore, React, and EJS. The more common presentation libraries include Kendo UI, Twitter Bootstrap, Topcoat.io, and Sencha Touch. And we can't forget Animations: Effeckt.css, Animate.css, and GSAP. For this chapter, I chose AngularJS as the MV* framework, Topcoat.io for styling, and a mix of Animate and GSAP for animations (more on animations at the end of the chapter). AngularJS offers simple two-way data binding as well as templates, routing, and jQuery Lite (jqLite). Topcoat is just CSS (and some images), no JavaScript. For icons, I chose FontAwesome, a library that includes an icon font and CSS declarations.

NOTE
This chapter assumes you have no familiarity with AngularJS and includes documentation and rabbit trails to help you become familiar with AngularJS.

Chapter 5 is all you need to successfully build mobile web applications. The point of the previous chapter was to demonstrate that mobile development really is simple. This chapter, on the other hand, is not light reading material. The content is challenging! If, however, you are a fearless programmer with a desire to control the finest detail of your application, then this chapter is for you.

Chapters 7 and 8 are each divided into two parts. The first half of each chapter shows you how to integrate PeopleSoft with the jQuery Mobile prototype. The second half shows how to integrate with AngularJS. With that in mind, you could actually skip this chapter and be no worse for it. Nevertheless, I packed some AMAZING stuff in this chapter, so I highly encourage you to be brave and read on. I have full confidence in you. Even if you don't master web development with AngularJS, you will definitely learn something of value. Carpe diem!

Preparing the Project

Back in the old days of web development (you remember when we walked to school in the snow and it was up hill both ways?)…we downloaded files manually, prepared directory structures, wrote code, and then packaged, tested, and deployed (FTP'd) web applications. Today front-end web developers use a variety of package and build management tools including Yeoman, Grunt, and Bower. These tools configure projects; download libraries; run automated tests; and process, minify, and package files. In this section, let's try both methods for preparing a project. First, we'll use the old-fashioned method of building a folder structure and downloading files. Then we will use the automated method. In math class, my math teacher would show us the *hard* way to solve a problem. Once we understood what we were doing, he would show us a shortcut; same concept here. Once you understand what the automated tools accomplish, then using them is great. Having a basic understanding will help you resolve problems when they arise.

The NetBeans/Manual Approach

Did I say we would create this project the old-fashioned way first? Well, not exactly. We will let NetBeans do most of it. Then we will manually add missing libraries.

NOTE
While working with code in the NetBeans project, you will see references to bower. Bower is the alternative to the manual approach. You will learn how to use bower later in this chapter.

Creating the NetBeans Angular-Seed Project

Launch NetBeans and create a new project by choosing File | New Project from the NetBeans menu bar. In step 1, choose HTML5 Application for the project type. Press the Next button to move to step 2. Name the project `PersonnelDirectory-ajs`. Note the Project Location and Project Folder. Later we will download additional libraries into this folder. Press the Next button to move to step 3; select the Download Online Template option and then select the AngularJS Seed template. Click Finish to create the project. Figures 6-1, 6-2, and 6-3 are screenshots of the various New Project wizard steps.

NOTE
Step 4 of the wizard will automatically download the additional libraries we plan to add to this project. During testing with NetBeans 7.4, however, I found NetBeans to be very inconsistent with its folder structures when downloading libraries into angularjs-seed.

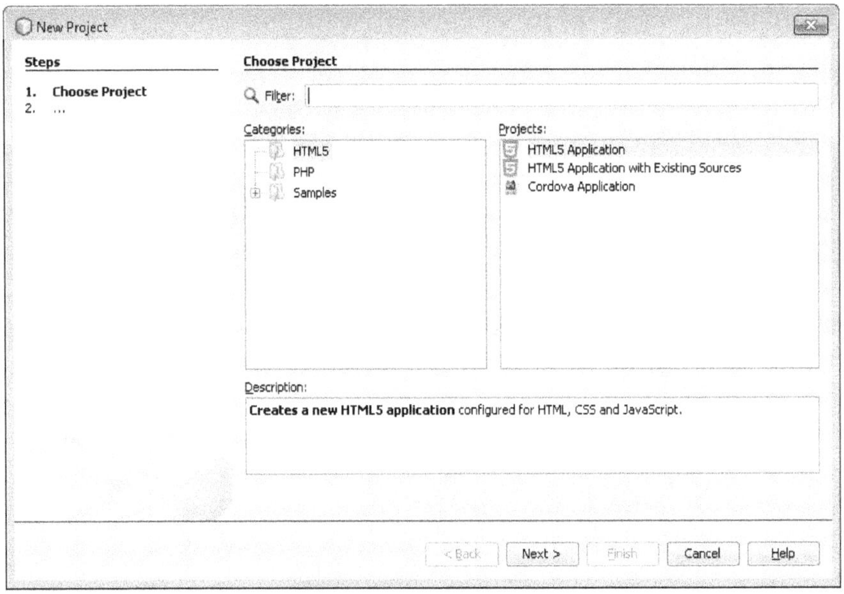

FIGURE 6-1. *Step 1 of the New Project wizard*

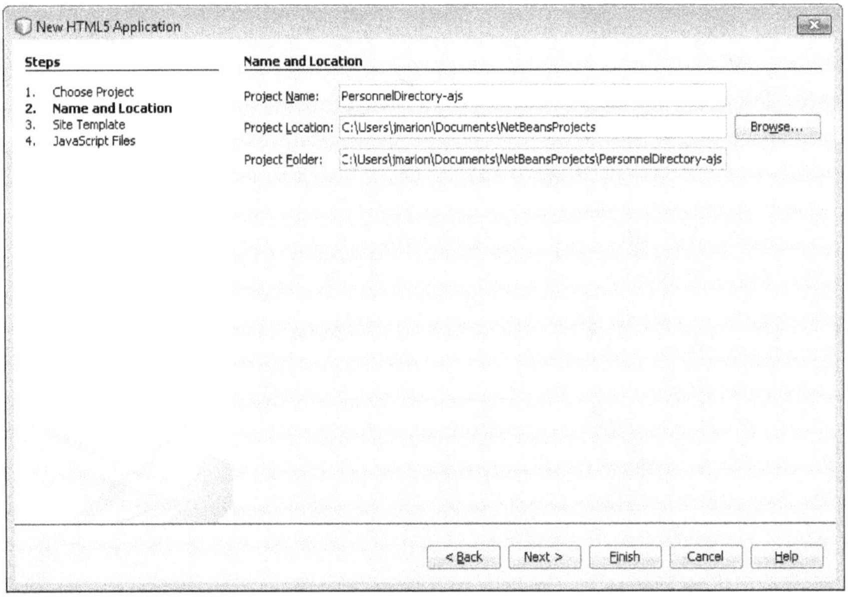

FIGURE 6-2. *Step 2 of the New Project wizard*

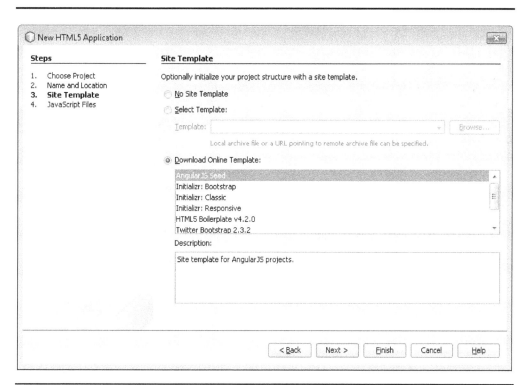

FIGURE 6-3. *Step 3 of the New Project wizard*

Alternatively, if you prefer a development environment other than NetBeans, you can use Git to clone angularjs-seed from https://github.com/angular/angular-seed. The angularjs-seed project contains complete instructions for downloading and running the seed template. We will discuss more on this later.

Examining and Modifying the Project Folder Structure

Step 2 of the NetBeans project wizard displayed the project root folder. If you did not save a copy of that location, you can find the folder by right-clicking the project name in NetBeans' project explorer and selecting Properties from the context menu. The Project Folder is the first field of the Sources category. Using Windows Explorer (or your operating system specific file browser), navigate to your project folder. Inside that folder, you should see a subfolder named app. The app folder contains our website content, including css, img, js, and partials folders.

Many of the project folders already contain content. For example, the css folder contains app.css and the js folder contains app.js, controllers.js, directives.js, and so on. This is the sample structure created by the angular-seed project and is the structure we will use for this chapter's iteration of the mobile Personnel Directory.

There are other AngularJS starter projects that organize files differently (for example, by feature rather than by type).

The seed project is designed for use with Bower, a JavaScript package management application and therefore contains no libraries—not even AngularJS libraries. Before downloading additional libraries, create a new folder named lib inside the app folder. We will place downloaded JavaScript libraries in this new folder.

Download AngularJS

AngularJS is an MV* JavaScript framework backed by Google. The AngularJS newsletter says "[AngularJS] is ideal for use when building client-side single-page apps. It is not a library, but a framework for building dynamic web pages. It focuses on extending HTML and providing dynamic data binding, and it plays well with other frameworks (e.g., jQuery). If you are building a single-page app, AngularJS will be perfect for you." (http://www.ng-newsletter.com/posts/beginner2expert-how_to_start.html).

Our project uses AngularJS for:

- Routing
- Two-way data binding
- Ajax
- HTML templates

The AngularJS project is modular, which means there is one JavaScript file for each feature. The mobile Personnel Directory project will use three AngularJS modules: the core angular module as well as the angular-route and angular-animate modules. You can find these files within a version specific subdirectory of https://code.angularjs.org/. This chapter was written using files from the https://code.angularjs.org/1.2.9/ download location (1.2.9 was the latest version when I wrote this chapter). Download the following files into the app\lib directory of your project:

- angular-animate.min.js
- angular-route.min.js
- angular.min.js

Download Topcoat

Topcoat.io is a light-weight skinning framework lead by Adobe. We will only use a small fraction of this already small framework: component CSS styling, the Source Sans font, and an image or two. Download the Topcoat framework by navigating to http://topcoat.io/ and clicking the Download button. When I wrote this chapter, the download button was in the upper right corner. Extract the downloaded zip file into your project app directory.

Download FontAwesome

FontAwesome is an AMAZING icon font originally designed for Twitter Bootstrap. Why use a font for icons? Here are a few reasons:

- Infinitely scalable—won't pixelate at larger sizes.

- Great for iOS Retina display (because they are scalable).

- Easily colored (CSS color attribute).

- You can add display effects such as drop shadow.

Download FontAwesome by using the Download button on the http://fontawesome .github.io/Font-Awesome/ website. Just like Topcoat, extract FontAwesome into the project app directory. Also just like Topcoat, we will only use a small fraction of the functionality provided by FontAwesome. Fortunately, FontAwesome CSS and font file are very small and will be cached by mobile browsers. Figure 6-4 is a screenshot of the file system structure after adding the lib, topcoat, and font-awesome library and folders.

FIGURE 6-4. *Project folder structure*

Download Animate.css

Animations can have a dramatic influence on usability. Imagine a shopping application where you search for and select items to add to a shopping cart. You probably don't have to imagine very hard because most of us use shopping applications like this regularly (Amazon perhaps?). As you add items to your shopping cart, how do you know the cart value? How many items are in the cart? Where is that shopping cart anyway? What if, as you selected items to purchase, you saw an animation move the item from the list into a cart representation in the upper right corner of the screen? An animation such as this would automatically train your eyes to look for the shopping cart in the upper right corner.

Animate.css is a CSS library that defines keyframes for several common CSS animations. We will use it later because it integrates well with AngularJS. Download the library by navigating to http://daneden.github.io/animate.css/ and choosing "Download Animate.css." Save the file in your project's app\css directory. Your CSS folder should now contain app.css and animate.css

Download GSAP

GreenSock Animation Platform (GSAP) is a very impressive JavaScript animation library. Many developers in the web industry left JavaScript animation in favor of hardware-accelerated CSS animations. There are many benefits to CSS animation, with the greatest being that you can change animations without modifying application code. The CSS-Tricks website, but makes a very compelling argument for JavaScript animations in their article "Myth Busting: CSS Animations vs. JavaScript" (http://css-tricks.com/myth-busting-css-animations-vs-javascript/). We will use the GSAP library later when we discuss animating the user experience.

Download GSAP by visiting the http://www.greensock.com/gsap-js/ website and clicking the Download JS button. When the download dialog appears, click the Download Zip button. From the downloaded file (a file named something like greensock-v12-js.zip) extract the src\minified\TweenMax.min.js file to your project's app\lib directory. Figure 6-5 is a screenshot showing the contents of the lib folder.

Documents library
lib

Name

angular.min.js
angular-animate.min.js
angular-route.min.js
TweenMax.min.js

FIGURE 6-5. *Contents of lib folder*

Test Data

In Chapter 4, we created test data: two files named DETAILS.json and SEARCH_
RESULTS.json. Copy these into a new folder named test-data. Rename DETAILS.json
to KU0001, the employee ID (EMPLID) of the first employee in the search results.

We also need a photo for our test data. In Chapters 7 and 8, we will create services
for employee photos. For this chapter, we will use the same static image we used in the
last chapter. Either copy the avatar.svg image from your last project or download it with
this book's sample code. Place avatar.svg in the project's app\img directory.

Your NetBeans project explorer should look something like Figure 6-6. I have
included a fully configured sample project zip file named ch06starter.zip in the
book's sample download.

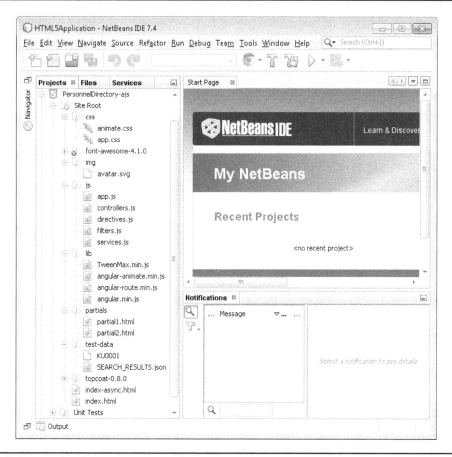

FIGURE 6-6. *NetBeans project explorer*

FIGURE 6-7. *Screenshot of index.html*

Running the Modified Angular-seed Example
Right-click on index.html and choose Run File from the context menu. The Chrome
web browser should launch and display a page that looks similar to Figure 6-7.
Click the view2 hyperlink to switch to an alternate view. Notice that the part after
the # in the URL changes, but you remain on index.html. AngularJS applications are
single-page applications, which mean they use Ajax to retrieve content and display
that content in a view region.

The Automated Way
The official angular-seed project is available in a Git repository website at https://
github.com/angular/angular-seed. Git is a popular distributed version control system
that integrates well with IDEs such as NetBeans, Eclipse, and JDeveloper. NetBeans
is great at creating a simple structure for an AngularJS project, but any serious AngularJS
development should start with the angular-seed project.

The following scenario and commands were run from a Linux laptop. Mac users
will find these listings very familiar. Windows users will need to slightly modify the
commands (for example, change the file path from a slash to a backslash, change
cp to copy, and mv to move).

NOTE
*If you are not using NetBeans or another IDE that
supports the angular-seed site template, then the
following steps will help you prepare your project.
The steps listed below are optional. Preparing the
project using the automation tools described here is
not required. If you prepared your project using the
manual method discussed earlier, then you are ready
to move to the Introduction to AngularJS section.*

Cloning the Angular-seed Repository

If you are familiar with git, you can clone the angular-seed repository into a directory using the following commands (commands in bold text):

```
sarah@laptop:~$ cd ~/Documents/NetBeansProjects
sarah@laptop:NetBeansProjects$ git clone\
https://github.com/angular/angular-seed.git
Cloning into 'angular-seed'...
remote: Reusing existing pack: 2472, done.
remote: Counting objects: 3, done.
remote: Compressing objects: 100% (3/3), done.
remote: Total 2475 (delta 0), reused 3 (delta 0)
Receiving objects: 100% (2475/2475), 10.91 MiB | 4.87 MiB/s, done.
Resolving deltas: 100% (1417/1417), done.
Checking connectivity... done.
sarah@laptop:NetBeansProjects$ mv angular-seed PersonnelDirectory-seed
sarah@laptop:NetBeansProjects$ cd PersonnelDirectory-seed/
sarah@laptop:PersonnelDirectory-seed$ ls
app  bower.json  LICENSE  package.json  README.md  test
sarah@laptop:PersonnelDirectory-seed$
```

First, I move into my NetBeans projects directory, and then I clone the angular-seed project. Next, I rename the project's folder. Since we aren't really working on the angular-seed project, but using that as a template, it makes sense to rename the folder to something meaningful. The final step navigates to the project's working directory and lists its contents.

If you are not a Git user, then you can download a compressed archive of the repository from the angular-seed repository at https://github.com/angular/angular-seed (search the page for Download Zip). Extract the archive into a directory, rename the angular-seed directory, and then open a command prompt into the seed project directory.

Installing Dependencies

The official angular-seed project uses tools including Karma, http-server, Bower, and so on, which are available from the Node.js repository. The angular-seed project includes a file (package.json) that tells Node Package Manager (npm) what to download and where to put it. From inside the project directory, run the following command:

```
sarah@laptop:PersonnelDirectory-seed$ npm install
```

NOTE
We installed Node.js in Chapter 1.

When you run this command, npm will download the dependencies listed in package.json and install them in a new directory name node_modules within the project directory. After installing all of these dependencies, package.json directs npm to run the command `bower install`. Bower is a JavaScript package manager. Angular-seed uses Bower to download JavaScript libraries used by the seed project, such as AngularJS and the various AngularJS modules. You should now see several new directories in your project's app/bower_components directory (don't worry if your bower_components directory is empty. Other build steps will add content to this directory). The project directory should now weigh in around 100 MB. That is quite a bit larger than the original 17 KB of the angular-seed project. Rather than package all the dependencies into angular-seed, the directors of angular-seed chose to distribute just the angular-seed files and use package managers (such as npm and Bower) to download all the dependencies. This ensures that you have the latest versions of the required libraries when you pull the angular-seed project.

NOTE
The .bowerrc file in the project's root directory tells Bower where to place library files.

Test the Sample
Here are the steps required to run the sample:

1. git clone https://github.com/angular/angular-seed.git

2. mv angular-seed PersonnelDirectory-seed

3. npm install

We can run the sample application by invoking the command `npm start` (a command that is defined in package.json) from the command line. Besides a bunch of other text, this command should display:

```
Starting up http-server, serving ./ on port: 8000
Hit CTRL-C to stop the server
```

When you see this text, it means you now have a web server running on port 8000. To view it, open a web browser and enter http://localhost:8000/app/. This will load the sample angular-seed project and navigate to the default application route (more about routing later). After reviewing the sample, press the CTRL-C keyboard combination (or whatever command was displayed when you started the server) to stop the web server.

Project Specific JavaScript Dependencies

When we created the project through NetBeans, we manually downloaded each JavaScript library. As we saw in this section, angular-seed is configured to use Bower to download libraries. That configuration is stored in the bower.json file. If you open that file in a text editor, you will see that it contains references for angular, angular-route, angular-loader, and so on.

NOTE
The angular-seed project also contains a reference for html5-boilerplate. We aren't using html5-boilerplate, so feel free to remove it from your bower .json file.

Since angular-seed uses Bower, we can just ask Bower to download our project's additional JavaScript dependencies. Tell Bower what to download by running the command `bower install <library>`. If you want Bower to remember your library choices, add the `--save` parameter.

How do you run Bower? The npm command installed Bower into the project's node_modules directory when you ran the `npm install` command. From the project's root directory (~/Documents/NetBeansProjects/PersonnelDirectory-seed), run the command `./node_modules/.bin/bower`. If you have a bash shell (Linux, Mac, or Cygwin), you can use the shortcut `$(npm bin)/bower`. The following listing contains a command for each additional library:

```
$(npm bin)/bower install animate.css --save
$(npm bin)/bower install fontawesome --save
$(npm bin)/bower install gsap --save
$(npm bin)/bower install topcoat --save
```

NOTE
The command `npm bin` returns the current project's bin directory containing references to all of the local node module binaries. From a bash command line you can execute bower using the shortcut `$(npm bin)/bower install`.

Running these commands will download the requested libraries to app/bower_components and add them to bower.json. As time progresses and new updates are available for the various JavaScript dependencies, you can run `bower update` to download the latest version.

NOTE
You can find information about the bower.json file structure online at https://github.com/bower/bower .json-spec. The semantics for the version attribute is quite flexible. You can find additional information about the version number syntax at https://github .com/isaacs/node-semver/.

You could run npm start again, but we haven't changed any of the code, so you wouldn't notice any difference.

Asynchronous JavaScript

If you review the contents of the app/ directory, you will see there are actually two different index files. The first is the one we already tested: index.html. The second is index-async.html. The index-async file doesn't actually work yet. I intentionally ignored it earlier when manually downloading files because index-async requires a special injected JavaScript file. I could have told you how to copy and paste the contents, but the minified contents would be rather difficult to work with. It is so much easier to let npm inject the appropriate content. Inside index-async.html you find the text:

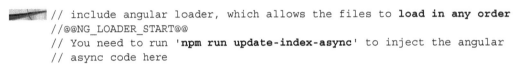

```
// include angular loader, which allows the files to load in any order
//@@NG_LOADER_START@@
// You need to run 'npm run update-index-async' to inject the angular
// async code here
```

From this comment, we see that the difference between index.html and index-async.html is that index-async.html "loads [files] in any order." Or, more specifically, it loads JavaScript files asynchronously. The default browser behavior is to load JavaScript files synchronously, blocking the entire load process for each script tag. Asynchronous file loading can significantly improve load-time performance. To enable asynchronous loading, at the command prompt navigate to your project's root directory (the directory with package.json...and you are probably already there) and enter the command npm run update-index-async. This will replace the content between the @@NG_LOADER_START@@ and @@NG_LOADER_END@@ lines with the contents of the file angular-loader.min.js (which is why that file is listed in the bower.json file).

Asynchronous JavaScript Loaders

The angular-seed project contains an alternate index file named index-async .html. The point of this file is to load JavaScript asynchronously. The default browser behavior is to block HTML parsing and rendering while reading JavaScript files. This default behavior can have a negative impact on rendering performance. The alternative is to inject JavaScript by inserting DOM nodes into the document after the DOM is available for manipulation. This allows the browser to render a user experience before downloading, parsing, and executing JavaScript files.

The key to successful asynchronous JavaScript is recognizing dependencies and executing JavaScript modules in the appropriate order. JavaScript developers use libraries such as require.js to implement asynchronous JavaScript loading. My favorite is the lightweight $script.js JavaScript library. AngularJS includes a minified version of $script embedded in index-async.html.

Execute the command `npm start` to start the embedded web server and then load http://localhost:8000/app/index-async.html in your web browser. If your web server is already running, you don't need to start it, just open index-async.html in your web browser. Verify that index-async.html performs the same as index.html. With a sample project as small as this one, you may not notice a performance difference between the index.html synchronous loading and the asynchronous features of index-async.html.

Extra Credit: Prepare a NetBeans Project

If you are not using NetBeans, then of course you won't be creating a NetBeans project. I like to use a combination of the approaches shown in this chapter. I prefer the development tools provided by NetBeans as well as the dependency automation included with the angular-seed project. With this in mind, I use the tools described in this section to git clone angular-seed and then run the npm and Bower install processes. When those complete, I create a NetBeans project from the seed source and manipulate the NetBeans metadata. If you prefer to use this approach, launch NetBeans and choose File | New Project from the NetBeans menu bar. In step 1 of the New Project wizard, choose the category HTML5 and the project HTML5 Application with Existing Sources. In step 2, for the Site Root, select the app directory of your seed project. The Project Directory is the seed project's root directory. Figure 6-8 is a screenshot of step 2.

Summary of Steps

The following listing contains the commands we ran to prepare our project:

```
git clone https://github.com/angular/angular-seed.git
mv angular-seed PersonnelDirectory-seed
npm install

$(npm bin)/bower install animate.css --save
$(npm bin)/bower install fontawesome --save
$(npm bin)/bower install gsap --save
```

```
$(npm bin)/bower install topcoat -save

# Optional step for async loader
npm run update-index-async

# Run server to ensure it all works
npm start
```

The remainder of this chapter uses the project you created using the NetBeans/ Manual method. I chose this approach because it has fewer dependencies. I encourage the use of angular-seed along with Bower, Node, and npm, but these tools can be difficult to install on certain operating systems. To ensure consistency for all readers, we will use the manual, NetBeans approach. If you are not using NetBeans and prefer the automated Bower approach, then feel free to continue using your new automated project. Just be sure to update paths and file references accordingly. For example, the seed project references libraries from the bower_ components directory, whereas I reference libraries from the lib directory.

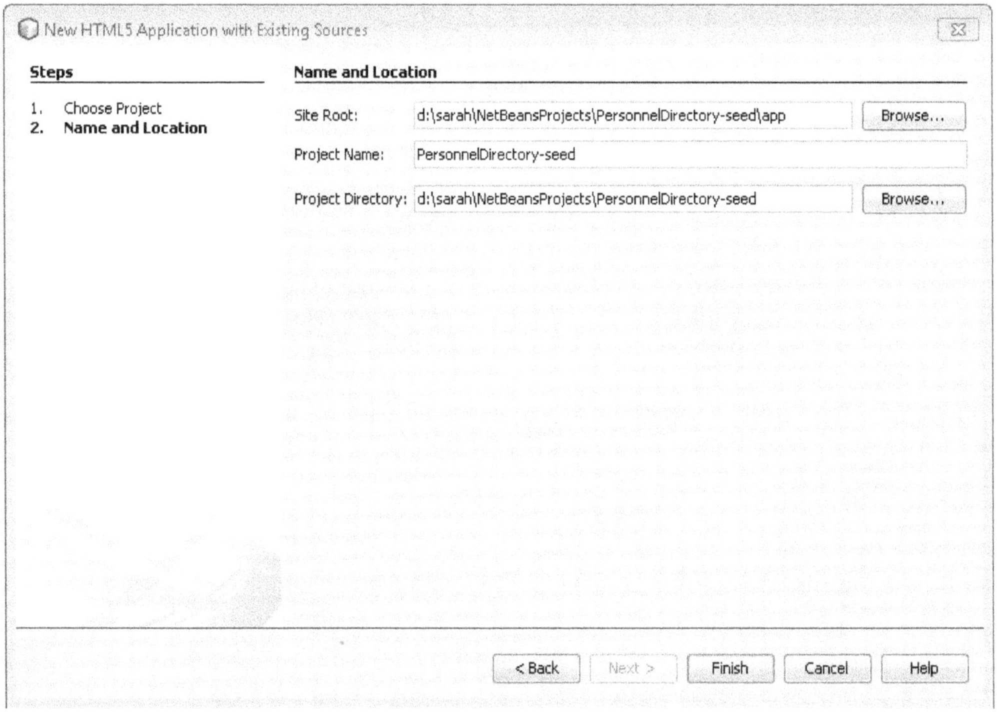

FIGURE 6-8. *NetBeans project folder locations*

Introduction to AngularJS

If you already know something about AngularJS, then feel free to skip this section. The point here is to help new AngularJS users become comfortable and familiar with the AngularJS platform. The Internet is packed with great AngularJS tutorials. I recommend starting with the AngularJS tutorial at https://docs.angularjs.org/tutorial. AngularJS even has its own YouTube channel: https://www.youtube.com/user/angularjs.

First, what is AngularJS? Is it a library? Is it a framework? The AngularJS team would prefer that we think of AngularJS as a toolset...or even an extension to HTML. It uses declarative directives for the user interface (views) and JavaScript configurations and dependency injection for the data model, services, and so on (model and controllers). AngularJS dramatically reduces DOM manipulation through two-way data binding and template views (also known as *partials*). For a great overview, visit http://en.wikipedia.org/wiki/AngularJS.

Enough with the abstract descriptions; let's build something so you can draw your own conclusions.

My First AngularJS Page

Let's create a sample page to see AngularJS in action. Select the PersonnelDirectory-ajs project in NetBeans. This is the project you created using the NetBeans/Manual method and contains a lib directory with JavaScript libraries. From the NetBeans menu bar, select File | New File. Choose the file type HTML5 | HTML File. On step 2, name your file `sample` (the name is not important, but for consistency, name it "sample"). NetBeans will create a new file with the necessary `html`, `head`, and `body` tags. To this file, we will add some AngularJS directives and some sample code.

The first thing we need to do is *bootstrap* our document. Bootstrapping involves adding an `ng-app` attribute (known as a directive) to the root of our application (usually the html element, but can be any element). To bootstrap `sample.html`, add the attribute `ng-app` to the `html` element (the `html` element should be the second line of the document...well, except for the generic licensing comments inserted by NetBeans). The following code listing contains the first two lines of the document after adding the `ng-app` attribute. Notice that we don't have to specify an attribute value for `ng-app`. HTML5 is a simplification of the HTML specification and does not require each attribute to have a value.

```
<!DOCTYPE html>
. . .
<html ng-app>
```

Now let's add some HTML and AngularJS directives to demonstrate two-way data binding. Replace the contents of the body element with the following (AngularJS directives are in bold):

```
<p>
  <input type="text" ng-model="p.userName" id="userNameField"/>
</p>
<p>Hello {{p.userName}}</p>
<script src="lib/angular.min.js"></script>
```

The ng-model attribute of the text field binds the input text element to the userName property of the p object (p.userName). We then display the value of the property using the template {{p.userName}}. Test it out by right-clicking the NetBeans text editor and choosing Run File from the context menu. Type a value into the text field and watch it appear below the text box. At this point, we have not written any JavaScript and we already have a working data-driven web application. This is the power of AngularJS two-way data binding: the model and view remain synchronized.

While reviewing this example in the Chrome web browser (or similar browser), right-click on the paragraph (the part that says "Hello") and choose Inspect Element from the context menu. Notice that AngularJS added a class attribute with the value ng-binding. Expand the paragraph above the "Hello" paragraph and inspect the input element. Notice the input element also has new classes: ng-valid and ng-dirty. Figure 6-9 is a screenshot of the AngularJS page showing the Chrome inspector.

Bootstrapping AngularJS

When constructing sample.html, our first step was to *bootstrap* the page by adding the ng-app attribute to the root html element. Bootstrapping identifies the current page as an AngularJS app and directs the AngularJS library to compile and link the current document. Compiling involves traversing the DOM to identify AngularJS directives (ng attributes and elements). Linking registers scope and listeners to DOM elements identified by the compile process.

The ng-app directive is not the only way to bootstrap an AngularJS application. For more control over the bootstrap process, we can manually bootstrap an application using JavaScript similar to the following:

```
window.onload = function() {
  // identify the element that is the root of our AngularJS app
  var $rootElement = angular.element(window.document);

  // specify which modules we plan to use in our app
  var modules = [
    'ng',
    //'myApp', // If our app had its own config module
    function($provide) {
      $provide.value('$rootElement', $rootElement);
    }
```

```
    ];

    var $injector = angular.injector(modules);

    // get a reference to the AngularJS compiler for our app
    var $compile = $injector.get('$compile');

    // compile the app (traverse the DOM looking for directives)
    var compositeLinkFn = $compile($rootElement);

    var $rootScope = $injector.get('$rootScope');

    // link the app (create watches and scope)
    compositeLinkFn($rootScope);

    // tell AngularJS we are done and it should synchronize data
    $rootScope.$apply();
};
```

Since we are using the ng-app directive with synchronous file loading, this chapter doesn't require any special bootstrap code.

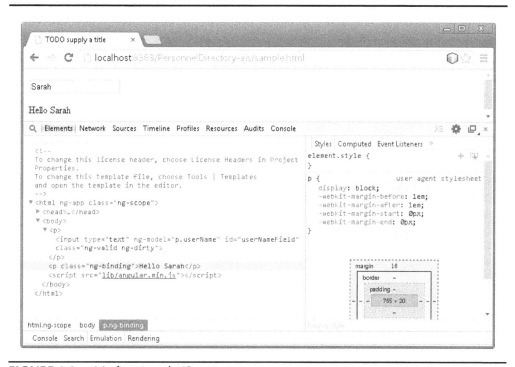

FIGURE 6-9. *My first AngularJS page*

AngularJS templates can evaluate standard JavaScript expressions. Add the following just before the angular.min.js script tag:

```
<p>Expression: 1 + 2 = {{1 + 2}}</p>
```

Save and view your page in Chrome (or another web browser). You should see the text "Expression: 1 + 2 = 3" displayed in a new paragraph below the "Hello" line.

We can further test two-way data binding by setting and inspecting data model values using JavaScript. For this next test, we will add two buttons below our new expression and a few lines of JavaScript. First, add two buttons:

```
<p><button onclick="sayHello()">Say Hello!</button></p>
<p><button onclick="changeMyName()">Change My Name</button></p>
```

Next, add the sayHello and changeMyName JavaScript functions:

```
<script>
  var sayHello = function() {
    var el = document.getElementById("userNameField");
    var scope = angular.element(el).scope();
    var name = scope.p.userName;

    alert("Hello " + name);
  };

  var changeMyName = function() {
    var el = document.getElementById("userNameField");
    var scope = angular.element(el).scope();

    scope.p.userName = "Jim";
    scope.$apply();
  };
</script>
```

Briefly, the sayHello function above first obtains a reference to the input field using the standard DOM method getElementById. It then uses the AngularJS jQuery Lite method angular.element. The point of using the angular/jQuery lite representation of the element is to access the element's AngularJS scope. Once we have a reference to the scope, we can read and/or change values within the scope.

The changeMyName function is very similar to the sayHello function. After obtaining a reference to the model and updating model values, changeMyName calls the special AngularJS scope method $apply().

If you are using NetBeans and Chrome and launched the current page through NetBeans' Run File command, then simply save your changes and switch to Chrome. The NetBeans plugin for Chrome automatically reloads changed files. If you are using a different browser, save your work and manually reload the file to

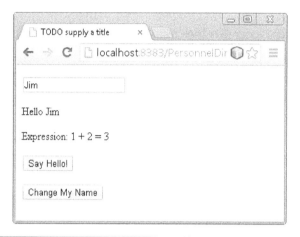

FIGURE 6-10. *Final screenshot of sample.html*

view your changes. Type a name into the input field and click the Say Hello! button. You should see a dialog box containing the text "Hello XXX" (where XXX represents the text you typed). This demonstrates that it is possible to retrieve AngularJS data model values. Clicking the Change My Name button will change the name displayed both in the paragraph and input field. This demonstrates that we can set AngularJS data model values and those changes are automatically synchronized with the view layer. Figure 6-10 is a final representation of the sample.html page. Notice that we didn't write any DOM manipulation JavaScript. All of our interactions were with the data model.

Now that you have tested the expected scenario and seen it perform as intended, try the following scenario:

- Refresh the page.
- Ensure that the input field is empty.
- Click the Change My Name button.

Did the page content change? Did the value change in the input field as it did in our prior test? When I perform this test, the input field stays blank and nothing appears after the text "Hello." If I open my web browser's JavaScript console and click the button again, I see the text, "Uncaught TypeError: Cannot set property 'userName' of undefined." What the browser is telling us is the scope does not contain `p.userName`. This is because AngularJS doesn't add the `p` object and its corresponding `userName` property to the scope until we enter some data. We can resolve this problem by changing our JavaScript to create the `p` attribute of the scope if it does not already exist. Later in this chapter, you will learn how to use controllers to initialize scope properties and values. The following is an updated JavaScript listing with changes in bold text:

```javascript
var initP = function(scope) {
  if (!scope.p) {
    scope.p = {};
  }
};

var sayHello = function() {
  var el = document.getElementById("userNameField");
  var scope = angular.element(el).scope();

  initP(scope);

  var name = scope.p.userName;

  alert("Hello " + name);
};

var changeMyName = function() {
  var el = document.getElementById("userNameField");
  var scope = angular.element(el).scope();

  initP(scope);
  scope.p.userName = "Jim";
  scope.$apply();
};
```

The following is a complete code listing of sample.html:

```html
<!DOCTYPE html>
<!--
To change this license header, choose License Headers in Project
Properties.
To change this template file, choose Tools | Templates
and open the template in the editor.
-->
<html ng-app>
  <head>
    <title>TODO supply a title</title>
    <meta charset="UTF-8">
    <meta name="viewport" content="width=device-width">
  </head>
  <body>
```

```
<p>
  <input type="text" ng-model="p.userName" id="userNameField"/>
</p>
<p>Hello {{p.userName}}</p>
<p>Expression: 1 + 2 = {{1 + 2}}</p>
<p><button onclick="sayHello()">Say Hello!</button></p>
<p><button onclick="changeMyName()">Change My Name</button></p>

<script src="lib/angular.min.js"></script>
<script>
  var initP = function(scope) {
    if (!scope.p) {
      scope.p = {};
    }
  };

  var sayHello = function() {
    var el = document.getElementById("userNameField");
    var scope = angular.element(el).scope();

    initP(scope);

    var name = scope.p.userName;

    alert("Hello " + name);
  };

  var changeMyName = function() {
    var el = document.getElementById("userNameField");
    var scope = angular.element(el).scope();

    initP(scope);
    scope.p.userName = "Jim";
    scope.$apply();
  };
</script>
</body>
</html>
```

NOTE

Did you see the template text ({{p.userName}}, etc.) while the page was loading? AngularJS includes a special directive called ng-cloak that you can use to hide template content that is visible during that fraction of a second between the browser loading the content and AngularJS bootstrapping the page.

Scope

You have already seen how we use controllers and $scope to bind data methods to a view. There is another type of scope, and that is the traditional variable scope. In programming languages, scope determines visibility. Most languages have the concept of a global scope. Anything declared at the global scope is accessible to any code accessed throughout the duration of the program. JavaScript running within a web browser has a type of global scope contained by the window object. Anything added to the window object is global and accessible as long as the current web page is loaded. If the browser loads a new page by navigating away from the current page, then anything declared by the current page is destroyed and garbage collected (garbage collection: the process of freeing memory used by variables that no longer exist). When a new page loads, the old window scope is destroyed and a new one is created. You can actually load JavaScript by adding a `<script>` node, delete that script node, and still run functions declared by that script. Any functions declared at the global scope or in some way attached to the global scope will exist until they go out of scope. The only way to remove them is to place them inside a scope that you manage and can delete. JavaScript developers manage scope through anonymous, self-executing functions and closures.

If AngularJS uses a single-page application pattern, how does it manage memory to ensure that controllers are dropped from memory when navigating between views? AngularJS manages scope through its module pattern. You invoke a method to identify the type (controller, directive, and so on) of module and you give the module a name. This binds an object to a name that you can later inject into other modules. The code for the module exists in a closure. AngularJS can create instances of the module when needed and then destroy them at the appropriate time, for example, when navigating between views.

I recommend the following articles if you are interested in learning more about AngularJS scope and memory management:

- http://stackoverflow.com/questions/16947957/how-does-angularjs-handle-memory-management-with-ngview

- http://tech.small-improvements.com/2013/09/10/angularjs-performance-with-large-lists/

- http://thenittygritty.co/angularjs-pitfalls-using-scopes

Dependency Injection

There is one more topic you need to understand before continuing: Dependency Injection. Dependency Injection is a common design pattern in strongly typed languages. Spring, Guice, and PicoContainer are well-known Java Dependency

Injection frameworks (also known as Inversion of Control [IoC] frameworks). The point of Dependency Injection is to decouple services from the code that uses those services. For example, if you want to round a number to the nearest Integer using JavaScript, you might write code that looks something like this:

```
var roundPhi = function() {
  return Math.round(1.61803);
};
```

The Dependency Injection version of the `roundPhi` function would not use the `Math` object directly, but would instead contain a `Math` parameter. The `Math` parameter would be known as a service. Here is what a Dependency Injection version might look like:

```
var roundPhiDI = function(math) {
  return math.round(1.61803);
};
```

You would invoke the Dependency Injection version like this: `roundPhiDI(Math)` and it would return the value 2. In this example, the function's dependency on the *Math* module is satisfied through the method's parameter. Why the hassle? Why not just use the Math module? What if you wanted to call `roundPhi`, but you wanted it to behave slightly differently? For example, what if you wanted to track each time someone invokes `Math.round`? Would you search your code for every usage of `Math.round` and add more code to account for its usage? If you are familiar with dynamic languages (such as JavaScript), you might actually take another approach: Monkey Patching (or Duck Punching). The Monkey Patching approach would replace, or *patch*, the original `Math.round` with a new version. Here is an example:

```
(function() {
  var oldRound = Math.round;
  Math.round = function(n) {
    console.log("round was called with parameter " + n);
    return oldRound(n);
  }
}());
```

Calling `Math.round(1.61803)` will still return 2, but will now print "round was called with parameter 1.61803" to the JavaScript console.

Here is another example: What if you wanted to call `roundPhi` but wanted to change the rounding rules? How would you change round's behavior for just `roundPhi` and not globally for all executions of `Math.round`?

One of the problems with Monkey Patching is that it changes the behavior of known objects without notification. When you call `Math.round`, you expect it to adhere to the ECMAScript specification. When you use a math service, however, all you know is you invoked the `round` method, and you expect a whole integer result conforming to the definition for the `round` method. Implementation details are unimportant. It does not matter to you whether the definition was provided by ECMAScript and implemented by Google V8 or defined by JimScript and implemented by Sarah V12. Your expectations change.

Dependency Injection improves testability. It is possible to test the original `roundPhi` function in its original state. We can invoke the function and verify the result. But, what are we really testing? How would we really know if it was rounding Phi? What if the result was hard coded to just return 2? Would that be wrong? What if we wanted to use different rounding rules, for example, to return more decimal places? By using Dependency Injection, we can test more than just the function result. We can also verify that its interactions with the Math service will satisfy our requirements. We can create a `MathMock` object with a `round` method and then validate the Phi value passed to the `round` method.

One of the problems with Dependency Injection within a framework is tracking dependency requirements. A simplistic approach is to use method and constructor parameters. This is not very flexible and requires declarations for variables that we may never use. Consider the following example:

```
var resultCtrl = myApp.controller("ResultsCtrl",
    function ($scope, $routeParams, $http, $location, searchService) {
  // do something with $scope and $http, but ignore others;
}
```

The framework controller method expects all of those parameters but the implementation only uses two of the parameters. Modern versions of Java use annotations to identify injection targets. AngularJS uses a parameter array:

```
.controller('ResultsCtrl', [
    '$scope',
    '$routeParams',
    'SearchService',
    function ($scope, $routeParams, searchService) {
      // code that uses parameters goes here
    }
  ]);
```

Not only does this allow us to inject any number of parameters in any order, it also allows us to inject parameters that the framework had not considered. This allows the developer to determine the parameters. In the above example, `SearchService` is not part of the AngularJS framework, it is a custom-defined service. When AngularJS encounters the parameter named `SearchService`, it searches its list of configured modules for a module named `SearchService` and injects that object into the method argument list.

That covers the basics. Here is a list of my favorite AngularJS resources:

- Official AngularJS Tutorial (https://docs.angularjs.org/tutorial)

- A Step-by-Step Guide to Your First AngularJS App (http://www.toptal.com/angular-js/a-step-by-step-guide-to-your-first-angularjs-app)

- AngularJS Fundamentals in 60-ish Minutes (https://www.youtube.com/watch?v=i9MHigUZKEM)

- Official AngularJS YouTube Channel (https://www.youtube.com/user/angularjs)

Learning from Angular-seed

With the basics of data binding out of the way, let's review the angular-seed template project and see what we can learn about AngularJS from this boilerplate example.

Comparing Index Files

The angular-seed project includes two index files:

- index.html

- index-async.html

NOTE
The angular-seed project is a living project, meaning it changes regularly. I wrote this book using version 0.1. Your angular-seed project contents may differ from what appears in this text.

There are a few differences between index.html and index-async.html, but the key difference is the loading pattern. The index.html file uses the standard synchronous loading pattern. With this pattern, the web browser will download images, resources, and so on, asynchronously until it encounters a script tag. Upon encountering a script tag, the browser will cease activity and download, interpret, and execute the script. This is a blocking, synchronous pattern and may have performance implications. Because this pattern blocks the browser from interpreting and rendering portions of the user interface, the angular-seed index file places JavaScript files at the end of the body tag, after the user interface renders. The benefit of this synchronous, blocking pattern is that it is easy to understand. You place your script tags in a logical, dependent order and the browser will load them in that order.

The index-async.html file uses an alternative, nonblocking asynchronous pattern. The async index file includes a small amount of JavaScript that it expects the browser to execute synchronously and then uses the $script.js (https://github.com/ded/script. js) library to execute the remainder of the JavaScript asynchronously. This allows the browser to parse and render the user interface before preparing and executing the JavaScript associated with the application.

In the version of angular-seed that I am using, there are a few other differences as well. For example, the index-async version uses `ng-cloak` to hide the body content until after the compile and link (bootstrap) process. Another difference is the bootstrap method. The synchronous index version uses the `ng-app` directive to bootstrap the AngularJS application, whereas the index-async version uses JavaScript to bootstrap the AngularJS application after $script finishes loading the JavaScript files associated with this application.

Resolving Dependencies

As with our sample.html file, we need to add a reference to the angular library we previously downloaded (angular-seed assumes you are using bower for dependency management). To make this change, scroll to the end of index.html and locate the following:

```
<script src="bower_components/angular/angular.js"></script>
<script src="bower_components/angular-route/angular-route.js"></script>
```

Change the src attribute to reference the files we downloaded into the lib directory as follows (changes are in bold):

```
<script src="lib/angular.min.js"></script>
<script src="lib/angular-route.min.js"></script>
```

NOTE
The angular-seed project references the uncompressed, human-readable JavaScript files. Since we don't intend to read or debug the AngularJS libraries, we chose to download the minified versions. Be sure to reference the ".min" versions in your script files.

Routes

Run the index.html file by right-clicking the code editor and choosing Run File from the context menu. Google Chrome should load the index.html file and display two links: view1 and view2 along with the contents of view1, "This is the partial for view1." Click the view2 link and watch the contents change. While transferring between view1 and view2, look at the URL in the browser address bar. Notice that it changes between /index.html#/view1 and /index.html#/view2. The browser stays on index.html but displays different content depending on the chosen link (also known as a route). Change the URL to just index.html and notice that it automatically directs to /index.html#view1. We will see how to configure this a little later when discussing routing.

While viewing #/view1, right-click on the phrase "This is the partial for view1" and select Inspect element from the context menu. Chrome Developer Tools will highlight the paragraph (p) element in the source tree. The parent of that paragraph is a div with the attribute ng-view. The ng-view directive is a placeholder for content. When transferring between routes, AngularJS loads content into the ng-view placeholder. The element containing the ng-view attribute becomes the container for the route-specific content.

An AngularJS application is a single-page application that uses Ajax to load content into ng-view, based on the chosen route (or URL). The content displayed by the route comes from a template referred to as a *partial*. The data displayed in the template is provided by a JavaScript object called a Controller.

Routes are configured in the AngularJS application module. We haven't talked about the application module yet. The application module is an AngularJS module containing application configuration information. For our application, the two critical configuration pieces are modules and routes. To view the application's routing information, open the file js/app.js. The following code listing displays the contents of app.js:

```javascript
'use strict';


// Declare app level module which depends on filters, and services
angular.module('myApp', [
  'ngRoute',
  'myApp.filters',
  'myApp.services',
  'myApp.directives',
  'myApp.controllers'
]).
config(['$routeProvider', function($routeProvider) {
  $routeProvider.when('/view1', {
    templateUrl: 'partials/partial1.html',
    controller: 'MyCtrl1'
  });
  $routeProvider.when('/view2', {
    templateUrl: 'partials/partial2.html',
    controller: 'MyCtrl2'});
  $routeProvider.otherwise({redirectTo: '/view1'});
}]);
```

NOTE
Do you see the AngularJS dependency injection pattern? The config method parameter is an array where the first elements in the array are named dependencies and the final parameter is a function containing parameters that correspond to the named dependencies listed in the array.

The bottom half of this file contains `$routeProvider.when`. Each of these *when* methods describes a different route. The angular-seed project only contains two routes: view1 and view2. The first parameter to the when method is the route URL pattern. The second parameter is an object describing what to do when AngularJS encounters that route.

How does AngularJS know which module to use as the application module? The application module is specified during the bootstrapping process. In index.html, the application module is specified as the ng-app attribute value:

```html
<html lang="en" ng-app="myApp" class="no-js">
```

The index.html file uses the synchronous auto-bootstrapping method. Earlier we used the ng-app attribute in the sample.html file, but we didn't specify a value. This is because our sample.html application did not need an application module.

The index-async.html file uses a different approach. After asynchronously loading all of the required JavaScript, bootstraps the document with the myApp module:

```javascript
angular.bootstrap(document, ['myApp']);
```

Notice that we can use the same JavaScript for both index.html and index-async .html. The modules are self-contained, meaning their only dependencies are specified as method parameters (dependency injection).

Partials

Partials are HTML fragments that represent templates. The angular-seed project includes two partials: partial1.html and partial2.html. Open the file partials/partial1 .html and review its contents. The partial1.html file is not very exciting. Notice that it is just plain HTML. When viewing index.html in your browser earlier, you saw that AngularJS loaded partial1.html into ng-view, based on the routing configuration.

Controllers

Besides URL patterns and templates, routing information also specifies a controller for each route. The controller prepares and manages the data used by a partial template. Open js/controllers.js to view the list of sample controllers defined in angular-seed.

Building with AngularJS

Now that you have an understanding of AngularJS, let's use it to build another
iteration of the Personnel Directory.

NOTE
*The following example uses the PersonnelDirectory-
ajs project and synchronous index.html file.*

Creating the Search Page

Similar to the jQuery Mobile version, our primary page is the search page. Let's start
by building the search partial.

In NetBeans, right-click on the partials folder and choose New | HTML File from
the context menu. Name the file search.html. When the new file appears in the editor,
replace the contents with the following:

```
<form>
    <input type="text" placeholder="Employee ID"/>
    <input type="text" placeholder="Name"/>
    <input type="text" placeholder="Last Name"/>
    <button>Search</button>
</form>
```

NOTE
*I intentionally left field labels off of this form. I felt
the HTML5 placeholder attribute provided enough
context and instruction to eliminate labels. Mobile
devices don't have much display area and I didn't
want to waste it with unnecessary information.*

Next, we need to connect these form fields to a data model. From Chapter 4 we
know that our future search service will expect the fields EMPLID, NAME, LAST_
NAME_SRCH. Let's bind those to an object named searchParms. We also want
something to happen when the user clicks search, so we will bind the form submit
button to a method appropriately named search. Adding the appropriate ng attributes
to our HTML would make it resemble the following (changes in bold type):

```
<form ng-submit="search()">
    <input type="text" placeholder="Employee ID"
        ng-model="searchParms.EMPLID"/>
    <input type="text" placeholder="Name"
        ng-model="searchParms.NAME"/>
    <input type="text" placeholder="Last Name"
        ng-model="searchParms.LAST_NAME_SRCH"/>
    <button type="submit">Search</button>
</form>
```

Every view requires a controller. Let's write just enough code to say we have a controller and then run index.html to see our progress. Inside the js folder, open the file controllers.js. Immediately following the line containing the text `angular .module`, place the following:

```
.controller('SearchCtrl', ['$scope', function($scope) {

}])
```

Notice the leading dot (.) before the word `controller`. My preference is to place the dot immediately before the method to which it refers. The angular-seed project uses the opposite convention, placing a trailing dot immediately following the object to which it refers. To me that trailing dot seems more like a period marking the end of a sentence than a coordinating conjunction linking two related constructs. Whichever convention you prefer, just be consistent. For purposes of this example, make sure you only have one dot. The sample controllers `MyCtrl1` and `MyCtrl2` are not required, so delete those before continuing. After making these changes your controllers.js file should contain the following:

```
'use strict';

/* Controllers */

angular.module('myApp.controllers', [])
    .controller('SearchCtrl', ['$scope', function($scope) {

    }]);
```

NOTE
The final semicolon is not required, but is good practice. If you delete that final semicolon, then NetBeans will display a warning and suggest you add a semicolon. Semicolons tell the JavaScript interpreter where a command ends. Adding semicolons makes your code easier to understand just as adding periods to sentences makes them easier to read. Even better, semicolons allow you to place multiple commands on the same line, something that is critical when you want to minimize file size by eliminating unnecessary white space.

We need to define a route before we can run the search page. Open the js/app.js file in NetBeans to add a new route. Delete the `view1` and `view2` routes as well. While you are there, change the default (`otherwise`) route from `/view1` to `/`

search. The final `$routeProvider` configuration should match the following code listing:

```
.config(['$routeProvider', function($routeProvider) {
    $routeProvider.when('/search', {
        templateUrl: 'partials/search.html',
        controller: 'SearchCtrl'
    });
    $routeProvider.otherwise({redirectTo: '/search'});
}]);
```

To view the search page in a web browser, right-click on index.html and choose Run File from the context menu. The search page should appear similar to Figure 6-11. Not very pretty yet. In fact, it isn't even functional.

While not completely functional, we have bound our input fields to a data model and can actually see that data model change. From your web browser, open the developer tools (F12 on most browsers). Right-click one of the input fields and choose Inspect Element from the context menu. This will highlight the data-bound field in the structure browser. The field chosen is not important. The important part is that a data-bound field is selected in the structure browser. Switch to the Console tab, type the following, and press ENTER:

```
angular.element($).scope()
```

The console will display an object representing the same scope that is available to our AngularJS controller. At this time, the scope doesn't contain much, just a few $xxx properties. Now enter a value into the Employee ID field and execute the same command again. The new object printed in the console now has a

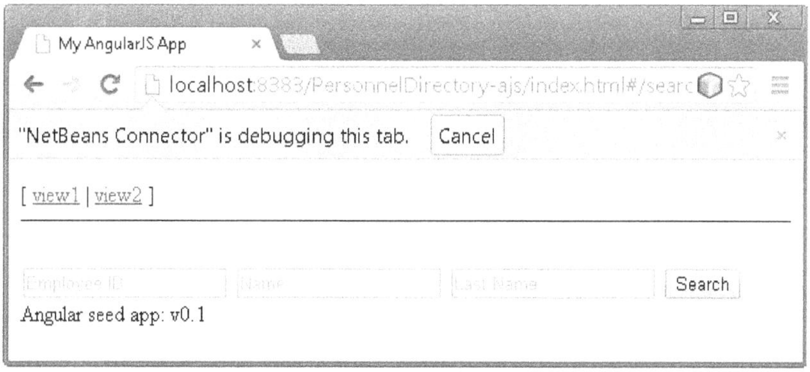

FIGURE 6-11.   *Screenshot of the unstyled search page*

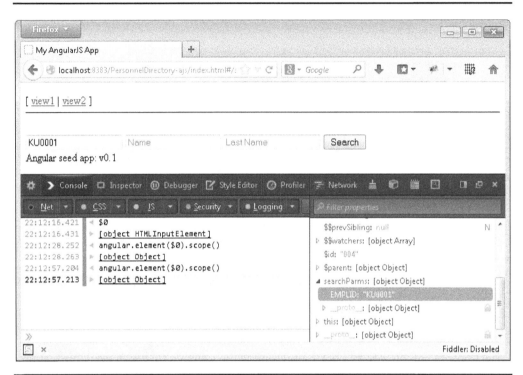

FIGURE 6-12. *Viewing the scope within the JavaScript console*

searchParms field, which is an object that contains the EMPLID field. Figure 6-12 is a screenshot of the Console window highlighting the EMPLID attribute in Firefox developer tools.

Cleaning up index.html

The index.html file contains sample code we won't use. For example, the top of the page contains references to two navigation cases that no longer exist in app.js. Actually, while viewing index.html in your web browser, click the view1 and view2 links. Nothing happens. Your page stays the same. The URL in the address bar does not change. This is because AngularJS did not find the requested routes #/view1 or #/view2, and the default (otherwise) route in app.js specifies search.html as the page to display for all unrecognized URLs.

Open index.html in your editor. We'll start at the top and delete items we won't use. First on the list are any stylesheet links and script elements that point to bower_components. The head HTML element should now just contain the following:

```html
<head>
  <meta charset="utf-8">
  <meta http-equiv="X-UA-Compatible" content="IE=edge">
  <title>My AngularJS App</title>
  <meta name="description" content="">
  <meta name="viewport"
      content="width=device-width, initial-scale=1">
  <link rel="stylesheet" href="css/app.css"/>
</head>
```

NOTE
The HTML above has the title set to "My AngularJS App." This is the default title from the angular-seed project. You may want to change the title to something more meaningful, such as "Personnel Directory."

Next, remove the ul element that represents the single-page application navigation. We will use the HTML nav element instead. Immediately following the navigation, you may see some IE browser comments suggesting that users of this page upgrade. If you are concerned that users might try to browse your mobile app with Internet Explorer browsers older than IE 7, then keep the comment. Otherwise, eliminate it also.

Immediately following the div with an ng-view attribute, you should find a div referencing a custom directive: Angular seed app: v... Delete this line as well. The body element should now consist of just the ng-view div and a handful of AngularJS JavaScript files:

```html
<body>

  <div ng-view></div>

  <script src="lib/angular.min.js"></script>
  <script src="lib/angular-route.min.js"></script>
  <script src="js/app.js"></script>
  <script src="js/services.js"></script>
  <script src="js/controllers.js"></script>
  <script src="js/filters.js"></script>
  <script src="js/directives.js"></script>
</body>
```

NOTE
I also deleted the comment suggesting that you use ajax.googleapis.com for production applications.

Reload the page and verify that it displays only the three form fields and a submit button.

Styling the Search Page

As you saw from your configuration section, we are using the Topcoat.io CSS library. There are many popular styling libraries, including Twitter Bootstrap. Bootstrap has some great style ideas, but comes with a lot of JavaScript components. Topcoat is just CSS (and some images, but we won't use those).

Let's add some style to the search page. Open the search.html page and make the following changes:

- To the form, add `class="margin"`.

- To each input field, add `class="topcoat-text-input"`.

- To the button, add `class="topcoat-button"` and `data-icon="search"`.

The search page HTML should now contain the following content:

```
<form ng-submit="search()" class="margin">
    <input type="text" placeholder="Employee ID"
        class="topcoat-text-input"
        ng-model="searchParms.EMPLID"/>
    <input type="text" placeholder="Name"
        class="topcoat-text-input"
        ng-model="searchParms.NAME"/>
    <input type="text" placeholder="Last Name"
        class="topcoat-text-input"
        ng-model="searchParms.LAST_NAME_SRCH"/>
    <button class="topcoat-button" data-icon="search"
        type="submit">Search</button>
</form>
```

I like to make small incremental changes and review those changes in a browser. You could do that now, but it won't be very thrilling because we haven't told the browser how to interpret any of the class attribute values, such as `class="topcoat-text-input"`. Let's do that now by adding the topcoat CSS file right before app.css in the head section of index.html. While we are here, we might as well add a reference for FontAwesome. We will use it on the search page to add a magnifying glass icon to the search button. Add the following bold lines to the head section of index.html. I included a few lines for reference but only add the four bold lines in the middle:

```
<meta name="viewport"
      content="width=device-width, initial-scale=1">
<link rel="stylesheet"
      href="topcoat-0.8.0/css/topcoat-mobile-light.css"/>
<link rel="stylesheet"
      href="font-awesome-4.1.0/css/font-awesome.min.css">
<link rel="stylesheet" href="css/app.css"/>
```

The reason we add these references right before app.css is so that we can place application specific overrides in app.css. This allows us to change the way the browser displays topcoat styles without modifying the topcoat CSS file.

Reload your page and enjoy the visual changes. It still isn't perfect, but we are a lot closer to the appearance of a mobile app. Resize your page and notice that it is already responsive, meaning the layout changes with the page width. Figure 6-13 is a screenshot of the search page at its smallest width.

FIGURE 6-13. *Small-width search page*

Proprietary CSS Frameworks

Let's stop here for a moment and consider the value we just entered into the class attribute: `topcoat-input-text` and `topcoat-button`. Don't those seem a bit redundant? Didn't the HTML already declare that we were styling the input text and button elements? Didn't our stylesheet link already specify that we were using Topcoat? Each CSS framework has its own prefix. Topcoat uses `topcoat-`. Pure uses `pure-`. Twitter Bootstrap doesn't have prefixes, but does have its own set of redundant classes. For example, to style a form input element, you have to use `form-control`. CSS is smart enough to handle this. Why do these frameworks require me to spell it out? If I want to switch to a new CSS framework, I have to modify my HTML, not just swap out the CSS library.

The rest of the search page appearance will come from custom defined CSS styles. The angular-seed project includes app.css for custom CSS. When you open this file, you will see that it already contains CSS class definitions. As you look through the contents of this file, notice the use of `before` and `after` pseudo selectors as well as how angular-seed uses the `content` attribute. We will use similar syntax to add icons to buttons. Unfortunately, none of these predefined styles relate to our project, so delete the entire contents of the file.

As we start adding content around the form, such as a header and sidebar, we will want the form to have some spacing, or margin, around it. We already added a class attribute to the form to associate the form with a style class named `margin`. Add the following text to the css/app.css file to define the `margin` style class:

```css
.margin {
    margin: 1rem;
}
```

When you save, NetBeans will reload index.html and display the search page with some margin around the form.

Define styling information for the search button icon by adding the following to app.css:

```css
[data-icon]:after {
  font-family: FontAwesome;
  padding-left: 1rem;
}

[data-icon=search]:after {
  content: "\f002";
}
```

Save and reload the page to see a magnifying glass appear inside the form's button.

Generic Selectors and Performance

I prefer generic selectors for reuse throughout an application to provide a consistent visual appearance. For example, in our Personnel Directory, now that we have a margin class, all elements that need a margin will have the same margin definition. Likewise, all elements requiring an icon will have the same icon specifications. I use attribute and wildcard selectors without regard for CSS selector performance.

There was a time when I used to consider performance when writing selectors. This is a holdover from my jQuery experience. Writing efficient selectors for early jQuery was critical to application performance. With jQuery, as with CSS, an ID selector is the fastest, so you start with an ID and begin qualifying descendants. jQuery allows us to chain selectors together as separate methods. CSS does not. Both jQuery and CSS start evaluation and qualification on the right, not the left, removing elements that don't qualify.

Since many of us read left to right, we think that selector engines do as well. We write selectors starting with something highly qualified to narrow down the list of matched elements, and then further qualify the elements within a container. Often times, we include selectors with pseudo and attribute selectors thinking the selector engine will only attempt to match elements of the parent. CSS selector engines don't work that way. They start from the right and find the subset of elements that match the most qualified part of the selector. For example, a selector engine matching against the CSS3 :last-of-type pseudo-class selector will first find all elements that are the last of their type in a collection and then will work to the left of the selector, eliminating elements that don't qualify.

The general wisdom around CSS selector performance today seems to be, "don't try to optimize selectors." CSS optimization involves a lot of DOM considerations. Each document will optimize differently. To further complicate the issue, each browser will optimize the same document differently. Rather than focus on selector speed, write selectors that make sense. Keep them small, and remove unused selectors. The CSS inside the selector seems to have more impact on performance than the selector itself.

For further reading, I recommend

- http://css-tricks.com/efficiently-rendering-css/
- http://benfrain.com/css-performance-revisited-selectors-bloat-expensive-styles/
- http://csswizardry.com/2011/09/writing-efficient-css-selectors/

If you prefer the way the form's layout displays fields in a single row on large displays and wraps for smaller displays, then you can stop styling the form now. If you would like each field on a separate line, then add the following to app.css:

```
.topcoat-text-input {
  display: block;
  width: 100%;
  margin: 1rem 0;
}
```

The above CSS declaration overrides attributes specified by Topcoat. For example, Topcoat defines the margin to be 0. So that we have vertical space between each input element, I redefined it to have top and bottom margins of 1rem. Figure 6-14 is a screenshot of the search page after making these changes.

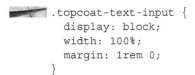

NOTE
Do you see the placeholder text in each field of 6-14? We used that in lieu of a label to save space on small devices. There are a couple of problems with this approach. The first is that screen readers prefer labels. A potential solution would be to add labels to describe the fields, but then use CSS to hide them. The other problem is with user expectations. I have seen users attempt to select placeholder text so they can delete it before entering data into a field. If you click inside a field with placeholder text, however, the text disappears. Trying to select text that disappears can be very frustrating.

Search Page Logic

The purpose of the search page is to gather information and submit it to the results page. AngularJS form processing works differently from the standard HTML/HTTP form-processing model. The HTML/HTTP form-processing model doesn't work well with single-page applications. Instead of posting to a server-side processor, AngularJS allows us to process the form results within the current page and controller. The code for the controller would receive the data, make an Ajax request, and then process the results. That seems like too much logic for this view and controller. To keep our sample simple, the search page controller will transfer the gathered requirements to the *results* controller and *results* view.

FIGURE 6-14.   *Final search page*

NOTE
*An alternative search/results pattern is to place the
search form in a collapsible region and display the
results immediately following the search form within
the same view.*

The search form inside the search.html partial page already has the ng-submit
attribute that tells AngularJS how to process the form. All we have to do is implement
the search method within the controller scope. Open js/controllers.js and change
the contents to match the following. The file doesn't have much, so I included the
entire file for reference. Add the text in bold:

```
'use strict';

/* Controllers */

angular.module('myApp.controllers', [])
    .controller('SearchCtrl', [
      '$scope',
      '$location',
      function($scope, $location) {
        // Declaration not necessary, but best practice. If someone
        // submits an empty form, searchParms won't exist unless we
```

```
// declare it inside the controller.
$scope.searchParms = {};

$scope.search = function() {
  // send to results route
  console.log($scope.searchParms);
  $location.path("/results").search($scope.searchParms);
};
}]);
```

Save and then switch to your web browser. Clicking the submit button won't appear to do anything. This is because we haven't created the /results route referenced in the search function. Open your JavaScript console, however, and click submit again. You should see the searchParms object printed in the JavaScript console. Enter some values into the search form and click submit again. Notice that the values in searchParms change to reflect the values within the form. This is the power of AngularJS two-way data binding.

The SearchCtrl controller introduces the $location service. The $location service is patterned after the JavaScript window.location object and manages the browser URL. It synchronizes routes with the browser URL. We use it here to switch to a different route just like we would use window.location.pathname to load a different resource from the same server.

The Results Page

Open app.js and add a new route for the path /results. The template will be partials/results.html, and the controller will be named ResultsCtrl. The code for this new route is as follows:

```
$routeProvider.when('/results', {
  templateUrl: 'partials/results.html',
  controller: 'ResultsCtrl'
});
```

Place this between the /search route and the otherwise route. The following listing contains the entire .config block for reference. The new route is in bold:

```
.config(['$routeProvider', function($routeProvider) {
  $routeProvider.when('/search', {
    templateUrl: 'partials/search.html',
    controller: 'SearchCtrl'
  });
  $routeProvider.when('/results', {
    templateUrl: 'partials/results.html',
    controller: 'ResultsCtrl'
  });
  $routeProvider.otherwise({redirectTo: '/search'});
}]);
```

Right-click on the partials folder inside the project explorer and choose New |
HTML File from the context menu. Name the new file results. NetBeans will
automatically add the .html extension and place the new file in the partials folder.
Our results list is exactly that: a list. So let's add an HTML list template to the results
.html file. Replace the contents of the result.html file with the following:

```
<ul class="topcoat-list">
  <li class="topcoat-list__item" ng-repeat="p in persons">
    <a ng-href="#/details/{{p.EMPLID}}"
       class="button">{{ p.NAME}}</a>
  </li>
</ul>
```

That's it. Our template is complete. When AngularJS compiles the template, it will
see the ng-repeat attribute and repeat the li element once for each p (abbreviation for
person) found in the persons array.

NOTE
*I used the abbreviation p for person instead of
spelling out person because person is too easy
to confuse with the plural form persons used to
represent the search results collection.*

Before seeing search results we have to populate $scope with a collection of
search results: the persons array identified in the results.html template. Add the
following controller to the controllers.js file:

```
.controller('ResultsCtrl', [
  '$scope',
  '$routeParams',
  '$http',
  function($scope, $routeParams, $http) {
    // view the route parameters in your console by uncommenting
    // the following:
    // console.log($routeParams);
    $http({
      method: 'GET',
      url: 'test-data/SEARCH_RESULTS.json',
      params: $routeParams
    }).then(function(response) {
      // view the response object by uncommenting the following
      // console.log(response);
      // closure -- updating $scope from outer function
      $scope.persons = response.data.SEARCH_RESULTS.SEARCH_FIELDS;
    });
  }]);
```

WARNING
When inserting a new controller, be careful of the terminating semicolon (;). There should be a semicolon at the end of the `SearchCtrl` controller we created earlier. Be sure to move that semicolon to the very end of the file, after the new `ResultCtrl` controller. Our controller definitions use method chaining. Including a semicolon in the middle will interrupt that chain.

You can test the route, partial, and controller by navigating to http://localhost:8383/PersonnelDirectory-ajs/index.html#/results. Since we are using hard-coded test data, the parameters are irrelevant. The controller will always access the same data. Your results page should appear similar to Figure 6-15. Verify that your search page is passing parameters to the results page by watching the URL change when you enter data into the search form and click the search button.

There isn't much to the controller. You will find that to be a common theme with AngularJS: There isn't much code to write. The framework handles most of the complicated stuff. This controller accepts the search page parameters passed to it through the `$routeParams` service and then forwards them along to another service using the `$http` service.

FIGURE 6-15. *Results page*

NOTE
Our controller currently uses Ajax to fetch a hard-coded text file. That text file doesn't know how to interpret search parameters so it ignores them. In Chapters 7 and 8, we will write back-end services using PeopleSoft and PeopleCode and then connect those services to this AngularJS application.

This code fragment introduces two new services:

- `$http`

- `$routeParams`

The `$http` service is the AngularJS service we use to interact with remote services—or more specifically, we use it to make Ajax requests. AngularJS prefers asynchronous interactions implemented through a promise object inspired by Kris Kowal's Q implementation. A promise represents a value that is not yet known, whereas a deferred represents work that is not yet finished. When making an Ajax request, `$http` returns before it has a response from a server. This is where the promise fits. The `$http` service returns a promise to complete the HTTP request and return a response. Promises have three methods: then, catch, and finally. We are only using the `then` method (which can have an optional error callback that matches the catch callback).

The promise returned by `$http` is a little different from the AngularJS `$q` promise. A `$http` promise contains the additional methods: `success` and `error`. The `success` and `then` methods are two sides of the same coin. They both receive the same information, just in two different ways. The `then` method receives one parameter, the response object, which exposes the response data, HTTP status code, headers, configuration, and HTTP status text. The `success` method receives the same information, but as one parameter for each item. I prefer to use `then` over `success` simply because I'm trying to get used to the promise pattern. You can read more about the `$http` service in the AngularJS documentation at https://docs.angularjs.org/api/ng/service/$http.

The `$routeParams` service is the AngularJS service that provides access to the URL parameters specified in the URL when accessing the route. In this example, we are accessing query string parameters. Later we will see how to access parameters embedded within the URL path. For additional information about the `$routeParams` service visit https://docs.angularjs.org/api/ngRoute/service/$routeParams.

Styling the Results Page

I'm not happy with the list style. As you saw in Figure 6-15, the links don't really look like links. The list items are supposed to appear more like mobile buttons. Right now it just looks like a plain list. Let's add some CSS to resolve this. To the project's css/app.css file, add the following rules:

```
.topcoat-list__item {
  padding: 0;
}

.topcoat-list__item > a {
  color: black;
  cursor: pointer;
  display:block;
  padding: 1.25rem;
  text-decoration:none;
}

.topcoat-list__item > a:hover {
  background-color:hsla(180,5%,83%,1);
}

.topcoat-list__item > a:active {
  background-color:hsla(180,5%,83%,1);
}

/* arrow after list item */
.topcoat-list__item > a:after {
    content: "\f054";
    float: right;
    font-family: FontAwesome;
}
```

Reload the page in your browser and you should now see arrows to the right of each list item. I also added a hover effect to list items. It won't help much on a mobile device, but this really helps a desktop user identify the list item as a link.

The Details Page

After selecting a result from the search results list, we should present the user with a detailed view of the result. The detail view route and controller are very similar to the code we've already written. The HTML partial (or template), however, is a bit more complicated. Add the following route to the app.js file. Place it between the results route and the otherwise route:

```
$routeProvider.when('/details/:EMPLID', {
  templateUrl: 'partials/details.html',
  controller: 'DetailsCtrl'
});
```

NOTE
We haven't created partials/details.html yet (just in case you were wondering why you don't have a details.html file).

The URL pattern for the details view follows the REST-ful pattern of identifying a resource by ID as part of the URL, rather than using a query string parameter. The `:EMPLID` portion of the route URL will become a property of the `$routeParam` service injected into the `DetailsCtrl` controller.

Details Controller

The following controller code should look very familiar. The only difference between the `DetailsCtrl` controller and the `ResultsCtrl` controller is the service endpoint. Be sure to move the final semicolon to the end of the file. Don't leave it on the line following the `ResultsCtrl` controller.

```
.controller('DetailsCtrl', [
  '$scope',
  '$routeParams',
  '$http',
  function($scope, $routeParams, $http) {
    // view the route parameters in your console by uncommenting
    // the following:
    // console.log($routeParams);
    $http.get('test-data/' + $routeParams.EMPLID)
        .then(function(response) {
          // view the response object by uncommenting the following
          // console.log(response);
          // closure -- updating $scope from outer function
          $scope.details = response.data.DETAILS;
        });
}]);
```

Modular AngularJS Files

This chapter places all controllers in the same file because the controllers are small. A larger scale application may require more code within controllers. Likewise, if you have more features, you may desire a modular approach where controllers, partials, directives, and related services reside together in a folder structure identified by feature. For example, we may want to place the details controller and partial in a folder named details, and separate that from

(Continued)

the search controller and partial by placing them in a folder named search. To implement this feature-based modular approach, create a JavaScript file named something simple like controller.js that contains the following contents:

```
angular.module('myApp.controllers', []);
```

This code fragment creates a new module named myApp.controllers. The [] parameter to the angular.module method is what notifies AngularJS that we are creating a module. Later we can retrieve a reference to the myApp .controllers module by invoking the same method without the additional [] parameter. Within each feature folder, we can add a controller.js file with contents similar to the following code. It is the same as the DetailsCtrl controller code above:

```
angular.module('myApp.controllers')
    .controller('DetailsCtrl', [
      '$scope',
      '$routeParams',
      '$http',
      function($scope, $routeParams, $http) {
        // view the route parameters in your console by uncommenting
        // the following:
        // console.log($routeParams);
        $http.get('test-data/' + $routeParams.EMPLID)
            .then(function(response) {
              // view the response object by uncommenting the following
              // console.log(response);
              // closure -- updating $scope from outer function
              $scope.details = response.data.DETAILS;
            });
      }]);
```

Look familiar? It is the same controller code we used with each of the other controllers. The only difference is the first line: Get a reference to the controller module rather than create a new controller module. In the index.html file, you will now have to load the initial controller.js file that creates the myApp .controllers module as well as each feature-specific controller. Be sure to load the controller.js file that defines the myApp.controllers module before loading any feature specific controllers.

Details View

Create a new HTML file named details.html and place it in the partials directory. Delete the contents of the file and insert the following:

```
<div>
  <div class="margin clearfix">
    <img src="img/avatar.svg" class="avatar"
        alt="{{details.NAME}}'s Photo">
    <h2>{{details.NAME}}</h2>
    <p>{{details.EMPLID}}</p>
    <p>{{details.CITY}}, {{details.STATE}} {{details.POSTAL}}<br/>
      {{details.COUNTRY}}</p>
  </div>
  <ul class="topcoat-list">
    <li class="topcoat-list__item">

      <a data-icon-before="phone"
        class="icon-pull-right big-icon"
        href="tel:{{details.COUNTRY_CODE.length > 0 &&
            details.COUNTRY_CODE || ''}}{{details.PHONE}}">
        <div>Call Phone</div>
        {{details.COUNTRY_CODE.length > 0 &&
            '+' + details.COUNTRY_CODE || ''}} {{details.PHONE}}
      </a>
    </li>
    <li class="topcoat-list__item">
      <a data-icon-before="location"
        class="icon-pull-right big-icon"
        href="https://maps.google.com/?q={{details.ADDRESS1}}
{{details.CITY}} {{details.STATE}} {{details.POSTAL}}
{{details.COUNTRY}}">
        <div>Location</div>
        <div>{{details.ADDRESS1}}</div>
      </a>
    </li>
  </ul>
</div>
```

Before applying any styling, test your page in a web browser. You should see something similar to Figure 6-16.

Styling the Details Page

The details.html partial page definition uses some classes defined earlier. For example, we defined the margin class earlier and then took advantage of it in the details header. The icons, however, we want to behave a little differently. We want the image *after* the text and we want it to float all the way to the right. We also want

FIGURE 6-16. *Unstyled details page*

it bigger than the text around it. To accomplish all of this, I created several CSS selectors, classes, and attributes. Could I have done it all with one CSS class selector? Yes, absolutely. Later we will leverage some of this work, however, when adding other icons that appear before list item elements. Here is the CSS. Add this to the project's css/app.css file:

```
[data-icon-before]:before {
   font-family: FontAwesome;
   padding-right: 1rem;
}

.icon-pull-right [data-icon-before]:before {
   float: right;
   padding-right: 0rem;
```

```
    padding-left: 1rem;
}

/* remove the arrow that an early rule placed on the right */
.topcoat-list__item >a.icon-pull-right[data-icon-before]:after {
    content: "";
}

.big-icon[data-icon-before]:before {
    font-size: 2em;
}

[data-icon-before=phone]:before {
    content: "\f095";
}

[data-icon-before=location]:before {
    content: "\f041";
}
```

NOTE
Are you wondering where I get those content values like \f041? They are all listed on http:// astronautweb.co/snippet/font-awesome/.

The only item left to style on this page is the avatar/information region. Add the following to the project's css/app.css file to resize the avatar and align the employee information to the right of the avatar:

```
.avatar {
    float: left;
    height: auto;
    margin: 0 20px 20px 0;
    max-width: 100px;
    width: 40%;
}

.clearfix {
    clear: both;
}

.clearfix:after {
    display: table;
    content: "";
}
```

NOTE
The clearfix class definition is based on the HTML5 Boilerplate/Twitter Bootstrap clearfix demonstrated at http://nicolasgallagher.com/micro-clearfix-hack/. The point is to make sure the contact details list appears below the avatar rather than beside the avatar.

After applying these CSS changes, your details page should resemble Figure 6-17.

The Profile Page

The profile page allows a user to update his/her contact details. It looks a lot like the details page, but with text fields for data entry. Before someone can access the profile page, we have to create a route. As with the other routes we created in this chapter, open the project's js/app.js file and add the following route before the otherwise route:

```
$routeProvider.when('/profile', {
    templateUrl: 'partials/profile.html',
    controller: 'ProfileCtrl'});
```

FIGURE 6-17. *Styled details page*

The partial for the profile is remarkably similar to the details page. Create a new HTML file in the partials directory named profile.html. Replace the contents of the file with the following HTML fragment:

```
<div class="margin">
  <div class="margin clearfix">
    <img src="img/avatar.svg" class="avatar"
        alt="{{profile.NAME}}'s Photo">
    <h2>{{profile.NAME}}</h2>
    <p>{{profile.EMPLID}}</p>
  </div>
  <form ng-submit="save()" class="margin">
    <input type="phone" class="topcoat-text-input"
        placeholder="Phone" ng-model="profile.PHONE"/>
    <input type="text" class="topcoat-text-input"
        placeholder="Address" ng-model="profile.ADDRESS1"/>
    <input type="text" class="topcoat-text-input"
        placeholder="City" ng-model="profile.CITY"/>
    <input type="text" class="topcoat-text-input"
        placeholder="State" ng-model="profile.STATE"/>
    <input type="text" class="topcoat-text-input"
        placeholder="Postal Code" ng-model="profile.POSTAL"/>
    <input type="text" class="topcoat-text-input"
        placeholder="Country" ng-model="profile.COUNTRY"/>
    <button class="topcoat-button" data-icon="save"
        type="submit">Save</button>
  </form>
</div>
```

NOTE
I used bold type in the listing above to highlight Controller and CSS requirements that differ from the earlier details.html partial.

From this listing, we see that our $scope must have a save method and a profile object. Since we don't have a back-end service available for data, we will just use our KU0001 test data file. Here is an example of the controller used for the profile partial. In Chapter 7, we will replace some of this code with a call to a real service. Add the following JavaScript to the project's js/controllers.js file right before the last semicolon:

```
.controller('ProfileCtrl', ['$scope',
  '$routeParams',
  '$http',
  function($scope, $routeParams, $http) {
    $http.get('test-data/KU0001')
        .then(function(response) {
            $scope.profile = response.data.DETAILS;
```

```
        });

    $scope.save = function() {
      // TODO: implement during Chapters 7 and 8
    };
  }])
```

As far as styling the page…well we did such a good job on the other pages that we were able to reuse existing style classes. We do have one new style class to add and that is the rule for the attribute [data-icon=save]. Add the following to app.css:

```
[data-icon=save]:after {
  content: "\f0c7";
}
```

Unlike the search | results | details flow presented above, we don't have a way to access the profile page. To view your profile page, change the URL to http://localhost:8383/PersonnelDirectory-ajs/index.html#/profile. Figure 6-18 is a screenshot of the styled profile page.

FIGURE 6-18.   *Profile page*

Adding a Header

Desktop applications have title bars that describe the overall theme of a site or page. Because mobile web browsers don't have the same amount of real estate as their desktop cousins, they don't always display these title bars. Let's add a header to our application to provide some type of context for our users. Inside index.html, just before the `<div ng-view>` element, add the following HTML:

```html
<header class="topcoat-navigation-bar">
  <div class="topcoat-navigation-bar__item left quarter">
    <a id="slide-menu-button"
       class="topcoat-icon-button--quiet slide-menu-button">
      <i class="fa fa-bars"></i>
    </a>
  </div>
  <div class="topcoat-navigation-bar__item center half">
    <h1 class="topcoat-navigation-bar__title">
      Personnel Directory
    </h1>
  </div>
  <div class="topcoat-navigation-bar__item right quarter">
    <a class="topcoat-icon-button--quiet" href="#/search">
      <i class="fa fa-search"></i>
    </a>
  </div>
</header>
```

Refresh any of the views in your web browser and you should now see a header. The "hamburger" icon doesn't work and the icons are too small. Let's correct the icon size by adding the following CSS to the project's css/app.css file:

```css
header .topcoat-icon-button--quiet {
  vertical-align: middle;
}
header .fa {
  font-size: 1.5em;
}
```

NOTE
Why do they call it a hamburger? It is called the "hamburger button" because it resembles a bun with a patty in the middle. That is pretty much it. It is a common icon used in responsive design to tell users that there are more options. If you touch the hamburger icon, something will happen.

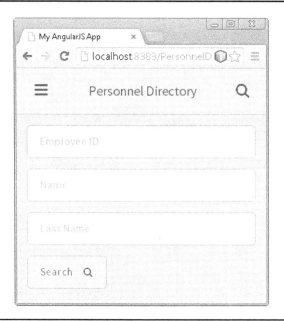

FIGURE 6-19. *Search page with header*

After saving and refreshing your browser, you should see a page that looks similar to Figure 6-19. If you don't, click the search button to navigate to the search page and confirm again.

Implementing a Navigation Sidebar

The application header provides an easy way to access the search page, but not a mechanism to access the user profile or the last search results. Let's implement a sidebar. Within index.html, between the header and the ng-view directive, add the following HTML:

```
<nav>
  <ul class="topcoat-list">
    <li class="topcoat-list__item">
      <a href="#/profile" class="fa-user">My Profile</a>
    </li>
    <li class="topcoat-list__item">
      <a href="#/search" class="fa-search">Search</a>
    </li>
    <li class="topcoat-list__item">
      <a href="#/results" class="fa-th-list">Results</a>
    </li>
  </ul>
</nav>
```

Don't refresh your page yet. It will look quite ugly…well, OK, refresh it to see what we just added, but I warned you, it isn't pretty. The navigation list sits inside the body of the main document rather than to the left. Let's straighten this out with a little CSS. To the project's css/app.css file, add the following:

```
nav {
  display:none;
  position:absolute;
  left:0;
  width: 14em;
  height: 100%;

  transition: padding-top .2s ease-out;
}
```

That CSS made the left navigation disappear. Now we need to come up with a clever way to make it appear, preferably without a lot of complicated JavaScript. How about toggling a class on the body element to change the CSS selector used by the nav? To the hamburger button, add the following onclick handler. I included the entire button markup for context. Just add the text in bold.

```
<div class="topcoat-navigation-bar__item left quarter">
  <a id="slide-menu-button"
    class="topcoat-icon-button--quiet slide-menu-button"
    onclick="document.body.classList.toggle('left-nav')">
    <i class="fa fa-bars"></i>
  </a>
</div>
```

I keep referring to an area in index.html file that represents the ng-view directive. It is represented by the HTML `<div ng-view></div>`. The div element is not very semantic. Let's change it to main. Replace `<div ng-view></div>` with `<main ng-view></main>`. Save and refresh your page to make sure everything still works as expected.

Let's add the left-nav CSS selector and see what happens. Add the following to css/app.css:

```
body.left-nav .topcoat-navigation-bar,
body.left-nav main {
  margin-left:14rem;
}

body.left-nav nav {
  display: block;
}
```

Now when you click the hamburger icon, the header and content area jump to the right and the sidebar appears. I'm not very happy with that jumping behavior. We can fix that nicely with some animation, but I'll refrain for now and save the animations for later in the chapter.

Styling the Navigation Sidebar

The sidebar is too similar to the list items. I think we should change the appearance to give it more contrast. To css/app.css, add the following:

```
nav .topcoat-list__item {
  border-top: none;
}

nav .topcoat-list__item > a {
  color: #c6c8c8;
}

nav .topcoat-list__item > a:hover {
  background-color:#747474;
}

nav .topcoat-list__item > a:active {
  background-color:#353535;
}
```

It seems like the sidebar background color should span the entire sidebar, not just the links area. Let's attempt to solve it by setting the body background color. Add the following to css/app.css:

```
body {
  background-color: #353535;
}
```

Well, that definitely changed the color of the navigation area. Unfortunately, it also changed the color of the main content region. Figure 6-20 is a representation of the mess we've created.

We can fix the appearance problem with the following CSS:

```
.topcoat-navigation-bar {
    position: absolute;
    width: 100%;
    z-index: 100;
    box-shadow: inset 0 -1px #9daca9, 0 1px rgba(0,0,0,0.15);
}

main {
```

```
  background: #dfe2e2;
  box-shadow: 0px 0px 8px 2px rgba(0, 0, 0, 0.57);
  left: 0;
  min-height: 100%;
  padding-top: 4.375rem;
  position: absolute;
  width:100%;
}
```

We just have one more item to fix in the navigation. If you look closely at Figure 6-20, you will see that the icons beside the list items contain cryptic symbols instead of recognizable icons. To resolve this issue, add the following CSS to the file css/app.css:

```
nav .topcoat-list__item > a:before {
  font-family: FontAwesome;
  margin-right: 2rem;
}
```

Figure 6-21 is a screenshot of the styled navigation bar.

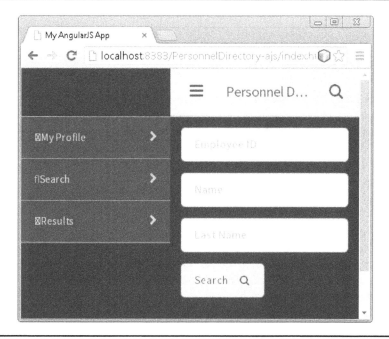

FIGURE 6-20. *Sidebar visible, but the form background color is incorrect*

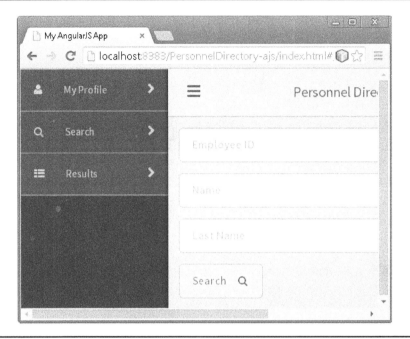

FIGURE 6-21. *Styled navigation bar*

Making the Navigation Sidebar Responsive

Our content region does not contain much information. With the navigation on the left and invisible until needed, our application is sized appropriately for a mobile phone. When displayed on a tablet, however, we have enough space to make the sidebar visible all the time. We will use media queries to facilitate this *responsive design* feature.

NOTE
I intentionally implemented the mobile CSS first and the desktop/tablet CSS second. Mobile phones have less processing power and usually run over wireless networks such as 3G and 4G. Tablets and desktops often have more power and more bandwidth. Rather than building for desktops and using media queries to scale back for phones, we will build for the phone and use media queries to enhance the display for desktops and tablets.

Add the following media query and CSS to the css/app.css file. It is critical that these definitions appear after the `nav` and `main` CSS declarations because they override some of the previously defined values.

```
/* !! override, must follow main and side-nav declarations !! */
/* sidebar navigation visible on wider screen */
@media screen and (min-width: 600px) {
  .slide-menu-button {
    opacity: 0;
  }
  main {
    /* left: 14rem; */
    right:0;
    width:auto;

    margin-left: 14rem;
  }
  nav {
    padding-top: 4.375rem;
    display: block;

  }
  /* if hamburger hides because of resize,
     need to pretend like left-nav not set */
  body.left-nav .topcoat-navigation-bar {
    margin-left:0;
  }
}
```

Save and refresh the page and then try changing the width of the page. Notice how the sidebar appears and hides based on the width of the browser window.

Custom Results Directive

The side navigation has a button labeled "Results" that is supposed to display the last search results. At this time, however, it is just a link to the results page. When transferring to the last search results, it doesn't actually display the last search results or carry forward the search page parameters to perform a new search. Our results controller is responsible for fetching data. Because that data is scoped to the results controller, it disappears when we transfer to another route. Likewise the search parameters only exist for the life of the search controller and then the results controller, but only because we pass them along to the results controller. To make the last search results exist beyond the life of the ResultsCtrl controller we have to create a service.

Another problem is that the Results button is always visible. If the sidebar existed inside a partial, we could set the visibility of the button based on information within the controller $scope. But the button doesn't exist inside a partial. The AngularJS way to control the user experience is through directives. A directive can exist outside a partial and has access to services. We can create a new directive and connect it to the Search Service to determine when to show the Results button.

AngularJS Services

AngularJS defines services as "substitutable objects that are wired together using dependency injection (DI)." Basically, that just means services represent objects with properties and methods that you can inject into other services and controllers. AngularJS services have two primary features: lazy instantiation and single instance, which means they aren't created until they are needed, and once they are created they exist for the life of the single-page application. What makes them valuable to us in this scenario is that we can use a service to store the last search results and then access those results multiple times—basically, a results cache.

We are going to create a service, but before we do, let's review the three mechanisms AngularJS provides for writing services:

- Factory

- Service

- Provider

A Factory and a Service are very similar. The only real difference seems to be the creation mechanism: A Factory is a function you call and that function returns a value. The Factory *creates* the service. A Service *is* the object you want created so AngularJS uses the JavaScript new reserved word to create an instance of the Service. A Provider also returns a service but the difference is you can configure them during the application configuration page. You can find a great overview of the differences between Factories, Services, and Providers on the AngularJS website at https://docs.angularjs.org/guide/providers. Look for the heading, "Note: A Word on Modules."

For our purposes, we can use any one of these options to define a search results Service. To keep things simple we will use the Factory option for this scenario. A more robust solution would be to use a Provider and add the service end point URL as a configuration parameter.

Let's review the requirements for our Search service:

- It will send search criteria to a web service endpoint.

- It has to cache the results between requests.

- It must notify observers that it has data.

We implemented the first requirement in our search controller. Since services exist for the life of the AngularJS application, we can implement the second requirement storing the search results in a variable and then providing access to those results. Let's implement the third requirement first because it requires a little more thought and code.

The Observer Service   The Observer pattern is a common software design pattern where a subject maintains a list of *observers* and notifies those observers of changes to the subject. Because this pattern is so common, let's create an injectable, reusable service called ObserverService. In NetBeans, open the file js/services.js. The services.js file contains a sample service that we aren't using. Replace the contents of the file with the following:

```
'use strict';

/* Services */
angular.module('myApp.services', [])
    .factory('ObserverFactory', function() {

      // result that factory will return
      var observerService = {};

      // createObserver method
      observerService.createObserver = function() {
        // private object data (closure/module pattern)
        var observers = [];

        return {
          /*
           * use data parameter to send information as a parameter
           * to callback when invoked.
           */
          notify: function(data) {
            var observerIdx = observers.length - 1;
            for (; observerIdx >= 0; observerIdx--) {
              // invoke callback
              observers[observerIdx](data);
            }
          },
          register: function(callback) {
            observers.push(callback);
          },
          remove: function(callback) {
            var index = observers.indexOf(callback);
            if (index > -1) {
              observers.splice(index, 1);
```

```
            }
          }
        };
    };

    return observerService;
});
```

Iterating Arrays

I am a huge fan of `Array.forEach`. I love the elegance of the callback design pattern, the internal closure, and control over `this`. So why didn't I use that pattern when iterating over the list of observers? I ran a test at http://jsperf .com/angularjs-foreach-vs-native-foreach/14 to see which iteration method offered the best performance. I tested the following scenarios:

```
// Native Array.forEach
arr.forEach(function(item) {
  item;
});

// AngularJS's forEach
angular.forEach(arr, function(item) {
  item;
});

// for key in Array
for (var key in arr) {
  arr[key];
}

// old-fashioned for loop
for (i = arr.length - 1; i >= 0; i--) {
  arr[i];
}
```

I ran this test on the following browsers:

- Google Chrome 35
- Chromium 31
- Firefox 24 ESR
- Internet Explorer 10
- iPad IOS7
- Andriod 4.0.4

With the exception of Firefox, the old-fashioned `for` loop was +90% faster than the other three iteration options. Firefox results were close enough to say it didn't matter which option I chose—all iterative constructs were bad to Firefox.

My conclusion? Use the old-fashioned `for` loop unless you need closures, control of `this`, or any of the other features unique to the `forEach` alternatives. Avoid the `for (var key in object)` pattern.

What about Objects? The `for (var key in object)` construct used to be the only way to iterate over properties of an object. With `Object.keys` we have a new alternative that appears to perform much better. Here is an example:

```
var obj = {
    fname: "Sarah",
    lname: "Marion",
    role: "Author"
};

var properties = Object.keys(obj);

// old-fashioned for loop
for(i=properties.length-1; i>=0; i--) {
    console.log(obj[properties[i]]);
}

// forEach alternative
Object.keys(obj).forEach(function(property) {
    console.log(obj[property]);
});
```

Personally, I think the `Array.forEach` alternative is more elegant, but if you want performance, it seems the old-fashioned `for` loop wins. Feel free to visit http://jsperf.com/angularjs-foreach-vs-native-foreach/14 and run the test for yourself.

The `ObserverFactory` returns an object with a single method: `createObserver`. The `createObserver` method creates a new object with the following methods:

- `register`
- `remove`
- `notify`

What we really have here is a factory that creates a factory. Since AngularJS creates one instance of `ObserverFactory` for an application and we may use the Observer pattern in various modules, we can't place the observers array right inside `ObserverFactory`. That would merge the observers for all modules into a single array. Instead, we use the `createObserver` method to return a new Observer for each module.

NOTE
At this point my thought is, "Why not create a plain old JavaScript file with an Observer object? Why do I need a factory that creates a factory?" The answer is dependency injection and test-driven development. Using dependency injection allows us to mock test cases and test code fragments as units.

The Search Service   While building the personnel directory application, we discovered that we really need access to the search results from more places than just the `ResultsCtrl` controller. We also realized there is value in caching the search results. Let's refactor the `ResultsCtrl` controller by moving the Ajax request from the controller into a new service called `SearchService`. To the js/services.js file, add the following right before the final semicolon (similar file layout to the controllers.js file):

```
.factory('SearchService', [
  '$http',
  'ObserverFactory',
  function($http, observerFactory) {
    var searchResults = [];
    var observers = observerFactory.createObserver();

    var searchService = {};

    searchService.search = function(parms) {
      var promise = $http({
        method: 'GET',
        url: 'test-data/SEARCH_RESULTS.json',
        params: parms
      }).then(function(response) {
        if (!!response.data) {
            searchResults =
              response.data.SEARCH_RESULTS.SEARCH_FIELDS;
        } else {
          // no data
          searchResults = [];
```

```
    }

    observers.notify(searchResults);

    return searchResults;
  });

  return promise;
};

searchService.getLastResults = function() {
  return searchResults;
};

searchService.registerObserver = observers.register;
searchService.removeObserver = observers.remove;

return searchService;
}])
```

Now open js/controllers.js and change the `ResultsCtrl` controller to contain the following. I included the entire controller code for context. You only need to change the JavaScript in bold text.

```
.controller('ResultsCtrl', [
  '$scope',
  '$routeParams',
  'SearchService',
  function($scope, $routeParams, searchService) {
    // view the route parameters in your console by uncommenting
    // the following:
    // console.log($routeParams);

    if (Object.keys($routeParams).length > 0) {
      // has parameters, must have come from search form
      searchService.search($routeParams)
          .then(function(results) {
            //console.log(results);
            $scope.persons = results;
          });
    } else {
      // no parameters, assuming came from sidebar Results button
      $scope.persons = searchService.getLastResults();
      console.log("using cache");
    }
}])
```

Reload your application and run through the scenarios. Entering search criteria on the search page should return your sample data. Clicking the Results button in the left sidebar should return the same three rows. If you open the JavaScript console, you should see that clicking the left sidebar Results button prints "using cache" to the JavaScript console.

Extra Credit   If you click the search button on the search page without entering any criteria the ResultsCtrl controller will think it is supposed to use the cache. The only problem is that there is no cache. Either create a status message that tells the user there are no search results or disable the search button on the search page until the user enters search criteria.

AngularJS Directives

Custom directives are elements, attributes, class names, or comments added to HTML documents to manipulate the DOM. In the Personnel Directory, we want to manipulate the visibility state of the Results button in the left sidebar.

To create a new directive, open the js/directives file. You will see a sample angular-seed directive. Delete that directive and insert the following. I included the entire file contents for context. Only add the text in bold:

```
'use strict';

/* Directives */


angular.module('myApp.directives', [])
    .directive('bmaResultsHideClass', [
      'SearchService',
      function(searchService) {
        return {
          restrict: 'A',
          link: function(scope, element, attrs, ctrl) {
            var hiddenClassName = attrs.bmaResultsHideClass;

            var updateClass = function(results) {
              if (results.length > 0) {
                element.removeClass(hiddenClassName);
              } else {
                element.addClass(hiddenClassName);
              }
            };

            // set initial state
            updateClass(searchService.getLastResults());
```

```
        // register a callback
        searchService.registerObserver(updateClass);
      }
    };
  }]);
```

This JavaScript declares a new attribute named `bma-results-hide-class`. That attribute expects a CSS class name as a value. When the `SearchService` reports that it has data, the directive will remove the class name identified by `bma-results-hide-class`. Alternatively, if the `SearchService` has no data then the directive will add the `bma-results-hide-class`. We know that the directive creates an attribute rather than an element, comment, or class name because of the `restrict: 'A'` property. We know the name of the attribute by looking at the first parameter to the directive method:

 `directive('`**`bmaResultsHideClass`**`'...`

When compiling a document AngularJS takes a directive such as `bma-results-hide-class` and converts it to a case-sensitive camelCase normalized name. That means AngularJS removes the dashes and upper cases the first letter of each word following a dash. That is why our directive is named `bmaResultsHideClass`. In HTML, however, we will refer to it as `bma-results-hide-class`.

To use this new directive, open index.html and search for the Results `li` within the `nav` element. In my file that is at line 50. Add the new attribute `bma-results-hide-class="ng-hide"`. Here is a sample code fragment:

```
        <li class="topcoat-list__item"
          bma-results-hide-class="ng-hide">
          <a href="#/results" class="fa-th-list">Results</a>
        </li>
```

NOTE
Editors like NetBeans appropriately identify the new attribute as an error. The HTML5 valid mechanism for adding a new attribute is to prefix that attribute with `data-`*. Using this valid mechanism, our attribute would be* `data-bma-results-hide-class`*. AngularJS is designed to adhere to standards and will strip the* `data-` *prefix from the attribute before matching it against its list of known directives.*

Save and reload index.html in your browser. Since you have not visited the results route, the Results button should not be visible. After performing a search and seeing a list of results, the Results button should appear.

Animation

When I talk to people about adding animation to applications, the typical response is, "Oh, right. Eye candy. Yes, if we have time and it doesn't get in the way, we can add some animations." It is true; you can use animations for eye candy, but I believe there is a much more enterprise worthy reason for animation: creating intuitive, usable apps. Animations provide transition between states. When a sidebar appears abruptly over the top of existing content, our mind has to figure out what is happening. What is this new content? Where did it come from? Where is my prior content? If the sidebar slides out from the left, or if the content slides to the right and reveals a sidebar, then our mind is prepared. It watched the entire scene unfold. It knows where the old content is. It knows how to get it back. It knows how the new sidebar appeared. Another example is the shopping cart. When you add items to an online shopping cart, how do you know if the item is really in the cart? For that matter, where is the cart? An animation that shows an item moving from a search list into a cart trains our mind where to look for the cart. We have no doubt that our item is in the cart because we watched it move into the cart. These are the types of animations we should add to our enterprise applications. It isn't about eye candy. It is about usable, intuitive apps built around the way people think and process information.

In the remainder of this chapter, we will review three different ways to add animations to our Personnel Directory application:

- CSS3 transitions

- Using the animate.css library with its predefined keyframes CSS3 animations

- The TweenMax GreenSock Animation Platform

Animating with CSS3 Transitions

The first thing we need to animate is the sidebar appearance. When activating the "hamburger" button in the upper right corner, the sidebar appears rather abruptly. As I mentioned before, the appearance is a bit jarring and requires the user to pause and figure out what just happened. Adding a reveal transition can reduce, or even eliminate the "jar" from the experience.

To the css/app.css file, add the following:

```
.topcoat-navigation-bar,
main {
    transition: margin-left 0.2s ease-out;
}
```

This animates the `margin-left` attribute of the `main` element as well as any element with the `topcoat-navigation-bar` CSS class. Whenever the value of `margin-left` changes, the CSS3 animation processor will move the object left or right between the original value and the new `margin-left` value. The entire animation will last 0.2 seconds.

Save and reload your page to view the animation. Change the browser width to see the animation activate when the browser crosses the size boundary we defined in our responsive media query. When the page is small enough for the hamburger button to be visible, click the button to display the sidebar. Click the button again to hide the sidebar. Because of the main content area box shadow, the sidebar has the appearance of residing below the main content. Clicking the hamburger button gives the appearance that the main content is sliding to the right to reveal the sidebar that resides underneath it.

Transitions are the easiest animations to apply. They are a simple, yet tasteful way to improve the user experience.

Using animate.css

The animate.css library is a CSS file containing CSS3 keyframes definitions for common animations. You may view a list of defined animations at http://daneden .github.io/animate.css/. Let's use animate.css to animate the transition between routes within our single-page application.

AngularJS provides support for animation through the angular-animate module. Before proceeding, open index.html and add a reference for the animate.css file to the head section. Add this reference right before the app.css file. The following code fragment includes the appropriate link element as well as the previous two lines and following line for context. Only add the line in bold text to your code.

```
<link rel="stylesheet"
      href="font-awesome-4.1.0/css/font-awesome.min.css">
<link rel="stylesheet" href="css/animate.css"/>
<link rel="stylesheet" href="css/app.css"/>
```

While still editing index.html, look for `<main ng-view` and insert the class `route-transition`. The main element will appear as follows (additions in bold text):

```
<main ng-view class="route-transition"></main>
```

Next, add a script tag to import angular-animate.min.js. The following code fragment includes the appropriate script tag as well as the previous and following line for context. Only add the line in bold text.

```
<script src="lib/angular-route.min.js"></script>
<script src="lib/angular-animate.min.js"></script>
<script src="js/app.js"></script>
```

Next, we need to tell AngularJS to use the animation module. Open the file js/ app.js and add the ngAnimate module to the list of modules in the myApp module constructor. The following code fragment contains the appropriate line to add as well as the previous and following line for context. Only add the line in bold text.

```
'ngRoute',
'ngAnimate',
'myApp.filters',
```

To the file css/app.css, add the following in its entirety:

```
main[ng-view].ng-enter {
    -webkit-animation: slideInRight 0.5s;
    animation: slideInRight 0.5s;
}
```

Reload index.html in your web browser and watch as the page slides in from the right. Navigate through the app and watch as each page enters from the right, stacking on top of the previous page.

AngularJS manages this animation by adding the `ng-animate`, `ng-enter`, and `ng-leave` CSS class names to the element in transition. When changing routes, for example, AngularJS creates a new element matching the element with the `ng-view` attribute (our `main` element). To the `main` element that is leaving, AngularJS adds the CSS class name `ng-leave`. To the element that is appearing, it adds the class name `ng-enter`. When the animation finishes, AngularJS deletes the element tagged with `ng-leave`.

Animating with the GreenSock Animation Platform

When browsers first adopted CSS3 animations, many web developers switched from JavaScript animations to CSS3 because CSS3 animations are (in theory) hardware accelerated, which means they take advantage of the graphics processor at the hardware level rather than using a timeline to manipulate the DOM and forcing the web browser to repaint itself with each transition. The hypothesis is that CSS3 hardware accelerated animations outperform JavaScript animations. GreenSock (GSAP) wants us to believe otherwise and they make a pretty compelling case. Navigate to http://www.greensock.com/js/speed.html and try the GSAP dots animation test. Try several different engines using the default 300 dots setting. When I run this on my laptop, I don't notice much difference. If I increase the number of dots to 2000, however, there is no comparison. Using the jQuery engine, I see one ring of dots. Using Zepto, which is very close to pure CSS animation, I see rings of dots slowly progress across the screen. If I switch to the pure GSAP engine, however, the dots start processing immediately and fly by as expected.

Let's use GSAP to create a complex page transition. Before we get started, we have to clean up the CSS3 animation we added using animate.css. Leave the `ngAnimate` module and angular-animate.min.js changes in tact. We will create an animations module that will require the `ngAnimate` module. You can also leave the animate.css file in index.html (although we won't use it). What we need to remove is the main[ng-view] .ng-enter rule we added to the end of the css/app.css file.

Next, create a new file in the js folder named animations.js and add the following JavaScript:

```
'use strict';

angular.module('myApp.animations', [])
    .animation('.route-transition', function() {
      return {
        enter: function(element, done) {
          var tween = TweenMax.from(element, 2, {
            left: "100%",
            rotation: "180deg",
            opacity: .2,
            scale: .1,
            ease: Power4.easeOut,
            onComplete: done}
          );
          return function(isCancelled) {
            if (isCancelled) {
              tween.kill();
            }
          };
        },
        leave: function(element, done) {
          var tween = TweenMax.to(element, 2, {
            rotation: "-180deg",
            opacity: 0,
            scale: 0,
            ease: Power4.easeOut,
            onComplete: done}
          );

          return function(isCancelled) {
            if (isCancelled) {
              tween.kill();
            }
          };
        }
      };
    });
```

Near the top of this file we tell AngularJS to animate any element with the class name route-transition. For elements with that class name, AngularJS will invoke the enter method when the element appears, and the leave method when the element disappears. The code inside the enter and leave methods tells GSAP (TweenMax) to animate the left, rotation, opacity, and scale attributes all at the same time.

What is Tweening?

Tweening is the process of generating frames between a start and end position. For example, if you want to animate the movement of an object from `left: 0px` to `left: 300px`, tweening would be the process of generating the intermediate states between 0 and 300 pixels. In the early days of JavaScript animation, it was common to divide the change in distance by the time allowed for the transition and move the animated element the derived number of pixels for each tick of the clock. The "tick of the clock" was triggered through the `setTimeout` or `setInterval` JavaScript methods. The problem with this approach is that `setInterval` and `setTimeout` are subject to the resources available on the system in which they run. If your laptop is performing a lot of calculations and has little CPU left for animations, that click tick interval is not going to come up as often as it should. Tweening in JavaScript involves determining the start and end positions as well as the start and stop times and then recalculating the movement distance on each interval. This accounts for the erratic behavior of the interrupt cycle giving a much smoother transition.

I first learned about Tweening from Thomas Fuchs's Amsterdam presentation available here: https://fronteers.nl/congres/2009/sessions/roll-your-own-effects-framework. You can find the very small emile framework here https://github.com/madrobby/emile.

Before running this file, we have to add TweenMax and our new module to index.html as well as load our new animations module into the AngularJS application configuration. Inside index.html, add a reference to TweenMax and a reference to the new animations module. The following listing contains all of the required JavaScript files with the new additions in bold:

```html
<script src="lib/TweenMax.min.js"></script>
<script src="lib/angular.min.js"></script>
<script src="lib/angular-route.min.js"></script>
<script src="lib/angular-animate.min.js"></script>
<script src="js/app.js"></script>
<script src="js/services.js"></script>
<script src="js/controllers.js"></script>
<script src="js/filters.js"></script>
<script src="js/directives.js"></script>
<script src="js/animations.js"></script>
```

Next, open js/app.js and include the new animations module in the application configuration. The following listing contains the full myApp module constructor with

the list of included modules. Only add the line in bold. Be sure every module
except the last module has a trailing comma delimiting it from the next row:

```
angular.module('myApp', [
  'ngRoute',
  'ngAnimate',
  'myApp.filters',
  'myApp.services',
  'myApp.directives',
  'myApp.controllers',
  'myApp.animations'
])
```

Reload index.html and watch the search page rotate, grow, and fade into view.
Enter search criteria and watch as the search form rotates out of view, shrinks, and
fades out while the results view rotates, grows, and fades in. Arguably, we have crossed
the line from subtle, enterprise enabling animations into eye candy. However, you have
to admit, it is pretty amazing and makes our applications a lot more fun to use.

Conclusion

In this chapter, you built a Personnel Directory search application using AngularJS.
You saw how to consume external services and how to make the application
responsive using media queries. We finished the chapter by experimenting with
various animation alternatives. Along the way you learned a lot about AngularJS.
In the next two chapters, you will learn how to connect this chapter's application to
PeopleSoft services. In Chapter 7, you will use iScripts to serve data to the Angular
JS Personnel Directory. In Chapter 8, you will use PeopleSoft REST web services.

CHAPTER

7

iScript-based Controllers

I n this chapter, you will learn how to use iScripts to connect an HTML5 user experience to PeopleSoft. Specifically, we will create iScripts that serve content and data to the HTML5 views we created in Chapters 5 and 6.

What is an iScript?

I describe iScripts in great detail in Chapter 5 of my book *PeopleSoft PeopleTools Tips & Techniques*. In fact, iScripts are the backbone of the entire user experience section of that book. Rather than repeat Chapter 5, here is a brief description (for a longer, but still brief description, read the blog post http://jjmpsj.blogspot.com/2008/02/what-is-iscript.html):

> iScripts are custom PeopleCode functions that can be invoked by URL. iScripts read URL parameters from the HTTP Request object and render a result through the HTTP Response object. iScripts are very similar to other PeopleCode programs in that they have full access to PeopleCode functions, objects, and the PeopleSoft application database.

We define iScripts as functions inside a record field event. PeopleTools requires the record name be prefixed with WEBLIB_. Although not a requirement, by convention we place iScript functions in the FieldFormula event.

jQuery Mobile with iScripts

In Chapter 5, you created a jQuery Mobile personnel directory prototype. That prototype contains hard-coded search results, details, and profile pages. Let's transform those pages into PeopleSoft iScripts that can execute SQL and return real results. Here are the steps required:

1. Create a Web library.

2. Write iScripts that process request parameters and return required data.

3. Add new iScripts to a permission list.

4. Create parameterized HTML templates.

5. Refactor the iScripts to return jQuery Mobile HTML fragments.

6. Update the jQuery Mobile application to reference the new iScripts.

7. Upload the jQuery Mobile application to the PeopleSoft web server.

The Search iScript

Launch PeopleTools Application Designer and create a new record definition. To this new record definition, add the delivered field ISCRIPT1. Set the record type to Derived/Work and then save the record as `WEBLIB_BMA_JQPD` (I know, not very descriptive, but after the required prefix and the site specific prefix, there aren't many characters left. The PeopleTools maximum record name length is 15 characters). Figure 7-1 is a screenshot of the new record definition.

Open the FieldFormula event of the ISCRIPT1 field and enter the following PeopleCode:

```
Function iScript_Search
   Local string &emplidParm =
         %Request.GetParameter("emplidSearch");
   Local string &nameParm = %Request.GetParameter("nameSearch");
   Local string &nameSrchParm =
      %Request.GetParameter("lastNameSearch");

   %Response.Write(&emplidParm | ", " | &nameParm | ", " |
         &nameSrchParm);
End-Function;
```

At this stage of development, we just want to write enough PeopleCode to test the iScript. After testing, we will add some SQL to perform a search and then HTML to format the results.

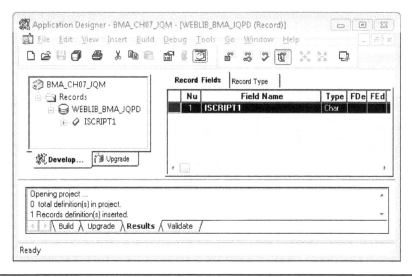

FIGURE 7-1. *WEBLIB_BMA_JQPD record definition*

iScript Security

Prior to testing, we have to add our new iScript to a permission list. Your organization may have a plan and recommendations for permission lists. If so, then please follow the guidance of your organization. Otherwise, create a new permission list and role and then use this same permission list and role for all secure content in this chapter and the next (Chapters 7 and 8).

To create a permission list, log into your PeopleSoft application online and navigate to PeopleTools | Security | Permissions & Roles | Permission Lists. Add the new value BMA_PERSON_DIR and set the description to something short and logical such as "Personnel Directory." Switch to the Web Libraries tab (hint, use the links across the bottom) and add the web library WEBLIB_BMA_JQPD. Next, click the edit link, and then the Full Access button. Figure 7-2 is a screenshot of the Web Libraries tab and Figure 7-3 is a screenshot of the Web Libraries permissions dialog.

Save the permission list and then navigate to PeopleTools | Permissions & Roles | Roles. Create a new role named BMA_PERSON_DIR. As with the Permission List, give this role a reasonable description. I used the clever description "Personnel Directory." Switch to the Permission Lists tab and add the permission list BMA_PERSON_DIR. Figure 7-4 is a screenshot of the Permission Lists tab of the new BMA_PERSON_DIR role.

Add the new BMA_PERSON_DIR role to your user profile.

Test the iScript by entering the URL http://<server>:<port>/psc/<site>/EMPLOYEE/HRMS/s/WEBLIB_BMA_JQPD.ISCRIPT1.FieldFormula.iScript_Search. Replace server, port, and site with your installation-specific values. Here is the URL from my

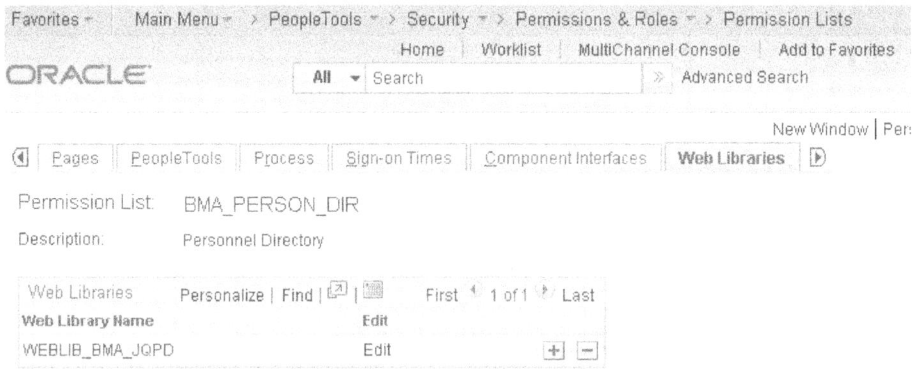

FIGURE 7-2. *Web Libraries tab*

Weblib Permissions

WEBLIB_BMA_JQPD

Web Library Permission	Personalize | Find | 🗗 | 🔲	First ◄ 1 of 1 ► Last	Full Access (All)
Function	*Access Permissions	View Content References for this Script	No Access (All)
ISCRIPT1.FieldFormula.iScript_search	Full Access ▼	View	

OK   Cancel

FIGURE 7-3.   *Web Library permissions dialog*

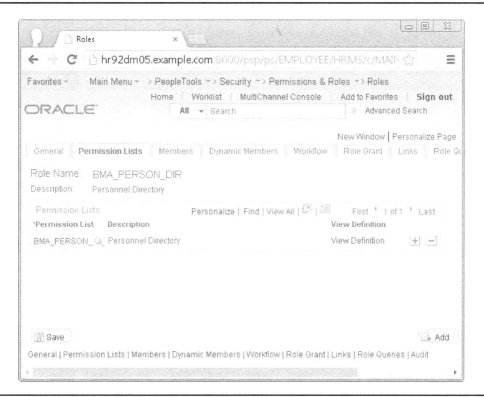

FIGURE 7-4.   *BMA_PERSON_DIR role*

VirtualBox demo image: http://hr92dm05.example.com:8000/psc/ps/EMPLOYEE/ HRMS/s/WEBLIB_BMA_JQPD.ISCRIPT1.FieldFormula.iScript_Search. Since we entered no parameters, you should see a couple of commas printed in your browser window.

NOTE
If you see the response "Authorization Error— Contact your Security Administrator" then check your URL. This error message tells you that PeopleTools could not find anything your user profile can access that matched the requested URL. It does not mean the target exists. I have encountered this error because I misspelled a record, field, event, or function name.

Let's add some query string parameters to our URL to match the fields the jQuery Mobile search form will send to the iScript. Here is an example URL with query string fields and values in bold: http://hr92dm05.example.com:8000/psc/ps/ EMPLOYEE/HRMS/s/WEBLIB_BMA_JQPD.ISCRIPT1.FieldFormula.iScript_ Search**?emplidSearch=KU0001&nameSearch=Sarah&lastNameSearch=Marion**. Loading this URL will print KU0001, Sarah, Marion as shown in Figure 7-5.

NOTE
Echoing query string parameters in this manner is considered a security risk. The most important rule of security is "don't trust your users." If anything I type in the address bar appears again in the browser, then it is possible for me to put something malicious in the URL that will run in the browser. Now, arguably, since I am echoing parameters to myself, I will be attacking my own computer. No one said hacking (or security rules) had to make sense.

FIGURE 7-5. *Query string parameter echo*

Implementing Search Behavior

We need to construct an SQL statement that returns a list of results that match the criteria entered on the search page. The search page is designed so that a user can enter information into any of the fields. None of them are required. Any field with a value adds to the SQL statement criteria. This means our SQL statement *where* clause may differ between requests. When writing SQL for PeopleCode we have to consider three rules:

- Prevent SQL Injection attacks.

- Don't embed managed object names in strings.

- Optimize SQL for performance.

The criteria values will come from query string parameters. Concatenating these values directly into an SQL statement is the easiest way to create dynamic SQL, but also poses the greatest risk for a SQL Injection attack (don't *ever* concatenate unchecked user entered values to create an SQL statement). The alternative is to use bind variables. Using bind variables also satisfies the optimization rule by allowing the SQL engine to cache statements between requests.

Since we will be generating the SQL statement dynamically, it is tempting to hard code object names such as table and field names within strings. Embedding strings renders some of the lifecycle management tools unreliable. An alternative is to use a combination of SQL managed definitions and named definitions. The benefit is that our usage of managed definitions will be visible to lifecycle management tools such as Find Definition References.

Let's start with a basic SQL select statement without criteria. Create an SQL definition in Application Designer and enter the following SQL. Name the statement BMA_PERSON_SRCH.

```
SELECT EMPLID
  , NAME
  , LAST_NAME_SRCH
  FROM PS_PERS_SRCH_ALL
```

The search iScript will have to test each input parameter for a value. If the parameter has a value, then it will need to add a field to a criteria list and a value to a parameter list. The presence of the word list in that last sentence suggests that we will need some arrays. One array will contain an entry for each criterion. The other array will contain a list of corresponding values. By using an array for the criteria, we can later join them into a single string using the word AND as the join method separator. This ensures that we place the word AND only between criterion.

To summarize, the iScript PeopleCode will

■ Extract the base SQL statement from an SQL definition named BMA_
PERSON_SRCH.

■ Evaluate query string parameters for valid criterion.

■ Construct a valid, secure WHERE clause.

■ Execute the constructed SQL statement.

■ Iterate over the results.

■ Send each result back to the client device as a new row.

Replace iScript_Search with code from the following listing:

```
Function iScript_Search
    Local string &emplidParm =
        %Request.GetParameter("emplidSearch");
    Local string &nameParm = %Request.GetParameter("nameSearch");
    Local string &nameSrchParm =
        %Request.GetParameter("lastNameSearch");

    REM ** build SQL based on parameters;
    REM ** careful of SQL injection!!;
    Local array of any &sqlParms = CreateArrayAny();
    Local array of string &criteriaComponents =
        CreateArrayRept("", 0);
    Local string &sql = FetchSQL(SQL.BMA_PERSON_SRCH);
    Local string &whereClause;

    REM ** query and column variables;
    Local SQL &cursor;
    Local string &emplid;
    Local string &name;
    Local string &nameSrch;

    REM ** build a WHERE clause;
    If (All(&emplidParm)) Then
       &sqlParms.Push(&emplidParm);
       &criteriaComponents.Push(Field.EMPLID | " LIKE :" |
            &sqlParms.Len | " %Concat '%'");
    End-If;

    If (All(&nameParm)) Then
       &sqlParms.Push(&nameParm);
       &criteriaComponents.Push(Field.NAME | " LIKE :" |
            &sqlParms.Len | " %Concat '%'");
    End-If;
```

```
If (All(&nameSrchParm)) Then
   &sqlParms.Push(&nameSrchParm);
   &criteriaComponents.Push(Field.LAST_NAME_SRCH |
        " LIKE :" | &sqlParms.Len | " %Concat '%'");
End-If;

&whereClause = &criteriaComponents.Join(" AND ", "", "");

If (All(&whereClause)) Then
   &whereClause = " WHERE " | &whereClause;
End-If;

REM ** iterate over rows, adding to response;
&cursor = CreateSQL(&sql | &whereClause, &sqlParms);

While &cursor.Fetch(&emplid, &name, &nameSrch);
   %Response.Write(&emplid | ", " | &name | ", " |
        &nameSrch | "<br/>");
End-While;
&cursor.Close();

End-Function;
```

After updating the iScript to contain the above content, test it again by entering query string values that match your data. For example, using the HCM demo database, I can search for all employees whose ID starts with KU, first name starts with C, and last name contains E by requesting the URL http://hr92dm05.example. com:8000/psc/ps/EMPLOYEE/HRMS/s/WEBLIB_BMA_JQPD.ISCRIPT1.FieldFormula. iScript_Search?emplidSearch=KU00&nameSearch=C&lastNameSearch=%25E.

NOTE
The %25 right before the E is URL encoding for %. % is the SQL wildcard we use to match the first portion of the last name. It also happens to be a reserved URL character so we have to replace it with the hexadecimal equivalent.

Parameterizing the Search Results Page

We now have all of the logic necessary to present search results. We just need to format them to fit our jQuery Mobile user experience. In Chapter 5, we created the *format* for the search results. Let's break the Chapter 5 results page into the following two HTML definitions:

- A page template
- A row template

The following code listing contains the HTML for the page template. Place this HTML in an Application Designer HTML definition named `BMA_JQPD_SEARCH_RESULT_PAGE`:

```
<div data-role="page" id="results">
  <div data-role="header">
    <h1>Personnel Directory</h1>
    <a href="#panel" class="show-panel-btn" data-icon="bars"
       data-iconpos="notext">Menu</a>
    <a href="#search" data-icon="search" data-iconpos="notext"
       class="ui-btn-right">Search</a>
  </div><!-- /header -->

  <div data-role="content">
    <ul id="resultsList" data-role="listview" data-filter="true"
        data-filter-placeholder="Filter results..."
        data-inset="true">
%Bind(:1)
    </ul>
  </div><!-- /content -->

  <div data-role="footer" data-position="fixed">
    <h4>
      Copyright &copy; Company 2014, All rights reserved
    </h4>
  </div><!-- /footer -->

</div><!-- /page -->
```

The `%Bind(:1)` character sequence in the prior code listing is a placeholder for row data. Create another HTML definition and name it `BMA_JQPD_SEARCH_RESULT_LINK`. To this new definition, insert the following HTML:

```
<li>
  <a href="%Bind(:1)">%Bind(:3) (%Bind(:2))</a>
</li>
```

The above template contains three parameters:

■ URL for the details iScript

■ Employee ID of the search result row

■ Description (name) of employee

Let's now refactor the search results iScript to use these new HTML templates. Scroll to the end of the iScript and find the while `&cursor.fetch`...loop. Starting from the `while` loop, replace the code for the loop through the end of the function with the following:

```
Local array of string &rows = CreateArrayRept("", 0);
Local string &detailsLink = GenerateScriptContentURL(%Portal,
      %Node, Record.WEBLIB_BMA_JQPD, Field.ISCRIPT1,
      "FieldFormula", "iScript_Details");

While &cursor.Fetch(&emplid, &name, &nameSrch);
   &rows.Push(GetHTMLText(HTML.BMA_JQPD_SEARCH_RESULT_LINK,
         &detailsLink | "?EMPLID=" | &emplid, &emplid,
         &name));
End-While;
&cursor.Close();

%Response.Write(GetHTMLText(HTML.BMA_JQPD_SEARCH_RESULT_PAGE,
      &rows.Join("", "", "")));
End-Function;
```

Briefly stated, the code above iterates over the resulting rows, pushing each row into an array. It then joins all the array elements into a single string, which becomes the body of the page template. The final step is to write the page template with the results to the client.

Test your changes by reloading the search results URL in your browser. Figure 7-6 is a screenshot of the raw, unstyled HTML that jQuery Mobile will later transform into a smashing user experience.

Each row contains a link to a details iScript that does not yet exist. Application Designer lets me save regardless. After refreshing the browser's results page and

FIGURE 7-6. *Unstyled search page*

clicking a link, PeopleTools presents me with the error message, "Missing function iScript_Details in PeopleCode program ???.???-Other. (180,127)." We will resolve this later when we create the `iScript_Details` function. Alternatively, add the following stub for this function to the end of the FieldFormula event editor:

```
Function iScript_Details
    %Response.Write("Details will appear here");
End-Function;
```

The Details iScript

Creating the Details iScript will follow a pattern similar to the search iScript:

1. Gather parameters from the request.

2. Query the database for details.

3. Display the results using an HTML template.

To the FieldFormula event of the record and field WEBLIB_BMA_JQPD ISCRIPT1, add the following PeopleCode:

```
Function iScript_Details
    Local string &emplid = %Request.GetParameter("EMPLID");
    Local string &NAME;
    Local string &ADDRESS1;
    Local string &CITY;
    Local string &STATE;
    Local string &POSTAL;
    Local string &COUNTRY;
    Local string &COUNTRY_CODE;
    Local string &PHONE;

    SQLExec(SQL.BMA_PERSON_DETAILS, &emplid, &NAME, &ADDRESS1,
        &CITY, &STATE, &POSTAL, &COUNTRY, &COUNTRY_CODE,
        &PHONE);
    Local string &photoUrl = GenerateScriptContentURL(%Portal,
        %Node, Record.WEBLIB_BMA_JQPD, Field.ISCRIPT1,
        "FieldFormula", "iScript_Photo");
    &photoUrl = &photoUrl | "?EMPLID=" | &emplid;

    %Response.Write(GetHTMLText(HTML.BMA_JQPD_DETAILS_PAGE,
        &emplid, &NAME, &ADDRESS1, &CITY, &STATE, &POSTAL,
        &COUNTRY, &COUNTRY_CODE, &PHONE, &photoUrl,
        "/pdjqm/css/details.css"));
End-Function;
```

NOTE

In Chapter 4, we created the SQL definition `BMA_`
`PERSON_DETAILS` *as part of our data model.*

From this code listing, we see that we also need a new HTML page template as well as an iScript: `iScript_Photo`. The HTML template is a derivative of the details page from Chapter 5. Place this HTML in an Application Designer HTML definition named `BMA_JQPD_DETAILS_PAGE`.

NOTE

The PeopleCode above contains the path `"/pdjqm/`
`css/details.css"`, *which does not yet exist on
your web server. We will create it later in this chapter.*

```html
<div data-role="page" id="details">
  <style type="text/css" scoped>
    @import url("%Bind(:11)");
  </style>

  <div data-role="header">
    <h1>Personnel Directory</h1>
    <a href="#panel" class="show-panel-btn" data-icon="bars"
       data-iconpos="notext">Menu</a>
    <a href="#search" data-icon="search" data-iconpos="notext"
       class="ui-btn-right">Search</a>
  </div><!-- /header -->

  <div data-role="content">
    <h2>%Bind(:2)</h2>
    <div>
      <img src="%Bind(:10)" class="avatar"
          alt="%Bind(:2)'s Photo">
      <p>%Bind(:1)</p>
      <p><a href="tel:%Bind(:8)%Bind(:9)">%Bind(:8) %Bind(:9)
         </a></p>
      <p>
        <a href="https://maps.google.com/?q=%Bind(:3)+%Bind(:4)+
%Bind(:5)+%Bind(:6)+%Bind(:7)">%Bind(:3)</a><br>
        %Bind(:4), %Bind(:5) %Bind(:6)<br>
        %Bind(:7)
      </p>
    </div>
  </div><!-- /content -->

  <div data-role="footer" data-position="fixed">
```

```
<h4>
   Copyright &copy; Company 2014, All rights reserved
</h4>
</div><!-- /footer -->

</div><!-- /page -->
```

NOTE
*Differences between the Chapter 5 version and
this chapter are displayed in bold text. Specifically
notice that I changed the path to details.css. The
path referenced here does not yet exist on your web
server. We will create it later in this chapter.*

The employee photo iScript comes from Chapter 5 of my book *PeopleSoft
PeopleTools Tips & Techniques*. The code is repeated below:

```
Function IScript_Photo
    Local string &emplid = %Request.GetParameter("EMPLID");
    Local any &data;

    SQLExec("SELECT EMPLOYEE_PHOTO FROM PS_EMPL_PHOTO " |
        "WHERE EMPLID = :1", &emplid, &data);
    %Response.SetContentType("image/jpeg");
    %Response.WriteBinary(&data);
End-Function;
```

NOTE
The original function from PeopleSoft PeopleTools
Tips & Techniques *was named IScript_
EmployeePhoto. I shortened the name to make it
easier to type.*

Be sure to add these new iScripts to the permission list BMA_PERSON_DIR
before testing. Here is a sample test URL for the details page: http://hr92dm05
.example.com:8000/psc/ps/EMPLOYEE/HRMS/s/WEBLIB_BMA_JQPD.ISCRIPT1
.FieldFormula.iScript_Details?EMPLID=KU0001. Unfortunately, my demo PeopleSoft
instance has no employee photos. To compensate, we can use the PeopleTools
placeholder avatar called PT_DUMMY_PHOTO. Here is a slightly modified version
of the iScript_Photo function that serves the "Dummy Photo" if the requested
employee does not have a photo. Changes are in bold text.

```
Function IScript_Photo
    Local string &emplid = %Request.GetParameter("EMPLID");
    Local any &data;
```

```
    SQLExec("SELECT EMPLOYEE_PHOTO FROM PS_EMPL_PHOTO " |
        "WHERE EMPLID = :1", &emplid, &data);
    If (None(&data)) Then
        %Response.RedirectURL(%Response.GetImageURL(
            Image.PT_DUMMY_PHOTO));
    Else
        %Response.SetContentType("image/jpeg");
        %Response.WriteBinary(&data);
    End-If;
End-Function;
```

Figure 7-7 is a screenshot of the unstyled details page.

Profile Page

The profile page is the only data-driven page in this mobile application that has no parameters. It is also the only page in this application that is both read and write. Because the page implements both read and write functionality, we will require two services:

- A read service to display information about the logged-in user.

- An update service to save changes.

FIGURE 7-7. *Unstyled details page*

We are going to implement the *read* service a little differently from the other pages in this application. Since the profile page does not require parameters, we can take advantage of a delivered iScript configuration tool built specifically for reading data from the database and then transforming that data into compelling user experiences: Pagelet Wizard.

Using Pagelet Wizard to Configure Mobile Displays

For most of North America, it was 2 weeks before the spring season officially began. To those of us attending the Higher Education Alliance conference in Las Vegas, however, it felt like the middle of summer. After a short, but pleasant stroll through the sunshine between the conference sessions and the demo grounds, I was greeted by my friend Chris Coutre of Ciber Consulting. Chris has been working on some amazing Enterprise Portal implementations and had some ideas he wanted to share with me. I am always curious to hear how our customers and partners are using Oracle products, and especially if Chris Coutre is the one talking. Chris is very intelligent, energetic, and implements a lot of innovative ideas. What he shared with me opened my mind to a whole new way of thinking about Pagelet Wizard. I have always known that Pagelet Wizard is the most flexible and underutilized PeopleTool in the PeopleSoft developer toolbox. Here is what Chris said, "We are using Pagelet Wizard to create mobile applications." What was that Chris? Come again? Pagelet Wizard for mobile applications? After thinking for a minute, I realized how much sense this makes. In this chapter, you have created two read-only pages. Each page required a separate iScript. That iScript required PeopleCode and security. What if you could create mobile applications without writing any code? This is the Pagelet Wizard sweet spot. It gives you the ability to query the database (through the query data type) and transform those results into any type of response...even a jQuery Mobile user experience. Let's see what this might look like.

iScript Data Source Query   Log into your PeopleSoft application online and navigate to Reporting Tools | Query | Query Manager. Create a new query and add the PERSONAL_DATA record to your query. On the Query tab, select the following fields:

- EMPLID
- NAME
- COUNTRY
- ADDRESS1
- CITY

- STATE

- POSTAL

- COUNTRY_CODE

- PHONE

NOTE
Pagelet Wizard–generated XSL refers to columns by ordinal (or position) within the Pagelet Wizard XML. The XSL described later in this chapter refers to fields by name. Field position within the query should not matter because we are using field names rather than positions. For consistency and to avoid errors, however, I suggest you list the query fields exactly as shown here.

Switch to the Criteria tab and add a prompt to the EMPLID field. Through Pagelet Wizard, we will bind the prompt to a system variable. The following listing contains the SQL for the query:

```
SELECT A.EMPLID
  , A.NAME
  , A.COUNTRY
  , A.ADDRESS1
  , A.CITY
  , A.STATE
  , A.POSTAL
  , A.COUNTRY_CODE
  , A.PHONE
  FROM PS_PERSONAL_DATA A
   , PS_PERALL_SEC_QRY A1
  WHERE ( A.EMPLID = A1.EMPLID
    AND A1.OPRID = 'PS'
    AND ( A.EMPLID = :1 ) )
```

NOTE
I did not add PS_PERALL_SEC_QRY or related criteria. These were added by PeopleSoft query to protect sensitive data.

Name the query BMA_JQPD_PROFILE and make it public. Figure 7-8 is a screenshot of the query save dialog.

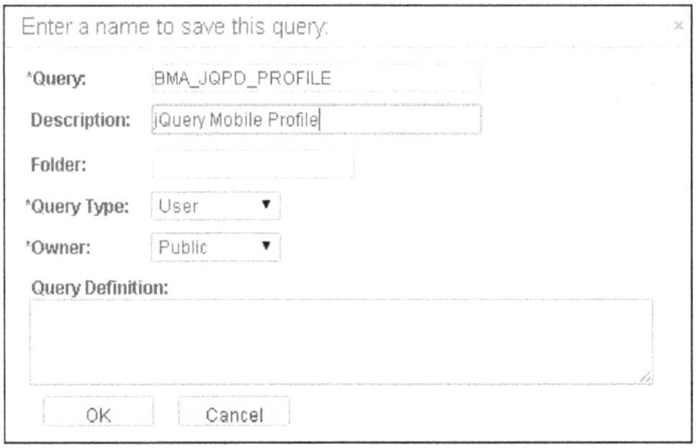

FIGURE 7-8. *Query save dialog*

Profile Pagelet Wizard Definition   Now that we have a valid query, let's configure the metadata necessary to expose the query to our jQuery Mobile application. Navigate to PeopleTools | Portal | Pagelet Wizard | Pagelet Wizard and create a new pagelet named BMA_JQPD_PROFILE. Click Add to move to step 1 of the Pagelet Wizard. None of the required information in step 1 is important for this example because we aren't actually publishing the pagelet. Nevertheless, enter meaningful values into each required field. For example, jQuery Mobile Profile into the Title field and then click the Next button to move to step 2.

In step 2, set the Data Type to PS Query and then select the query BMA_JQPD_ PROFILE (which is the query you just created). Figure 7-9 is a screenshot of step 2. Click the Next button to move to step 3.

Step 3 allows us to specify values for prompts. This is where we specify that the Pagelet Wizard should only display results for the logged-in user. For the EMPLID field, select the System Variable usage type and then set the Default Value to %EmployeeId. Figure 7-10 is a screenshot of step 3. Click the Next button to move to step 4.

Step 4 allows us to determine how to display the query results. Each data type has its own list of Display Formats. Some formats, such as the Custom format, are shared by other Data Types. Others, such as Table, are specific and apply to only one Data Type. The Display Formats shown in Figure 7-11 are delivered for the PS Query Data Type. You can also create your own Display Formats. My favorite custom Display Format is one that I created to perform meta-HTML transforms. For example, in the XSL we are about to create, we will hardcode the path to an iScript. I am not fond of hardcoding paths like these because URLs differ between development, test, and production systems. I wrote a custom Display Format that allows me to use

FIGURE 7-9. *Step 2 of the Pagelet Wizard*

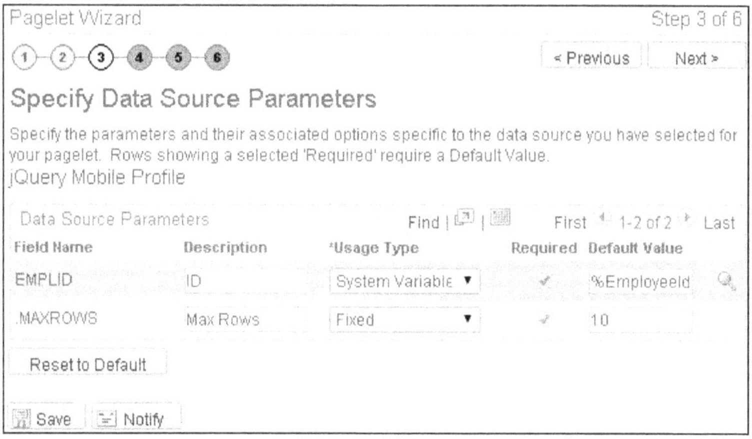

FIGURE 7-10. *Step 3 of the Pagelet Wizard*

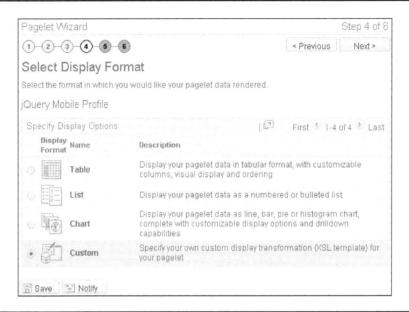

FIGURE 7-11. *Step 4 of the Pagelet Wizard*

meta-HTML sequences such as `%ScriptContentURL(...)` instead of hardcoded URLs. In step 4, choose the Custom Display Format. This will allow us to use XSL to transform the query results into a jQuery Mobile page fragment. Figure 7-11 is a screenshot of step 4. Click the Next button to move to step 5.

Step 5 is our last stop on the Pagelet Wizard train. In this step, we have the opportunity to enter the XSL that will transform our Query XML into jQuery Mobile markup. The XSL is really just our Chapter 5 profile.html page with some XSL template tags for context and XSL and XPath selection statements for values. When working with Pagelet Wizard XSL, I like to copy the XML from Pagelet Wizard into a local file and then build my XSL, applying the transforms locally in an editor like NetBeans or Eclipse. I can then validate the XSL as well as visually inspect the output prior to pasting the XSL into Pagelet Wizard. The following listing contains the XSL I generated for transforming the query's results into the jQuery Mobile profile page fragment.

```
<?xml version="1.0" encoding="UTF-8"?>

<!--
    Document    : profile2jqm.xsl
    Created on : July 20, 2014, 5:13 PM
    Author      : sarah
    Description:
        Transform query results into jQuery Mobile markup.
-->
```

```xsl
<xsl:stylesheet xmlns:xsl="http://www.w3.org/1999/XSL/Transform"
    version="1.0">
  <xsl:output method="html"/>

  <xsl:template match="/">
    <div data-role="page" id="profile">
      <style type="text/css" scoped="true">
        @import url("/pdjqm/css/details.css");

        @media (min-width:28em) {
          img.avatar {
            margin-bottom: 20px;
          }
        }
      </style>

      <div data-role="header">
        <h1>Personnel Directory</h1>
        <a href="#panel" class="show-panel-btn" data-icon="bars"
          data-iconpos="notext">Menu</a>
        <a href="#search" data-icon="search"
          data-iconpos="notext" class="ui-btn-right">Search</a>
      </div><!-- /header -->

      <xsl:apply-templates/>

      <div data-role="footer" data-position="fixed">
        <h4>
          Copyright (c) Company 2014, All rights reserved
        </h4>
      </div><!-- /footer -->

    </div><!-- /page -->
  </xsl:template>

  <xsl:template match="row">
    <div data-role="content">
      <form action="#" method="POST">
        <img src="/psc/ps/EMPLOYEE/HRMS/s/
WEBLIB_BMA_JQPD.ISCRIPT1.FieldFormula.iScript_Photo
?EMPLID={querydata[@fieldname='EMPLID']}"
            class="avatar"
            alt="{querydata[@fieldname='NAME']}'s Photo"/>
        <h2>
          <xsl:value-of select="querydata[@fieldname='NAME']"/>
        </h2>
        <div>
          <xsl:value-of
              select="querydata[@fieldname='EMPLID']"/>
        </div>
```

```
        <div class="ui-field-contain">
          <label for="phone">Phone:</label>
          <input type="tel"
              value="{querydata[@fieldname='PHONE']}"
              name="phone" id="phone"/>
        </div>
        <div class="ui-field-contain">
          <label for="address">Address:</label>
          <input type="text"
              value="{querydata[@fieldname='ADDRESS1']}"
              name="address" id="address"/>
        </div>
        <div class="ui-field-contain">
          <label for="city">City:</label>
          <input type="text"
              value="{querydata[@fieldname='CITY']}"
              name="city" id="city"/>
        </div>
        <div class="ui-field-contain">
          <label for="state">State:</label>
          <input type="text"
              value="{querydata[@fieldname='STATE']}"
              name="state" id="state"/>
        </div>
        <div class="ui-field-contain">
          <label for="postal">Postal Code:</label>
          <input type="text" value="30014"
              name="{querydata[@fieldname='POSTAL']}"
              id="postal"/>
        </div>
        <div class="ui-field-contain">
          <label for="country">Country:</label>
          <input type="text"
              value="{querydata[@fieldname='COUNTRY']}"
              name="country" id="country"/>
        </div>

        <input type="submit" value="Save" data-theme="b"/>
      </form>
    </div><!-- /content -->
  </xsl:template>


  <!-- delete unmatched text -->
  <xsl:template
      match="@*|text()|comment()|processing-instruction()">
  </xsl:template>
</xsl:stylesheet>
```

FIGURE 7-12. *Screenshot of step 5 of the Pagelet Wizard*

NOTE
The XSL template contains an HTML form that points to #. This means that the save button does not actually work.

Figure 7-12 is a screenshot of step 5. After entering the XSL and clicking outside the XSL box (to trigger the FieldChange event of the XSL field), save your Pagelet.

You can test this iScript outside of Pagelet Wizard by accessing the Pagelet Wizard runtime iScript URL. Here is an example from my demo instance: http://hr92dm05.example.com:8000/psc/ps/EMPLOYEE/HRMS/s/WEBLIB_PTPPB.ISCRIPT1 .FieldFormula.IScript_PageletBuilder?PTPPB_PAGELET_ID=BMA_JQPD_PROFILE. Similar to the other iScript pages created thus far, this one is not very pretty. We are just a few steps from hooking these page fragments into the jQuery Mobile app we created in Chapter 5, allowing jQuery Mobile to progressively enhance each page.

Integrating These iScripts with jQuery Mobile

We now have fully functional page fragments that include

- Search results page with live data

- A person detail page

- A personal profile detail page

These page fragments contain some minor jQuery Mobile markup but they aren't very pretty, responsive, or mobile. They are just fragments designed to be used in the context of a container page that includes jQuery Mobile. By making a couple of changes to the search.html page we built in Chapter 5, we can transform the appearance of these new iScript page fragments.

Updating the Chapter 5 Source Code

Open your Chapter 5 jQuery Mobile project in your favorite Integrated Development Environment (NetBeans perhaps?). Locate and open the search.html page. This is the starting point for our application and is the only page we have to update. In fact, search.html is the only HTML page we still need from this project (for now). The rest of the pages were just prototypes used to develop our iScripts. Within search.html, find the text `profile.html` and replace it with /psc/ps/EMPLOYEE/HRMS/s/ WEBLIB_PTPPB.ISCRIPT1.FieldFormula.IScript_PageletBuilder?PTPPB_PAGELET_ ID=BMA_JQPD_PROFILE. Here is a sample code fragment, with the changed URL in bold text:

```
    <nav data-role="panel" id="panel" data-display="push"
        data-theme="b">
      <ul data-role="listview">
        <li data-icon="delete" class="hide-panel-btn">
          <a href="#" data-rel="close">Close menu</a>
        </li>
        <li data-icon="user">
          <a href="/psc/ps/EMPLOYEE/HRMS/s/WEBLIB_PTPPB.ISCRIPT1
.FieldFormula.IScript_PageletBuilder?PTPPB_PAGELET_ID=
BMA_JQPD_PROFILE">My Profile</a>
        </li>
      </ul>
    </nav><!-- /panel -->
```

Next, find the search form within search.html. It has the attribute `action` with a value of `results.html`. Replace the text `results.html` with the URL for the search iScript we created earlier: /psc/ps/EMPLOYEE/HRMS/s/WEBLIB_BMA_JQPD. ISCRIPT1.FieldFormula.iScript_Search.

Uploading the Project

The mobile prototype currently runs through an embedded NetBeans web server. The PeopleSoft iScript, on the other hand, runs in a PeopleSoft web server on an entirely different host name and/or port. For jQuery Mobile Ajax page loading to work, the browser needs to think both are running in the same web server instance. There are a handful of ways to accomplish this. Here are four:

1. Proxy PeopleSoft through the same web server as our jQuery Mobile application.

2. Use the jQuery and jQuery Mobile version included with PeopleTools, and move everything from the Chapter 5 project into a PeopleTools managed definition.

3. Deploy the jQuery Mobile prototype into the PeopleSoft web server.

4. Deploy the jQuery Mobile libraries to the PeopleSoft web server, but upload all of the application files as iScript accessible pages.

For this chapter, let's choose option three: deploy to the PeopleSoft web server. We will save the proxy example for Chapter 8. Copy the Chapter 5 project's public_ html folder into your PeopleSoft web server. In my HCM demo image, the web server's root directory is located at /home/psadm2/psft/pt/8.53/webserv/peoplesoft/ applications/peoplesoft/PORTAL.war. I used pscp to copy a zip archive of the public_html folder.

NOTE
There are many different mechanisms to transfer files. pscp is common to Linux and Unix servers because it uses the SSH service, which is usually running for remote administration. Other copy methods include FTP, SFTP, FTPS, and just standard SAMBA file transfers.

What is pscp?

The pscp utility is a Secure file CoPy (scp) client program that is part of the very popular PuTTY suite. The scp protocol uses the same data transfer and authentication mechanisms as Secure SHell (SSH). You can download the PuTTY suite from http://www.chiark.greenend.org.uk/~sgtatham/putty/ download.html. After unzipping the downloaded archive, I recommend adding the PuTTY suite folder to your %PATH% environment variable.

Here is the command line transcript showing how I used 7zip and pscp to upload the modified Chapter 5 project to my PeopleSoft web server. I am using the HCM 9.2 VirtualBox demo image available from My Oracle Support.

```
C:\>cd C:\Users\sarah\Documents\NetBeansProjects\
PersonnelDirectory-jqm>
PersonnelDirectory-jqm>"C:\Program Files\7-Zip\7z" a -r
PersonnelDirectory-jqm.zip public_html
PersonnelDirectory-jqm>pscp PersonnelDirectory-jqm.zip
root@hr92dm05:/home/psadm2/psft/pt/8.53/webserv/peoplesoft
/applications/peoplesoft/PORTAL.war/PersonnelDirectory-jqm.zip
```

NOTE
Since I am using a VirtualBox demo image, I know the root password. Unless you are the system administrator for your PeopleSoft server, chances are high that you do not know the root user password. All that matters is that you have write access to the PeopleSoft web server directory. If your production systems and credentials are like mine, you have credentials for the Linux server, but don't know the password for the user with write access to the web server directory. In this scenario, I copy the file as myself, log in using SSH, and then use sudo to become the web server user. As the web server user, I can move and expand the zip file.

Once the file is on the server, I become the web server owner and then expand the file into my PeopleSoft Web server root directory. Here are the commands I executed from a PuTTY SSH session:

```
[root@hcm92 ~]# su - psadm2
[psadm2@hcm92 PORTAL.war]$ cd psft/pt/8.53/webserv/peoplesoft/\
> applications/peoplesoft/PORTAL.war/
[psadm2@hcm92 PORTAL.war]$ unzip PersonnelDirectory-jqm.zip
[psadm2@hcm92 PORTAL.war]$ mv public_html pdjqm
```

Test your uploaded version to ensure that the iScripts execute properly from the jQuery user interface. Start by navigating to the search.html file in the pdjq directory we created earlier. The URL from my VirtualBox VM looks like this: http://hr92dm05.example.com:8000/pdjqm/search.html. After entering search criteria, you should see search results similar to the contents shown in Figure 7-13 (but with your data, of course).

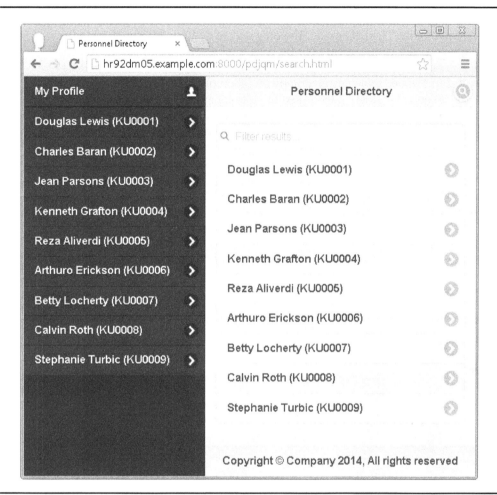

FIGURE 7-13.   *Search results page*

NOTE
*We did not implement authentication. One of the
benefits of using the PeopleTools 8.53 delivered
jQuery Mobile is that authentication is handled by the
PeopleSoft application. Be sure to log into PeopleSoft
before attempting to access the mobile URL.*

Handling Authentication

iScripts require a PS_TOKEN cookie. The only way to acquire this cookie is to log into PeopleSoft. Just for fun, clear your browser cookies and then load the jQuery mobile app from http(s)://<yourserver>/pdjqm/search.html. The search page will appear, just fine. Enter some search criteria and then press the search button. You should see a PeopleSoft login page. Attempting to login, however, doesn't work! Figure 7-14 is a screenshot of the login page viewed through jQuery Mobile.

jQuery Mobile attempts to perform all of the server side interactions through Ajax. jQuery Mobile parses Ajax responses and attempts to place page content in the correct location. The PeopleSoft login doesn't work because the JavaScript supplied by PeopleSoft is outside of the body tag—jQuery Mobile ignores content that is outside the body tag.

One way to solve this problem is to authenticate before showing the search page. This requires us to place the search page under PeopleSoft control—move it into PeopleSoft managed metadata. The easiest way to make this switch would be to use Pagelet Wizard as we did for the profile page, but unfortunately the contents of search.html conflicts with step 5 of the Pagelet Wizard. Step 5 is required before we can use the Pagelet Wizard iScript.

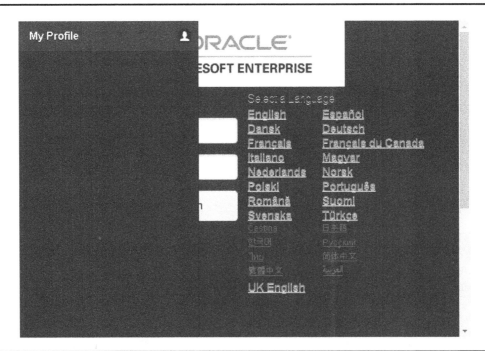

FIGURE 7-14. *Defective login screen*

An alternative is to create our own iScript. Log into Application Designer and create a new HTML definition. Before (or after) pasting the existing search.html page contents into this the new HTML definition we need to change a couple of file paths. The search.html file paths reference libraries using relative paths, but we need to change them to semi-absolute paths (absolute, but without the server name). Since we are modifying the HTML anyway, let's update the search form's action attribute and the profile link to use bind variables as URLs. We can then let PeopleTools build the correct iScript URLs rather than hardcode node names, portal names, and so on. The following HTML fragment identifies the lines that require modification. I included several lines for context. Changes are in bold text. After making these changes, name the new HTML definition BMA_JQPD_SEARCH_PAGE.

```
<!DOCTYPE html>
<html>
  <head>
    <title>Search</title>
    <meta charset="UTF-8">
    <meta name="viewport" content="width=device-width">

    <link rel="stylesheet"
        href="/pdjqm/js/libs/jquery-mobile/jquery.mobile.css">
    <style>
      @media (min-width:42em) {

        ...
      }
    </style>

    <script src="/pdjqm/js/libs/jquery/jquery.js"></script>
    <script src="/pdjqm/js/libs/jquery-mobile/jquery.mobile.js">
    </script>
...
  </head>
  <body class="ui-responsive-panel">
    <main data-role="page" id="search">

      <header data-role="header">
        <h1>Personnel Directory</h1>
        <a href="#panel" class="show-panel-btn" data-icon="bars"
           data-iconpos="notext">Menu</a>
      </header><!-- /header -->

      <article data-role="content">
        <form action="%Bind(:1)" method="GET">
...
        </form>
      </article><!-- /content -->
```

```
...
    </main><!-- /page -->

    <nav data-role="panel" id="panel" data-display="push"
        data-theme="b">
      <ul data-role="listview">
        <li data-icon="delete" class="hide-panel-btn">
          <a href="#" data-rel="close">Close menu</a>
        </li>
        <li data-icon="user">
          <a href="%Bind(:2)?PTPPB_PAGELET_ID=BMA_JQPD_PROFILE">
            My Profile
          </a>
        </li>
      </ul>
    </nav><!-- /panel -->
  </body>
</html>
```

Next, open the `WEBLIB_BMA_JQPD` record definition and then open the `ISCRIPT1` FieldFormula event editor. We need to create a new iScript to serve `BMA_JQPD_SEARCH`. Scroll to the end of the event and add the following PeopleCode:

```
Function iScript_SearchForm
    Local string &searchUrl = GenerateScriptContentURL(%Portal, %Node,
        Record.WEBLIB_BMA_JQPD, Field.ISCRIPT1, "FieldFormula",
        "iScript_Search");
    Local string &profileUrl = GenerateScriptContentURL(%Portal, %Node,
        Record.WEBLIB_PTPPB, Field.ISCRIPT1, "FieldFormula",
        "IScript_PageletBuilder");

    %Response.Write(GetHTMLText(HTML.BMA_JQPD_SEARCH_PAGE,
        &searchUrl, &profileUrl));
End-Function;
```

Before testing, be sure to add this new iScript function to the `BMA_PERSON_DIR` permission list. Next, test the search page by navigating to your version of the URL http(s)://<yourserver>/psc/<site>/EMPLOYEE/HRMS/s/WEBLIB_BMA_JQPD.ISCRIPT1 .FieldFormula.iScript_SearchForm (modified with your server's connection information). Here is the URL for my virtual machine (for reference purposes): http://hr92dm05 .example.com:8000/psc/ps/EMPLOYEE/HRMS/s/WEBLIB_BMA_JQPD.ISCRIPT1 .FieldFormula.iScript_SearchForm. With this URL PeopleSoft will display a signon page when authentication is required. In the next chapter, we will learn how to use REST services to create an anonymous personnel directory.

AngularJS with iScripts

Let's turn our attention to the Chapter 6 prototype. Chapter 6 was difficult. If you have a working prototype, now is the time to convert the static JSON files to dynamic data sources. Even if you don't have a working prototype, I encourage you to continue reading. The Chapter 6 prototype requires JavaScript Object Notation (JSON). Through the next few pages you will learn how to use PeopleCode to produce JSON.

We will follow the same pattern as we did with jQuery Mobile by creating a new web library and several iScripts that serve required data. After confirming the iScript services work as expected, we will connect them to the AngularJS prototype. Here is a summary of the steps we will complete:

1. Create iScript data sources using the Document definitions we created in Chapter 4.

2. Create an iScript entry point to manage authentication.

3. Update the AngularJS service URLs to the new iScript URLs.

4. Upload the modified AngularJS application.

The Search iScript

Launch PeopleTools Application Designer and create a new record definition. To this new record definition, add the delivered field ISCRIPT1. Set the record type to Derived/Work and then save the record as WEBLIB_BMA_AJPD. Figure 7-15 is a screenshot of the new record definition.

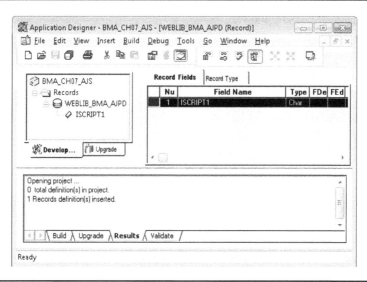

FIGURE 7-15. *AngularJS iScript web library*

We already created the logic for the search results and details iScripts, so we will copy that logic into our new web library. We can't use the exact same iScripts, however, because the jQuery Mobile version of these iScripts used HTML templates, whereas the AngularJS version requires JSON data. The following `iScript_Search` code listing is similar to the jQuery Mobile version, but with the following changes:

- Parameter names are different.

- Rather than new HTML definitions, this code listing uses the Documents we created in Chapter 4 to generate JSON data.

To the FieldFormula event of field ISCRIPT1, add the following PeopleCode. Differences from the jQuery Mobile version are noted in bold text.

```
Function iScript_Search
    Local string &emplidParm = %Request.GetParameter("EMPLID");
    Local string &nameParm = %Request.GetParameter("NAME");
    Local string &nameSrchParm =
        %Request.GetParameter("LAST_NAME_SRCH");

    REM ** build SQL based on parameters;
    REM ** careful of SQL injection!!;
    Local array of any &sqlParms = CreateArrayAny();
    Local array of string &criteriaComponents =
        CreateArrayRept("", 0);
    Local string &sql = FetchSQL(SQL.BMA_PERSON_SRCH);
    Local string &whereClause;

    REM ** query and column variables;
    Local SQL &cursor;
    Local string &emplid;
    Local string &name;
    Local string &nameSrch;

    REM ** build a WHERE clause;
    If (All(&emplidParm)) Then
       &sqlParms.Push(&emplidParm);
       &criteriaComponents.Push(Field.EMPLID | " LIKE :" |
            &sqlParms.Len | " %Concat '%'");
    End-If;

    If (All(&nameParm)) Then
```

```
      &sqlParms.Push(&nameParm);
      &criteriaComponents.Push(Field.NAME | " LIKE :" |
            &sqlParms.Len | " %Concat '%'");
   End-If;

   If (All(&nameSrchParm)) Then
      &sqlParms.Push(&nameSrchParm);
      &criteriaComponents.Push(Field.LAST_NAME_SRCH |
            " LIKE :" | &sqlParms.Len | " %Concat '%'");
   End-If;

   &whereClause = &criteriaComponents.Join(" AND ", "", "");

   If (All(&whereClause)) Then
      &whereClause = " WHERE " | &whereClause;
   End-If;

   REM ** iterate over rows, adding to response;
   &cursor = CreateSQL(&sql | &whereClause, &sqlParms);

   Local Document &resultsDoc =
         CreateDocument("BMA_PERSONNEL_DIRECTORY",
         "SEARCH_RESULTS", "v1");
   Local Compound &resultsRoot = &resultsDoc.DocumentElement;
   Local Collection &resultsColl =
         &resultsRoot.GetPropertyByName("RESULTS");
   Local Compound &item;
   Local boolean &ret;

   While &cursor.Fetch(&emplid, &name, &nameSrch);
      &item = &resultsColl.CreateItem();
      &item.GetPropertyByName("EMPLID").Value = &emplid;
      &item.GetPropertyByName("NAME").Value = &name;
      &item.GetPropertyByName("LAST_NAME_SRCH").value =
            &nameSrch;
      &ret = &resultsColl.AppendItem(&item);
   End-While;

   &cursor.Close();

   %Response.SetContentType("application/json");
   %Response.Write(&resultsDoc.GenJsonString());
End-Function;
```

JSON before PeopleTools 8.53

The Documents module is first mentioned in PeopleBooks for PeopleTools 8.51. While the intention of the Documents module has always been to provide an abstraction between rendered data and programming structures, until 8.53 the Documents module only generated XML formatted data. 8.53 added support for JSON rendering and parsing. How can an organization that uses an earlier PeopleTools release generate a JSON response?

Generating JSON is a little tricky because JSON looks a lot like JavaScript but with the following requirements:

■ JSON structures are either arrays or objects (or arrays of objects) which means they either start with [or {.

■ Property names must be quoted. JavaScript allows for object definitions whose properties aren't quoted, but JSON requires each property name to be surrounded with quotes.

■ Within strings certain characters *must* be escaped even though they may represent valid JavaScript strings.

NOTE
You can find more information about the JSON data format on the json.org website.

It is these special requirements that keep us from using the EscapeJavascriptString PeopleCode built-in function to generate JSON. Here are two options:

■ Use a Java JSON library such as json.simple or json.org.

■ Use a combination of HTML definitions, string concatenation, and PeopleCode to build JSON structures.

The first option is the safest alternative because it guarantees valid JSON. You can find an example of using the json.simple Java library with PeopleCode in my book *PeopleSoft PeopleTools Tips and Techniques*. I also have an example of using the json.org parser on my blog at http://jjmpsj.blogspot.com/2008/09/parsing-json-with-peoplecode.html. The problem with using custom Java libraries is that custom libraries require special treatment during upgrades. Specifically, you have to update the Java class path for each app server and/or process scheduler after an upgrade.

Option two is a little more risky. You are responsible for escaping values, joining strings properly, and so on. To help properly escape string values, I posted a PeopleCode JSON Encoder on my blog at http://jjmpsj.blogspot .com/2010/04/json-encoding-in-peoplecode.html. It is still your responsibility, however, to ensure proper concatenation. When generating JSON on earlier versions of PeopleTools, I test my results at http://jsonlint.org/ to confirm that the result produced valid JSON.

Add this new web library and iScript to the BMA_PERSON_DIR permission list and test the iScript by navigating to your environment's version of http(s)://<yourserver>/ psc/<site>/EMPLOYEE/HRMS/s/WEBLIB_BMA_AJPD.ISCRIPT1.FieldFormula.iScript_ Search?EMPLID=KU00&NAME=C&LAST_NAME_SRCH=%25E. Using my server, the URL is http://hr92dm05.example.com:8000/psc/ps/EMPLOYEE/HRMS/s/WEBLIB_ BMA_AJPD.ISCRIPT1.FieldFormula.iScript_Search?EMPLID=KU00&NAME=C&LAST_ NAME_SRCH=%25. If you are not using a demo database, then be sure to change the parameters to match data that exists in your instance. Here is what my demo database returns:

```
{"SEARCH_RESULTS": {
"SEARCH_FIELDS": [
{"EMPLID": "KU0015","NAME": "Carmichael Espinosa",
"LAST_NAME_SRCH": "ESPINOSA"},{
"EMPLID": "KU0020","NAME": "Christelle Stevenson",
"LAST_NAME_SRCH": "STEVENSON"}
]}
}
```

NOTE
If your web browser prompts you to download the file rather than display the file, then change the parameter for `%Response.SetContentType()` *from* `application/json` *to* `text/plain`.

Just to confirm the response is valid JSON, I recommend copying the response, navigating to http://jsonlint.org, and then pasting the response into the Validation box. JSON lint will reformat the data and display a notification telling you whether or not the response data is valid. Here is the formatted response:

```
{
    "SEARCH_RESULTS": {
        "SEARCH_FIELDS": [
            {
                "EMPLID": "KU0015",
```

```
            "NAME": "Carmichael Espinosa",
            "LAST_NAME_SRCH": "ESPINOSA"
        },
        {
            "EMPLID": "KU0020",
            "NAME": "Christelle Stevenson",
            "LAST_NAME_SRCH": "STEVENSON"
        }
    ]
  }
}
```

Using Documents

Documents describe a hierarchical data structure. We use PeopleCode to interact with the data in these structures. The Document object model is very similar to an XML document's object model (the `XmlDoc` object). Just like an `XmlDoc`, a Document has a root element known as the `DocumentElement`. That root element is a Compound, which is a fancy way of saying that it contains two or more separate elements. The children of a Compound can be one of the following three types:

- Collection
- Compound
- Primitive

Our example used all three of these types. We started at the root element, the `SEARCH_RESULTS` compound and then found the `RESULTS` collection (an array of `SEARCH_FIELDS` compound objects). The end of each Document tree contains one or more Primitive leaves. In our example, the leaves are `EMPLID`, `NAME`, and `LAST_NAME_SRCH`.

The Details iScript

The logic for the AngularJS details iScript is the same as the jQuery Mobile iScript. We just have to swap out the HTML templates for the Document definition we created in Chapter 4. Here is the PeopleCode for the AngularJS version of the details iScript with differences noted in bold text.

```
Function iScript_Details
    Local string &emplid = %Request.GetParameter("EMPLID");

    If (None(&emplid)) Then
        &emplid = %EmployeeId;
```

```
    End-If;

    Local string &NAME;
    Local string &ADDRESS1;
    Local string &CITY;
    Local string &STATE;
    Local string &POSTAL;
    Local string &COUNTRY;
    Local string &COUNTRY_CODE;
    Local string &PHONE;

    SQLExec(SQL.BMA_PERSON_DETAILS, &emplid, &NAME, &ADDRESS1,
            &CITY, &STATE, &POSTAL, &COUNTRY, &COUNTRY_CODE, &PHONE);

    Local Document &detailsDoc = CreateDocument(
            "BMA_PERSONNEL_DIRECTORY", "DETAILS", "v1");
    Local Compound &detailsRoot = &detailsDoc.DocumentElement;
    &detailsRoot.GetPropertyByName("EMPLID").Value = &emplid;
    &detailsRoot.GetPropertyByName("NAME").Value = &NAME;
    &detailsRoot.GetPropertyByName("ADDRESS1").Value = &ADDRESS1;
    &detailsRoot.GetPropertyByName("CITY").Value = &CITY;
    &detailsRoot.GetPropertyByName("STATE").Value = &STATE;
    &detailsRoot.GetPropertyByName("POSTAL").Value = &POSTAL;
    &detailsRoot.GetPropertyByName("COUNTRY").Value = &COUNTRY;
    &detailsRoot.GetPropertyByName("COUNTRY_CODE").Value =
            &COUNTRY_CODE;
    &detailsRoot.GetPropertyByName("PHONE").Value = &PHONE;

    %Response.SetContentType("application/json");
    %Response.Write(&detailsDoc.GenJsonString());
End-Function;
```

NOTE

The string parameters to the CreateDocument function are case sensitive. A common mistake is to use an uppercase V in the Document definition and then a lowercase v (or vice versa) when invoking the CreateDocument function.

I added a parameter test to the beginning of this iScript. The jQuery Mobile version of the Personnel Directory sends data mixed with display markup. The AngularJS version does not. The separation of data from display logic allows us to use the AngularJS version's service URL for multiple displays. For this example, it means we can use the same iScript for both the details and profile pages. The EMPLID parameter test at the top of the iScript assumes that if this iScript is called without an EMPLID then the user is requesting his or her profile.

Add this new iScript to the `BMA_PERSON_DIR` permission list and test the iScript by navigating to your environment's version of http(s)://<yourserver>/psc/<site>/EMPLOYEE/ HRMS/s/WEBLIB_BMA_AJPD.ISCRIPT1.FieldFormula.iScript_Details?EMPLID=KU0015. On my server the URL is http://hr92dm05.example.com:8000/psc/ps/EMPLOYEE/ HRMS/s/WEBLIB_BMA_AJPD.ISCRIPT1.FieldFormula.iScript_Details?EMPLID=KU0015. Be sure to update the EMPLID to match data that exists in your system. When I access this URL, the web browser displays the following JSON (formatted using jsonlint.org):

```
{
    "DETAILS": {
        "EMPLID": "KU0015",
        "NAME": "Espinosa,Carmichael",
        "ADDRESS1": "4122 West Avenue",
        "CITY": "San Antonio",
        "STATE": "TX",
        "POSTAL": "78220",
        "COUNTRY": "USA",
        "COUNTRY_CODE": "",
        "PHONE": "925\/694-7915"
    }
}
```

Integrating Our iScripts with AngularJS

We integrate our iScripts into the AngularJS application by updating five URLs:

- `SearchService` service
- `DetailsCtrl` controller
- `ProfileCtrl` controller
- The details photo URL
- The profile photo URL

Updating the searchService

In your AngularJS project, open the js/services.js file and find the `searchService` URL. In my sample, it is line 53. Replace the URL with the iScript URL. The following code fragment contains a couple of lines for context. The changed line is in bold text.

```
searchService.search = function(parms) {
  var promise = $http({
    method: 'GET',
    url: '/psc/ps/EMPLOYEE/HRMS/s/WEBLIB_BMA_AJPD.
ISCRIPT1.FieldFormula.iScript_Search',
    params: parms
  }).then(function(response) {
```

Updating the DetailsCtrl Controller

Open the js/controller.js file in your AngularJS project. Find the `DetailsCtrl` controller and update the URL to your details iScript URL. The following code fragment contains the entire `DetailsCtrl` controller with the modified URL in bold text:

```
.controller('DetailsCtrl', [
  '$scope',
  '$routeParams',
  '$http',
  function($scope, $routeParams, $http) {
    // view the route parameters in your console by uncommenting
    // the following:
    // console.log($routeParams);
    $http.get('/psc/ps/EMPLOYEE/HRMS/s/WEBLIB_BMA_AJPD.
ISCRIPT1.FieldFormula.iScript_Details?EMPLID=' +
        $routeParams.EMPLID)
      .then(function(response) {
        // view the response object by uncommenting the
        // following:
        // console.log(response);
        // closure -- updating $scope from outer function
        $scope.details = response.data.DETAILS;
      });
  }])
```

Updating the ProfileCtrl Controller

The profile controller looks strikingly similar to the details controller. Make the same URL change to the profile controller (without the EMPLID parameter). I reprinted the profile controller here with the URL in bold text:

```
.controller('ProfileCtrl', ['$scope',
  '$routeParams',
  '$http',
  function($scope, $routeParams, $http) {
    $http.get('/psc/ps/EMPLOYEE/HRMS/s/WEBLIB_BMA_AJPD.
ISCRIPT1.FieldFormula.iScript_Details')
      .then(function(response) {
        // closure -- updating $scope from outer function
        $scope.profile = response.data.DETAILS;
      });

    $scope.save = function() {
      // TODO: implement during Chapters 7 and 8
    };
  }]);
```

Updating the Details Template Photo URL

Open partials/details.html and identify the `img` tag near the top of the template. Replace the `src` attribute name and value with `ng-src` as follows:

```
<img ng-src="/psc/ps/EMPLOYEE/HRMS/s/WEBLIB_BMA_JQPD.ISCRIPT1.
FieldFormula.iScript_Photo?EMPLID={{details.EMPLID}}"
    class="avatar" alt="{{details.NAME}}'s Photo">
```

NOTE
We are switching from the `src` attribute to `ng-src` to keep the browser from resolving the `src` attribute before AngularJS has bound and replaced all of the values.

Updating the Profile Template Photo URL

Open partials/profile.html and identify the `img` tag near the top of the template. Replace the `src` attribute name and value with `ng-src` as follows:

```
<img ng-src="/psc/ps/EMPLOYEE/HRMS/s/WEBLIB_BMA_JQPD.ISCRIPT1.
FieldFormula.iScript_Photo?EMPLID={{profile.EMPLID}}"
    class="avatar" alt="{{details.NAME}}'s Photo">
```

Uploading the Project

Uploading the AngularJS project is very similar to uploading the jQuery Mobile project. Just like jQuery Mobile, AngularJS uses Ajax to fetch data. We need to make the browser think that the iScript data sources come from the same domain as the web application. The easiest way to accomplish this is to copy the AngularJS application into the PeopleSoft web server. Inside the PersonnelDirectory-ajs folder of your AngularJS project, copy the app folder into your PeopleSoft web server. The steps required are the same as the jQuery Mobile project. In the spirit of brevity, I am just including the commands I used to compress, copy, and then expand the project files into the correct location on the web server.

At the Windows command prompt, I executed

```
C:\>cd C:\Users\sarah\Documents\NetBeansProjects\
PersonnelDirectory-ajs
PersonnelDirectory-ajs>"C:\Program Files\7-Zip\7z" a -r
PersonnelDirectory-ajs.zip app
PersonnelDirectory-jqm>pscp PersonnelDirectory-ajs.zip
root@hr92dm05:/home/psadm2/psft/pt/8.53/webserv/peoplesoft
/applications/peoplesoft/PORTAL.war/PersonnelDirectory-ajs.zip
```

Within an SSH session, I executed

```
[root@hcm92 ~]# su - psadm2
[psadm2@hcm92 PORTAL.war]$ cd psft/pt/8.53/webserv/peoplesoft/\
> applications/peoplesoft/PORTAL.war/
[psadm2@hcm92 PORTAL.war]$ unzip PersonnelDirectory-ajs.zip
[psadm2@hcm92 PORTAL.war]$ mv app pdajs
```

NOTE
*The zip file expanded into a folder named app. I
used the mv command to rename that folder to
pdajs (Personnel Directory AngularJS) which is a
little more meaningful than the original.*

Test the application by navigating to your server's version of http://hr92dm05
.example.com:8000/pdajs/ (pdajs is the name of the folder on your web server).
Figure 7-16 is a screenshot of the uploaded application using iScripts as data sources.

NOTE
*If the application doesn't work properly with the
/pdajs/ URL, then rename the folder to /app/ and try
using the /app/ URL.*

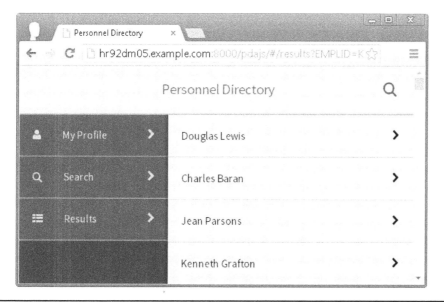

FIGURE 7-16.   *Screenshot of the AngularJS app connected to PeopleSoft iScripts*

Extra Credit

The profile templates used by each of the solutions presented in the chapter included save buttons. Demonstrate your understanding of the concepts in this chapter by creating an iScript that implements save functionality. Hint: read form parameters using `%Request.GetParameter()` and use a component interface to update the database.

Conclusion

In this chapter, you learned how to connect the prototypes from Chapters 5 and 6 to real PeopleSoft data using iScripts. The iScript method presented here is just one approach. Some developers believe this approach is easier than others because it requires the fewest number of managed definitions. What it gains in efficiency, however, it gives up in flexibility. As you will learn in the next chapter, the REST service approach has many advantages including anonymous access.

CHAPTER

8

REST Controllers

In this chapter, you will learn how to connect an HTML5 user experience to PeopleSoft through REST services. While working through the content in this chapter you will gain experience with JSON, PeopleSoft Query, and the Apache web server.

What is REST?

The word REST is an acronym for REpresentational State Transfer. The term was coined by Roy Fielding in his doctoral dissertation *Architectural Styles and the Design of Network-based Software Architectures*. Chapter 5 of the dissertation introduces REST and is available online at http://www.ics.uci.edu/~fielding/pubs/dissertation/rest_arch_style.htm.

I describe REST as the opposite of SOAP web services. Rather than add new standards and vocabularies (like SOAP), REST leverages that which already exists. The focus of REST is the target resource (or data), whereas SOAP is more concerned with remote method invocation. This makes REST well-suited for standard Create, Read, Update, and Delete data operations. The nature of the REST request makes it much easier to use in client-side web requests because it doesn't require complex WSDLs, data structures, security policies, and "envelopes."

Building REST Service Operations

PeopleSoft REST service operations require the following metadata definitions:

- Documents

- Messages

- Services

- Service Operations

- PeopleCode Service Operation Handlers

- Routings

PeopleTools REST support varies by release. PeopleTools 8.52 was the first PeopleTools release with the RESTListeningConnector. REST-like services have been possible, however, since PeopleTools hit the Internet. For this chapter, we are most concerned with passing values to PeopleCode through a URL and then receiving a properly formatted result. PeopleTools 8.42 through 8.51 offered this through the `IBConnectorInfo` object and only supported URL values through query string parameters (see http://jjmpsj.blogspot.com/2011/10/rest-like-peoplesoft-services.html

for more details). PeopleTools 8.52 gives us a true REST URL pattern as well as HTTP(S) authorization headers and common REST content types. In this chapter, we will use the RESTListeningConnector to read REST URLs and serve both JSON and HTML responses. Our jQuery Mobile and AngularJS applications will both use the BMA_PERSONNEL_DIRECTORY.SEARCH_FIELDS and BMA_PERSONNEL_DIRECTORY.EMPLID documents we created in Chapter 4. Since the jQuery Mobile and AngularJS applications both require a different response file format, we will create separate Service Operations for each.

jQuery Mobile with the RESTListeningConnector

Similar to Chapter 7, in this chapter we are going to transform the jQuery Mobile static application into a data-driven tool.

Creating Message Definitions

A Message definition is an abstract descriptor for a Service Operation payload. It is the web service structural synonym of an Interface or Abstract Class. Service Operations point to Messages without regard for Message implementation details. To use our Documents in Service Operations, we need to create corresponding Message definitions. Through your online PeopleSoft application, navigate to PeopleTools | Integration Broker | Integration Setup | Messages.

Defining the Search Parameter Document Message Definition

When you navigate to the Messages component online, PeopleSoft presents you with a search page. Click the Add a New Value link to transfer to Add mode. Enter the values from Table 8-1 into the Add New Message page.

Field Label	Value
Type	Document
Message Name	BMA_PERS_DIR_SEARCH_PARMS
Message Version	v1
Package	BMA_PERSONNEL_DIRECTORY
Document	SEARCH_FIELDS
Version	v1

TABLE 8-1. *BMA_PERS_DIR_SEARCH_PARMS values*

When you click the Add button, the following screen will look suspiciously like the original Document definition screen. This is intentional. A Document already contains all of the metadata required for Integration Broker. Nevertheless, Integration Broker needs a Message definition to act as an abstraction layer between the Service Operation and its structure definition. Be sure to save the new definition or your Message will not exist.

NOTE
Even though the Message definition looks exactly like
the underlying Document definition, be sure to click
the Save button.

Defining the Details Parameter Document Message Definition

From the search results page we want to be able to select an item from the list and view the item details. To view the item (person) details, we need to send a unique identifier (employee ID) to the Service Operation to identify the desired item. Create a new Message definition named BMA_PERS_DIR_DETAILS_PARMS. Use the values from Table 8-2 to populate the Message metadata.

NOTE
When adding another Message, if your navigation
breadcrumbs show that you are on the Messages
component, but the content looks like the Documents
component, then don't click the Return to Search
link. Clicking this link will take you to the Document
search page, not the Messages search page.

Field Label	Value
Type	Document
Message Name	BMA_PERS_DIR_DETAILS_PARMS
Message Version	v1
Package	BMA_PERSONNEL_DIRECTORY
Document	EMPLID
Version	v1

TABLE 8-2. *BMA_PERS_DIR_DETAILS_PARMS values*

The REST Service Container

PeopleTools requires all Service Operations to belong to a Service definition. Let's create a Service definition container for our jQuery Mobile Service Operations. Log into your PeopleSoft application online and navigate to PeopleTools | Integration Broker | Integration Setup | Services. Add the new value BMA_PERS_DIR_JQM and check the REST Service box. Figure 8-1 is a screenshot of the Add New Service page. Click the Add button to move to the next page.

When the Service definition page appears, enter the description Personnel Directory JQ Mobile and then click the Save button. Figure 8-2 is a screenshot of the Service definition.

Creating Service Operations

We add Service Operations directly to Service definitions. The new service operations will be very similar to the iScripts we created in the last chapter. They will receive criteria in the URL and return jQuery Mobile page fragments. In fact, many of them will use the same HTML templates we created in Chapter 7. The only difference will be the URL pattern and delivery mechanism.

The Details Service Operation

When we consider how our users will interact with a Personnel Directory application, the search results page is the first dynamically generated page. Because it links to the details page, however, we will start with the details Service Operation. As with the iScript example, we want to dynamically generate that link for the details service. Unlike the iScript example, however, we can't generate that link unless the target exists.

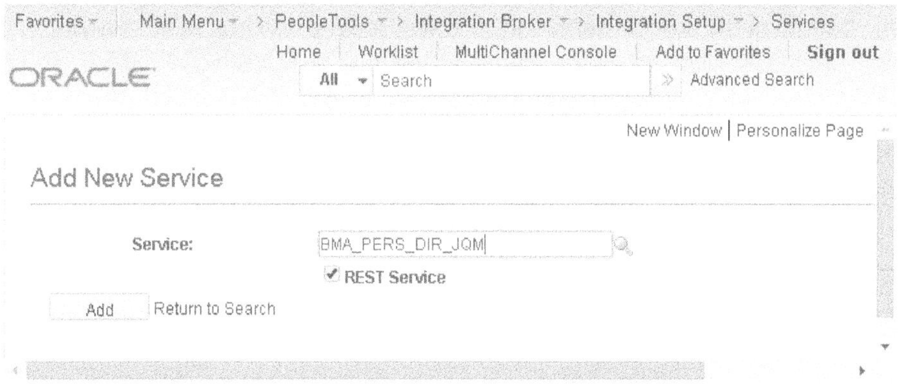

FIGURE 8-1. *Add New Service page*

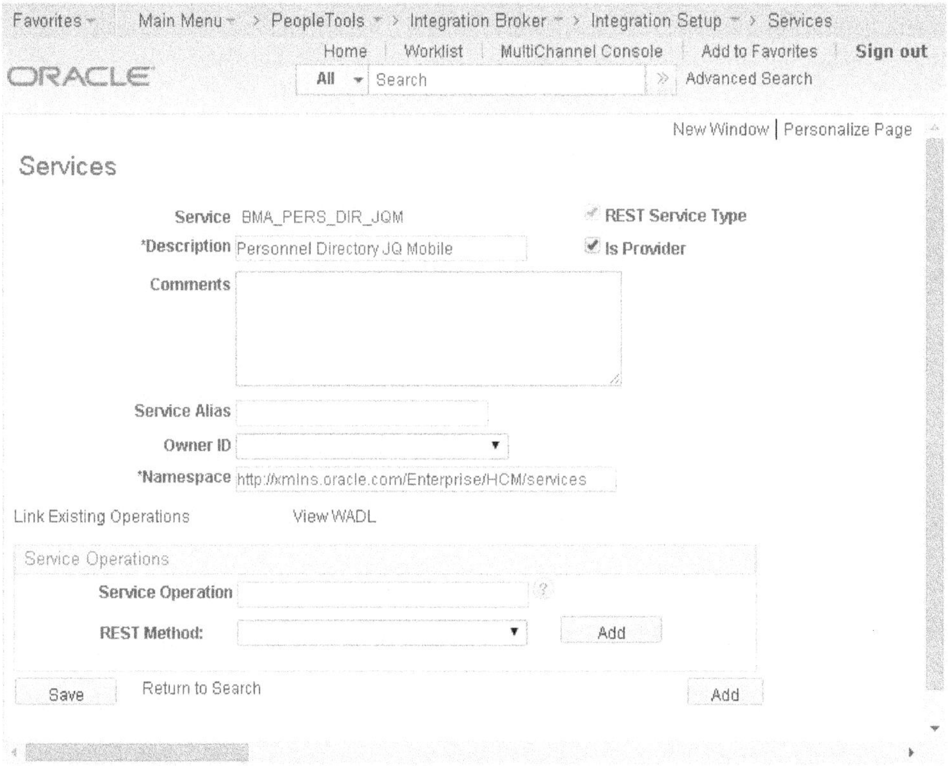

FIGURE 8-2. *Service definition*

At the bottom of the Service definition, you will see a group box titled "Service Operation." In the Service Operation field, enter the text BMA_PERS_DIR_DTL_ JQM. This will be the name (or alias) used to identify the Service Operation. Select the value Get as the REST method. The GET HTTP verb tells the REST provider (PeopleSoft) to fetch data. This stands in contrast to other verbs such as POST, PUT, and DELETE which all manipulate data. Figure 8-3 is a screenshot of the

FIGURE 8-3. *Service Operation group box*

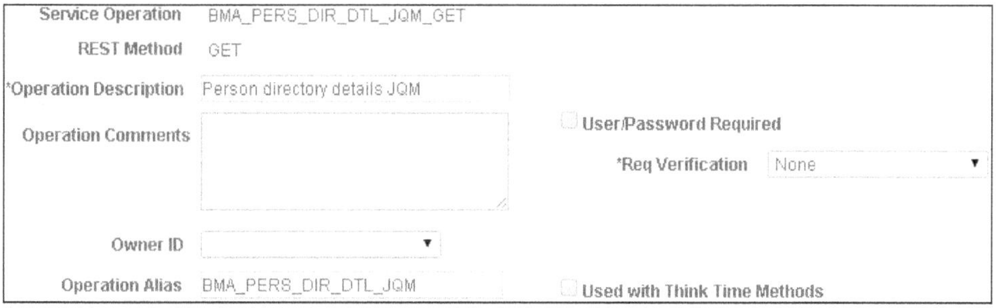

Service Operation	BMA_PERS_DIR_DTL_JQM_GET		
REST Method	GET		
*Operation Description	Person directory details JQM		
Operation Comments		☐ User/Password Required	
		*Req Verification	None ▼
Owner ID	▼		
Operation Alias	BMA_PERS_DIR_DTL_JQM	☐ Used with Think Time Methods	

FIGURE 8-4.   *Top of the Service Operation page*

Service Operation group box. Click the Add button to create and define the Service Operation.

On the Service Operation page, enter the description Person directory details JQM. Figure 8-4 is a screenshot of the top section of the Service Operation page.

NOTE
When creating the Service Operation, we entered the name BMA_PERS_DIR_DTL_JQM. PeopleTools, however, created a Service Operation named BMA_PERS_DIR_DTL_JQM_GET. PeopleTools appends the REST method to the Service Operation name when creating new REST Service Operations.

Moving further down the page, you will see the REST Resource Definition group box. The REST Resource Definition describes the URL patterns associated with this Service Operation. Integration Broker uses the information in this section to map fragments of the URL into properties of a Document structure. In this section, select the Document Template BMA_PERS_DIR_DETAILS_PARMS.v1. After selecting the Document, you can either:

■ Manually enter a URL template that matches the jQuery Mobile search form's input fields.

■ Use the Build button to create the URL template.

Here is the URL template text:

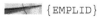 {EMPLID}

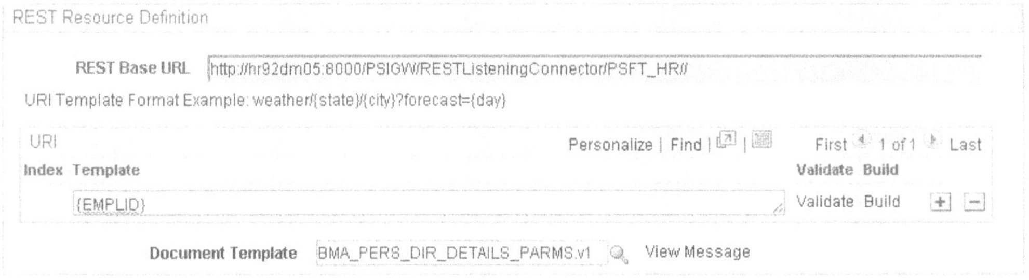

REST Resource Definition

REST Base URL http://hr92dm05:8000/PSIGW/RESTListeningConnector/PSFT_HR//

URI Template Format Example: weather/{state}/{city}?forecast={day}

URI		Personalize	Find			First 1 of 1 Last
Index Template			Validate Build
{EMPLID}			Validate Build ＋ －

Document Template BMA_PERS_DIR_DETAILS_PARMS.v1   View Message

FIGURE 8-5. *REST Resource Definition*

Figure 8-5 is a screenshot of the REST Resource Definition section of the Service Operation definition.

NOTE
If your REST Base URL is blank, then navigate to PeopleTools | Integration Broker | Configuration | Service Configuration and click the Setup Target Locations link. Verify that the REST Target Location has a value.

Move down to the Default Service Operation group box and enter an appropriate version description. Since the version identifier is v1, the value Version 1 seems appropriate. While still in the Default Service Operation section, move down to the Message Instance group box. Specify a Message.Version value of IB_GENERIC_REST.V1. Our jQuery Mobile REST responses will be HTML page fragments, and not structured data, so we can use an unstructured, delivered Message definition. Select text/html for the Content-Type. Save the new Service Operation. Figure 8-6 is a screenshot of the Default Service Operation Version section after saving.

After saving the Service Operation, a new link appears near the top and is labeled Service Operation Security. Select this link to add this Service Operation to a permission list. For development purposes, we can add this Service Operation to PTPT1000 and PTPT1200. Before deploying to a production system, work with your system security administrator to determine the appropriate permission list for this Service Operation.

NOTE
Service Operation Security opens as a popup. Be sure your browser allows popups from your PeopleSoft instance.

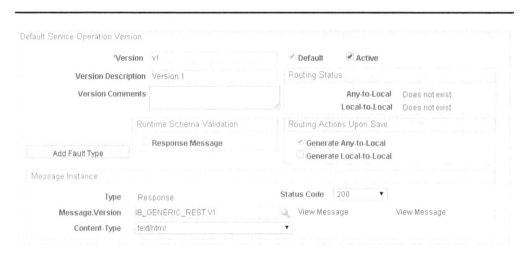

FIGURE 8-6. *Default Service Operation Version*

Details Service Operation Handler   The metadata generated thus far tells Integration Broker *what* data to generate (response Message definition), *who* can generate it (Service Operation security and routings), and *when* to generate the response (URL pattern). Next, we need to tell Integration Broker *how* to generate the response. The Service Operation Handler tells Integration Broker the PeopleCode to execute when it receives a request for the BMA_PERS_DIR_DTL_JQM service. Before configuring the handler, we need to write some PeopleCode. The handler's PeopleCode will look very similar to the iScript request handler from Chapter 7 but with the following changes:

- The REST handler does not have %Request and %Response system variables. Instead, the Service Operation Handler must collect its incoming parameters from the &MSG method parameter and return a new Message object containing the Service Operation response.

- We cannot use %Response.WriteBinary to send the employee's picture to the client browser.

Item one will be trivial because we will use a standard Service Operation Handler design pattern. Item two is more difficult. To send photos to the browser through a Service Operation Handler, we will need to convert image data into a text format that the browser can interpret.

Log into PeopleTools Application Designer and create a new Application Package named BMA_PERS_DIR_JQM. To this new package, add the class

`DetailsRequestHandler`. Open the `DetailsRequestHandler` PeopleCode event editor and enter the following PeopleCode. Differences between the handler PeopleCode and Chapter 7 `iScript_Details` function are emphasized with bold type.

```
import PS_PT:Integration:IRequestHandler;

class DetailsRequestHandler implements
      PS_PT:Integration:IRequestHandler
   method OnRequest(&MSG As Message) Returns Message;
   method OnError(&MSG As Message) Returns string;

   method getPhotoDataUrl(&emplid As string) Returns string;

private
   method getImageB64(&sqlId As string, &imgId As string,
      &size As number) Returns string;

end-class;

method OnRequest
   /+ &MSG as Message +/
   /+ Returns Message +/
   /+ Extends/implements
      PS_PT:Integration:IRequestHandler.OnRequest +/

   REM ** read parameters from URI using a document;
   Local Compound &parmCom = &MSG.GetURIDocument().DocumentElement;
   Local string &emplid = &parmCom.GetPropertyByName("EMPLID").value;

   REM ** write response to a document;
   Local Message &response = CreateMessage(
      Operation.BMA_PERS_DIR_DTL_JQM_GET, %IntBroker_Response);

   Local string &NAME;
   Local string &ADDRESS1;
   Local string &CITY;
   Local string &STATE;
   Local string &POSTAL;
   Local string &COUNTRY;
   Local string &COUNTRY_CODE;
   Local string &PHONE;
   Local string &photoUrl;

   SQLExec(SQL.BMA_PERSON_DETAILS, &emplid, &NAME, &ADDRESS1, &CITY,
      &STATE, &POSTAL, &COUNTRY, &COUNTRY_CODE, &PHONE);
```

```
    &photoUrl = %This.getPhotoDataUrl(&emplid);

    Local boolean &tmp = &response.SetContentString(GetHTMLText(
        HTML.BMA_JQPD_DETAILS_PAGE, &emplid, &NAME, &ADDRESS1, &CITY,
        &STATE, &POSTAL, &COUNTRY, &COUNTRY_CODE,  &PHONE,
        &photoUrl, "/pdjqm/css/details.css"));
    Return &response;

end-method;

method OnError
    /+ &MSG as Message +/
    /+ Returns String +/
    /+ Extends/implements PS_PT:Integration:IRequestHandler.OnError +/
    Return "He's dead, Jim";
end-method;
```

Our PeopleCode first declares the Application Class structure and then implements the OnRequest method. The OnRequest method is really defined in the class base interface PS_PT:Integration:IRequestHandler. We are required to implement this method because Integration Broker will execute the OnRequest method when it receives a REST request.

This OnRequest handler uses the same logic, SQL, and HTML definitions as the iScript version from Chapter 7. A critical difference is the way we handle the photo's URL. Instead of generating a URL, we are going to convert the binary image into a base64 representation. This is because Integration Broker does not contain a mechanism for serving binary data. The result will contain approximately one-third more bytes than the original image.

The database contains binary data that we need to convert into base64 text. One way to accomplish this is to use a combination of PeopleCode and database-specific functions to perform the base64 encoding. Why not use PeopleCode? PeopleCode does not contain functions or data types for manipulating binary data. Here is the PeopleCode for generating the &photoUrl. Add this to the end of the Application Class event handler.

```
method getPhotoDataUrl
    /+ &emplid as String +/
    /+ Returns String +/
    Local number &size;

    SQLExec(SQL.BMA_EMPL_PHOTO_LENGTH, &emplid, &size);

    If (All(&size)) Then
        Return "data:image/jpeg;base64," |
            %This.getImageB64(SQL.BMA_EMPL_PHOTO_B64, &emplid,
            &size);
```

```
   Else
      SQLExec(SQL.BMA_DUMMY_PHOTO_LENGTH, Image.PT_DUMMY_PHOTO,
            &size);
      Return "data:image/jpeg;base64," |
            %This.getImageB64(SQL.BMA_DUMMY_PHOTO_B64,
            Image.PT_DUMMY_PHOTO, &size);
   End-If;
end-method;

method getImageB64
   /+ &sqlId as String, +/
   /+ &imgId as String, +/
   /+ &size as Number +/
   /+ Returns String +/
   Local number &start = 1;
   Local number &chunkSize = 1455;
   Local string &b64;
   Local string &result;

   Repeat
      If ((&start + &chunkSize) > &size) Then
         &chunkSize = &size - &start;
      End-If;

      SQLExec("%SQL(" | &sqlId | ", :1, :2, :3)", &chunkSize,  &start,
            &imgId, &b64);

      &result = &result | &b64;

      &start = &start + &chunkSize;
   Until ((&start >= &size) Or
      (&start < 1));

   Return &result;
end-method;
```

The above code listing contains two methods:

- `getPhotoDataUrl`

- `getImageDataUrl`

The `getPhotoDataUrl` method determines if an employee photo exists. If it does, then it invokes `getImageDataUrl` with the employee photo SQL statement. If the photo does not exist, then it uses the "dummy photo" SQL statement.

The `getImageDataUrl` method is the method that actually executes the base64 conversion SQL. Since the Oracle database base64 conversion routine (`UTL_ENCODE.BASE64_ENCODE`) has a size limitation, the `getImageDataUrl` method performs the base64 conversion in chunks and then concatenates the converted text into a final result.

Before saving the new Application Class, you will need to create the following four SQL definitions:

BMA_EMPL_PHOTO_LENGTH:

```
SELECT DBMS_LOB.GETLENGTH(EMPLOYEE_PHOTO)
  FROM PS_EMPL_PHOTO
 WHERE EMPLID = :1
```

BMA_EMPL_PHOTO_B64:

```
SELECT UTL_RAW.CAST_TO_VARCHAR2(UTL_ENCODE.BASE64_ENCODE(
    DBMS_LOB.SUBSTR(EMPLOYEE_PHOTO
, %P(1)
, %P(2))))
  FROM PS_EMPL_PHOTO
 WHERE EMPLID = %P(3)
```

BMA_DUMMY_PHOTO_LENGTH:

```
SELECT DBMS_LOB.GETLENGTH(CONTDATA)
  FROM PSCONTENT
 WHERE CONTNAME = :1
```

NOTE
The data in PSCONTENT may span multiple rows. The PT_DUMMY_PHOTO image is small enough to fit in one row. If your placeholder image is larger, then you may have to alter the `getImageDataUrl` PeopleCode method to iterate over multiple rows.

BMA_DUMMY_PHOTO_B64:

```
SELECT UTL_RAW.CAST_TO_VARCHAR2(UTL_ENCODE.BASE64_ENCODE(
    DBMS_LOB.SUBSTR(CONTDATA
, %P(1)
, %P(2))))
  FROM PSCONTENT
 WHERE CONTNAME = %P(3)
```

NOTE
Microsoft SQL Server and other PeopleTools database platforms have their own platform-specific base64 routines. Another alternative to the Oracle PL/SQL solution is to use `File.WriteRaw` *to move binary data into a file and then* `File` `.GetBase64StringFromBinary` *to convert the binary data into base64 text.*

We can now associate our PeopleCode OnRequest handler with the BMA_ PERS_DIR_DTL_JQM_GET Service Operation. Return to the BMA_PERS_DIR_ DTL_JQM_GET Service Operation definition in your PeopleSoft online application and switch to the Handlers tab. Within the Handlers section, enter a Name, select the On Request Type, and Application Class Implementation. The name you enter within this grid is not important. After entering the Application Class details, the component will automatically set the Name field to REQUESTHDLR. Figure 8-7 is a screenshot of the configured handler prior to clicking the Details link.

Click the details link and enter the Package Name BMA_PERS_DIR_JQM, the Path ":", and Class ID DetailsRequestHandler. Select the Method OnRequest. Figure 8-8 is a screenshot of the handler details.

After saving, test the Service Operation by navigating to http://<server>:<port>/ PSIGW/RESTListeningConnector/<default local node>/BMA_PERS_DIR_DTL_JQM .v1/<emplid>, replacing values in the URL to match your environment-specific values. Here is the URL for my demo system: http://hr92dm05:8000/PSIGW/ RESTListeningConnector/PSFT_HR/BMA_PERS_DIR_DTL_JQM.v1/KU2001. When the page loads, you should see the details page for the selected employee. Figure 8-9 is a screenshot of employee KU2001's details (who happens to be one of the authors of this book).

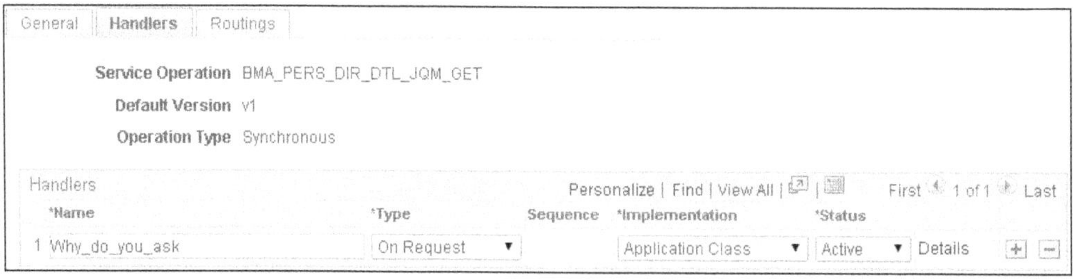

| General | Handlers | Routings | | | | | | | | |

Service Operation BMA_PERS_DIR_DTL_JQM_GET
Default Version v1
Operation Type Synchronous

Handlers — Personalize | Find | View All | 🗗 | 🔣 — First ◀ 1 of 1 ▶ Last

	*Name	*Type	Sequence	*Implementation	*Status		
1	Why_do_you_ask	On Request ▼		Application Class ▼	Active ▼	Details	＋ －

FIGURE 8-7. *On Request PeopleCode handler*

Handler Details

Handler Name	REQUESTHDLR
Handler Type	On Request
Description	
Comments	
Handler Owner	

Application Class

'Package Name	BMA_PERS_DIR_JQM
'Path	
Class ID	DetailsRequestHandler
Method	OnRequest

OK   Cancel

FIGURE 8-8. *Service Operation OnRequest handler details*

FIGURE 8-9. *Details jQuery Mobile page fragment accessed as a REST service*

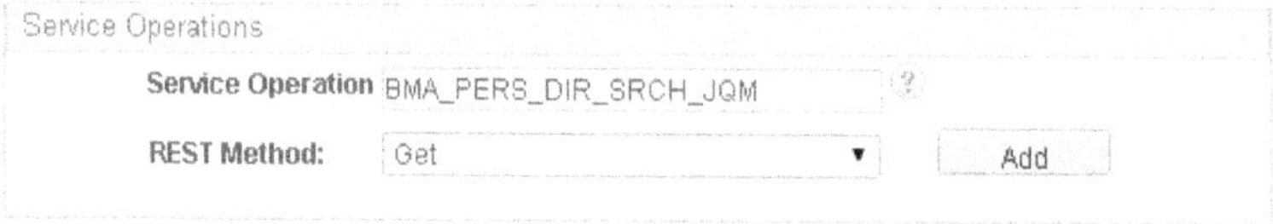

Service Operations

Service Operation BMA_PERS_DIR_SRCH_JQM

REST Method: Get   ▼   Add

FIGURE 8-10. *Service Operation group box*

NOTE
PSFT_HR is the delivered name of the default local node. One of the first steps you should take when configuring a PeopleSoft system is renaming the default local node. The node name is used to create a trust relationship between PeopleSoft instances. Failure to change your node name may compromise your application security.

The Search Service Operation

The Search Service Operation receives search criteria as query string parameters in a manner very similar to the Chapter 7 `iScript_Search` function.

Return to the `BMA_PERS_DIR_JQM` Service definition. In the Service Operation field, create a new Service Operation by entering the text `BMA_PERS_DIR_SRCH_JQM`. Select the value Get as the REST method. Figure 8-10 is a screenshot of the Service Operation group box. Click the Add button to create and define the Service Operation.

On the Service Operation page, enter the description `Person directory search JQM`. Figure 8-11 is a screenshot of the top section of the Service Operation page.

REST Method   GET

*Operation Description   Person directory search JQM

Operation Comments   ☐ User/Password Required

                                                       *Req Verification   None   ▼

Owner ID   ▼

Operation Alias   BMA_PERS_DIR_SRCH_JQM   ☐ Used with Think Time Methods

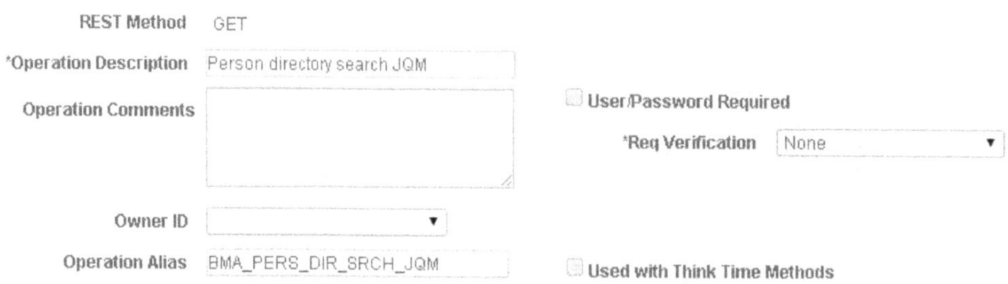

FIGURE 8-11. *Top of the Service Operation page*

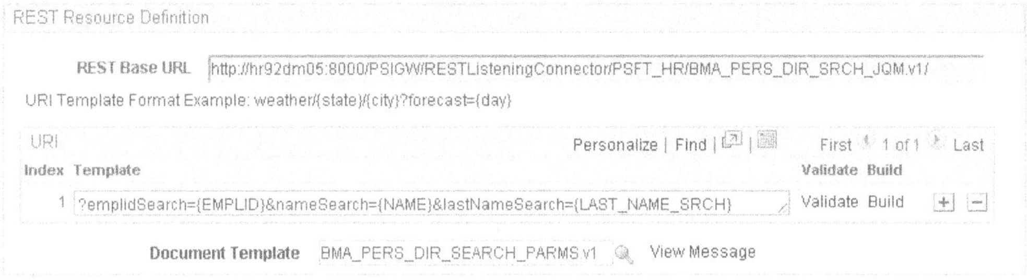

REST Resource Definition

REST Base URL http://hr92dm05:8000/PSIGW/RESTListeningConnector/PSFT_HR/BMA_PERS_DIR_SRCH_JQM.v1/

URI Template Format Example: weather/{state}/{city}?forecast={day}

URI		Personalize	Find	🗗	🖼	First ◀ 1 of 1 ▶ Last
Index	Template	Validate Build
1	?emplidSearch={EMPLID}&nameSearch={NAME}&lastNameSearch={LAST_NAME_SRCH}	Validate Build ➕ ➖

Document Template BMA_PERS_DIR_SEARCH_PARMS v1 🔍 View Message

FIGURE 8-12. *REST Resource Definition*

In the REST Resource Definition section, select the Document Template `BMA_PERS_DIR_SEARCH_PARMS.v1`. Set the URL template text to:

```
?emplidSearch={EMPLID}&nameSearch={NAME}&lastNameSearch={LAST_NAME_SRCH}
```

Figure 8-12 is a screenshot of the REST Resource Definition section of the Service Operation definition.

NOTE
Figure 8-12 was taken after saving the Service Operation. Prior to saving, the REST Base URL was http://hr92dm05:8000/PSIGW/RESTListeningConnector/PSFT_HR// and was enabled for editing.

Move down to the Default Service Operation group box and enter an appropriate version description. Since the version identifier is `v1`, the value `Version 1` seems appropriate. While still in the Default Service Operation section, move down to the Message Instance group box. Specify a Message.Version value of `IB_GENERIC_REST.V1`. Our jQuery Mobile REST responses will be HTML page fragments, and not structured data, so we can use an unstructured, delivered Message definition. Select `text/html` for the Content-Type. Save your Service Operation. Figure 8-13 is a screenshot of the Default Service Operation Version section after saving.

Scroll back to the top of the Service Operation and select the Service Operation Security link. Add the appropriate permission lists. In the absence of an application-specific permission list, PTPT1000 and PTPT1200 will work.

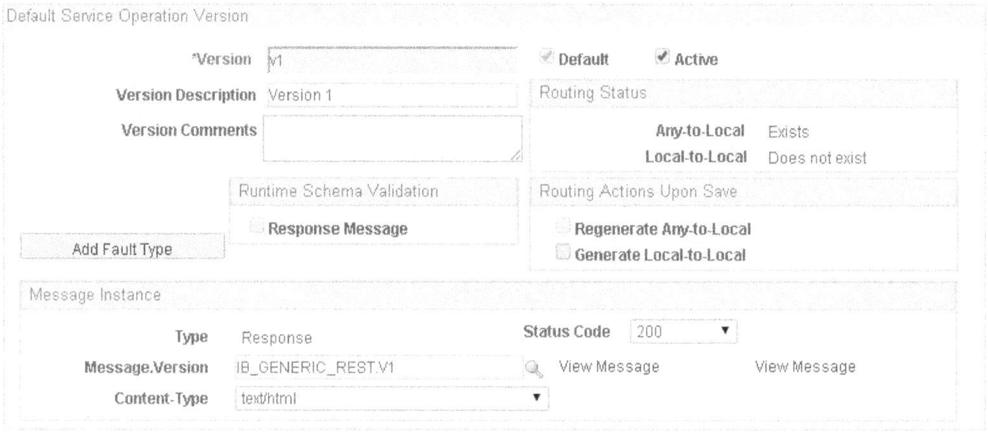

FIGURE 8-13. *Default Service Operation Version*

Search Service Operation Handler   Log into PeopleTools Application Designer and open the Application Package BMA_PERS_DIR_JQM. To this Application Package add the class SearchRequestHandler. Open the SearchRequestHandler's PeopleCode event editor and enter the following PeopleCode. Deviations from the Chapter 7 jQuery Mobile iScript_Search function are emphasized with bold type.

```
import PS_PT:Integration:IRequestHandler;

class SearchRequestHandler implements
        PS_PT:Integration:IRequestHandler
   method OnRequest(&MSG As Message) Returns Message;
   method OnError(&MSG As Message) Returns string;
end-class;

method OnRequest
   /+ &MSG as Message +/
   /+ Returns Message +/
   /+ Extends/implements
        PS_PT:Integration:IRequestHandler.OnRequest +/

   REM ** read parameters from URI using a document;
   Local Compound &parmCom = &MSG.GetURIDocument().DocumentElement;
   Local string &emplidParm = &parmCom.GetPropertyByName(
        "EMPLID").value;
   Local string &nameParm = &parmCom.GetPropertyByName("NAME").value;
   Local string &nameSrchParm = &parmCom.GetPropertyByName(
        "LAST_NAME_SRCH").value;
```

```
REM ** write response to a document;
Local Message &response = CreateMessage(
     Operation.BMA_PERS_DIR_SRCH_JQM_GET, %IntBroker_Response);


REM ** build SQL based on parameters -- careful of SQL injection!!;
Local array of any &sqlParms = CreateArrayAny();
Local array of string &criteriaComponents = CreateArrayRept("", 0);
Local string &sql = FetchSQL(SQL.BMA_PERSON_SRCH);
Local string &whereClause;

REM ** query and column variables;
Local SQL &cursor;
Local string &emplid;
Local string &name;
Local string &nameSrch;

REM ** build a WHERE clause;
If (All(&emplidParm)) Then
   &sqlParms.Push(&emplidParm);
   &criteriaComponents.Push(Field.EMPLID | " LIKE :"
        | &sqlParms.Len | " %Concat '%'");
End-If;

If (All(&nameParm)) Then
   &sqlParms.Push(&nameParm);
   &criteriaComponents.Push(Field.NAME | " LIKE :" |
        &sqlParms.Len | " %Concat '%'");
End-If;

If (All(&nameSrchParm)) Then
   &sqlParms.Push(&nameSrchParm);
   &criteriaComponents.Push(Field.LAST_NAME_SRCH | " LIKE :" |
        &sqlParms.Len | " %Concat '%'");
End-If;

&whereClause = &criteriaComponents.Join(" AND ", "", "");

If (All(&whereClause)) Then
   &whereClause = " WHERE " | &whereClause;
End-If;

REM ** iterate over rows, adding to response;
&cursor = CreateSQL(&sql | &whereClause, &sqlParms);

Local array of string &rows = CreateArrayRept("", 0);
Local string &detailsLink;
```

```
Local Document &linkDoc = CreateDocument(
    "BMA_PERSONNEL_DIRECTORY", "EMPLID", "v1");
Local Compound &linkCom = &linkDoc.DocumentElement;

While &cursor.Fetch(&emplid, &name, &nameSrch);
    &linkCom.GetPropertyByName("EMPLID").Value = &emplid;
    &detailsLink = %IntBroker.GetURL(
        Operation.BMA_PERS_DIR_DTL_JQM_GET, 1, &linkDoc);

    &rows.Push(GetHTMLText(HTML.BMA_JQPD_SEARCH_RESULT_LINK,
        &detailsLink, &emplid, &name));
End-While;

&cursor.Close();

Local boolean &tmp = &response.SetContentString(GetHTMLText(
    HTML.BMA_JQPD_SEARCH_RESULT_PAGE, &rows.Join("", "", "")));
Return &response;

end-method;

method OnError
    /+ &MSG as Message +/
    /+ Returns String +/
    /+ Extends/implements PS_PT:Integration:IRequestHandler.OnError +/
    Return "He's dead, Jim";
end-method;
```

NOTE
The PeopleCode above uses SQL definitions from Chapter 4 and HTML definitions from Chapter 7.

Besides the obvious differences of wrapping this code in an Application Class and using Documents and Service Operations, the REST event handler differs from the iScript version in the way it generates URLs. Since REST has no concept of %Portal and other online interactive variables, we can't use the standard GenerateXxx functions to create URLs. Instead, we use the %IntBroker.GetURL method, passing in a parameter the Document object to use when populating the target Service Operation URL template.

Return to the BMA_PERS_DIR_SRCH_JQM_GET Service Operation online and switch to the Handlers tab. Within the Handlers section, enter a Name, select the On Request Type, and Application Class Implementation. Click the details link and enter the Package Name BMA_PERS_DIR_JQM, the Path ":" and Class ID SearchRequestHandler. Select the Method OnRequest.

FIGURE 8-14. *REST search results*

Search Service URL Templates   Test the Service Operation by navigating to your version of http://hr92dm05:8000/PSIGW/RESTListeningConnector/PSFT_HR/BMA_PERS_DIR_SRCH_JQM.v1?emplidSearch=KU00&nameSearch=A&lastNameSearch =S using test data that matches your environment data. You should see a basic search results list similar to the one in Figure 8-14.

Our search page is supposed to accept a variable number of parameters. Try removing one of the parameters (lastNameSearch, for example) and verify your results. Depending on your tools release and cache state, you will either see the search page fragment with no results or an Exception message. The reason it doesn't work with fewer parameters is because Integration Broker is not able to find a URI template that matches the URL in the browser address bar. Return to the BMA_PERS_DIR_SRCH_JQM_GET Service Operation and add the following additional URI templates:

```
?emplidSearch={EMPLID}
?emplidSearch={EMPLID}&nameSearch={NAME}
?emplidSearch={EMPLID}&lastNameSearch={LAST_NAME_SRCH}
?nameSearch={NAME}
?nameSearch={NAME}&lastNameSearch={LAST_NAME_SRCH}
?lastNameSearch={LAST_NAME_SRCH}
```

Save and then test a few different URL search patterns. You should now see valid results. Just for fun, swap some of the parameters and view the results. For example, place nameSearch at the front of the query string and emplidSearch at the back. Notice that changing parameter placement won't match a URI template and therefore won't return results. Figure 8-15 is a screenshot of the URI templates.

URI				
Index Template	Personalize | Find | ⟨⟩ | 🔲	First ◁ 1-7 of 7 ▷ Last		
		Validate Build		
1	?emplidSearch={EMPLID}&nameSearch={NAME}&lastNameSearch={LAST_NAME_SRCH}	Validate Build	+	−
2	?emplidSearch={EMPLID}	Validate Build	+	−
3	?emplidSearch={EMPLID}&nameSearch={NAME}	Validate Build	+	−
4	?emplidSearch={EMPLID}&lastNameSearch={LAST_NAME_SRCH}	Validate Build	+	−
5	?nameSearch={NAME}	Validate Build	+	−
6	?nameSearch={NAME}&lastNameSearch={LAST_NAME_SRCH}	Validate Build	+	−
7	?lastNameSearch={LAST_NAME_SRCH}	Validate Build	+	−

FIGURE 8-15.   *URI templates*

My Profile Service Operation

The personal profile page Service Operation differs from the details Service Operation in the following ways:

- It returns information about the logged-in user.

- Requires authentication to identify the current user.

Create the profile Service Operation by returning to the BMA_PERS_DIR_JQM Service definition and creating the new Service Operation BMA_PERS_DIR_PROF_ JQM. Just like the other Service Operations, select the value Get as the REST method and then click the Add button.

When the Service Operation definition page appears, enter the description Person directory profile JQM. Check the box labeled User/Password Required and then select Req Verification of Basic Authorization. This will force the user to authenticate prior to accessing the profile service. Figure 8-16 is a screenshot of the top section of the Service Operation definition.

NOTE
PeopleTools 8.54 adds the Req Verification values
PeopleSoft Token and PeopleSoft Token
and SSL.

Even though this Service Operation requires no parameters, Integration Broker requires each Service Operation to contain at least one URI template. In the REST Resource Definition section, create a URI template containing the single word profile. Figure 8-17 is a screenshot of the REST Resource Definition.

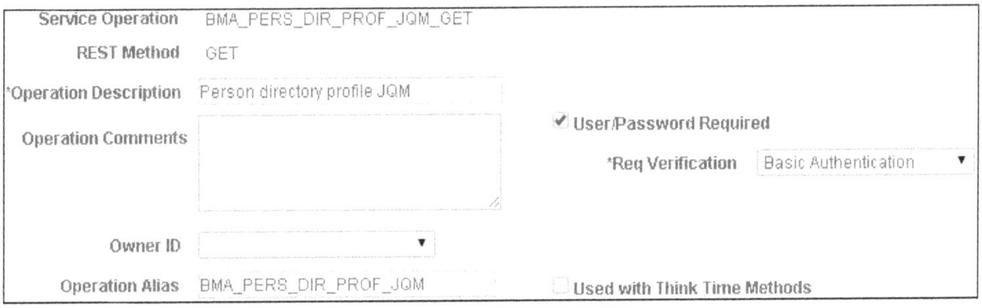

Service Operation	BMA_PERS_DIR_PROF_JQM_GET		
REST Method	GET		
'Operation Description	Person directory profile JQM		☑ User/Password Required
Operation Comments			'Req Verification Basic Authentication ▼
Owner ID	▼		
Operation Alias	BMA_PERS_DIR_PROF_JQM		☐ Used with Think Time Methods

FIGURE 8-16. *Top section of secure Service Operation*

Scroll down to the Default Service Operation Version and fill in the same values that were used for the search Service Operation (described earlier in Figure 8-13). After saving, scroll back to the top of the Service Operation and select the Service Operation Security link. Add the appropriate permission lists. For development purposes we can use PTPT1000 and PTPT1200.

My Profile Service Operation Handler   The profile page is similar to the details page, but with a different template. We could use the same SQL as the details page, but let's do something a little different this time. In Chapter 7, we used PeopleSoft Query and Pagelet Wizard to display the profile page. Let's use the same query inside a REST service handler. For the HTML, rather than create an HTML definition using Application Designer, we will upload it using the online Branding Objects component that was added to PeopleTools in 8.53. By moving both the data and display template into online components, we convert this portion of the application into something that designers, developers, and super users can maintain without Application Designer access.

REST Resource Definition

REST Base URL	http://hr92dm05:8000/PSIGW/RESTListeningConnector/PSFT_HR/BMA_PERS_DIR_PROF_JQM.v1/

URI Template Format Example: weather/{state}/{city}?forecast={day}

URI		Personalize | Find | 🔲 | 🔲	First ◄ 1 of 1 ► Last
Index Template			Validate Build
1 profile			Validate Build + −

Document Template   🔍 View Message

FIGURE 8-17. *Profile Service Operation URI definition*

NOTE
If you are using a version of PeopleTools older than 8.53, then create your HTML definition using Application Designer.

First, let's write a PeopleCode handler that runs the query we created in the last chapter. Log into PeopleTools Application Designer and open the Application Package `BMA_PERS_DIR_JQM`. To this package, add the class `ProfileRequestHandler`. Open the `ProfileRequestHandler`'s PeopleCode event editor and enter the following PeopleCode.

```
import BMA_PERS_DIR_JQM:DetailsRequestHandler;
import PS_PT:Integration:IRequestHandler;

class ProfileRequestHandler implements
        PS_PT:Integration:IRequestHandler
   method OnRequest(&MSG As Message) Returns Message;
   method OnError(&MSG As Message) Returns string;
end-class;

method OnRequest
   /+ &MSG as Message +/
   /+ Returns Message +/
   /+ Extends/implements
        PS_PT:Integration:IRequestHandler.OnRequest +/

   REM ** write response to a document;
   Local Message &response = CreateMessage(
        Operation.BMA_PERS_DIR_PROF_JQM_GET, %IntBroker_Response);

   Local BMA_PERS_DIR_JQM:DetailsRequestHandler &photoEncoder;
   Local Rowset &rs;
   Local Row &row;
   Local Record &promptRec;
   Local Record &rec;
   Local ApiObject &qry;
   Local string &photoUrl;
   Local boolean &tmp;

   &qry = %Session.GetQuery();

   REM ** The SQL for the query BMA_JQPD_PROFILE is in Chapter 7;
   &tmp = &qry.Open("BMA_JQPD_PROFILE", True, False);
   &promptRec = &qry.PromptRecord;
   &promptRec.GetField(Field.EMPLID).Value = %EmployeeId;

   &rs = &qry.RunToRowset(&promptRec, 1);
```

```
    &rec = &rs.GetRow(1).GetRecord(1);

    &photoEncoder = create BMA_PERS_DIR_JQM:DetailsRequestHandler();
    &photoUrl = &photoEncoder.getPhotoDataUrl(%EmployeeId);

    &tmp = &response.SetContentString(GetHTMLText(
        HTML.BMA_JQPD_PROFILE_PAGE, &rec.GetField(1).Value,
        &rec.GetField(2).Value, &rec.GetField(4).Value,
        &rec.GetField(5).Value, &rec.GetField(6).Value,
        &rec.GetField(7).Value, &rec.GetField(3).Value,
        &rec.GetField(8).Value, &rec.GetField(9).Value, &photoUrl));

    Return &response;

end-method;

method OnError
   /+ &MSG as Message +/
   /+ Returns String +/
   /+ Extends/implements PS_PT:Integration:IRequestHandler.OnError +/
   Return "He's dead, Jim";
end-method;
```

Just like the details page, the profile page displays a photo. By making the `DetailsRequestHandler` photo-encoding method `getPhotoDataUrl` public, we are able to use the same method in the profile handler.

Return to your PeopleSoft online application and open the `BMA_PERS_DIR_PROF_JQM_GET` Service Operation. Within the Handlers section, enter a Name, select the `On Request` Type, and `Application Class` Implementation. Figure 8-18 is a screenshot of the configured handler prior to clicking the Details link. Remember, the name you choose is irrelevant because the component PeopleCode will automatically rename the handler `REQUESTHDLR`.

General	Handlers	Routings					

Service Operation	BMA_PERS_DIR_PROF_JQM_GET
Default Version	v1
Operation Type	Synchronous

Handlers   Personalize | Find | View All | First ◀ 1 of 1 ▶ Last

	*Name	*Type		Sequence	*Implementation		*Status	
1	overwrite_me	On Request	▼		Application Class	▼	Active	▼ Details + −

FIGURE 8-18. *Profile Service Operation handler metadata*

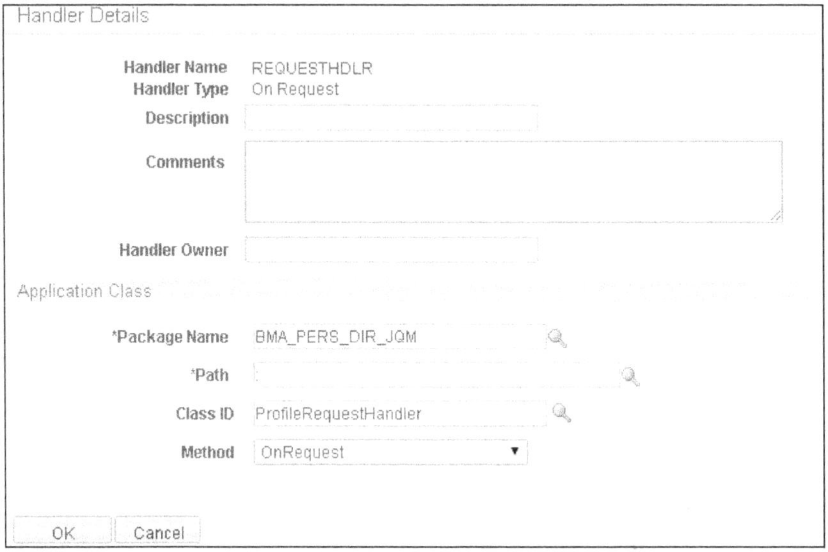

FIGURE 8-19. *Application Class metadata*

Click the Details link and fill in the handler's Application Class information:

- Package Name: BMA_PERS_DIR_JQM

- Path: " : "

- Class ID: ProfileRequestHandler

- Method: OnRequest

Figure 8-19 is a screenshot of the handler's Application Class metadata.

Save the Service Operation and copy the REST Base URL. For my demo server the REST Base URL is http://hr92dm05:8000/PSIGW/RESTListeningConnector/PSFT_HR/BMA_PERS_DIR_PROF_JQM.v1/. Set this URL aside for testing after we create the HTML definition.

Using your web browser, log into your PeopleSoft application and then navigate to PeopleTools | Portal | Branding | Branding Objects. On the HTML tab, click the Upload HTML Object link to create a new HTML definition. Name the new HTML definition BMA_JQPD_PROFILE_PAGE and provide a reasonable description. Paste the following into the main long edit field of the Add/Edit Branding Object dialog:

```
<div data-role="page" id="profile">
  <style type="text/css" scoped>
    @import url("css/details.css");
```

```
  @media (min-width:28em) {
    img.avatar {
      margin-bottom: 20px;
    }
  }
</style>

<div data-role="header">
  <h1>Personnel Directory</h1>
  <a href="#panel" class="show-panel-btn" data-icon="bars"
     data-iconpos="notext">Menu</a>
  <a href="#search" data-icon="search" data-iconpos="notext"
     class="ui-btn-right">Search</a>
</div><!-- /header -->

<div data-role="content">
  <form action="#" method="POST">
      <img src="%Bind(:10)" class="avatar" alt="%Bind(:2)'s Photo">
    <h2>%Bind(:2)</h2>
    <div>%Bind(:1)</div>
    <div class="ui-field-contain">
      <label for="phone">Phone:</label>
      <input type="tel" value="%Bind(:9)" name="phone"
             id="phone">
    </div>
    <div class="ui-field-contain">
      <label for="address">Address:</label>
      <input type="text" value="%Bind(:3)" name="address"
             id="address">
    </div>
    <div class="ui-field-contain">
      <label for="city">City:</label>
      <input type="text" value="%Bind(:4)" name="city" id="city">
    </div>
    <div class="ui-field-contain">
      <label for="state">State:</label>
      <input type="text" value="%Bind(:5)" name="state" id="state">
    </div>
    <div class="ui-field-contain">
      <label for="postal">Postal Code:</label>
      <input type="text" value="%Bind(:6)" name="postal"
          id="postal">
    </div>
    <div class="ui-field-contain">
      <label for="country">Country:</label>
      <input type="text" value="%Bind(:7)" name="country"
          id="country">
```

```
    </div>

    <input type="submit" value="Save" data-theme="b">
  </form>
</div><!-- /content -->

  <div data-role="footer" data-position="fixed">
    <h4>
      Copyright &copy; Company 2014, All rights reserved
    </h4>
  </div><!-- /footer -->

</div><!-- /page -->
```

Figure 8-20 is a screenshot of the HTML definition online editor.

Save the HTML definition and then test the Service Operation. To test this Service Operation, use the REST Base URL you copied and append the text

FIGURE 8-20. *Online HTML definition editor*

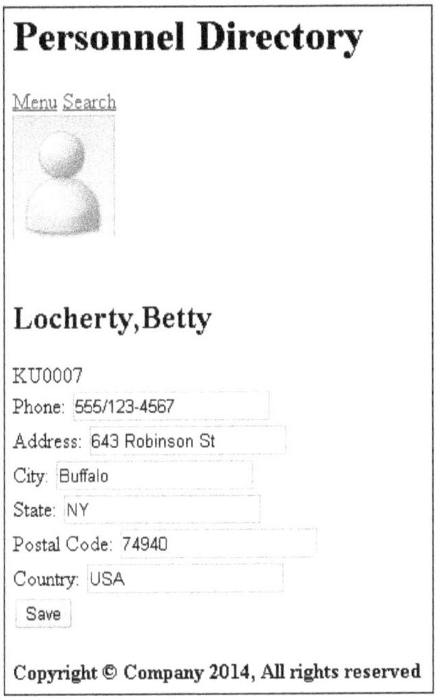

FIGURE 8-21. *Unstyled profile page*

`profile` as in: http://hr92dm05:8000/PSIGW/RESTListeningConnector/PSFT_HR/
BMA_PERS_DIR_PROF_JQM.v1/profile. When your browser attempts to load the
target URL, it will prompt you for credentials. Enter your PeopleSoft user name and
password. This is a critical difference from the Chapter 7 iScript prototype: through
configuration we can determine what to secure. Your results should appear similar
to Figure 8-21.

Preparing the jQuery Mobile Application

Do you still have a copy of the jQuery Mobile prototype from Chapter 5? If not, see
the sidebar titled "Resetting your jQuery Mobile Prototype" on the next page. When
you are ready, open the search page (search.html) and find the form element. Replace
the action URL with /PSIGW/RESTListeningConnector/<DEFAULT_LOCAL_NODE_
NAME> /BMA_PERS_DIR_SRCH_JQM.v1. Now scroll to the bottom of the
page and identify the profile hyperlink. Replace the links' URL with /PSIGW/

RESTListeningConnector/<DEFAULT_LOCAL_NODE_NAME>/BMA_PERS_DIR_ PROF_JQM.v1/profile. After making the change, your search.html file should contain the following code fragment. I included a couple of lines on each side of the change for context. The required change is in bold text.

NOTE
The HTML sample that follows uses the delivered default local node PSFT_HR. For security reasons you should rename your default local node.

```
    </header><!-- /header -->
    <article data-role="content">
      <form action="/PSIGW/RESTListeningConnector/PSFT_HR
/BMA_PERS_DIR_SRCH_JQM.v1" method="GET">
        <div class="ui-field-contain">
          <label for="emplidSearch">Employee ID:</label>
          <input type="text" name="emplidSearch" id="emplidSearch">
...
      <li data-icon="user">
        <a href="/PSIGW/RESTListeningConnector/PSFT_HR/
BMA_PERS_DIR_PROF_JQM.v1/profile">My Profile</a>
      </li>
```

Resetting your jQuery Mobile Prototype

Don't have a backup copy of the Chapter 5 jQuery Mobile prototype? The search page is the only page you have to update to reset the application. The rest of the pages are served form REST services. Within search.html, identify the `<link rel="stylesheet"`...and `<script` tags and eliminate the /pdjqm/ URL prefixes. The following listing contains some sample fragments:

```
<meta name="viewport" content="width=device-width">

<link rel="stylesheet"
    href="js/libs/jquery-mobile/jquery.mobile.css">

...

<script src="js/libs/jquery/jquery.js"></script>
<script src="js/libs/jquery-mobile/jquery.mobile.js"></script>
```

Scroll to the end of the search.html file and look for the My Profile hyperlink. It should be approximately six lines from the bottom.

Configuring a Reverse Proxy

The REST services are served by the PeopleSoft server, whereas the jQuery Mobile app runs locally through a NetBeans embedded web server. Just like the iScript version from last chapter, we need to get both running in the same domain since browsers block cross domain AJAX requests. Rather than upload our modified jQuery Mobile app to the PeopleSoft server, this time we will reverse proxy the PeopleSoft REST services through the local Apache web server instance we installed in Chapter 1.

Configuring Apache httpd

Each operating system (and Linux distribution) configures the Apache web server a little differently. The Apache configuration for some Linux distributions, for example, contains the rule `Include conf.d/*.conf`, which means you configure the Apache httpd instance by adding configuration files to the conf.d directory. The installation for other operating systems, such as Microsoft Windows, however, requires you to add your own Include directives and configurations to the default httpd.conf. The following instructions assume a Windows installation similar to the installation described in Chapter 1. Please adjust accordingly for your operating system.

Creating a URL Alias

Using your favorite text editor, open the httpd.conf file located inside your c:\Apache2.4\conf directory. Scroll to the end of the file and add the following directive:

```
Include conf/bma/*.conf
```

Now while still inside the c:\Apache2.4\conf directory, create a new directory named bma. We will place our custom Apache configurations inside this directory.

NOTE
If your httpd.conf file already contains
`conf/*.conf`, *then you don't need to add the custom bma rule. Instead, any file you add to the conf directory will automatically be added to the Apache web server configuration. The benefit of using the delivered conf rule is that you can upgrade Apache without having to modify your configuration.*

Inside the bma directory, create a new text file named pdjqm.conf. We will add rules to this file that tell the Apache web server to access our jQuery Mobile application from the NetBeans project directory. First, let's map the project's long folder path into an alias that is shorter and easier to access from a URL. The following code listing contains two references to the public_html folder of my NetBeans project. Open the new pdjqm.conf file and add the following text, changing the file references to match your project's directory location. Each directive should be on its own line. For formatting purposes, the path and file names in the code listing span multiple lines.

```
Alias /pdjqm C:/Users/sarah/Documents/NetBeansProjects/
PersonnelDirectory-jqm/public_html

<Directory "C:/Users/sarah/Documents/NetBeansProjects/
PersonnelDirectory-jqm/public_html">
  ## directives for older httpd versions
  # Order allow,deny
  # Allow from all
  Require all granted
</Directory>
```

NOTE
Apache 2.4 uses the `Require` *directive, whereas older releases use the* `Allow` *directive. Adjust the directives to match your version*

Now is a good time to test your configuration to make sure you can access the jQuery Mobile application from a web browser. First, save the changes to pdjqm .conf file and then start the Apache web server. To start Apache, open a command prompt and navigate to c:\Apache2.4\bin. From this directory run httpd.exe. Now open a web browser and attempt to load http://localhost/pdjqm/search.html. You should see your jQuery Mobile search page. If the page won't load properly, check your web browser's JavaScript console and network resource tab for errors.

Don't try to execute a search yet. We haven't added proxy rules to reverse proxy a PeopleSoft instance into the same URL as our jQuery Mobile application. Let's add those rules now.

Configuring a Reverse Proxy

WARNING
Improperly configuring an Apache web server will turn it into an open relay. See http://httpd.apache .org/docs/current/mod/mod_proxy.html#access for more information.

Some rules are application specific, such as the Alias we just defined. Other rules apply to the entire server and should be defined in a central location (such as httpd.conf). Loading modules is one of those common configurations. It is possible to load Apache modules from application-specific configuration files. A decentralized approach, however, makes it difficult to enable and disable modules. Therefore, we will make the following changes directly to httpd.conf. Ensure that your Apache web server instance is configured to load the proxy modules by searching the httpd.conf file for the following lines:

- LoadModule headers_module

- LoadModule proxy_module

- LoadModule proxy_html_module

- LoadModule proxy_http_module

- LoadModule xml2enc_module

If you find these lines, but they are prefixed with a hash (#), then delete the hash (the presence of the hash symbol disables a line). Your LoadModule section should appear similar to the following:

```
LoadModule headers_module modules/mod_headers.so
...
LoadModule proxy_module modules/mod_proxy.so
...
LoadModule proxy_html_module modules/mod_proxy_html.so
LoadModule proxy_http_module modules/mod_proxy_http.so
...
LoadModule xml2enc_module modules/mod_xml2enc.so
```

Next, scroll to the bottom and add the following proxy configuration right before the line `Include conf/bma/*.conf`:

```
ProxyRequests Off
<Proxy *>
  ## directives for 2.3 and earlier
  # Order allow,deny
  #Allow from all
  # directive for Apache 2.4 and later
  Require all granted
</Proxy>
```

The rest of our proxy configuration is application (or PeopleSoft) specific and belongs in a less generic (but still somewhat generic) configuration file. Create the file bma\proxy.conf and add the following:

```
# In the following listing, replace <server:port> with your
# PeopleSoft webserver name and port number
# Mine is http://hr92dm05:8000/PSIGW/
ProxyPass /PSIGW/ http://<server:port>/PSIGW/
```

```
<Location /PSIGW/ >
    ProxyPassReverse /PSIGW/
    ProxyHTMLEnable On
    ProxyHTMLURLMap http://<server:port>/PSIGW /PSIGW

    # Eliminate compression -- more network traffic, less CPU
    RequestHeader unset Accept-Encoding

    # mod_deflate alternative if compression desired
    # -- more CPU, less network traffic
    #SetOutputFilter INFLATE;DEFLATE
</Location>
```

NOTE
This generic proxy configuration allows anyone to access a PeopleSoft Integration Broker service through the reverse proxy. This loose configuration will come in handy later when we want to reverse proxy different PeopleSoft Service Operations.

A few pages ago we used `%IntBroker.GetURL` to turn search result items into hyperlinks that point to the details service. That worked great when we tested the search Service Operation directly from Integration Broker. Unfortunately, when we reverse proxy this content, the links retain pointers to the original PeopleSoft server, not the reverse proxy server. The configuration described here uses mod_proxy_html directives to rewrite hyperlink URLs to match the reverse proxy configuration.

The configuration uses mod_headers to turn off compression. The browser normally sends a request header telling PeopleSoft that it can accept compressed responses. The benefit of this compression is smaller network downloads that use less bandwidth. This is especially valuable for mobile applications. Unfortunately, mod_proxy_html cannot directly inflate PeopleSoft responses. Alternatively, you can use mod_deflate with mod_proxy_html to inflate PeopleSoft responses and then deflate the content before it travels over the Internet to the client browser. I included the SetOutputFilter directive required to enable mod_deflate with mod_proxy_html, but commented the line for this prototype. Inflating and deflating requires extra processing time. Considering that most reverse proxy scenarios involve content inside a closed network in very close proximity, the performance degradation caused by wasted CPU cycles will not likely be recovered through the network benefit of compression.

NOTE
The document at http://www.apachetutor.org/ admin/reverseproxies contains great information describing how to configure the Apache web server as a reverse proxy server.

Creating Reverse Proxy Rules

The reverse proxy rules presented here are very generic. The point is to help developers get their applications up and running with minimal complexity. This oversimplified configuration could be tuned for better performance. For example, the configuration in this chapter enables HTML rewriting on all Integration Broker Service Operations even though we only want to rewrite URLs from the search results Service Operation. Here are some sample rules that target just the search Service Operation:

```
# Replace <default_local_node> with your PeopleSoft node name
# Replace <server:port> with your web server's host name and port
# number
ProxyPass /PSIGW/RESTListeningConnector/default_local_node\
/BMA_PERS_DIR_SRCH_JQM.v1 http://<server:port>/PSIGW/\
RESTListeningConnector/PSFT_HR/BMA_PERS_DIR_SRCH_JQM.v1

<Location /PSIGW/RESTListeningConnector/<default_local_node>\
/BMA_PERS_DIR_SRCH_JQM.v1 >
    ProxyPassReverse /PSIGW/RESTListeningConnector\
/<default_local_node>/BMA_PERS_DIR_SRCH_JQM.v1
    ProxyHTMLEnable On
    # Replace <server:port> with your server's host name and port
    # number
    ProxyHTMLURLMap http://<server:port>/PSIGW /PSIGW
    RequestHeader   unset   Accept-Encoding

</Location>
```

Restart Apache httpd and then perform a search. For example, try the URL http://localhost/PSIGW/RESTListeningConnector/PSFT_HR/BMA_PERS_DIR_SRCH_JQM.v1?emplidSearch=KU%25&nameSearch=&lastNameSearch=.You should see a rather unattractive, basic HTML list of search results similar to what you saw earlier in Figure 8-14. The only difference should be the host name used to access this content.

Click one of the search result hyperlinks and then look at the address bar. Notice that the URL changed to match the reverse proxy server's host name. Verify that the details page appears as expected; just plain HTML with no styling.

Testing the Reverse Proxied jQuery Mobile Application

Test the jQuery Mobile application by navigating to http://localhost/pdjqm/search.html. You should see the styled jQuery Mobile search page appear just as it did in Chapters 5 and 7. Now search for employees. You should see fully styled results.

Clicking a details link should display the employee's details and picture. Try clicking the profile link. Notice anything different? If you haven't logged into PeopleSoft yet, then clicking the profile hyperlink will cause the web browser to prompt you for your PeopleSoft credentials. I know I am repeating myself but this is an important point: The ability to apply different security rules to content is a critical difference between the iScript solution from Chapter 7 and the Service Operation solution presented in this chapter. Through configuration, we were able to provide anonymous access to browse the personnel directory and then require authentication for sensitive information. The iScript alternative, on the other hand, required authentication before a user could access the search page.

AngularJS with the RESTListeningConnector

Integrating AngularJS with the RESTListeningConnector is similar to the jQuery Mobile solution but with one difference: Our Service Operations will populate Document definitions and return JSON results.

Creating Message Definitions

The jQuery Mobile solution presented earlier in this chapter required Message definitions in order to map URI variables into Document definitions. We will reuse those same Message definitions for our AngularJS URIs and then create new Messages for the JSON responses.

Defining the Results Document Message Definition

Log into your PeopleSoft online application and navigate to PeopleTools | Integration Broker | Integration Setup | Messages. Create a new Message definition using the values from Table 8-3.

Field Label	Value
Type	Document
Message Name	BMA_PERS_DIR_SRCH_RESULTS
Message Version	v1
Package	BMA_PERSONNEL_DIRECTORY
Document	SEARCH_RESULTS
Version	v1

TABLE 8-3. *BMA_PERS_DIR_SRCH_RESULTS Message values*

Field Label	Value
Type	Document
Message Name	BMA_PERS_DIR_DETAILS_PARMS
Message Version	v1
Package	BMA_PERSONNEL_DIRECTORY
Document	EMPLID
Version	v1

TABLE 8-4. *BMA_PERS_DIR_DETAILS_PARMS Message values*

Defining the Details Parameter Document Message Definition

Create another message definition named BMA_PERS_DIR_DETAILS_PARMS using the values from Table 8-4. Remember to save your new Message definition.

Defining the Details Document Message Definition

Return to the Messages component one last time to create the BMA_PERS_DIR_DETAILS Message definition. Use the values from Table 8-5.

REST Service Operations

Just like the jQuery Mobile application, let's create some Service Operations for our AngularJS derivative.

Defining the Personnel Directory Service

Log into your PeopleSoft online application and navigate to PeopleTools | Integration Broker | Integration Setup | Services. On the Service search page, click the Add a New Value link that is to the right of the Service search box. Now that you are in Add

Field Label	Value
Type	Document
Message Name	BMA_PERS_DIR_DETAILS
Message Version	v1
Package	BMA_PERSONNEL_DIRECTORY
Document	DETAILS
Version	v1

TABLE 8-5. *BMA_PERS_DIR_DETAILS Message values*

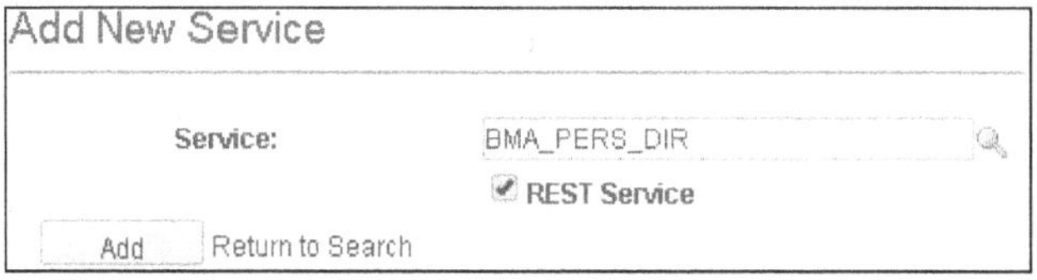

FIGURE 8-22. *Adding a Service*

mode, name the new Service BMA_PERS_DIR and check the REST Service checkbox. Figure 8-22 is a screenshot of the Add Service dialog. Click the Add button to define this Service and its related Service Operations.

Set the Service definition Description field value to Personnel Directory and ensure that both the REST Service Type and Is Provider checkboxes are checked. Figure 8-23 is a screenshot of the Service definition. Click the Save button located in the lower left corner of the page.

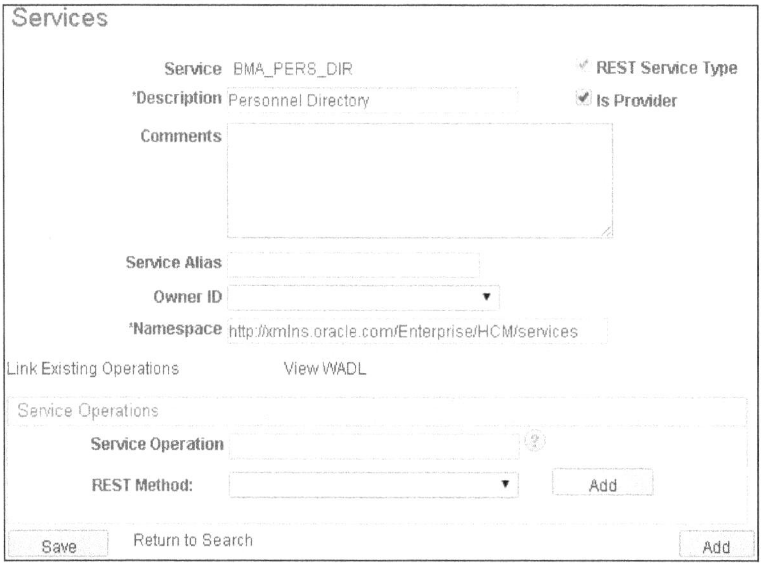

FIGURE 8-23. *Service definition*

FIGURE 8-24. *BMA_PERS_DIR_ SEARCH Service Operation definition*

Defining the Search Service Operation

The search request page will submit search parameters to PeopleSoft and expects to receive a list of matching results. Service Operations are the metadata definitions Integration Broker uses to map incoming requests to response handlers.

Search Service Operation General Settings While still viewing the BMA_PERS_ DIR Service definition, move down to the Service Operations group box and enter BMA_PERS_DIR_SEARCH. From the REST Method drop-down box, select Get. Figure 8-24 is a screenshot of the Service Operation definition.

Next, click the Add button that is to the right of the REST method drop-down box (not the Add button located at the bottom of the screen). This will take you to the Service Operation definition page.

In the Service Operation definition component, set the description to Person directory search. The top half of the BMA_PERS_DIR_SEARCH_GET Service Operation will look similar to Figure 8-25.

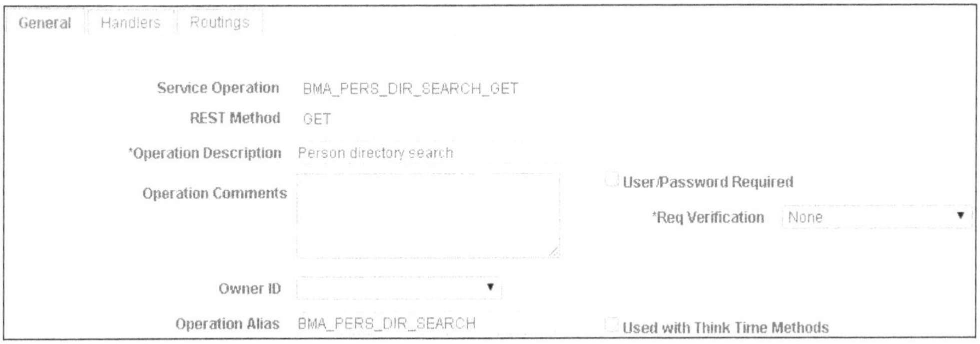

FIGURE 8-25. *Top half of Service Operation definition*

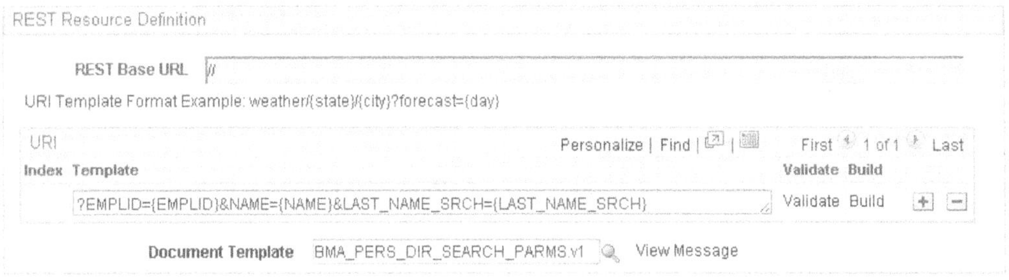

FIGURE 8-26. *REST Resource Definition*

Search Service Operation URI Definition Move down to the REST Resource Definition area of the Service Operation definition. We use this region to map the Service Operation URI pattern to a Document's structural properties. We are actually going to start at the bottom of this group box and work our way to the top. In the Document Template field, select the `BMA_PERS_DIR_SEARCH_PARMS.v1` message. This is the message encompassing our search parameters Document. Enter the following for the Template URI: `?EMPLID={EMPLID}&NAME={NAME}&LAST_NAME_SRCH={LAST_NAME_SRCH}`. Figure 8-26 is a screenshot of the REST Resource Definition prior to save (after saving, it will show additional information).

Search Service Operation Response Definition After configuring the request portion of the Service Operation, we continue to the response metadata. Move down the page to the Default Service Operation Version information. Complete this section as shown in Figure 8-27. Enter `v1` in the Version field and `Version 1` in the Version

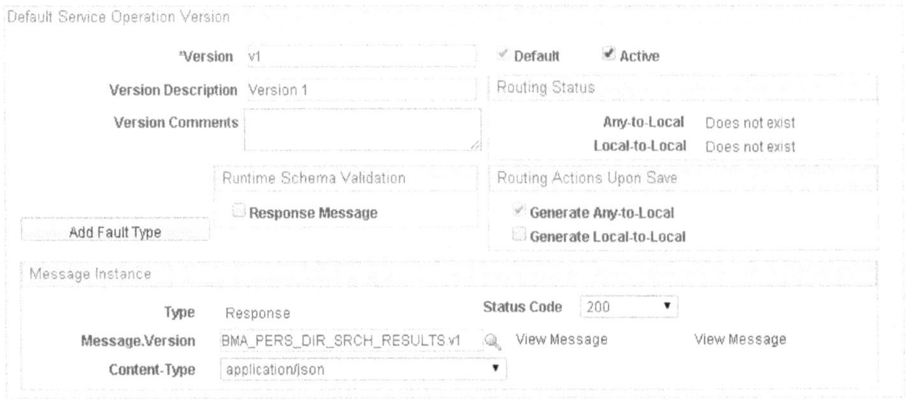

FIGURE 8-27. *BMA_PERS_DIR_SEARCH_GET Service Operation Version*

Description field. For the Message Instance section, enter `BMA_PERS_DIR_SRCH_`
`RESULTS.v1` into the Message.Version field and choose `application/json` for
the Content-Type.

NOTE
*If you are using PeopleTools 8.52, you may choose
the* `application/xml` *content type instead of*
`application/json`.

Save your Service Operation before continuing. After saving, move back to the
top and click the Service Operation Security link. Add a permission list for which
you have access so you can test this Service Operation. If you are using demo data
in a demo system, then add either permission list `PTPT1000` or `PTPT1200`.

Search Service Operation Handler PeopleCode   Launch Application Designer and
create a new Application Package named `BMA_PERS_DIR`. To this new Application
Package, add an Application Class named `SearchRequestHandler`. Open the
`SearchRequestHandler` Application Class PeopleCode editor and enter the
following Service Operation stub handler. All Service Operation handlers start with
this same boilerplate code.

```
import PS_PT:Integration:IRequestHandler;

class SearchRequestHandler implements
        PS_PT:Integration:IRequestHandler
   method OnRequest(&MSG As Message) Returns Message;
   method OnError(&MSG As Message) Returns string;
end-class;

method OnRequest
   /+ &MSG as Message +/
   /+ Returns Message +/
   /+ Extends/implements
        PS_PT:Integration:IRequestHandler.OnRequest +/
   Return null;
end-method;

method OnError
   /+ &MSG as Message +/
   /+ Returns String +/
   /+ Extends/implements PS_PT:Integration:IRequestHandler.OnError +/
   Return "He's dead, Jim";
end-method;
```

Our Service Operation–specific code goes inside the `OnRequest` method. Let's build the OnRequest method a few segments at a time. First, let's write some code to access the incoming request parameters:

```
REM ** read parameters from URI using a document;
Local Compound &parmCom = &MSG.GetURIDocument().DocumentElement;
Local string &emplidParm =
      &parmCom.GetPropertyByName("EMPLID").value;
Local string &nameParm = &parmCom.GetPropertyByName("NAME").value;
Local string &nameSrchParm =
      &parmCom.GetPropertyByName("LAST_NAME_SRCH").value;
```

Notice the hierarchical structure of a Document. First, we start with the request Message. From there we traverse into the URI Document. The URI Document was described in our Service Operation metadata using the `BMA_PERS_DIR_SEARCH_PARMS.v1` Document Template. Next, we traverse into the root Compound object—the object containing the three URI query string values: `EMPLID`, `NAME`, and `LAST_NAME_SRCH`.

Now let's add a code fragment that declares our Response Message and Document structure:

```
REM ** write response to a document;
Local Message &response = CreateMessage(
      Operation.BMA_PERS_DIR_SEARCH_GET, %IntBroker_Response);
Local Compound &responseCom =
      &response.GetDocument().DocumentElement;

Local Collection &items =
      &responseCom.GetPropertyByName("RESULTS");
Local Compound &resultItem;
Local boolean &result;
```

The REST response variables and Document declarations look very similar to the request PeopleCode above. This is because we are working with the exact same types of definitions. Documents have no concept of request or response. They are simply structural containers. There is one key difference between our request and response PeopleCode: the response includes a `Collection` definition. Our search results may contain multiple rows. We must add each row to the response collection.

The next fragment contains the same variable declarations as Chapter 7. Add the following code to your `OnRequest` method:

```
REM ** build SQL based on parameters -- careful of SQL injection!!;
Local array of any &sqlParms = CreateArrayAny();
Local array of string &criteriaComponents = CreateArrayRept("", 0);
Local string &sql = FetchSQL(SQL.BMA_PERSON_SRCH);
Local string &whereClause;
```

Notice that this code fragment contains two arrays. The first one is for our SQL bind values (`&sqlParms`). The second is for our dynamic SQL where clause (`&criteriaComponents`). This second array exhibits a string builder design pattern that I use when assembling text fragments. Later you will see how we use the Array `Join` method to connect these fragments into a single string.

This code fragment also demonstrates the use of the lesser known function `FetchSQL`. The `FetchSQL` function returns the SQL statement stored in a PeopleTools SQL definition. Best practices recommend that we store SQL statements in SQL definitions, not as text in PeopleCode definitions. The `FetchSQL` function allows us to retrieve the SQL fragment we previously stored so we can embellish it with a very important, dynamic SQL where clause.

Let's finish our variable declarations by adding variables corresponding to our SQL select columns:

```
REM ** query and column variables;
Local SQL &cursor;
Local string &emplid;
Local string &name;
Local string &nameSrch;
```

The next step is to construct a dynamic SQL where clause. This code is very similar to the Chapter 7 search iScript PeopleCode.

```
REM ** build a WHERE clause;
If (All(&emplidParm)) Then
   &sqlParms.Push(&emplidParm);
   &criteriaComponents.Push("EMPLID LIKE :" | &sqlParms.Len |
      " %Concat '%'");
End-If;

If (All(&nameParm)) Then
   &sqlParms.Push(&nameParm);
   &criteriaComponents.Push("NAME LIKE :" | &sqlParms.Len |
      " %Concat '%'");
End-If;

If (All(&nameSrchParm)) Then
   &sqlParms.Push(&nameSrchParm);
   &criteriaComponents.Push("LAST_NAME_SRCH LIKE :" |
      &sqlParms.Len | " %Concat '%'");
End-If;

&whereClause = &criteriaComponents.Join(" AND ", "", "");

If (All(&whereClause)) Then
   &whereClause = " WHERE " | &whereClause;
End-If;
```

This code fragment checks each parameter for a value. If the parameter has a value, then the value is added to the collection of bind values and the represented field is added to the SQL where clause. When building dynamic SQL statements, it is critical that we don't append any information that came from the request. In the code above, you will see that I used the database platform independent meta-SQL `%Concat`. This is another PeopleTools best practice. Whenever possible, avoid using platform-specific constructs to improve cross-platform compatibility and avoid vendor lock-in. Here we are using the database-specific concatenation operator to add a wildcard search character to the end of the search string. For this scenario, we are assuming that a user intended a *begins with* type of search. We could give the user more control over the results by removing this wildcard concatenation and expect the user to enter wildcards where desired.

As a final step, let's iterate over the SQL results and append matching rows to the response:

```
REM ** iterate over rows, adding to response;
&cursor = CreateSQL(&sql | &whereClause, &sqlParms);

While &cursor.Fetch(&emplid, &name, &nameSrch);
   &resultItem = &items.CreateItem();
   &resultItem.GetPropertyByName("EMPLID").Value = &emplid;
   &resultItem.GetPropertyByName("NAME").Value = &name;
   &resultItem.GetPropertyByName("LAST_NAME_SRCH").Value =
        &nameSrch;
   &result = &items.AppendItem(&resultItem);
End-While;

Return &response;
```

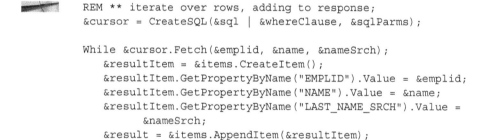

NOTE
The complete code listing is available from this book's download site as described in the introduction.

Search Service Operation Handler Metadata   While still viewing the BMA_PERS_ DIR_SEARCH_GET Service Operation, switch to the Handlers tab. Within the Handlers section, enter a Name, select the On Request Type and Application Class Implementation. The name you enter within this grid is not important. After entering the Application Class details, the component will automatically set the Name field to REQUESTHDLR. Figure 8-28 is a screenshot of the Handlers tab.

Click the Details link to select an Application Class. Set the Description to Search request handler, the Package Name to BMA_PERS_DIR, the Path to :, the Class ID to SearchRequestHandler, and the Method to OnRequest. Save the Service Operation before continuing.

| General | Handlers | Routings |

Service Operation	BMA_PERS_DIR_SEARCH_GET
Default Version	v1
Operation Type	Synchronous

Handlers   Personalize | Find | View All | | First   1 of 1   Last

	*Name	*Type	Sequence	*Implementation	*Status		
1	REQUESTHDLR	On Request		Application Class	Active ▼	Details	＋ －

FIGURE 8-28. *Screenshot of the Handlers overview tab*

Testing the Search Service Operation We now have enough information to test the BMA_PERS_DIR_SEARCH_GET Service Operation. From the General tab of the Service Operation, select the REST Base URL and the URI Template. Concatenate these two values into a single string and then replace each of the template bracketed items with a real value. Here is a sample URL from the HCM 9.2 demo image: http://hr92dm05:8000/PSIGW/RESTListeningConnector/PSFT_HR/BMA_PERS_DIR_SEARCH.v1/?EMPLID=KU00&NAME=A&LAST_NAME_SRCH=S. In my demo image, this URL returns the following JSON (formatting from http://jsonlint.com/):

```
{
    "SEARCH_RESULTS": {
        "SEARCH_FIELDS": [
            {
                "EMPLID": "KU0010",
                "NAME": "Antonio Santos",
                "LAST_NAME_SRCH": "SANTOS"
            },
            {
                "EMPLID": "KU0032",
                "NAME": "Alice Summer",
                "LAST_NAME_SRCH": "SUMMER"
            }
        ]
    }
}
```

Let's try one more test before moving onto the next Service Operation. In your URL, eliminate values for each of the fields except EMPLID. For the EMPLID field, enter a full EMPLID. From the example results above, I chose KU0010. Here is my sample URL: http://hr92dm05:8000/PSIGW/RESTListeningConnector/PSFT_HR/ BMA_PERS_DIR_SEARCH.v1/?EMPLID=KU0010&NAME=&LAST_NAME_SRCH=. Here is the response:

```
{
    "SEARCH_RESULTS": {
        "SEARCH_FIELDS": {
            "EMPLID": "KU0010",
            "NAME": "Antonio Santos",
            "LAST_NAME_SRCH": "SANTOS"
        }
    }
}
```

Compare this to the prior response. Specifically, look at the JavaScript notation immediately following the SEARCH_FIELDS property declaration. The prior results used bracket ([) JavaScript array notation. This last test that only returned one row, however, uses the curly brace ({) JavaScript object notation. If a JSON response includes multiple rows, Integration Broker will use array notation. Otherwise, it will use object notation. It does not matter that the underlying Document specifies that the SEARCH_FIELDS Compound is a member of a Collection.

Search Service Operation Optional Parameters   Let's finish this Service Operation definition by creating URI templates for each of the optional query string parameters. Add the following URI templates:

- ?EMPLID={EMPLID}

- ?EMPLID={EMPLID}&NAME={NAME}

- ?EMPLID={EMPLID}&LAST_NAME_SRCH={LAST_NAME_SRCH}

- ?NAME={NAME}

- ?NAME={NAME}&LAST_NAME_SRCH={LAST_NAME_SRCH}

- ?LAST_NAME_SRCH={LAST_NAME_SRCH}

Content-Type Extra Credit   Just for fun, return to your Service Operation and change the Message Instance Content Type to application/xml and rerun your test in the browser. Notice that the response is now XML. This is one of the benefits of using Documents to model data: It abstracts the rendered data format from the Document structure. Be sure to change the response content type back to application/ json before continuing.

Defining the Details Service Operation

Return to the `BMA_PERS_DIR` Service definition and add a new Service Operation named `BMA_PERS_DIR_DETAILS` that uses the Get REST Method. When the Service Operation definition appears, set the description to `Personnel Directory Details`. Move down to the URI section and select the BMA_PERS_DIR_DETAILS_PARMS.v1 Document Template. For the URI template, enter `{EMPLID}`. The URI template has the same values as the jQuery Mobile Details Service Operation described earlier in this chapter and portrayed in Figure 8-5.

Move to the end of the Service Operation definition and select the response message `BMA_PERS_DIR_DETAILS.v1`. Set the Response Content Type to `application/json`. Save, and then return to the top of the Service Operation to click the Service Operation Security link. For testing purposes, add this Service Operation to the PTPT1000 and PTPT1200 permission lists.

Details Service Operation Handler   Launch Application Designer and open the Application Package `BMA_PERS_DIR`. Add the new Application Class `DetailsRequestHandler`. To the PeopleCode editor, add the following code:

```
import PS_PT:Integration:IRequestHandler;

class DetailsRequestHandler implements
        PS_PT:Integration:IRequestHandler
   method OnRequest(&MSG As Message) Returns Message;
   method OnError(&MSG As Message) Returns string;
end-class;

method OnRequest
   /+ &MSG as Message +/
   /+ Returns Message +/
   /+ Extends/implements
        PS_PT:Integration:IRequestHandler.OnRequest +/

   REM ** read parameters from URI using a document;
   Local Compound &parmCom = &MSG.GetURIDocument().DocumentElement;
   Local string &emplid = &parmCom.GetPropertyByName("EMPLID").value;

   REM ** write response to a document;
   Local Message &response = CreateMessage(
        Operation.BMA_PERS_DIR_DETAILS_GET, %IntBroker_Response);
   Local Compound &responseCom =
        &response.GetDocument().DocumentElement;
```

```
    Local string &NAME;
    Local string &ADDRESS1;
    Local string &CITY;
    Local string &STATE;
    Local string &POSTAL;
    Local string &COUNTRY;
    Local string &COUNTRY_CODE;
    Local string &PHONE;

    SQLExec(SQL.BMA_PERSON_DETAILS, &emplid, &NAME, &ADDRESS1, &CITY,
            &STATE, &POSTAL, &COUNTRY, &COUNTRY_CODE, &PHONE);

    &responseCom.GetPropertyByName("EMPLID").Value = &emplid;
    &responseCom.GetPropertyByName("NAME").Value = &NAME;
    &responseCom.GetPropertyByName("ADDRESS1").Value = &ADDRESS1;
    &responseCom.GetPropertyByName("CITY").Value = &CITY;
    &responseCom.GetPropertyByName("STATE").Value = &STATE;
    &responseCom.GetPropertyByName("POSTAL").Value = &POSTAL;
    &responseCom.GetPropertyByName("COUNTRY").Value = &COUNTRY;
    &responseCom.GetPropertyByName("COUNTRY_CODE").Value =
            &COUNTRY_CODE;
    &responseCom.GetPropertyByName("PHONE").Value = &PHONE;

    Return &response;
end-method;

method OnError
    /+ &MSG as Message +/
    /+ Returns String +/
    /+ Extends/implements PS_PT:Integration:IRequestHandler.OnError +/
    Return "He's dead, Jim";
end-method;
```

Return to the Service Operation online and create an OnRequest Application Class handler with the following details.

Package Name: `BMA_PERS_DIR`

Path: " : "

Class ID: `DetailsRequestHandler`

Method: `OnRequest`

Test the Service Operation by using a URL similar to http://hr92dm05:8000/PSIGW/RESTListeningConnector/PSFT_HR/BMA_PERS_DIR_DETAILS.v1/KU0007. Here is a sample template: http://<server>:<port>/PSIGW/RESTListeningConnector/<default_local_node>/BMA_PERS_DIR_DETAILS.v1/<employee_id>. Be sure to update the server name, port, node, and employee ID to match your system data. Your results should appear similar to the following:

```json
{
    "DETAILS": {
        "EMPLID": "KU0007",
        "NAME": "Locherty,Betty",
        "ADDRESS1": "643 Robinson St",
        "CITY": "Buffalo",
        "STATE": "NY",
        "POSTAL": "74940",
        "COUNTRY": "USA",
        "COUNTRY_CODE": "",
        "PHONE": "555/123-4567"
    }
}
```

Creating an Employee Photo Service

For the detail view photo we could add a base64 member to the details Document, but that doesn't seem quite right considering the potential length of a base64-encoded photo. Instead, let's create a new service that returns the same base64 data generated by our earlier jQuery Mobile employee photo method.

From the BMA_PERS_DIR service, create the Service Operation BMA_PERS_DIR_PHOTO using the Get REST Method. The Document and URI template are the same as the BMA_PERS_DIR_DETAILS Service Operation. The Document template is BMA_PERS_DIR_DETAILS_PARMS.v1 and the URI is {EMPLID}.

For the response message we will just return plain text so set the Content Type to text/plain. We can use the IB_GENERIC_REST.V1 message since our response has no structure. Save, and then return to the top to add permission lists through the Service Operation Security hyperlink.

Employee Photo Service Operation Handler   In Application Designer, open the BMA_PERS_DIR Application Package and add the class PhotoRequestHandler. Open the PeopleCode event editor and enter the following PeopleCode:

```
import BMA_PERS_DIR_JQM:DetailsRequestHandler;
import PS_PT:Integration:IRequestHandler;

class PhotoRequestHandler implements PS_PT:Integration:IRequestHandler
   method OnRequest(&MSG As Message) Returns Message;
   method OnError(&MSG As Message) Returns string;
end-class;

method OnRequest
   /+ &MSG as Message +/
   /+ Returns Message +/
   /+ Extends/implements
```

```
            PS_PT:Integration:IRequestHandler.OnRequest +/

   REM ** read parameters from URI using a document;
   Local Compound &parmCom = &MSG.GetURIDocument().DocumentElement;
   Local string &emplid = &parmCom.GetPropertyByName("EMPLID").value;

   REM ** write response to a document;
   Local Message &response = CreateMessage(
         Operation.BMA_PERS_DIR_PHOTO_GET, %IntBroker_Response);

   Local BMA_PERS_DIR_JQM:DetailsRequestHandler &photoEncoder =
         create BMA_PERS_DIR_JQM:DetailsRequestHandler();

   Local boolean &tmp = &response.SetContentString(
         &photoEncoder.getPhotoDataUrl(&emplid));

   Return &response;

end-method;

method OnError
   /+ &MSG as Message +/
   /+ Returns String +/
   /+ Extends/implements PS_PT:Integration:IRequestHandler.OnError +/
   Return "He's dead, Jim";
end-method;
```

Return to the BMA_PERS_PHOTO_GET Service Operation and switch to the Handlers tab. Add an On Request Application Class handler. In the Application Class details enter the following:

Package Name: BMA_PERS_DIR

Path: ":"

Class ID: PhotoRequestHander

Method: OnRequest

Test the Service Operation using a URL similar to http://hr92dm05:8000/PSIGW/RESTListeningConnector/PSFT_HR/BMA_PERS_DIR_PHOTO.v1/KU0007. Your browser should display a lot of unintelligible base64 data.

Defining the Profile Service
The profile service differs from the details service in that it uses the employee ID of the logged-in user. Let's create the profile service now. Return to the Service BMA_PERS_DIR definition and create a Get Service Operation named BMA_PERS_DIR_

PROFILE. Set the description to something meaningful such as `Person directory profile`. Check the User/Password Required checkbox and set the Req Verification to `Basic Authentication`.

Moving down to the REST Resource Definition group box, set the URI template to the text: `profile`. This REST Service Operation has no parameters, and, therefore no Document Template or complex URIs.

In the Default Service Operation Version section set the Message.Version to `BMA_PERS_DIR_DETAILS.v1`. Next, set the Content-Type to `application/json`. Save the Service Operation.

After saving the Service Operation, the Service Operation Security link will appear. Be sure to add a permission list to which your test user belongs. PTPT1000 are PTPT1200 common permission lists. They work great when testing content from a book, but I don't recommend using them to deploy a real solution.

Profile Service Operation Handler   Return to Application Designer to write a Service Operation handler for the profile Service Operation. This will be really easy because it is the same code as the `DetailsRequestHandler`, but without parameters. Open the `BMA_PERS_DIR` Application Package and add the class `ProfileRequestHandler`. Save the Application Package and then open the `ProfileRequestHandler` PeopleCode editor. Enter the following PeopleCode. Alternatively, if you already have the `DetailsRequestHandler` PeopleCode you can copy the `DetailsRequestHandler` and implement the changes noted in bold text.

```
import PS_PT:Integration:IRequestHandler;

class ProfileRequestHandler implements
        PS_PT:Integration:IRequestHandler
   method OnRequest(&MSG As Message) Returns Message;
   method OnError(&MSG As Message) Returns string;
end-class;

method OnRequest
   /+ &MSG as Message +/
   /+ Returns Message +/
   /+ Extends/implements PS_PT:Integration:IRequestHandler.OnRequest +/

   REM ** write response to a document;
   Local Message &response = CreateMessage(
        Operation.BMA_PERS_DIR_PROFILE_GET, %IntBroker_Response);
   Local Compound &responseCom =
        &response.GetDocument().DocumentElement;

   Local string &NAME;
   Local string &ADDRESS1;
```

```
    Local string &CITY;
    Local string &STATE;
    Local string &POSTAL;
    Local string &COUNTRY;
    Local string &COUNTRY_CODE;
    Local string &PHONE;

    SQLExec(SQL.BMA_PERSON_DETAILS, %EmployeeId, &NAME, &ADDRESS1,
        &CITY, &STATE, &POSTAL, &COUNTRY, &COUNTRY_CODE, &PHONE);

    &responseCom.GetPropertyByName("EMPLID").Value = %EmployeeId;
    &responseCom.GetPropertyByName("NAME").Value = &NAME;
    &responseCom.GetPropertyByName("ADDRESS1").Value = &ADDRESS1;
    &responseCom.GetPropertyByName("CITY").Value = &CITY;
    &responseCom.GetPropertyByName("STATE").Value = &STATE;
    &responseCom.GetPropertyByName("POSTAL").Value = &POSTAL;
    &responseCom.GetPropertyByName("COUNTRY").Value = &COUNTRY;
    &responseCom.GetPropertyByName("COUNTRY_CODE").Value =
        &COUNTRY_CODE;
    &responseCom.GetPropertyByName("PHONE").Value = &PHONE;

    Return &response;
end-method;

method OnError
    /+ &MSG as Message +/
    /+ Returns String +/
    /+ Extends/implements PS_PT:Integration:IRequestHandler.OnError +/
    Return "He's dead, Jim";
end-method;
```

Composition over Inheritance

The `DetailsRequestHandler` and `ProfileRequestHandler` classes contain nearly identical code. The DRY (don't repeat yourself) principle suggests that we move this common code into a single location and then parameterize it. Object-oriented programming best practices offer three options:

- Move the code into a base class using inheritance.
- Move the code into a completely separate, unrelated class.
- Move the common code into a parameterized FUNCLIB function.

Because Integration Broker handlers have to directly implement the interface `PS_PT:Integration:IRequestHandler` we can't actually implement inheritance, leaving composition as our only option. Composition forces us to think differently and generally results in better code. Here is how Wikipedia describes composition:

> Composition over inheritance (or Composite Reuse Principle) in object-oriented programming is a technique by which classes may achieve polymorphic behavior and code reuse by containing other classes that implement the desired functionality instead of through inheritance (http://en.wikipedia.org/wiki/Composition_over_inheritance).

Just because we are talking about object-oriented programming doesn't mean we have to ignore functional design patterns. Since our OnRequest PeopleCode is stateless, we could just as easily use a FUNCLIB function to implement the handler's common code.

Save the Application Package and Class and then return to the BMA_PERS_DIR_ PROFILE_GET Service Operation online. Switch to the Handlers tab and fill in the Handlers table as we have for every other Service Operation. Give the handler a name (REQUESTHDLR seems appropriate), set the Type to On Request, and choose Application Class for the Implementation. Click the Details link and enter the following:

Package Name: BMA_PERS_DIR

Path: ":"

Class ID: ProfileRequestHandler

Method: OnRequest

After saving, test the Service Operation by visiting your environments version of the URL: http://hr92dm05:8000/PSIGW/RESTListeningConnector/PSFT_HR/BMA_ PERS_DIR_PROFILE.v1/profile (change the server, port, and node to match your URL).

Reverse Proxying the AngularJS Prototype

We already created reverse proxy rules for Integration Broker when we created the proxy.conf file. You can test the existing proxy configuration with the following URLs. Be sure to change the node to match your environment's node name (node name is in bold type):

- http://localhost/PSIGW/RESTListeningConnector/**PSFT_HR**/BMA_PERS_DIR_ SEARCH.v1?EMPLID=KU00&NAME=A

- http://localhost/PSIGW/RESTListeningConnector/**PSFT_HR**/BMA_PERS_DIR_ DETAILS.v1/KU0007

- http://localhost/PSIGW/RESTListeningConnector/**PSFT_HR**/BMA_PERS_DIR_
  PHOTO.v1/KU0007

- http://localhost/PSIGW/RESTListeningConnector/**PSFT_HR**/BMA_PERS_DIR_
  PROFILE.v1/profile

Updating the AngularJS Project's Source Code

Open PersonnelDirectory-ajs project in NetBeans and then locate the services.js and
controllers.js files. Both of these files contain JavaScript that points to static text files.
We need to replace the static text file references with references to our new Integration
Broker REST Services

Controllers.js   Find the DetailsCtrl Controller and update the URL as shown in the
following code listing. Required code changes are in bold text:

```
.controller('DetailsCtrl', [
   '$scope',
   '$routeParams',
   '$http',
   function($scope, $routeParams, $http) {
      // view the route parameters in your console by uncommenting
      // the following:
      // console.log($routeParams);
      $http.get('/PSIGW/RESTListeningConnector/PSFT_HR/
BMA_PERS_DIR_DETAILS.v1/' + $routeParams.EMPLID)
            .then(function(response) {
               // view the response object by uncommenting the following:
               // console.log(response);
               // closure -- updating $scope from outer function
               $scope.details = response.data.DETAILS;
            });
      $http.get('/PSIGW/RESTListeningConnector/PSFT_HR/
BMA_PERS_DIR_PHOTO.v1/' + $routeParams.EMPLID)
            .then(function(response) {
               $scope.photo = response.data;
            });
   }])
```

Did you notice that I snuck in some code to call the photo service as well? Let's
update the partials/details.html file to use the new `photo` scope field:

```
<img ng-src="{{photo}}" class="avatar"
    alt="{{details.NAME}}'s Photo">
```

NOTE
I switched from the `src` attribute to the `ng-src` attribute. This keeps the browser from attempting to render something until we are ready.

The `ProfileCtrl` controller is very similar to the details controller. Find the ProfileCtrl controller in js/controllers.js and update it as follows:

```
.controller('ProfileCtrl', ['$scope',
  '$routeParams',
  '$http',
  function($scope, $routeParams, $http) {
    $http.get('/PSIGW/RESTListeningConnector/PSFT_HR/
BMA_PERS_DIR_PROFILE.v1/profile')
           .then(function(response) {
              // closure -- updating $scope from outer function
              $scope.profile = response.data.DETAILS;
              $http.get('/PSIGW/RESTListeningConnector/
PSFT_HR/BMA_PERS_DIR_PHOTO.v1/' + $scope.profile.EMPLID)
                    .then(function(response) {
                      $scope.photo = response.data;
                    });
           });

    $scope.save = function() {
      // TODO: implement during Chapters 7 and 8
    };
}]);
```

NOTE
I once again snuck in a call to the photo service. This time, instead of invoking the photo service asynchronously, I intentionally waited for the profile service to return a value. This is because the photo service expects an employee ID, and we don't have the logged-in user employee ID until the profile service returns.

Besides updating the controller, we also need to update the partials/profile.html.

Services.js Open the file js/services.js and find the `SearchService` factory. Inside $http replace the URL `test-data/SEARCH_RESULTS.json` with

/PSIGW/RESTListeningConnector/PSFT_HR/BMA_PERS_DIR_SEARCH.v1.
After changing the URL your code should appear similar to the following fragment:

```
searchService.search = function(parms) {
    var promise = $http({
        method: 'GET',
        url: '/PSIGW/RESTListeningConnector/PSFT_HR/
BMA_PERS_DIR_SEARCH.v1',
        params: parms
    }).then(function(response) {
```

NOTE
As with all URLs presented in this book. Verify site-specific information, such as node names, and update the URL accordingly. For example, if your HRMS default local node is HC92SBX, then replace PSFT_HR with HC92SBX.

Aliasing the AngularJS Project for Apache httpd

Let's make the AngularJS project available to our local Apache web server by creating an alias. From within the c:\apache24\conf\bma\ directory, copy the file pdjqm.conf into pdajs.conf. Now open the new pdajs.conf file and replace each instance of jqm with ajs. Your pdajs.conf file should contain text similar to the following (paths may vary, of course):

```
Alias /pdajs C:/Users/sarah/Documents/NetBeansProjects/
PersonnelDirectory-ajs/app

<Directory "C:/Users/sarah/Documents/NetBeansProjects/
PersonnelDirectory-ajs/app">
  ## directives for older httpd versions
  # Order allow,deny
  # Allow from all

  Require all granted
</Directory>
```

Save the file and restart Apache httpd. Now verify that your AngularJS mobile application works as expected by using your web browser to visit the URL http://localhost/pdajs/. If it does, congratulate yourself on a job well done. If it doesn't work, congratulate yourself anyway because you accomplished a lot in this chapter; now troubleshoot your application using tools such as Firefox Firebug, Chrome developer tools, etc. The JavaScript console and network tabs will show you errors the browser identified, but didn't necessarily tell you about.

Conclusion

In this chapter you learned how to:

- Create REST services that return JSON and HTML.

- Use PeopleSoft Query to create configurable data sources.

- Edit HTML definitions online using the Branding Objects component.

- Configure Apache web server as a reverse proxy.

- Convert database binary objects into base64.

- Wire all of these ideas together to serve both anonymous and secure mobile applications.

PART

III

Constructing Native
Applications

CHAPTER
9

Native Apps for
Best Results

I n this section of the book, you will learn how to create native and hybrid applications. Native applications run on a mobile device and require development using an operating system-specific toolkit. Android native development, for example, requires the Android SDK. Hybrid applications are HTML5 applications that run in a native container and have access to native services, such as geolocation, camera, contacts, and so on. In this part of the book, you will build native and hybrid solutions using

- Eclipse and Android Developer Tools (more commonly referred to as Eclipse + ADT)

- Apache Cordova hybrid containers

- Oracle Mobile Application Framework

Each of these chapters will revolve around the same demo scenario: the Personnel Directory (just in case you forget who works with you). I don't know about you, but I'm getting a little tired of creating personnel directories. So why are we creating more? We are utilizing the same tautological example repeatedly so that we have the opportunity to compare various development patterns. This helps us make an "apples to apples" comparison between mobile technologies. Another good reason for continuing to solve the same problem is that it allows us to leverage the PeopleTools definitions we created in prior chapters so we can focus on the development method and non-PeopleSoft development tools rather than distracting ourselves with new PeopleTools definitions. In Part III we will create a few novel PeopleTools definitions, but the PeopleTools and mobile fundamentals are described in Parts I and II of this book.

Introduction to Part III

Here is what to expect from the remainder of this book.

Chapter 9

In this chapter, you will create a native Android version of the personnel directory. We will use the REST Service Operations we created in Chapter 8 as well as the data model from Chapter 4. We will write code using Eclipse and ADT, and then test our applications with an Android emulator. The primary purpose of Chapter 9 is to teach you how to consume PeopleSoft REST services with the Android SDK.

Chapter 10

Chapter 10 will show you how to build a hybrid mobile application. You will learn how to run the AngularJS mobile application from Chapter 6 (and Chapter 8) in the Apache Cordova/PhoneGap container. We will use the Cordova JavaScript API to access a mobile device camera to upload a *selfie* as an employee photo.

Chapter 11

Oracle has its own hybrid container called Mobile Application Framework (MAF). Rather than building applications in HTML, JavaScript, and CSS, MAF allows developers to create hybrid applications using a combination of Java and declarative constructs. In Chapter 11, you will learn how to use JDeveloper and Oracle MAF to create yet another iteration of the personnel directory.

A word about iOS

What about iOS? Where is the chapter on creating a mobile personnel directory for iPhone and iPad? From a PeopleTools perspective there is no difference between an Android and an iOS application. If you already know how to create iOS applications, then the PeopleTools data and REST service definitions described in Chapters 4 and 8 are all you need to be successful. And, if you aren't familiar with iOS, there are many great online and print resources available for learning iOS development.

NOTE
Chapters 10 and 11 will describe two different ways to create hybrid mobile applications, which are mobile applications that run on both Android and iOS.

Now let's build some high-performance native PeopleSoft apps!

Building a Mobile Android Personnel Directory

Writing about native mobile development is sort of like digging a hole in dry sand. The digger makes progress, but the landscape changes as fast as the laborer's shoveling. With each shovel full, the worker knows that a portion of it will end up back in the hole. I compare this to Android development because the Android application development landscape is constantly changing. Today we build Android applications using Eclipse and the ADT plugin. Before this book goes to print, however, it is likely that developers will be building Android applications using the Android Studio (currently in beta). With this in mind, this chapter will expend the least amount of effort to create a mobile application that connects to a PeopleSoft instance. I will expound those areas that seem static, but minimize those subjects that will likely change. The point of this chapter is not to teach you Android development. Instead, my intention is to show you how to invoke a PeopleSoft REST service from a native Android application.

Why Native?

The most commonly cited reason for choosing native over mobile web or hybrid applications is performance. Within the performance justification, we find network utilization, memory, and CPU overhead, as well as file install size. You can achieve many of these objectives through good mobile web and hybrid application design. Web and hybrid applications, however, live in a container abstracted from the native Android API. Native mobile application development offers a greater level of control that is not possible with the alternatives.

Introduction to Android Development

Even though I said this isn't a book about Android development, let's go ahead and create a simple Android application just to get the feel for the ADT SDK.

Creating a Project

Launch the Eclipse instance you installed in Chapter 1 with Android SDK. I installed mine in C:\apps\adt-bundle-windows-x86_64-20140702\eclipse. When the Eclipse IDE appears, select File | New | Android Application Project from the Eclipse menu bar. In the New Android Application dialog, enter an Application Name such as `HelloAndroid`. The name doesn't matter too much because this is just an example application. The Project and Package Name fields will update automatically to match the Application Name. Figure 9-1 is a screenshot of the New Android Application dialog. Notice the yellow triangle with the exclamation mark? It tells me that I should not use `com.example` as the Package Name prefix. The Package Name is a unique identifier that *must* stay the same throughout the life of the application. I am using com.example, because the HelloAndroid application is an example, and not meant to be deployed anywhere except to an emulator.

Just below the application name, select the device target platform range. The minimum required SDK determines the APIs available to your application. Select the lowest platform you expect to support, but no lower. Selecting a platform too low will limit your development opportunities by reducing the available APIs. Click the Next button to move to the next step in the New Android Application wizard.

In step 2, verify that the Create custom launcher icon, Create activity, and Create Project in Workspace checkboxes are selected. Selecting these checkboxes will create the default application structure required to install and launch our new HelloAndroid application. Figure 9-2 is a screenshot of step 2. Click Next to move onto step 3.

Click the Next button when asked to configure a launcher icon. We will use the default icon configuration for this example. On step 4, select Blank Activity for the activity template and click the Next button. The final step of the wizard allows you to change the name of the activity. Keep the default activity name of `MainActivity`

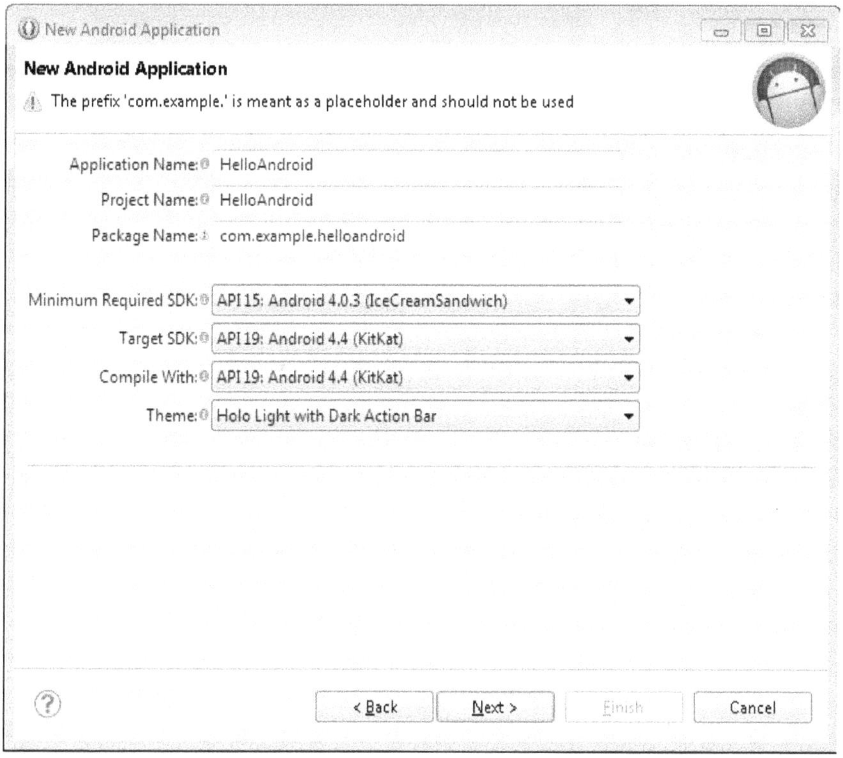

FIGURE 9-1. *New Android Application wizard step 1*

and the default layout name of `activity_main`. Figure 9-3 is a screenshot of the final step of the wizard. Click the Finish button to complete the wizard.

Reviewing the Project

Your new project contains several important files:

- AndroidManifest.xml

- res/layout/activity_main.xml

- res/values/strings.xml

- src/com/example/helloandroid/MainActivity.java

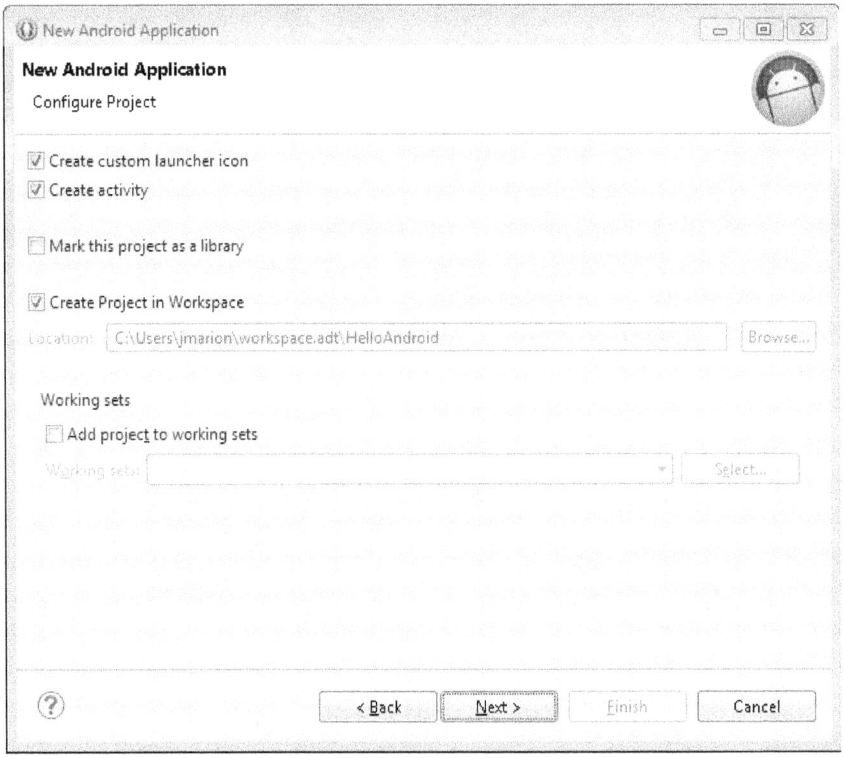

FIGURE 9-2. *New Android Application wizard step 2*

The Android Eclipse ADT plugin contains a different editor for each of these files. The AndriodManifest.xml file contains all of the metadata necessary to run an application including activities and permissions.

The resources folder of an Android project contains images, page designs (called layouts), string tables, and other noncode resources. Specifically review the activity_main.xml layout file. This file describes the content of the application's MainActivity activity. Notice that it contains a single text box containing the text `Hello World`. Rather than hard coding the text, the value Hello World comes from a string resource that exists in file values/strings.xml.

Inside the src folder you will find a file named MainActivity.java. This file contains the Java code required to initialize the activity including specifying the layout definition and any activity specific menu items.

FIGURE 9-3.   *Final step of the New Android Application wizard*

Launching an Application

Launch the HelloAndroid application by selecting Run | Run from the Eclipse menu
bar. When prompted, select Run as Android Application. Eclipse will prompt for the
target device, and then deploy and launch the new HelloAndroid application.
Figure 9-4 is a screenshot of the HelloAndroid application running in a NexusOne
emulator with the WQVGA400 skin.

Networking with Android

Our personnel directory is a little more complex than the HelloAndroid example,
although, not by much. Besides making a few modifications to the layout, the
personnel directory will require external information gathered through a network
connection. Networking is a common Android application task. Many applications,

FIGURE 9-4. *HelloAndroid application running in an emulator*

such as Facebook, LinkedIn, and TripCase use Android networking capabilities to send and receive information. Android includes two HTTP client libraries: `java .net.HttpURLConnection` and Apache `HttpClient`, neither of which is a good fit for mobile development. These are just bare HTTP client protocol handlers that don't consider scheduling, caching, concurrency, and many other factors that make mobile networking unique. Developers building high-performance native applications often write their own networking clients on top of the delivered `HttpClient` and `HttpURLConnection` client libraries. At the 2013 Google I/O conference, Ficus Kirkpatrick of Google introduced the world to a new networking library named Android Volley. Android Volley is designed to promote performance and Android networking best practices with very little code. In this chapter, we will use Android Volley to manage network requests.

Preparing Android Volley
Android Volley exists as a separate project and is not included with the Android developer tools. To use it we need to download and either package it as a Java library (JAR file) or include it in Eclipse as an Android library project. In this chapter, we will choose the latter: include it in Eclipse as an Android library.

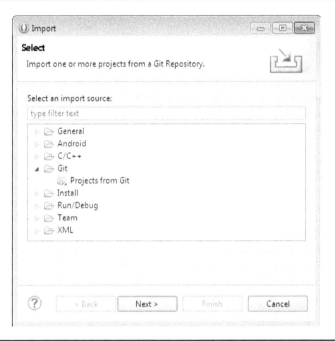

FIGURE 9-5. *Select import source dialog*

Launch the ADT bundled instance of Eclipse (if it is not already running) and select File | Import from the Eclipse menu bar. When the Import dialog appears, select Git | Projects from Git as shown in Figure 9-5. Click Next to continue to the next step.

In step 2, select a repository source, select URI. Click Next to move to step 3. When step 3 appears, enter the URI https://android.googlesource.com/platform/frameworks/volley. Eclipse will automatically fill in the Host and Repository path. Figure 9-6 is a screenshot of repository location dialog. Click Next to move to the Branch Selection dialog

Git repositories can have many branches. We are only interested in the *master* branch. When the Branch Selection dialog appears, select the *master* branch (Tip: Click the Deselect All button, and then just select master). Click Next to move to the Local Destination selection step. Accept the defaults and click Next to move to the Select a project import wizard type step. Select the Import existing projects option as shown in Figure 9-7.

When you click the Next button, Eclipse will present you with a list of projects found within the downloaded Git repository. Select the Volley project and unselect the VolleyTests project. Figure 9-8 is a screenshot of the final step in the import wizard. Click Finish to complete the import wizard.

FIGURE 9-6. *Import Git repository location selection dialog*

NOTE
There is nothing wrong with importing the VolleyTests project along with the Volley project. We just won't be using it. If you already imported it, you can either delete it or ignore it.

As soon as you click finish, Eclipse will process and compile the Volley project. You may see an error appear in the console telling you that Android tools were not able to find the Volley project's res directory. Your error message may appear similar to the following:

```
[2014-11-11 20:35:46 - Volley] ERROR: resource directory
'C:\Users\jmarion\git\volley\res' does not exist
```

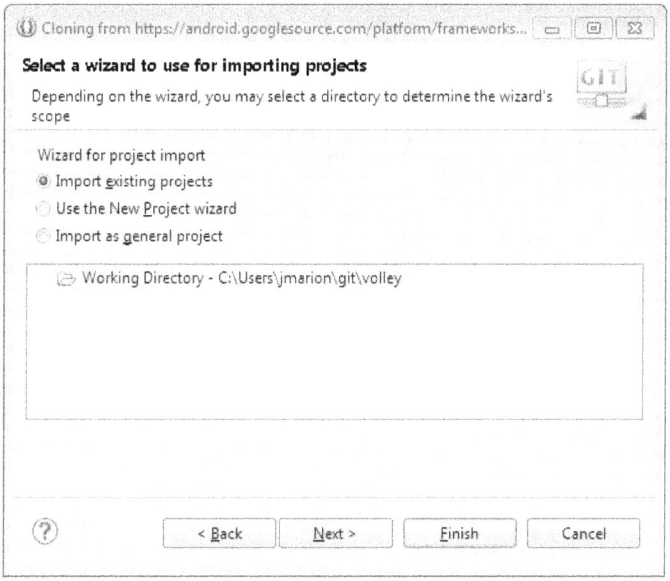

FIGURE 9-7.   *Select a project import wizard type*

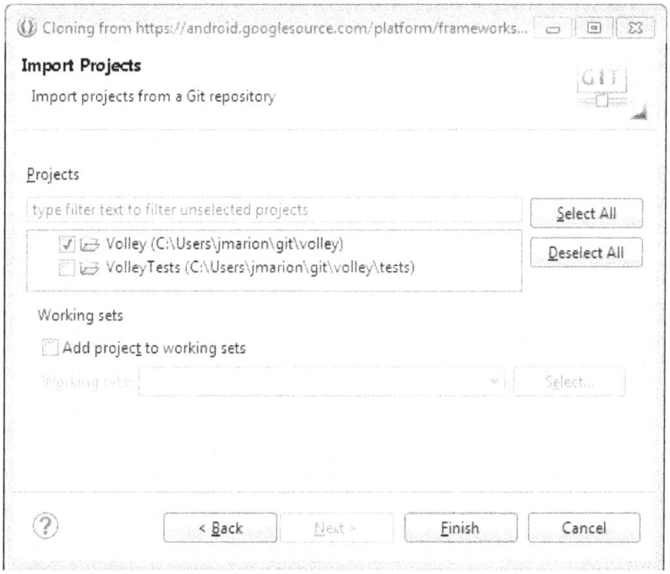

FIGURE 9-8.   *Final step of the import wizard*

Ignore this error. Volley is a library project with no user interface. A container project will supply layouts, string tables, icons, and any other Android resources necessary to create an Android application.

Right-click on the new Volley project and select Properties from the context menu. Find and select the Android item in the list on the left. In the lower right, select the Is Library checkbox to mark this project as an Android library. Figure 9-9 is a screenshot of the properties dialog.

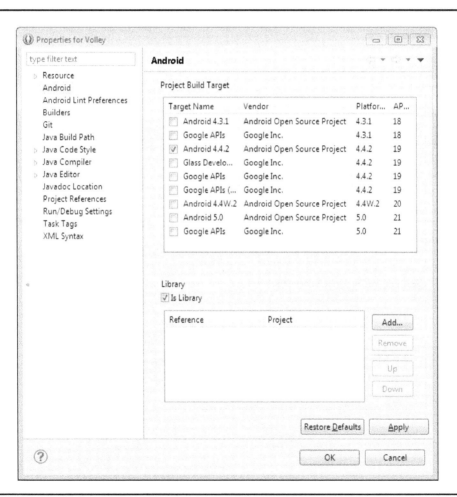

FIGURE 9-9. *Volley Android library properties*

Building a Native Directory

Create a new Android Application Project named PersonnelDirectory. In the New Android Application dialog, allow Eclipse to fill in the Project Name and Package Name details. Specify values for the Minimum, Target, and Compile SDK. I chose IceCreamSandwich for the minimum and KitKat for the Target and Compile SDK. Figure 9-10 is a screenshot of the New Android Application dialog. Click the Next button to move to the next step. Click the Next button for the remainder of the steps, accepting all of the defaults. On the final step, click the Finish button. Just as with our HelloAndroid project, Eclipse will create a project with all of the files necessary to immediately deploy the new application to an Android emulator.

Next, let's associate this project with the Volley library. Right-click on the PersonnelDirectory project node within the Package Explorer and select Properties from the context menu. When the Properties window appears, use the outline on the left to select the Android node. Locate the Library section in the lower half of the

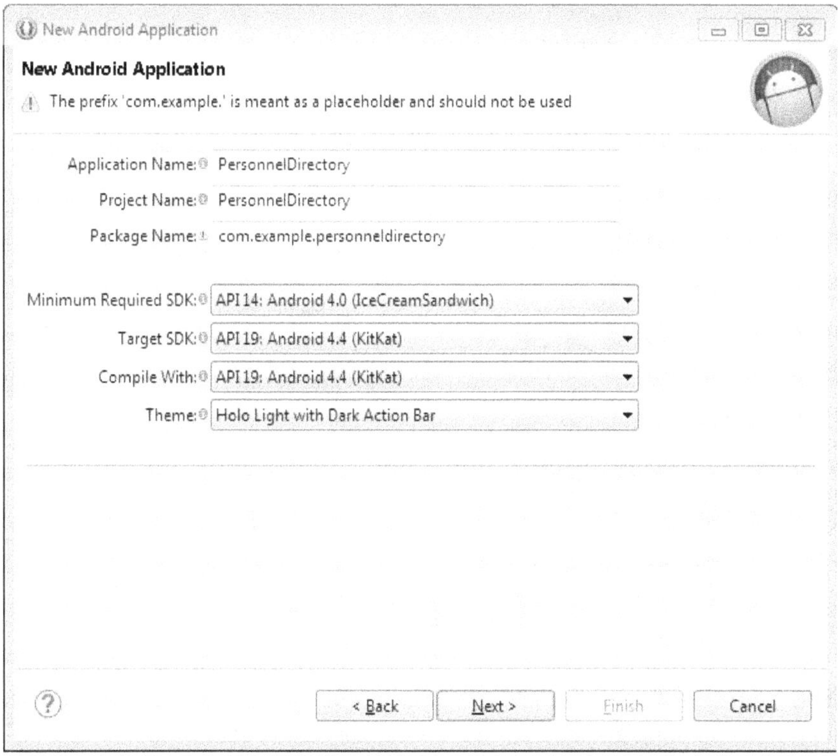

FIGURE 9-10.   *New Android Application dialog*

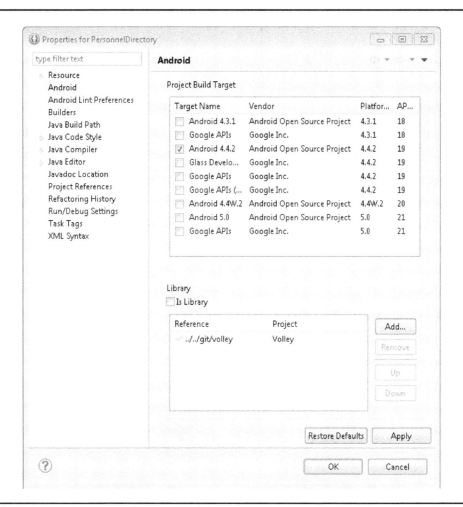

FIGURE 9-11. *Android project properties dialog*

Properties window and use the Add button to select the Volley library. Click OK to save your changes and close the Properties dialog. Figure 9-11 is a screenshot of the Properties window after selecting the Volley library.

Design the Search Layout

You should now be looking at the Graphical Layout tab of the activity_main.xml file. If you are not, locate the res/layout/activity_main.xml file in the Eclipse Package Explorer and then open activity_main.xml. We want to turn activity_main.xml into a search page that resembles Figure 9-12.

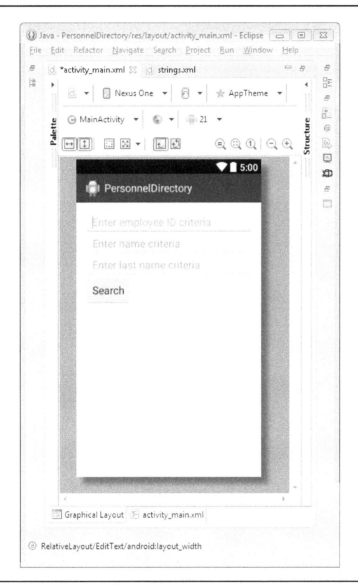

FIGURE 9-12. *activity_main.xml search page*

We can make the current activity_main.xml look like Figure 9-12 by first removing the existing "Hello world" Text view and adding three Plain Text EditText fields to activity_main.xml. After adding the new fields, change the Id property of each field to @+id/emplid_search, @+id/name_search, and @+id/last_

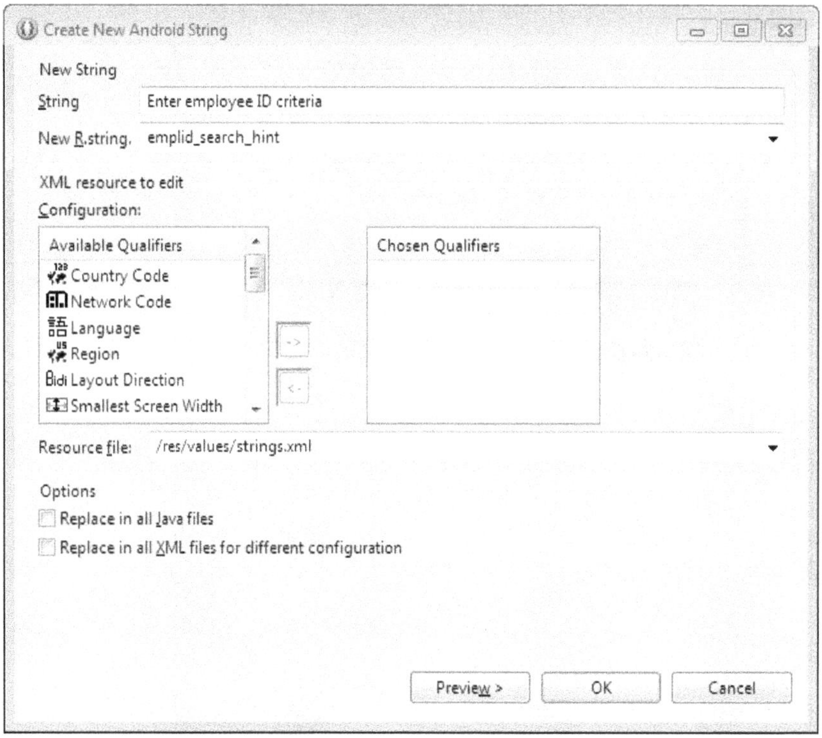

FIGURE 9-13. *Create New Android String dialog*

name_search. When prompted, select Yes to update references. We also need to update the hint text for each field. To change the hint text for a field, select the field in the graphical editor and then find the Hint property in the structure viewer on the right. Click the ellipses button (… three dots) and then click the New String button in the Resource Chooser dialog. The Create New Android String dialog will appear. Enter a string value of Enter employee ID criteria and Resource ID of emplid_search_hint. Figure 9-13 is a screenshot of the Create New Android String dialog.

Click the OK button to save the new string resource. When you return to the Resource chooser, click the OK button again to update the EditText field hint property. Repeat these steps for the remaining EditText fields, substituting the values from Table 9-1.

The final step in creating the search layout is to drag a button from the Palette's form widgets onto the layout just below the last name search field. After dragging a

Field ID	String Value	Resource ID
name_search	Enter name criteria	name_search_hint
last_name_search	Enter last name criteria	last_name_search_hint

TABLE 9-1. *EditText hint values*

new button to the layout, and with the button still selected, find the Text property in the Properties window. Use the ellipses build button to create a new string resource. Set the new string's resource ID (R.string) to `search_button_label` and give it a value of `Search`.

NOTE
We could hard code string values for each display field, but that would be neither reusable nor translatable.

While still viewing the Properties window and with the Search button still selected, find the On Click event. Set the value to `execSearch`. We will create the `execSearch` method later.

Switch to the layout's XML view by clicking the activity_main.xml tab to the right of the Graphical Layout tab. For each EditText element, change the `android:layout_width` attribute value from `wrap_content` to `match_parent`. This will stretch the text field width to match the width of the parent container. The following listing contains the XML used to describe the activity_main.xml layout. The layout_width attribute values are in bold print.

```
<RelativeLayout
        xmlns:android="http://schemas.android.com/apk/res/android"
    xmlns:tools="http://schemas.android.com/tools"
    android:layout_width="match_parent"
    android:layout_height="match_parent"
    android:paddingBottom="@dimen/activity_vertical_margin"
    android:paddingLeft="@dimen/activity_horizontal_margin"
    android:paddingRight="@dimen/activity_horizontal_margin"
    android:paddingTop="@dimen/activity_vertical_margin"
    tools:context="com.example.personneldirectory.MainActivity" >

    <EditText
        android:id="@+id/emplid_search"
        android:layout_width="match_parent"
```

```
        android:layout_height="wrap_content"
        android:layout_alignParentLeft="true"
        android:layout_alignParentTop="true"
        android:ems="10"
        android:hint="@string/emplid_search_hint" >

        <requestFocus />
    </EditText>

    <EditText
        android:id="@+id/name_search"
        android:layout_width="match_parent"
        android:layout_height="wrap_content"
        android:layout_alignParentLeft="true"
        android:layout_below="@+id/emplid_search"
        android:ems="10"
        android:hint="@string/name_search_hint" />

    <EditText
        android:id="@+id/last_name_search"
        android:layout_width="match_parent"
        android:layout_height="wrap_content"
        android:layout_alignParentLeft="true"
        android:layout_below="@+id/name_search"
        android:ems="10"
        android:hint="@string/last_name_search_hint" />

    <Button
        android:id="@+id/button1"
        android:layout_width="wrap_content"
        android:layout_height="wrap_content"
        android:layout_alignLeft="@+id/last_name_search"
        android:layout_below="@+id/last_name_search"
        android:onClick="execSearch"
        android:text="@string/search_button_label" />

</RelativeLayout>
```

Implement Search Behavior

When we created the PersonnelDirectory project, we told Eclipse to create a default activity named MainActivity. We also identified the activity layout as activity_main .xml. We just finished designing activity_main.xml, the search page layout. Now we need to write some Java to implement the layout behavior. Specifically, we have to tell the Android device how to respond when a user taps the Search button.

When I Tap an Icon, How does Android Know What to Do?

Before we touch MainActivity.java, it already contains a few dozen lines of code. Look specifically at the onCreate method. Notice that this method references R.layout.activity_main. This is the layout we just described. Here is the relationship:

AndroidManifest.xml → MainActivity.java → activity_main.xml

The manifest file identifies the default activity (MainActivity.java) and the default activity loads its layout (activity_main.xml).

From within the Package Explorer, find and open the MainActivity.java file located inside the src/com.example.personneldirectory folder. We need to add a button click handler to this file. The button click handler will package the search values entered by the user and transfer those values to a new activity. Find the line near the top of MainActivity.java that defines the MainActivity class. It looks something like:

```
public class MainActivity extends Activity {
```

Just below that line, add the following:

```
public final static String EMPLID_SEARCH_KEY =
    "com.example.personneldirectory.EMPLID_SEARCH_KEY";
public final static String NAME_SEARCH_KEY =
    "com.example.personneldirectory.NAME_SEARCH_KEY";
public final static String LAST_NAME_SEARCH_KEY =
    "com.example.personneldirectory.LAST_NAME_SEARCH_KEY";
```

We will use these three declarations to identify search field values after passing them to the next activity. Now scroll to the bottom, just above the final closing curly brace (}) and enter the following:

```
public void execSearch(View v) {
    Intent intent = new Intent(this, SearchResultsActivity.class);

    EditText emplidText = (EditText) findViewById(
            R.id.emplid_search);
    intent.putExtra(EMPLID_SEARCH_KEY,
            emplidText.getText().toString());

    EditText nameText = (EditText) findViewById(R.id.name_search);
    intent.putExtra(NAME_SEARCH_KEY,
```

```
                    nameText.getText().toString());

        EditText lastNameText = (EditText) findViewById(
                R.id.last_name_search);
        intent.putExtra(LAST_NAME_SEARCH_KEY,
                lastNameText.getText().toString());

        startActivity(intent);
    }
```

Users of our personnel directory trigger the `execSearch` method by tapping the search button on the activity_main.xml layout. When invoked, this method copies the user-entered search criteria into a reserved area of an Android Intent object. The method then uses the Android Intent to launch a new activity. That new activity, `SearchResultsActivity`, doesn't exist yet so Eclipse will mark it as an error. We will resolve that error later. First, we need to create a data model to hold the user's search results.

Search Results Data Model

After tapping the search button, our users expect the application to connect to a PeopleSoft server and fetch a list of matching results. Android has a built-in list view that will display those results for us. We just have to create an object that can transform each result item into a displayable String. Create this *transformation* object by selecting File | New | Class from the Eclipse menu bar. When the New Java Class dialog appears, set the Package value to `com.example.personneldirectory.model` and then set the Name value to `Person`. Click the Finish button to close the dialog and create the new class. Figure 9-14 is a screenshot of the New Java Class dialog.

Replace the contents of the new Java class with the following:

```
package com.example.personneldirectory.model;

import org.json.JSONException;
import org.json.JSONObject;

public class Person {
    private String employeeId;
    private String name;

    public Person(JSONObject json) throws JSONException {
        this.employeeId = json.getString("EMPLID");
        this.name = json.getString("NAME");
    }

    public String getEmployeeId() {
        return employeeId;
```

```
    }

    public String getName() {
        return name;
    }

    @Override
    public String toString() {
        return this.getName() + " (" + this.getEmployeeId() + ")";
    }
}
```

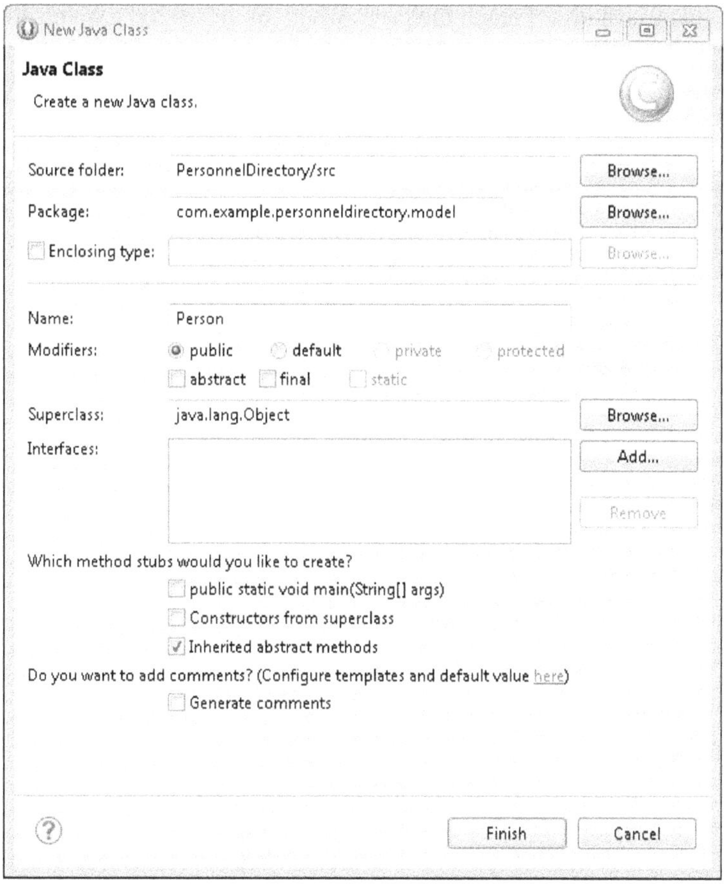

FIGURE 9-14.   *New Java Class dialog*

This class is an unexciting, plain old Java object with two important features:

- The constructor for this class uses the `JSONObject` parameter to initialize itself.

- The class overrides the `toString` method to give the Android built-in list view some text to display.

Creating the Search Results Activity

Browsing through the Package Explorer, I see that Eclipse marked MainActivity.java as having an error. Figure 9-15 is a screenshot of MainActivity.java. Notice Eclipse places an error icon next to MainActivity.java inside the Package Explorer. After opening MainActivity.java, I can find the exact location of the error by scrolling through MainActivity.java until I reach the point where there are red markers in the gutters on each side of file. In Figure 9-15 these markers point to a problem with `SearchResultsActivity.class`. The problem is that we haven't defined `SearchResultsActivity.class`.

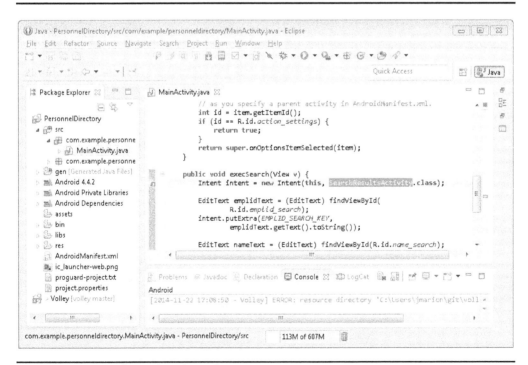

FIGURE 9-15. *Eclipse identifying the MainActivity error*

The easiest way to create the `SearchResultsActivity` Java class is to attempt to resolve the error Eclipse identified in MainActivity.java by clicking the error marker in the left-hand gutter. When the context menu appears below the underlined text, select the Create class "SearchResultsActivity" option. The New Java Class dialog will appear with everything prefilled except the Superclass. Change the value of the Superclass to `android.app.ListActivity`. This will give our class access to list specific behavior. Figure 9-16 is a screenshot of the New Java Class dialog.

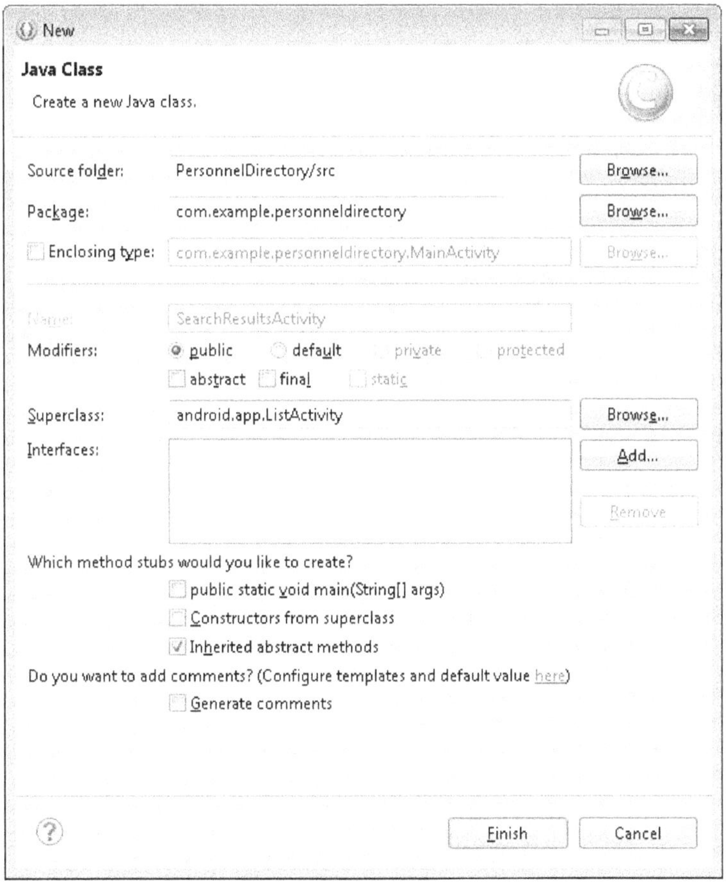

FIGURE 9-16. *New Java Class dialog*

Click OK to close the dialog and then add the following declarations just inside the class definition. I included the first line of the class definition for context. Additions are in bold.

```
public class SearchResultsActivity extends ListActivity {
    private static final String BASE_URL =
        "http://192.168.56.102:8000/PSIGW/RESTListeningConnector/PSFT_HR/" +
        "BMA_PERS_DIR_SEARCH.v1";
    private List<Person> people = new ArrayList<Person>();
    private ArrayAdapter<Person> adapter;
```

The first variable, BASE_URL, points to a Service Operation we created in Chapter 8 that is running on my local VirtualBox demo image. Replace the IP address with your development server IP address or host name.

NOTE
If you are using a real device rather than an emulator to test applications, then replace the IP address in BASE_URL with your development server's IP address or host name. The IP address above points to the host-only adapter on my VirtualBox image. Most PeopleSoft Update Manager images use a host-only adapter with a very similar IP address.

Do I Have to Hard Code an IP Address?

The example here embeds an IP address directly in the code. I did this to keep the example as simple as possible. When developing a mobile application for reuse by a variety of PeopleSoft customers, you may want to create a configuration page where users can enter a target PeopleSoft server. On the other hand, if the mobile application is just for consumption within your organization, you may want to hard code a host name rather than require a configuration. Why make it harder for your users? Facebook, for example, doesn't require users to enter the target Facebook URL before using their mobile application.

If you prefer to hard code a host name, but aren't ready to point your mobile application at production servers, then you can trick your emulator into thinking your development server is really your production server by adding a line to the emulator's hosts file (you might remember this trick from Chapter 1). Open a terminal (cmd on Windows) window and enter the following commands at the prompt (commands are in bold):

```
C:\>adb remount
remount succeeded

C:\>adb shell
root@generic_x86:/ # echo '192.168.56.102 hcmdb.example.com' >>
 /etc/hosts
echo '192.168.56.102 hcmdb.example.com' >> /etc/hosts
```

You can verify the contents of the emulator's hosts file by typing the following at the adb shell prompt:

```
root@generic_x86:/ # cat /etc/hosts
cat /etc/hosts
127.0.0.1                           localhost
192.168.56.102 hcmdb.example.com
```

Android will overwrite your custom hosts file the next time it launches the emulator so you will need to apply this change each time you launch the emulator...kind of makes you wonder if it would just be easier to use the development server URL until you are ready to deploy.

Add the following method declaration just below the private member declarations:

```
@Override
protected void onCreate(Bundle savedInstanceState) {
  super.onCreate(savedInstanceState);

  adapter = new ArrayAdapter<Person>(this,
      android.R.layout.simple_list_item_1, people);
  setListAdapter(adapter);
}
```

This code tells an Android device that the `SearchResultsActivity` Activity will display a list. Unlike MainActivity, which requires a Java class and a layout, this activity just requires a Java class. Instead of defining our own custom layout, we are using a special Android defined layout named `simple_list_item_1`. Now we just have to specify some data.

NOTE
Android contains several built-in layouts. Refer to the blog post: http://arteksoftware.com/androids-built-in-list-item-layouts/ describes list specific layouts.

Place the following code just after the `setListAdapter` line inside the `onCreate` method.

```
// Get the message from the intent
Intent intent = getIntent();
String emplid = intent
    .getStringExtra(MainActivity.EMPLID_SEARCH_KEY);
String name =
    intent.getStringExtra(MainActivity.NAME_SEARCH_KEY);
String lastName = intent
    .getStringExtra(MainActivity.LAST_NAME_SEARCH_KEY);
```

These lines retrieve the search criteria passed to `SearchResultsActivity` from `MainActivity`. Next, we will use the Android `Uri.Builder` to construct the search service URL using parameters sent to `SearchResultsActivity` through an `Intent` object. Add the following lines to the end of the `onCreate` method, just inside the closing curly brace:

```
// Build the target URL with parameters from search page
Uri.Builder builder = Uri.parse(BASE_URL).buildUpon();

if ((emplid != null) && (emplid.length() > 0)) {
  builder.appendQueryParameter("EMPLID", emplid);
}

if ((name != null) && (name.length() > 0)) {
  builder.appendQueryParameter("NAME", name);
}

if ((lastName != null) && (lastName.length() > 0)) {
  builder.appendQueryParameter("LAST_NAME_SRCH", lastName);
}
```

The final step is to dispatch the asynchronous request. On response, our code will convert the service JSON response into a list of `Person` objects and then tell Android to update the results list. Add the following code to the end of the `onCreate` method:

```
// Instantiate the RequestQueue.
RequestQueue queue = Volley.newRequestQueue(this);
```

```
// Request a string response from the provided URL.
JsonObjectRequest request = new JsonObjectRequest(
    Request.Method.GET, builder.toString(), null,
    new Response.Listener<JSONObject>() {
      @Override
      public void onResponse(JSONObject response) {
        try {
          JSONArray results = response.getJSONObject(
              "SEARCH_RESULTS").getJSONArray("SEARCH_FIELDS");
          for (int i = 0; i < results.length(); i++) {
            Person p = new Person(results.getJSONObject(i));

            people.add(p);

          }
          // notifying list adapter about data changes
          // so that it renders the list view with updated
          // data
          adapter.notifyDataSetChanged();
        } catch (JSONException e) {
          // TODO: Tell user something went wrong
          e.printStackTrace();
          return;
        }

      }
    }, new Response.ErrorListener() {
      @Override
      public void onErrorResponse(VolleyError error) {
        // TODO: Tell user something went wrong
      }
    });
// Add the request to the RequestQueue.
queue.add(request);
```

The Java code in this section creates a new Volley request, queues the request, and specifies how to handle the response. Using Volley allows us to focus on what matters to us: packaging a valid request and consuming the response. We do not have to concern ourselves with caching, chunking, state, or any other protocol specific matters. Volley handles these for us.

This code section is critical for another reason. It satisfies the primary requirement of this chapter: Demonstrate how to invoke a PeopleSoft REST service and process the service response.

At this point, Eclipse is likely to be very upset with you and is trying to let you know how it feels by placing lots of red squiggly lines under many of the words in the `SearchResultsActivity` class. Most of these squiggly lines identify class definitions that need to be imported into the `SearchResultsActivity` class. You can resolve these errors now by hovering over the word marked with an error and then selecting the suggested class. Be careful to select the correct import class. Some of the suggestions contain multiple options. Validate your selections against the following listing that contains the entire `SearchResultsActivity` definition including import statements:

```java
package com.example.personneldirectory;

import java.util.ArrayList;
import java.util.List;

import org.json.JSONArray;
import org.json.JSONException;
import org.json.JSONObject;

import com.android.volley.Request;
import com.android.volley.RequestQueue;
import com.android.volley.Response;
import com.android.volley.VolleyError;
import com.android.volley.toolbox.JsonObjectRequest;
import com.android.volley.toolbox.Volley;
import com.example.personneldirectory.model.Person;

import android.app.ListActivity;
import android.content.Intent;
import android.net.Uri;
import android.os.Bundle;
import android.view.View;
import android.widget.ArrayAdapter;
import android.widget.ListView;

public class SearchResultsActivity extends ListActivity {
  private static final String BASE_URL =
      "http://192.168.56.102:8000/PSIGW/RESTListeningConnector/PSFT_HR/" +
      "BMA_PERS_DIR_SEARCH.v1";
  private List<Person> people = new ArrayList<Person>();
  private ArrayAdapter<Person> adapter;

  @Override
  protected void onCreate(Bundle savedInstanceState) {
    super.onCreate(savedInstanceState);
```

```
adapter = new ArrayAdapter<Person>(this,
    android.R.layout.simple_list_item_1, people);
setListAdapter(adapter);

// Get the message from the intent
Intent intent = getIntent();
String emplid = intent
    .getStringExtra(MainActivity.EMPLID_SEARCH_KEY);
String name = intent.getStringExtra(MainActivity.NAME_SEARCH_KEY);
String lastName = intent
    .getStringExtra(MainActivity.LAST_NAME_SEARCH_KEY);

// Build the target URL with parameters from search page
Uri.Builder builder = Uri.parse(BASE_URL).buildUpon();

if ((emplid != null) && (emplid.length() > 0)) {
  builder.appendQueryParameter("EMPLID", emplid);
}

if ((name != null) && (name.length() > 0)) {
  builder.appendQueryParameter("NAME", name);
}

if ((lastName != null) && (lastName.length() > 0)) {
  builder.appendQueryParameter("LAST_NAME_SRCH", lastName);
}

// Instantiate the RequestQueue.
RequestQueue queue = Volley.newRequestQueue(this);

// Request a string response from the provided URL.
JsonObjectRequest request = new JsonObjectRequest(
    Request.Method.GET, builder.toString(), null,
    new Response.Listener<JSONObject>() {
      @Override
      public void onResponse(JSONObject response) {
        try {
          JSONArray results = response.getJSONObject(
              "SEARCH_RESULTS").getJSONArray("SEARCH_FIELDS");
          for (int i = 0; i < results.length(); i++) {
            Person p = new Person(results.getJSONObject(i));

            people.add(p);

          }
```

```
                    // notifying list adapter about data changes
                    // so that it renders the list view with updated
                    // data
                    adapter.notifyDataSetChanged();
                } catch (JSONException e) {
                    // TODO: Tell user something went wrong
                    e.printStackTrace();
                    return;
                }

            }
        }, new Response.ErrorListener() {
          @Override
          public void onErrorResponse(VolleyError error) {
            // TODO: Tell user something went wrong
          }
        });
    // Add the request to the RequestQueue.
    queue.add(request);

    }

    @Override
    protected void onListItemClick(ListView l, View v, int position,
        long id) {
      // TODO: Add some code here to transfer to the details view
      super.onListItemClick(l, v, position, id);
    }

}
```

NOTE
The code above will display a list, but tapping an item in the list will not navigate to a new details activity. The code listing contains a stub for the onListItemClick event. To view the list item details you would add an Intent to the onListItemClick method to transfer to a new activity.

Let's register this Activity class with Android. Open AndroidManifest.xml and switch to the Application tab. Scroll to the bottom of the page and find the Application Nodes section. It should contain one entry named .MainActivity. Click the Add button and then select Activity from the list as shown in Figure 9-17.

FIGURE 9-17. *Select Activity from the list*

Eclipse will add a new activity to the list of application nodes. With the node named Activity selected, find the Activity properties to the right of the application nodes list and then type `.SearchResultsActivity` into the Name field. A few fields below the Name field you will see the Label field. Click the browse button and then add a new string with the key (New R.string.) `title_activity_search_results` and a value of `Search Results`. The final value for the label should be `@string/title_activity_search_results`. Scroll near the end of the properties list and find the Parent activity name field. Set the Parent activity name to `.MainActivity`. Specifying a parent activity will add a back button to the activity header, which allows the user to return to the prior step: entering search criteria.

Switch to the Permissions tab of the PersonnelDirectory.xml manifest file and add a Uses Permission item to the Permissions collection. Set the name of the new Uses Permission to `android.permission.INTERNET`. This tells Android that the PersonnelDirectory application requires Internet access. At install time, an Android device will read this permission collection and prompt the user to accept or deny access to the Internet service. The following code listing contains the complete PersonnelDirectory.xml manifest file contents:

```xml
<?xml version="1.0" encoding="utf-8"?>
<manifest xmlns:android="http://schemas.android.com/apk/res/android"
    package="com.example.personneldirectory"
    android:versionCode="1"
    android:versionName="1.0" >

    <uses-sdk
        android:minSdkVersion="16"
        android:targetSdkVersion="21" />

    <uses-permission android:name="android.permission.INTERNET" />

    <application
        android:allowBackup="true"
        android:icon="@drawable/ic_launcher"
        android:label="@string/app_name"
        android:theme="@style/AppTheme" >
        <activity
            android:name=".MainActivity"
            android:label="@string/app_name" >
            <intent-filter>
                <action android:name="android.intent.action.MAIN" />

                <category
                    android:name="android.intent.category.LAUNCHER" />
            </intent-filter>
        </activity>
        <activity
            android:name=".SearchResultsActivity"
            android:label="@string/title_activity_search_results"
            android:parentActivityName=".MainActivity" >
        </activity>
    </application>
</manifest>
```

Deploy and Test the Android Application

Our Personnel Directory app contains enough code to demonstrate web service access. Deploy the Personnel Directory to an Android Emulator by right-clicking the PersonnelDirectory project name in the Package Explorer and selecting Run As | Android Application from the context menu. When prompted, select an emulator. Eclipse will deploy and launch the application inside your chosen emulator. Within the mobile application on the emulator, enter search criteria. I chose KU000%. Tap search and wait for results. Figure 9-18 is a screenshot of the Search Results list displayed in a NexusOne emulator.

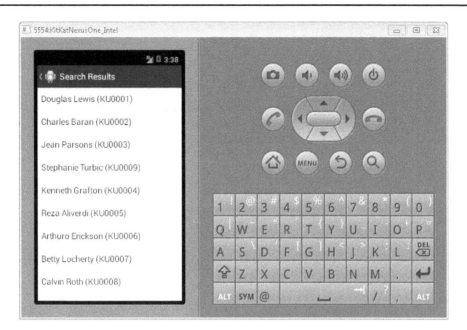

FIGURE 9-18. *Search Results list displayed in a NexusOne emulator*

Conclusion

We started this chapter with some custom PeopleSoft REST web services borrowed from Chapter 8. We then built enough of an Android native personnel directory to demonstrate invoking PeopleSoft REST services. There are many reasons to choose native development over HTML5, including exerting more control over network requests, performance, and access to device capabilities. In this chapter, we focused on performance by maintaining a thin user interface and exerting more control over network requests. In the next chapter, we will wrap our Chapter 8 HTML5 personnel directory in a Cordova wrapper, which will improve performance and provide access to on-device capabilities.

CHAPTER
10

Power-Using Cordova

I n this chapter, you will learn how to transform an HTML5 mobile web application into a hybrid multidevice native application using the Apache Cordova platform. We will use the NetBeans IDE, Apache Cordova command line interface, and Android SDK to convert the AngularJS personnel directory we started in Chapter 6 (but finished in Chapter 8) into a native, on-device Android application.

Why Apache Cordova? The most common reason to use Apache Cordova is platform independence. Cordova allows a developer to create a single application using standard HTML5 technology and deploy that application to multiple device operating systems (iOS, Android, etc.) without learning device-specific development tools. Another good reason to use Cordova is because it exposes a JavaScript interface to native device capabilities allowing web developers to access protected device features without learning device-specific APIs.

About the Apache Cordova Platform

Apache Cordova is an open source project donated to the Apache Software Foundation by Adobe Systems. Cordova provides a command line interface for assembling native applications from HTML, CSS, JavaScript, and images. Using plugins, Cordova exposes device-specific features, such as the camera and geolocation, to developers through a JavaScript API. The original open source project, named PhoneGap, was purchased by Adobe, and still exists as an extension of Cordova. There are a lot of similarities between the two platforms. In this chapter, we use Apache Cordova instead of PhoneGap, so that we can leverage the Cordova build tools included with NetBeans.

Cordova allows developers to create cross-platform applications using common development languages, such as JavaScript, HTML, and CSS, and deploy those applications to a variety of mobile operating systems. This allows a developer to write one version of an application and then deploy that application to multiple target operating systems (Android, iOS, BlackBerry, Windows Mobile, and so on). Cordova does not directly compile applications. Instead, it uses platform-specific development kits to compile and deploy applications. For example, if you want to create an Android application, then Cordova requires the Android SDK. Likewise, if you want to create an iPhone or iPad application, then Cordova requires Xcode.

Installing the Apache Cordova Platform

Even though NetBeans integrates with Apache Cordova, it doesn't include the Cordova Platform with the NetBeans installation. Instead, NetBeans will prompt you to install Cordova the first time you attempt to create a Cordova project. Let's get a head start by installing the required pieces ourselves. NetBeans requires Node.js, Git, and a mobile platform SDK. Chapter 1 described how to install Node.js as part of the

Weinre installation. If you didn't install Node.js in Chapter 1, head over to http://nodejs.org/download/ now and install the Node.js binaries appropriate for your operating system (Windows, Linux, Mac, and so on). You will also need Git installed. There are a multiple Windows Git packages. I use the one available at http://git-scm.com/downloads. As with Node.js, download the Git package appropriate for your operating system. The final prerequisite is a mobile SDK. Since we downloaded and installed the Android SDK in Chapter 1 and then used it to build a mobile application in Chapter 9, we have already satisfied that prerequisite. To summarize, the prerequisites for installing Cordova are

- Node.js

- Git

- Mobile SDK

After satisfying these prerequisites, install the Apache Cordova platform from a command prompt by entering the command npm install -g cordova as follows:

```
C:\Users\jmarion>npm install -g cordova
```

NOTE
Oracle maintains a brief NetBeans/Cordova "Getting Started" guide on the http://netbeans.org website. When I wrote this book, the getting started guide was available at https://netbeans.org/kb/docs/webclient/cordova-gettingstarted.html.

Creating a NetBeans Cordova Project

Creating a Cordova project in NetBeans is very similar to creating an HTML5 project (because a Cordova project IS an HTML5 project). Launch NetBeans and choose File | New Project from the NetBeans menu bar. When step 1 of the New Project appears, select the HTML5 category and then the Cordova Application Project. Click Next to Continue. In step 2, name the project PersonnelDirectoryCordova. In step 3, choose the Cordova Hello World Online Template. Figure 10-1 is a screenshot of step 3.

NOTE
If NetBeans raises an exception when trying to create a new Cordova project, then make sure you are running the most current version of NetBeans.

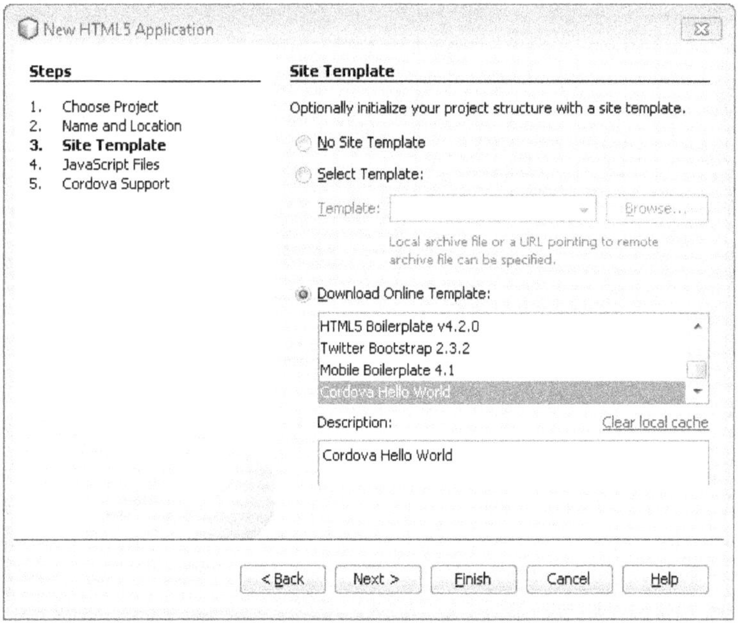

FIGURE 10-1. *Step 3 of the New HTML5 Application wizard*

On step 4, click Next to move to step 5. We don't need to select any libraries because we will be using the project source from Chapter 6. In step 5, you are prompted for an Application ID and Application Name. Keep the default Application ID but change the Application Name to `Personnel Directory`. Figure 10-2

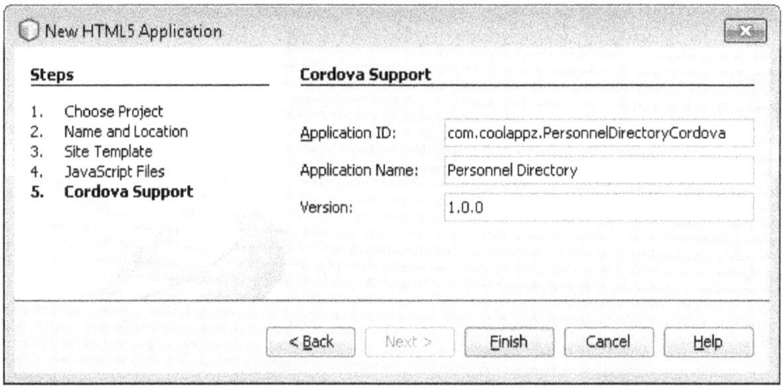

FIGURE 10-2. *Step 5 of the New HTML5 Application wizard*

is a screenshot of step 5. Click the Finish button to complete the wizard and create the project.

In the Project Explorer, identify the Important Files node and then the Cordova Plugins node. Double-click the Cordova plugins node to open the plugin.properties file. This file contains one row for each plugin used by a Cordova application. The Cordova Hello World template is preconfigured with entries for common plugins. We will only use the camera and console plugins so delete every line *except* the camera and console lines. After deletion, your plugin.properties file should contain the following:

```
# This is a list of plugins installed in your project
# You can delete or add new plugins
#
# Format is following:
# name.of.plugin=url_of_repository
#
# This list contains all core cordova plugins.
#
# For more information about plugins see
http://cordova.apache.org/blog/releases/2013/07/23/cordova-3.html
#

org.apache.cordova.camera=
https://git-wip-us.apache.org/repos/asf/cordova-plugin-camera.git
org.apache.cordova.console=
https://git-wip-us.apache.org/repos/asf/cordova-plugin-console.git
```

The first time you run a Cordova application, NetBeans will download each plugin listed in plugins.properties. This could take a significant amount of time. Since we won't be using any of the other plugins, it is better to delete them now rather than waste our time waiting for them to download.

Running a Cordova Project from NetBeans

After your emulator is running, return to NetBeans and locate the *Browser Select* toolbar icon. It should be one icon to the left of the two "hammer" icons. Click this icon and select Cordova (Android Emulator). Figure 10-3 is a screenshot of the browser selection menu.

Launch the new application by either clicking the green run (play) button in the toolbar or choosing Run | Run Project from the NetBeans menu bar. If this is your first time running a Cordova application from NetBeans, then NetBeans will display the error described in Figure 10-4.

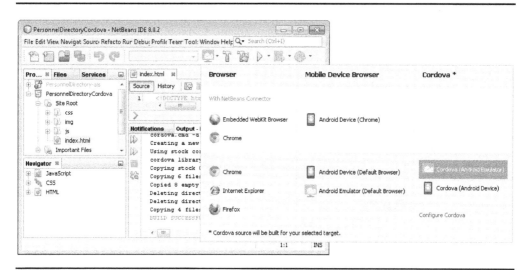

FIGURE 10-3. *Browser selection menu*

Click the OK button to open the NetBeans options dialog so you can enter the location of your Android SDK. Figure 10-5 is a screenshot of my NetBeans options showing the path to the Android SDK (downloading the Android SDK was part of Chapter 1). NetBeans should proceed with the build and deploy process. If not, run the project again.

NOTE
You must be connected to the Internet the first time you launch your project so that Apache Cordova can download the plugins identified in the plugins .properties file.

FIGURE 10-4. *Android Platform not configured error*

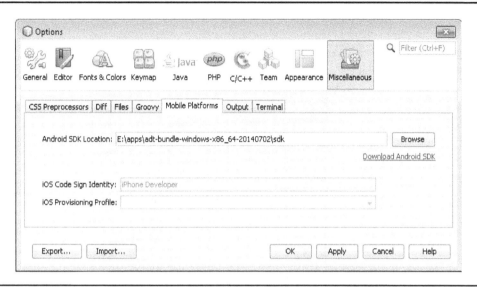

FIGURE 10-5. *NetBeans mobile platform options*

After running the project, switch to your emulator. You should see something that resembles Figure 10-6. If you don't, then return to NetBeans and review both tabs of the Output window.

NOTE
The Android emulator should automatically launch the Cordova Hello World application. You should not need to launch it yourself. If it isn't running, then look for the Personnel Directory icon on the emulator home screen.

From Website to On-device

Let's convert our Chapter 6 AngularJS Personnel Directory HTML5 remote mobile website into an on-device application running in the Cordova container. Here is how we will perform this transformation:

- Copy source files from the AngularJS Personnel Directory we created in Chapter 6 and finalized in Chapter 8.

- Change URLs so the emulator can connect to our PeopleSoft instance.

- Implement authentication for the profile page.

FIGURE 10-6. *Cordova Hello World template running in an Android emulator*

Copying Source Files

Locate your PersonnelDirectory-ajs\app directory on your file system. We created this folder in Chapter 8 through the PersonnelDirectory-ajs NetBeans project. Copy the contents of the app directory into your new project's (PersonnelDirectoryCordova) www directory. For example, I copied C:\Users\ jmarion\Documents\NetBeansProjects\PersonnelDirectory-ajs\app to C:\Users\ jmarion\Documents\NetBeansProjects\PersonnelDirectoryCordova\www. Say yes when prompted to overwrite files or merge folders.

NOTE
You can identify a project's source directory by right-clicking the project's node in the NetBeans project explorer and choosing Properties from the context menu.

Connecting the Emulator to Your PeopleSoft Instance

In Chapter 8, we ran a local web server for development purposes. Since our PeopleSoft web services were hosted by a different web site (domain), we had to reverse proxy those services to make the web browser think the web service content was coming from the same web server as the HTML files. Chapter 9, on the other hand, used the same web services, but didn't require a reverse proxy. The Chapter 9 application was able to connect directly to remote PeopleSoft services. The two chapters differed in that all content for Chapter 8 came from a remote location, whereas most of the Chapter 9 content was installed directly on the device. Even though this chapter uses the same source files as Chapter 8, we won't access them from a web server. Instead, the mobile device will behave more like Chapter 9—with locally installed content and allowing us to connect directly to remote services. This means the Chapter 9 URL rules and concepts apply. You can access the target Service Operations by

- IP address

- Host name

- IP address to host name mapping in the emulator hosts file (see Chapter 9 for example)

The Chapter 8 code we just copied into our PersonnelDirectoryCordova project references REST Service Operations as relative URLs. Since this project's HTML and JavaScript will run locally on the device with no need to reverse proxy content, we need to change the Service Operation URLs into absolute URLs that point to a PeopleSoft instance. Open the file js/controllers.js and search for the `DetailsCtrl` controller definition. Inside the `DetailsCtrl` controller function, identify the `$http.get` method invocations and convert the relative URLs into absolute URLs. For example, instances of `/PSIGW/RESTListeningConnector/` become `http://192.168.56.102:8000/PSIGW/RESTListeningConnector/`. The following is my `DetailsCtrl` with updated URLs in bold:

```
.controller('DetailsCtrl', [
  '$scope',
  '$routeParams',
  '$http',
  function($scope, $routeParams, $http) {
    // view the route parameters in your console by uncommenting
    // the following:
    // console.log($routeParams);
    $http.get('http://192.168.56.102:8000/PSIGW/
RESTListeningConnector/PSFT_HR/BMA_PERS_DIR_DETAILS.v1/' +
$routeParams.EMPLID)
        .then(function(response) {
          // view the response object by uncommenting the following
          // console.log(response);
          // closure -- updating $scope from outer function
```

```
            $scope.details = response.data.DETAILS;
        });
    $http.get('http://192.168.56.102:8000/PSIGW/
RESTListeningConnector/PSFT_HR/BMA_PERS_DIR_PHOTO.v1/' +
$routeParams.EMPLID)
        .then(function(response) {
            $scope.photo = response.data;
        });
    }])
```

Make the same change to the `ProfileCtrl` controller:

```
.controller('ProfileCtrl', ['$scope',
    '$routeParams',
    '$http',
    function($scope, $routeParams, $http) {

    $http.get('http://192.168.56.102:8000/PSIGW/
RESTListeningConnector/PSFT_HR/BMA_PERS_DIR_PROFILE.v1/profile')
            .then(function(response) {
                // closure -- updating $scope from outer function
                $scope.profile = response.data.DETAILS;
                $http.get('http://192.168.56.102:8000/PSIGW/
RESTListeningConnector/PSFT_HR/BMA_PERS_DIR_PHOTO.v1/' +
$scope.profile.EMPLID)
                        .then(function(response) {
                            $scope.photo = response.data;
                        });
            });
```

The js/services.js file also contains a reference to a relative Service Operation URL. Open js/services.js and find the `SearchService` factory method. A few lines down from the factory definition you should find the `searchService` `.search` method definition. Inside that method, you will see the URL /PSIGW/ RESTListeningConnector/PSFT_HR/BMA_PERS_DIR_SEARCH.v1. Convert this URL into an absolute URL. The following is a fragment of the services.js file with the necessary changes in bold. I included a few lines before and after for reference:

```
searchService.search = function(parms) {
    var promise = $http({
        method: 'GET',
        url: 'http://192.168.56.102:8000/PSIGW/RESTListeningConnector/
PSFT_HR/BMA_PERS_DIR_SEARCH.v1',
        params: parms
    }).then(function(response) {
```

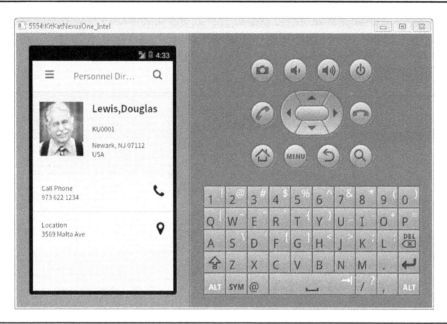

FIGURE 10-7. *AngularJS PersonnelDirectory*

Test your changes to ensure connectivity by selecting Run | Run Project from the NetBeans menu bar. Figure 10-7 is a screenshot of the AngularJS Personnel Directory running as a Cordova application inside a NexusOne Android emulator.

Debugging Cordova Applications

In Chapter 1 you learned how to use Weinre. Weinre is a great tool for debugging CSS and page layout as well as JavaScript. In this chapter, you already have a working application. At most, we just need to debug connectivity issues. I find Fiddler to be very helpful when debugging connection issues. Basically, we just need to find out what the Cordova application attempted to access and why it didn't receive the response we expected. Chapter 1 described how to configure Fiddler to accept connections from an emulator as well as how to get an

(Continued)

emulator to use Fiddler as its proxy server. Review the steps from Chapter 1 and then reload the Personnel Directory Cordova application. Figure 10-8 is a screenshot of both the Cordova application and Fiddler with the Cordova PeopleSoft HTTP request highlighted.

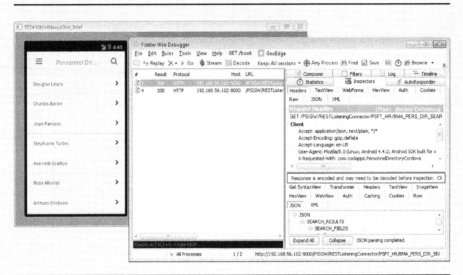

FIGURE 10-8. *Cordova HTTP request displayed in Fiddler*

Another option is to litter your JavaScript with `console.log` statements. The output of these statements is visible in the Android Device Monitor (monitor.bat) as well as the NetBeans Browser Log (visible when you launch a Cordova application from NetBeans).

Fixing Annoyances

In Part II of this book, we created the user interface that we are now porting to Cordova. While building that user interface, we primarily used a desktop web browser, which has a much larger form factor than a mobile phone. In this chapter, however, we are using an emulator with a significantly smaller screen size. I don't know about you, but I'm getting really annoyed that the side menu doesn't automatically close when I click one of the links. If you haven't experienced this, tap the "hamburger" menu button in the upper left corner of the Personnel Directory application. Now tap one of the links from the menu that appears. The new content will load but the menu will remain visible. We can hide the menu on click by adding a couple of lines to the index.html file. In NetBeans, open index.html and scroll through the text until you find the `<nav>` element. To each link within the nav element, add the attribute `onclick="document.body.classList .remove('left-nav')"`. Here is the nav fragment after making this change. The attribute additions are in bold.

```
<nav>
  <ul class="topcoat-list">
    <li class="topcoat-list__item">
      <a href="#/profile" class="fa-user"
      onclick="document.body.classList.remove('left-nav')">
        My Profile</a>
    </li>
    <li class="topcoat-list__item">
      <a href="#/search" class="fa-search"
      onclick="document.body.classList.remove('left-nav')">Search</a>
    </li>
    <li class="topcoat-list__item"
        data-bma-results-hide-class="ng-hide">
      <a href="#/results" class="fa-th-list"
      onclick="document.body.classList.remove('left-nav')">
        Results</a>
    </li>
  </ul>
</nav>
```

After implementing this change, run the Cordova application again and verify that the side menu slides out of view when you tap a link from the menu bar.

Implement Authentication

Try to access My Profile from the side menu. Were you prompted for your credentials? When the page loaded, did you see any data? The answer is no. The Cordova application did not prompt for credentials. Since you aren't authenticated, you won't see any data. This is a critical difference between an HTML application running in Cordova and a web application delivered through a web browser. Basic authentication is built into a web browser. If you use one of the debugging techniques described above, such as Fiddler, you will see the 401 status code returned by PeopleSoft Integration Broker. What this means is that we have to handle authentication ourselves.

Let's implement authentication by creating the following:

■ A service to hold credentials for the duration of the user session.

■ A login page to capture credentials.

■ A controller to marshal data between the login data model and the service.

The Authentication Service

Open your project's js/services.js file and scroll to the end. Find the very last semicolon in the file and delete it. Next, add the following JavaScript to the end of the file:

```
.factory('AuthenticationService', [
  '$location',
  function($location) {
    var username;
    var password;
    var token;
    var haveCredentials = false;
    var lastUrl;

    return {
      getToken: function() {
        if(haveCredentials) {
          return token;
        } else {
          lastUrl = $location.url();
          $location.path("/login");
        }
      },
      setCredentials: function(user, pwd) {
        username = user;
        password = pwd;
        token = window.btoa(username + ":" + password);
        console.log("setCredentials token: " + token);
        haveCredentials = true;
        $location.url(lastUrl);
      }
    };
}]);
```

This factory method creates a service named `AuthenticationService` with two methods: `getToken` and `setCredentials`. The `setCredentials` method requires a user name and a password.

The Login Template

Now we need a way to prompt the user for the parameters to `setCredentials`. Inside the partials folder, create a new HTML file named login.html. Replace the contents of the login.html file with the following:

```
<div class="margin">
  <form ng-submit="login()" class="margin">
    <input type="username" class="topcoat-text-input"
           placeholder="Username" ng-model="username"/>
    <input type="text" class="topcoat-text-input"
           placeholder="Password" ng-model="password"/>
    <button class="topcoat-button" data-icon="lock"
```

```
              type="submit">Login</button>
   </form>
</div>
```

I added extra emphasis to the `data-icon="lock"` attribute in the code sample. The point of this attribute is to insert a lock icon into the login/submit button. The CSS for this icon, however, does not yet exist. Open the css/app.css file from your PersonnelDirectoryCordova project and add the following:

```
[data-icon=lock]:after {
   content: "\f023";
}
```

Login Controller

Open the js/controller.js file and scroll to the very bottom. Delete the last semicolon present in that file and then append the following:

```
.controller('LoginCtrl', [
   '$scope',
   'AuthenticationService',
   function($scope, auth) {
      // Declaration not necessary, but best practice. If someone
      // submits an empty form, searchParms won't exist unless we
      // declare it inside the controller.
      $scope.username;
      $scope.password;

      $scope.login = function() {
         // send to results route
         //console.log($scope.searchParms);
         auth.setCredentials($scope.username, $scope.password);
      };
   }]);
```

This code creates a controller for the login.html partial. It manages the data model for the login.html partial and then sends data to the `AuthenticationService` when a user taps the login button.

Unfortunately, it isn't enough to just add a new controller. We also have to tell the profile controller (`ProfileCtrl`) to use the new `AuthenticationService` service. Locate the `ProfileCtrl` controller and insert the `AuthenticationService` dependency as shown in the following fragment:

```
.controller('ProfileCtrl', ['$scope',
   '$routeParams',
   '$http',
   'AuthenticationService',
   function($scope, $routeParams, $http, auth) {

      var token = auth.getToken();
```

I snuck an extra line into that last code fragment. Now that we have a reference to the `AuthenticationService`, the extra line at the bottom of the fragment asks the service for its token. If the service has a token, then we can invoke the PeopleSoft REST service. If it does *not* have a token, however, well…we don't have to worry about that. Our previous call to `getToken` will redirect to the login partial and ask the user for credentials.

The next fragment inside the `ProfileCtrl` controller contains a `$http.get` followed by a `$scope.save`. Wrap the `$http.get` in a logical `if` statement, but end that statement right before the `$scope.save`. Next, we need to add credentials to each of the profile's `$http.get` requests. Here is the code for the complete `ProfileCtrl` controller after making these modifications (changes are in bold text):

```
.controller('ProfileCtrl', ['$scope',
    '$routeParams',
    '$http',
    'AuthenticationService',
    function($scope, $routeParams, $http, auth) {

      var token = auth.getToken();

      if(!!token) {
        $http.get('http://192.168.56.102:8000/PSIGW/
RESTListeningConnector/PSFT_HR/BMA_PERS_DIR_PROFILE.v1/profile',
            {headers: {'Authorization': "Basic " + token}})
                .then(function(response) {
                  // closure -- updating $scope from outer function
                  $scope.profile = response.data.DETAILS;
                  $http.get('http://192.168.56.102:8000/PSIGW/
RESTListeningConnector/PSFT_HR/BMA_PERS_DIR_PHOTO.v1/' +
$scope.profile.EMPLID,
                        { headers: {'Authorization': 'Basic ' + token} })
                            .then(function(response) {
                              $scope.photo = response.data;
                            });
                }, function(response) {
                  console.log(response);
                });
      }

      $scope.save = function() {
      };
    }])
```

NOTE
Since getToken will redirect to the login partial and prompt for credentials, you may be wondering why we need to test the token variable for a value. This is because the redirect doesn't happen until after the controller finishes. The logical if statement helps us get to the finish line a little faster.

Now we just need a route to tie everything together. Open the js/app.js file and locate the otherwise route near the bottom. Just before that route, insert the following:

```
$routeProvider.when('/profile', {
  templateUrl: 'partials/profile.html',
  controller: 'ProfileCtrl'});
$routeProvider.when('/login', {
  templateUrl: 'partials/login.html',
  controller: 'LoginCtrl'});
$routeProvider.otherwise({redirectTo: '/search'});
}]);
```

NOTE
I included the profile and otherwise routes for context.

Deploy and test the Cordova application again. This time when you attempt to access your profile page, you will be presented with a login page as shown in Figure 10-9. After authenticating you should see data appear in the profile page.

NOTE
The code in this example assumes the profile service is protected and preemptively inserts credentials. This is how custom applications access known protected resources, but is not the way basic authentication works on the Internet. When a browser attempts to access a protected resource, the server will return a 401 Not Authorized response. It is this response that tells a web browser to prompt the user for credentials. We could modify this example to test for a 401 return code before performing authentication. The tradeoff would be reduced performance over a broadband network due to the extra HTTP request to ensure you didn't send credentials to a service that doesn't require credentials.

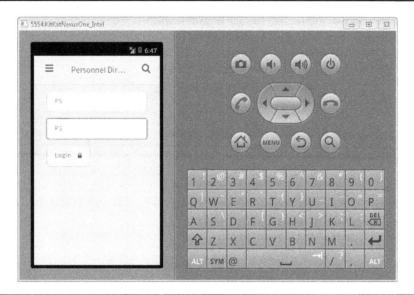

FIGURE 10-9. *Personnel Directory authentication page*

Implementing Native Features

By using Cordova for our web application container we have already gained several benefits:

- Reduced bandwidth consumption by only sending data (no images, CSS, HTML, and so on)

- Easy access through an on-screen icon

- Cross domain AJAX

One of the primary reasons for choosing a native implementation over a mobile web application, however, is the ability to leverage secure device capabilities such as the camera. Let's extend this Cordova application to use the device camera. We can add on-click behavior to the profile page's photo to launch the camera. This will allow the user to replace his or her profile photo with a selfie.

Updating the ProfileCtrl Controller

Normally the first step would be downloading and installing the camera Cordova plugin (or configuring it in NetBeans). We already have this plugin installed because we chose to keep it in the plugins.properties file when we were first configuring this project. The next step is to make Cordova features available to our application by adding the Cordova JavaScript file to index.html. Open index.html and scroll near the end, just before the first `<script>` tag. Insert the following below the `<main>` element and before the first `<script>` tag:

```
<script type="text/javascript" src="cordova.js"></script>
```

To the `ProfileCtrl` controller we need to add a scope method for taking photos. Later we will bind this to the ng-click attribute of the avatar img tag within the profile partial. Open the js/controllers.js file and scroll to the `ProfileCtrl` controller definition (it is pretty close to the bottom of the file). Add the following JavaScript just before the `$scope.save` method definition:

```
$scope.takePhoto = function() {

  var cameraOptions = { quality : 75,
    destinationType : Camera.DestinationType.DATA_URL,
    sourceType : Camera.PictureSourceType.CAMERA,
    allowEdit : true,
    encodingType: Camera.EncodingType.JPEG,
    targetWidth: 100,
    targetHeight: 100,
    saveToPhotoAlbum: false };

  navigator.camera.getPicture(function(imageURI) {
    $scope.$apply(function(){
      $scope.photo = "data:image/jpeg;base64," + imageURI;
      console.log($scope.photo);
    });
  }, function(err) {
    console.log(err);
  }, cameraOptions);
};
```

The above JavaScript configures the camera to return an image as base64 encoded data. As we learned in a previous chapter, we can specify base64 encoded data as the source for an HTML image tag. After configuring the camera, the code invokes the camera (`navigator.camera.getPicture`), passing in a reference to an anonymous callback function. The callback then updates the `$scope.photo` variable with the proper data URL containing the base64 encoded photo taken by the camera. An interesting feature of this code is the `$scope.$apply`. Since the callback will be invoked outside the AngularJS framework, AngularJS will not be notified of scope changes. `$scope.$apply` tells AngularJS to update references to variables updated within the `$apply` closure. Here is a complete listing of the `ProfileCtrl` controller with changes in bold:

```
.controller('ProfileCtrl', ['$scope',
  '$routeParams',
  '$http',
  'AuthenticationService',
```

```
function($scope, $routeParams, $http, auth) {

  var token = auth.getToken();
  console.log(token);
  // Note: the $scope.photo declaration here is optional
  $scope.photo;

  if(!!token) {
    $http.get('http://192.168.56.102:8000/PSIGW/
RESTListeningConnector/PSFT_HR/BMA_PERS_DIR_PROFILE.v1/profile',
        {headers: {'Authorization': "Basic " + token}})
          .then(function(response) {
            // closure -- updating $scope from outer function
            $scope.profile = response.data.DETAILS;
            $http.get('http://192.168.56.102:8000/PSIGW/
RESTListeningConnector/PSFT_HR/BMA_PERS_DIR_PHOTO.v1/' +
$scope.profile.EMPLID,
                  { headers: {'Authorization': 'Basic ' + token} })
                    .then(function(response) {
                      $scope.photo = response.data;
                    });
          }, function(response) {
            console.log(response);
          });
  }

  $scope.takePhoto = function() {

    var cameraOptions = { quality : 75,
      destinationType : Camera.DestinationType.DATA_URL,
      sourceType : Camera.PictureSourceType.CAMERA,
      allowEdit : true,
      encodingType: Camera.EncodingType.JPEG,
      targetWidth: 100,
      targetHeight: 100,
      saveToPhotoAlbum: false };

    navigator.camera.getPicture(function(imageURI) {
      $scope.$apply(function(){
        $scope.photo = "data:image/jpeg;base64," + imageURI;
        console.log($scope.photo);
      });
    }, function(err) {
      console.log(err);
    }, cameraOptions);
  };

  $scope.save = function() {
  };
}])
```

Updating the Profile Partial

It is now time to bind the avatar to the $scope.photo model property and the ng-click attribute of the avatar to the $scope.takePhoto method. Open the partials/profile.html file and locate the <img> element. Update its attributes to resemble the following (changes in bold text):

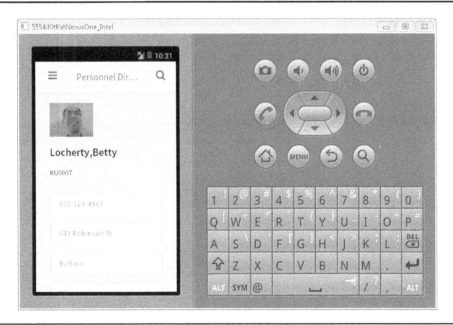

```
<img ng-src="{{photo}}" ng-click="takePhoto()" class="avatar"
    alt="{{profile.NAME}}'s Photo">
```

Run the project by choosing Run | Run Project from the NetBeans menu bar. When your Personnel Directory application appears in the emulator, expose the side bar menu and access the Profile item. After the profile loads, tap the photo. The emulator camera should appear. Snap a photo of yourself and watch the emulator update the Profile page to display your photo. Figure 10-10 is a screenshot of the profile page after I took a selfie in my hotel room.

FIGURE 10-10.   *Selfie on the Profile page ready for upload*

Conclusion

Through the example in this chapter, you learned how to install Apache Cordova, how to access PeopleSoft REST Service Operations from a Cordova hybrid application, and how to use the Cordova camera plugin. What about uploading the selfie to your PeopleSoft application? Implementing the PeopleSoft side of this service operation is beyond the scope of this chapter, but let me give you a few hints:

- Since the photo will contain a lot of information, you will POST to the REST service operation instead of using the GET HTTP method.

- The server will receive a JSON document containing values from the profile page. You would therefore create a Document containing a matching structure to allow you to access properties of the JSON Document.

- The browser will send base64-encoded data. How you decode base64 is a matter of preference. You could, for example, use the PeopleTools 8.52+ `File.WriteBase64StringToBinary` method. After moving the image into a file, you could then use the `PutAttachment` PeopleCode function to copy the file into PeopleSoft application tables. Another option would be to stream the base64 data directly into the database using database-specific procedures to convert base64 to binary.

The next chapter will conclude this section of the book by showing you how to use the Oracle Mobile Application Framework (MAF) to consume PeopleSoft REST Service Operations. The development approach will be similar to using the Android SDK in Chapter 9, but the result will be a hybrid application, which is what we built in this chapter.

CHAPTER
11

Building Mobile
Applications with
Oracle Mobile
Application Framework

Oracle Mobile Application Framework (MAF) is a hybrid platform for building enterprise mobile applications that allows developers to build single-source applications which deploy to both Android and iOS devices. With MAF, developers use Java, HTML5, CSS, JavaScript, and Cordova plugins to declaratively construct cross-platform hybrid applications. In this chapter, you will use Oracle MAF to build yet another Personnel Directory by consuming our Chapter 8 REST services (perhaps I should have named this book *101 Ways to Build a Personnel Directory?*). Although this chapter may offer a good introduction to MAF, the primary purpose is to show you how to consume PeopleSoft REST services with MAF. This chapter is not intended to be a definitive reference. While working through this chapter, I highly recommend reading *Oracle Mobile Application Framework Developer Guide* by Luc Bors, Oracle Press. I found it to be an invaluable resource.

Another important aspect of mobile application development is the user experience. This chapter will show you the basics of skinning MAF applications. You can learn more about Oracle mobile design guidelines at http://www.oracle .com/webfolder/ux/mobile/index.html.

Up and Running with JDeveloper 12*c*

Oracle maintains a great set of tutorials describing how to install Oracle JDeveloper and the MAF extension. When I wrote this book, the latest tutorial was located at http://docs.oracle.com/cd/E53569_01/tutorials/tut_jdev_maf_setup/tut_jdev_maf_ setup.html. The following is a summary of the steps required to install and configure JDeveloper with the MAF extension.

The first step is to download and install JDeveloper 12*c* Studio Edition. When writing this book, JDeveloper was available at http://www.oracle.com/technetwork /developer-tools/jdev/downloads/index.html. Download and install JDeveloper. When downloading, be sure to choose the *Studio Edition*. When JDeveloper finishes installing, choose Help | Check for Updates from the JDeveloper menu bar. The Update Center dialog will appear. Select the Oracle Fusion Middleware Products and Official Oracle Extensions and Updates options, choose next, and then select Mobile Application Framework.

NOTE
JDeveloper requires JDK 7. The MAF extension, however, requires Java 8. After JDeveloper restarts, it will prompt you for the location of JDK 8. Make sure you have a copy of JDK 8 installed before continuing.

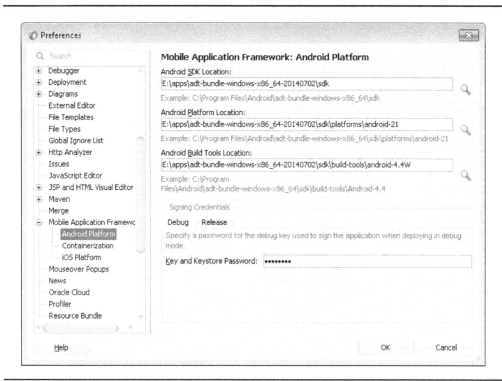

FIGURE 11-1. *MAF preferences*

Next, we have to configure the MAF preferences. Specifically, we need to tell JDeveloper MAF where to find the Android (and iOS if running on a Mac) SDK. From the JDeveloper menu bar, choose Tools | Preferences. Select the Mobile Application Framework node. If you see the Load Extension button, then click Load Extension. Otherwise, select the Android Platform (or iOS Platform) child node and specify the location of the Android SDK. Figure 11-1 is a screenshot of the MAF preferences.

Creating an MAF Project

Let's create a new MAF project so we can build yet another Personnel Directory. From the Applications sidebar, choose New Application. Alternatively, choose File | New | Application from the JDeveloper menu bar. From the New Gallery dialog, select General | Applications | Mobile Application Framework Application. Figure 11-2 is a screenshot of the New Gallery dialog.

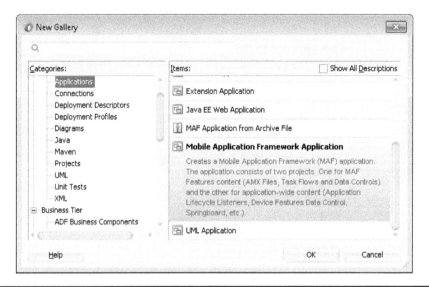

FIGURE 11-2. *New Gallery dialog*

The Create MAF Application dialog will appear. In step 1, enter the Application Name `PersonnelDirectory`. For the Application Package Prefix enter `com .example.ps.hcm`. Figure 11-3 is a screenshot of step 1. Click Next to move to the next step.

Continue through the wizard, accepting the defaults for steps 2 through 5, and then click the Finish button. JDeveloper will respond by creating a new Application named PersonnelDirectory that contains two projects: ApplicationController and ViewController. We will perform most of our work in the ViewController project.

The Client-Side Data Model

As we have seen in other chapters, our client-side user interface (UI) consists of four primary views:

- Search parameter page
- Search results list
- Detail view
- Editable profile view

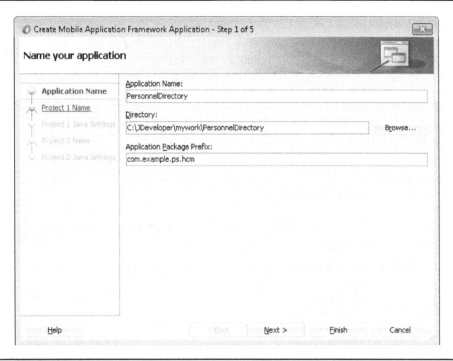

FIGURE 11-3. *Step 1 of the Create Mobile Application Framework wizard*

We also know that our server-side REST handlers consist of four services:

■ Search service

■ Details service

■ Photo service

■ Profile details service

The data model will contain structures that we can map to on-screen display attributes as well as methods to invoke remote services. From the PersonnelDirectory iterations and mockups we already created, we know what we expect to see on each page within the application. Just to recap…what do we expect to see on the search page? Data-entry fields requesting…what? Employee attributes. What about the search results page? We expect to see a list of employees, which is really a list of employee attributes. And then on the details page we expect to see even more employee attributes. All of the pages within our application deal with just one entity: Employee.

Each view within our application will capture or display attributes about an employee or a group of employees.

You may be familiar with JDeveloper Web Service Data Control. JDeveloper 12c with MAF 2.1 has great support for XML-based web services, but not for JSON. At this time, developing for JSON services requires invoking service operations directly through Java. While it may seem a little more complicated from a developer perspective, using JSON and REST reduces network strain resulting in better performing applications.

The Employee Entity

Let's create the entity Java class that we have determined will satisfy our requirements. Create a new Java class within the ViewController project in JDeveloper. There are several ways to create a new Java class:

- Right-click the ViewController project and select New | Java Class from the context menu.

- Select File | New | Java Class from the JDeveloper menu bar.

- Click the drop-down arrow beside the *New* toolbar button in the JDeveloper toolbar and select Java Class.

Whichever mechanism you choose, just be sure that the ViewController project is the active project. The easiest way to confirm this is to select the ViewController node in the Projects explorer sidebar. We want JDeveloper to create the new Java class in the ViewController project rather than in the ApplicationController project.

When the JDeveloper Create Java Class dialog appears, name the new class Employee and set the Package to `com.example.ps.hcm.mobile.entities`. Leave all other fields at their default values. Figure 11-4 is a screenshot of the Create Java Class dialog.

The Employee Java class will have an attribute for each field displayed on any screen, or view, within the mobile application. Here is a list of attributes:

- emplid

- name

- address1

- city

- state

- postal

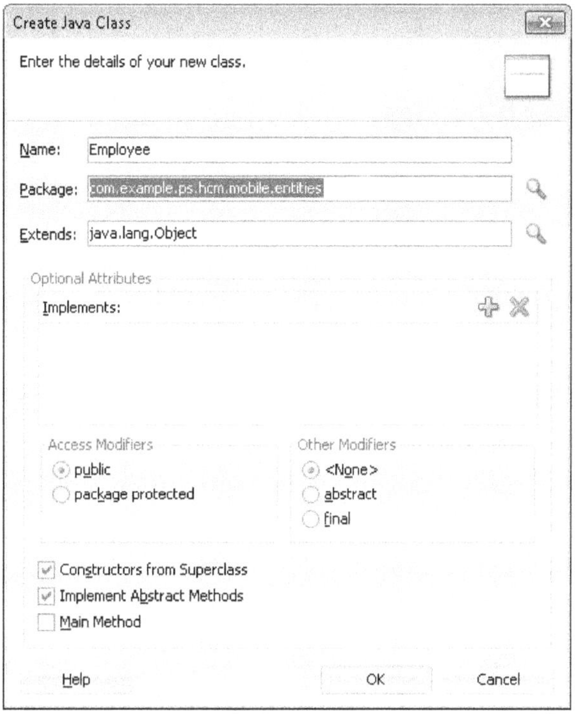

FIGURE 11-4. *Create Employee entity class dialog*

- country

- countryCode

- phone

- photoDataUrl

Each of these attributes contains string, or text, data. Add them as private String fields to the Employee class as follows:

```
public class Employee {
    private String emplid;
    private String name;
    private String address1;
```

```
private String city;
private String state;
private String postal;
private String country;
private String countryCode;
private String phone;
private String phototDataUrl;
...
}
```

NOTE
I included the class declaration for context. Place your field definitions directly below the first line of the class declaration.

After adding these new fields, JDeveloper will provide you with feedback via markers in the right-hand gutter. These markers tell you that the class contains unused field definitions, which can be very valuable after you have written a fair amount of code. Ignore these warnings for now. They will go away as soon as we implement getter and setter methods. Right-click near the end of the Java class editor and choose Generate Accessors from the context menu. The Generate Accessors dialog will appear. Check the box next to the Employee node at the very top of the list. Checking this box will select all child nodes. We want to generate accessors for all fields within the Employee class. Ensure that the scope for these accessors is set to public and that the Notify listeners when property changes box is selected. The Notify listener when property changes functionality ensures the UI is updated when we use Java to change entity attributes. Figure 11-5 is a screenshot of the Generate Accessors dialog. When you click the OK button, JDeveloper will generate a getter and a setter method for each field selected in the Generate Accessors dialog. After creating accessors, the markers in the right-hand gutter should disappear and the overview marker at the top will turn to green, providing you with instant feedback that your Java code is in good order.

NOTE
It is very important that you right-click at the end of the Java class file rather than somewhere in the middle. JDeveloper will use your click location as the insert location when adding accessor methods. It is not likely that you want JDeveloper to insert these anywhere except after the constructor definition.

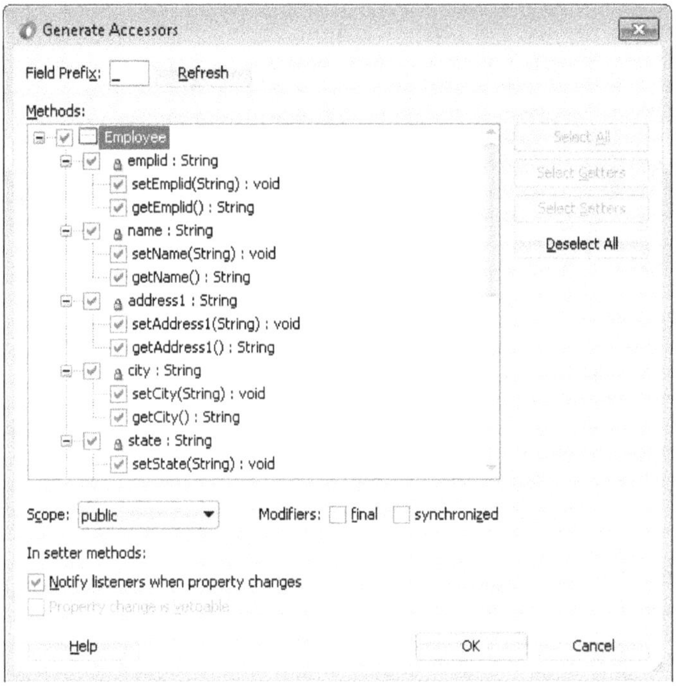

FIGURE 11-5.   *Generate Accessors dialog*

Getters/Setters or Constructor Parameters?

Our Employee entity starts life without an identity. We know this because the constructor contains no parameters. We assign an identity to the Employee entity by invoking the `setEmplid` method. Alternatively, we could create a constructor that expects an employee ID as a parameter, thereby assigning an identity at creation. Which method is the correct method? It depends. A constructor should contain a parameter for every attribute required to create a fully functional instance of a class. Likewise, read-only properties should be assigned through a constructor rather than a setter.

In a few pages, we will create Java classes that convert JSON objects and JSON arrays into Employee objects. At that time, we may once again ask ourselves, "should we have used constructors or setters for creating instances of Employee entities?" When we get there, I think you will agree with me that for this use case, setters are easier to read (although sometimes annoying to type). Specifically, setters clearly state the attribute we are updating. Constructors, on the other hand, rely on position, which offers no visual queue.

Here is a complete listing of the Employee class:

```
package com.example.ps.hcm.mobile.entities;

import oracle.adfmf.java.beans.PropertyChangeListener;
import oracle.adfmf.java.beans.PropertyChangeSupport;

public class Employee {
    private String emplid;
    private String name;
    private String address1;
    private String city;
    private String state;
    private String postal;
    private String country;
    private String countryCode;
    private String phone;
    private String phototDataUrl;
    private PropertyChangeSupport propertyChangeSupport =
            new PropertyChangeSupport(this);

    public Employee() {
        super();
    }


    public void setEmplid(String emplid) {
        String oldEmplid = this.emplid;
        this.emplid = emplid;
        propertyChangeSupport.firePropertyChange("emplid", oldEmplid,
                emplid);
    }

    public String getEmplid() {
        return emplid;
    }

    public void setName(String name) {
        String oldName = this.name;
        this.name = name;
        propertyChangeSupport.firePropertyChange("name", oldName,
                name);
    }

    public String getName() {
        return name;
    }
```

```
public void setAddress1(String address1) {
    String oldAddress1 = this.address1;
    this.address1 = address1;
    propertyChangeSupport.firePropertyChange("address1",
            oldAddress1, address1);
}

public String getAddress1() {
    return address1;
}

public void setCity(String city) {
    String oldCity = this.city;
    this.city = city;
    propertyChangeSupport.firePropertyChange("city", oldCity,
            city);
}

public String getCity() {
    return city;
}

public void setState(String state) {
    String oldState = this.state;
    this.state = state;
    propertyChangeSupport.firePropertyChange("state", oldState,
            state);
}

public String getState() {
    return state;
}

public void setPostal(String postal) {
    String oldPostal = this.postal;
    this.postal = postal;
    propertyChangeSupport.firePropertyChange("postal", oldPostal,
            postal);
}

public String getPostal() {
    return postal;
}

public void setCountry(String country) {
    String oldCountry = this.country;
    this.country = country;
```

```
        propertyChangeSupport.firePropertyChange("country",
                oldCountry, country);
    }

    public String getCountry() {
        return country;
    }

    public void setCountryCode(String countryCode) {
        String oldCountryCode = this.countryCode;
        this.countryCode = countryCode;
        propertyChangeSupport.firePropertyChange("countryCode",
                oldCountryCode, countryCode);
    }

    public String getCountryCode() {
        return countryCode;
    }

    public void setPhone(String phone) {
        String oldPhone = this.phone;
        this.phone = phone;
        propertyChangeSupport.firePropertyChange("phone", oldPhone,
                phone);
    }

    public String getPhone() {
        return phone;
    }

    public void setPhototDataUrl(String phototDataUrl) {
        String oldPhototDataUrl = this.phototDataUrl;
        this.phototDataUrl = phototDataUrl;
        propertyChangeSupport.firePropertyChange("phototDataUrl",
                oldPhototDataUrl, phototDataUrl);
    }

    public String getPhototDataUrl() {
        return phototDataUrl;
    }

    public void addPropertyChangeListener(PropertyChangeListener l) {
        propertyChangeSupport.addPropertyChangeListener(l);
    }

    public void removePropertyChangeListener(PropertyChangeListener l)
            {
        propertyChangeSupport.removePropertyChangeListener(l);
    }
}
```

JSON Helper Classes

Unfortunately, the JSON data structure returned by the PeopleSoft REST service doesn't match the Employee object. A matching JSON data structure would look like this:

```
{
    "EMPLID": "KU0001",
    "NAME": "Lewis,Douglas",
    "ADDRESS1": "3569 Malta Ave",
    "CITY": "Newark",
    "STATE": "NJ",
    "POSTAL": "07112",
    "COUNTRY": "USA",
    "COUNTRY_CODE": "",
    "PHONE": "973 622 1234"
}
```

The PeopleSoft REST Service Operation, however, insists on including an object identifier. We named that identifier DETAILS. Here is a sample (relevant text in bold):

```
{
    "DETAILS": {
        "EMPLID": "KU0001",
        "NAME": "Lewis,Douglas",
        "ADDRESS1": "3569 Malta Ave",
        "CITY": "Newark",
        "STATE": "NJ",
        "POSTAL": "07112",
        "COUNTRY": "USA",
        "COUNTRY_CODE": "",
        "PHONE": "973 622 1234"
    }
}
```

If our structures matched, we could let the MAF JSONBeanSerializationHelper convert the employee details JSON response directly to an Employee object. Instead, we have to write a few lines of conversion code. First, we will create a class that converts a JSON object into an Employee entity and then we will create a class that converts the search results service response into an array of Employee entities.

Converting a JSON Object into an Employee Entity   The JSONBeanSerializationHelper.fromJSON(java.lang.Class type, java.lang.String jsonString) method will convert a JSON string (the second parameter) into an object where the return type matches the first parameter…or at least that is the design. Actually, if the type specified implements

FIGURE 11-6. *Create Java Class dialog*

JSONDeserializable, it will return an object with a type that matches the return value of the JSONDeserializable.fromJSON method. It is this design feature that we will leverage to keep our converters separate from our entities.

Create a new Java class in the ViewController project named JsonObjectToEmployee with a package name of com.example.ps.hcm .mobile.json.converters. In the *Implements* section, add the JSONDeserializable interface. Figure 11-6 is a screenshot of the Create Java Class dialog.

Implement the fromJSON method as follows. I included the complete class definition for reference purposes even though you only need to implement the fromJSON method (in bold text). JDeveloper will write the rest of the Java code for you.

```
package com.example.ps.hcm.mobile.json.converters;

import com.example.ps.hcm.mobile.entities.Employee;
```

```java
import oracle.adfmf.framework.api.JSONDeserializable;
import oracle.adfmf.json.JSONObject;

public class JsonObjectToEmployee implements JSONDeserializable {
    public JsonObjectToEmployee() {
        super();
    }

    @Override
    public Object fromJSON(Object json) throws Exception {
        JSONObject outer = (JSONObject) json;
        Employee e = new Employee();

        JSONObject inner = outer.getJSONObject("DETAILS");
        e.setAddress1(inner.getString("ADDRESS1"));
        e.setCity(inner.getString("CITY"));
        e.setCountry(inner.getString("COUNTRY"));
        e.setCountryCode(inner.getString("COUNTRY_CODE"));
        e.setEmplid(inner.getString("EMPLID"));
        e.setName(inner.getString("NAME"));
        e.setPhone(inner.getString("PHONE"));
        e.setPostal(inner.getString("POSTAL"));
        e.setState(inner.getString("STATE"));

        return e;
    }
}
```

As noted in the JSON example above, the details Service Operation JSON response contains a nested object. The Java code in our `fromJSON` method first identifies the input parameter as a `JSONObject` and then extracts that inner employee details object.

NOTE
Rather than creating an `Employee` converter class we could have modified the `Employee` entity to implement the `JSONDeserializable` interface. How you implement `JSONDeserializable` is a matter of preference.

Create another Java class named `JsonArrayToEmployeeArray` with a package name of `com.example.ps.hcm.mobile.json.converters` that also implements `JSONDeserializable`. The following code listing contains the Java code for the `JsonArrayToEmployeeArray` class. As before, I included the entire class definition even though you only need to enter code into the `fromJSON` method.

NOTE
JDeveloper will automatically resolve missing imports. You can speed up the process by pressing the ALT-ENTER keyboard combination whenever JDeveloper identifies an unknown definition.

```java
package com.example.ps.hcm.mobile.json.converters;

import com.example.ps.hcm.mobile.entities.Employee;

import oracle.adfmf.framework.api.JSONDeserializable;
import oracle.adfmf.json.JSONArray;
import oracle.adfmf.json.JSONObject;

public class JsonArrayToEmployeeArray implements JSONDeserializable {
    public JsonArrayToEmployeeArray() {
        super();
    }

    @Override
    public Object fromJSON(Object json) throws Exception {
        JSONObject outer = (JSONObject) json;

        JSONObject inner = outer.getJSONObject("SEARCH_RESULTS");

        JSONArray list = inner.getJSONArray("SEARCH_FIELDS");
        Employee[] empls = new Employee[list.length()];
        for (int i = 0; i < list.length(); i++) {
            JSONObject item = list.getJSONObject(i);
            empls[i] = new Employee();
            empls[i].setEmplid(item.getString("EMPLID"));
            empls[i].setName(item.getString("NAME"));
        }

        return empls;
    }
}
```

NOTE
The Oracle A-Team created a Mobile Persistence Accelerator that eases the consumption of REST services as well as providing SQLite offline persistence. You can learn more about the A-Team Mobile Persistence Accelerator at http://www.ateam-oracle.com/getting-started-with-the-a-team-mobile-persistence-accelerator/.

URI Utility Class

Our application will invoke four different REST URLs. Each of these URLs shares common segments. Rather than littering our Java classes with URL references, let's create a utility class responsible for constructing REST service URLs. Create a new class named `UriUtil`. Set the package name to `com.example.ps.hcm.mobile .uri`. To this new class, add the following Java code:

```java
package com.example.ps.hcm.mobile.uri;

import java.util.ArrayList;
import java.util.Iterator;

public class UriUtil {
    private static String BASE_URI = "/";

    public UriUtil() {
        super();
    }

    public static String searchURI(String emplid, String name,
            String lastName) {
        StringBuilder uri = new StringBuilder(BASE_URI +
                "BMA_PERS_DIR_SEARCH.v1?");
        ArrayList<String> parmsList = new ArrayList<String>();

        if (emplid != null && emplid.length() > 0) {
            parmsList.add("EMPLID=" + emplid);
        }

        if (name != null && name.length() > 0) {
            parmsList.add("NAME=" + name);
        }

        if (lastName != null && lastName.length() > 0) {
            parmsList.add("LAST_NAME_SRCH" + lastName);
        }

        boolean isFirst = true;
        Iterator<String> parmsIt = parmsList.iterator();

        while (parmsIt.hasNext()) {
            if (isFirst) {
                uri.append(parmsIt.next());
                isFirst = false;
            } else {
                uri.append("&" + parmsIt.next());
            }
        }
    }
```

```
        return uri.toString();
    }

    public static String employeeURI(String emplid) {
        return BASE_URI + "BMA_PERS_DIR_DETAILS.v1/" + emplid;
    }

    public static String photoURI(String emplid) {
        return BASE_URI + "BMA_PERS_DIR_PHOTO.v1/" + emplid;
    }

    public static String profileURI() {
        return BASE_URI + "BMA_PERS_DIR_PROFILE.v1/profile";
    }

}
```

All of these methods concatenate Service Operation parameters into proper REST URLs. The only method with any substance is the searchURI method. The searchURI method takes several optional parameters and converts them into query string key/value pairs, but only for parameters with values.

If you review the methods of the UriUtil class, you will notice that they return a URL fragment; specifically, something like /BMA_PERS_DIR_DETAILS.v1/KU0001. This is the fragment of the URL that is unique to each Service Operation. Later we will create an Application Resource REST connection that identifies the primary, static portion of the URL.

Data Control JavaBean

Next, we need a Java class to invoke service operations. For example, after collecting search parameters we need to invoke the PeopleSoft search REST Service Operation. Likewise, after selecting a result we then have to invoke a Service Operation to fetch details. From the UI perspective, we want to call these Service Operations in response to clicking a button or selecting an item from a list.

With the ViewController project selected, add a new Java class named PersonnelDirectoryDC. Set the package name to com.example.ps.hcm .mobile.datacontrol. We will bind UI events to methods of this Java class through a JavaBean data control. JDeveloper will create a basic Java class with the following definition:

```
package com.example.ps.hcm.mobile.datacontrol;

public class PersonnelDirectoryDC {
    public PersonnelDirectoryDC() {
        super();
    }
}
```

Data Bound Accessors   Our UI will have a view that displays search results and another view that displays employee details. Let's add member fields to hold data for these two views. Just before the Java class constructor, add the following field definitions. I included the full class definition for context. Additions are in bold text.

```
package com.example.ps.hcm.mobile.datacontrol;

public class PersonnelDirectoryDC {
    private Employee selectedEmployee;
    private Employee[] searchResults;

    public PersonnelDirectoryDC() {
        super();
    }
}
```

Now we need public methods we can bind to UI elements. As with the other Java classes, move to the end of the file, right-click, and then select Generate Accessors from the context menu. Check the very top box to generate getters and setters for all fields. Make sure the scope is set to public. Unlike the other times we used the Generate Accessors routine, this time deselect the Notify listeners when property changes option. Later we will implement `ProviderChangeSupport` instead. Provider Change support is the collections equivalent of Notify listeners. After JDeveloper generates accessors, change the scope of the two `setXXX` methods from public to private. Our use case only requires read access to these members, not write access. The reason we generate write (or set) accessors is to provide a central mechanism for updating member field values from within other methods of the class. Specifically, we will set values internally after invoking web services. The `PersonnelDirectoryDC` Java class should now contain the following additional four methods. Notice that I changed the scope qualifier of `setSelectedEmployee` and `setSearchResults` to `private`.

```
    private void setSelectedEmployee(Employee selectedEmployee) {
        this.selectedEmployee = selectedEmployee;
    }

    public Employee getSelectedEmployee() {
        return selectedEmployee;
    }

    private void setSearchResults(Employee[] searchResults) {
        this.searchResults = searchResults;
    }

    public Employee[] getSearchResults() {
        return searchResults;
    }
```

Data Provider Change Support   The first page a user experiences within our mobile application is the search page. When viewing the search page the first time, the `searchResults` collection and `selectedEmployee` object will be empty. Later when we actually have values assigned to these member fields we want to make sure UI knows about data control changes. We notify the framework of bound variable changes through a class called `ProviderChangeSupport`. Let's add `ProviderChangeSupport` to the `PersonnelDirectoryDC`. Add the following field and method declarations to the `PersonnelDirectoryDC` Java class:

```
//***** provider change support *****//
//Enable provider change support
protected transient ProviderChangeSupport providerChangeSupport =
        new ProviderChangeSupport(this);

public void addProviderChangeListener(ProviderChangeListener l) {
    providerChangeSupport.addProviderChangeListener(l);
}

public void removeProviderChangeListener(
        ProviderChangeListener l) {
    providerChangeSupport.removeProviderChangeListener(l);
}
```

NOTE
The providerChangeSupport member field is marked as transient even though the PersonnelDirectoryDC class is not marked as serializable. We write code for two audiences. The first audience is the computer that will interpret the code. The second is other developers that have to maintain our code. The computer doesn't require the transient attribute, but other developers will appreciate knowing that this field should not be serialized.

Next, update the `setSelectedEmployee` and `setSearchResults` methods to fire a provider refresh when the corresponding property changes. The following is a listing of the two methods with additions in bold text:

```
private void setSelectedEmployee(Employee selectedEmployee) {
    this.selectedEmployee = selectedEmployee;
    providerChangeSupport.fireProviderRefresh("selectedEmployee");
}

...
```

```
private void setSearchResults(Employee[] searchResults) {
    this.searchResults = searchResults;
    providerChangeSupport.fireProviderRefresh("searchResults");
}
```

NOTE
*You can find a great YouTube video discussing MAF
provider and property change support at https://
www.youtube.com/watch?v=ZJePFhfVqMU.*

Invoking Service Operations   Our UI will invoke two primary service operations.
The first operation expects search criteria and returns a list of matching search results.
Converting those requirements into a data control method declaration would result
in a method signature resembling the following:

```
public void searchForEmployees(String emplid, String name,
        String lastName) {
    // TODO: implementation goes here
}
```

The UI will invoke `searchForEmployees` through a search button on a search
form. Wait…didn't I say that it would return a list of search results? That method
signature says the method does not return *any* results. Instead of returning results,
the method will make the results available through the `searchResults` member
field. Our UI will bind to the `searchResults` bean property exposed through
the `getSearchResults()` method.

The other method we need to implement is the select employee method. Here is
its method signature:

```
public void selectEmployee(String emplid) {
    // TODO: implementation goes here
}
```

The user will invoke the `selectEmployee` method by selecting an employee
from a list of search results.

Since both methods invoke REST service operations, they share a lot of similar
code. Rather than writing that code twice, let's create a private helper method named
`invokeRestRequest`. The following code listing provides the implementation for
this new method:

```
private String invokeRestRequest(String requestURI) {

    RestServiceAdapter restServiceAdapter =
            Model.createRestServiceAdapter();
    restServiceAdapter.clearRequestProperties();
    restServiceAdapter.setConnectionName("PersonnelDirectoryRestConn");
```

```
restServiceAdapter.setRequestType(
        RestServiceAdapter.REQUEST_TYPE_GET);

restServiceAdapter.addRequestProperty("Content-Type",
        "application/json");
restServiceAdapter.addRequestProperty("Accept",
        "application/json; charset=UTF-8");
restServiceAdapter.setRequestURI(requestURI);
restServiceAdapter.setRetryLimit(0);

//variable holding the response
String response = null;

try {
    response = restServiceAdapter.send("");
} catch (Exception e) {
    //log error
    Trace.log(Utility.APP_LOGNAME, Level.SEVERE, this.getClass(),
            "invokeRestRequest",
            "Invoke of REST Resource failed to " + requestURI);
    Trace.log(Utility.APP_LOGNAME, Level.SEVERE, this.getClass(),
            "invokeRestRequest", e.getLocalizedMessage());
}
return response;
};
```

NOTE
This method introduces the `oracle.adfmf.util` `.logging.Trace` *class and its* `log` *method. I will write more about the* `Trace` *class later.*

Inside the body of the `invokeRestRequest` method you will see the following line:

```
restServiceAdapter.setConnectionName("PersonnelDirectoryRestConn")
```

The connection `PersonnelDirectoryRestConn` does not exist yet. MAF maintains a separate connection descriptor so we don't have to hard code the REST end point in our URI utility class. Create a new connection by invoking the New Gallery through the File | New | From Gallery menu item and then selecting Connections | REST Connection from the Gallery. Choose the Create Connection in Application Resources option. Name the connection `PersonnelDirectoryRestConn` and set the URL to the portion of the REST service URL that is common across all REST services used by the application. To connect to my VirtualBox PUM environment configuration, the URL is http://192.168.56.102:8000/PSIGW/RESTListeningConnector/PSFT_HR. Figure 11-7 is a screenshot of the new REST connection.

Create REST Connection

Configure a new REST Web Service Connection. Choose Application Resources to add this connection to the current application. Choose IDE Connections if you don't want a single application to own it.

ADF
REST

Create Connection In: ⦿ Application Resources ⦿ IDE Connections

Name:

```
PersonnelDirectoryRestConn
```

URL Endpoint:

```
http://192.168.56.102:8000/PSIGW/RESTListeningConnector/PSFT_HR
```

Authentication Type:

```
None
```

Username:

Password:

Test Connection
Status:

Help   OK   Cancel

FIGURE 11-7. *Create REST Connection dialog*

NOTE
The Create REST Connection dialog contains a Test Connection button near the bottom. Attempting to test the connection with that button will result in an error because our REST Connection points to a URL fragment, not the entire REST URL.

With the common service operation code written, let's implement the remainder of the searchForEmployees and selectEmployee methods. First the searchForEmployees method:

```
public void searchForEmployees(String emplid, String name,
        String lastName) {
    String uri = UriUtil.searchURI(emplid, name, lastName);

    Trace.log(Utility.APP_LOGNAME, Level.INFO, this.getClass(),
            "searchForEmployees",
```

```
                    "Searching for employees matching emplid[ " + emplid +
                    "], name[" + name + "], lastName[" + lastName +
                    "] from uri " + uri);
        String response = invokeRestRequest(uri);

        Trace.log(Utility.APP_LOGNAME, Level.INFO, this.getClass(),
                "searchForEmployees", "JSON string: " + response);

        if (response != null) {
            try {
                setSearchResults((Employee[])
                        JSONBeanSerializationHelper.fromJSON(
                        JsonArrayToEmployeeArray.class, response));
            } catch (Exception e) {
                Trace.log(Utility.APP_LOGNAME, Level.SEVERE,
                        this.getClass(), "searchForEmployees",
                        "JSON => Search Results object conversion " +
                        "failed for JSON string: " + response);
                Trace.log(Utility.APP_LOGNAME, Level.SEVERE,
                        this.getClass(), "searchForEmployees",
                        e.getLocalizedMessage());
            }
        }
    }
}
```

The code in the above listing performs the following tasks:

- Asks `UriUtil` to compose a URL for the search service given the input parameters.

- Calls our `invokeRequest` method to fetch results from the REST search service.

- Uses the MAF `JSONBeanSerializationHelper` and our custom `JsonArraytoEmployeeArray` class to convert the service JSON response into an array of `Employee` objects.

The `selectEmployee` method is very similar:

```
public void selectEmployee(String emplid) {
    String uri = UriUtil.employeeURI(emplid);
    Trace.log(Utility.APP_LOGNAME, Level.INFO, this.getClass(),
            "selectEmployee",
            "Selecting employee " + emplid + " from uri " + uri);
    String response = invokeRestRequest(uri);
    Trace.log(Utility.APP_LOGNAME, Level.INFO, this.getClass(),
            "selectEmployee", "JSON string: " + response);
```

```
        if (response != null) {
            try {
                setSelectedEmployee((Employee)
                        JSONBeanSerializationHelper.fromJSON(
                                JsonObjectToEmployee.class,
                                response));
                getSelectedEmployee().setPhototDataUrl(
                        invokeRestRequest(UriUtil.photoURI(emplid)));
            } catch (Exception e) {
                Trace.log(Utility.APP_LOGNAME, Level.SEVERE,
                        this.getClass(), "selectEmployee",
                        "JSON => Employee object conversion failed " +
                        "for JSON string: " + response);
                Trace.log(Utility.APP_LOGNAME, Level.SEVERE,
                        this.getClass(), "selectEmployee",
                        e.getLocalizedMessage());
            }
        }
    }
}
```

Besides the obvious fact that this method invokes a different rest service and creates a different object, this method has one very important difference from the `searchForEmployees` method: `selectEmployee` calls two REST services. The first REST service selects an employee's details and the second selects the employee's photo. Considering that all of our use cases require both the image and the employee's details, it may make sense to combine these two services into one.

The complete class listing follows:

```
package com.example.ps.hcm.mobile.datacontrol;

import com.example.ps.hcm.mobile.entities.Employee;

import com.example.ps.hcm.mobile.json.converters.JsonArrayToEmployeeArray;
import com.example.ps.hcm.mobile.json.converters.JsonObjectToEmployee;
import com.example.ps.hcm.mobile.uri.UriUtil;

import java.util.logging.Level;

import oracle.adfmf.dc.ws.rest.RestServiceAdapter;
import oracle.adfmf.framework.api.JSONBeanSerializationHelper;
import oracle.adfmf.framework.api.Model;
import oracle.adfmf.java.beans.ProviderChangeListener;
import oracle.adfmf.java.beans.ProviderChangeSupport;
import oracle.adfmf.util.Utility;
import oracle.adfmf.util.logging.Trace;

public class PersonnelDirectoryDC {
    private Employee selectedEmployee;
```

```
private Employee[] searchResults;

public PersonnelDirectoryDC() {
    super();
}

private void setSelectedEmployee(Employee selectedEmployee) {
    this.selectedEmployee = selectedEmployee;
    providerChangeSupport.fireProviderRefresh("selectedEmployee");
}

public Employee getSelectedEmployee() {
    return selectedEmployee;
}

private void setSearchResults(Employee[] searchResults) {
    this.searchResults = searchResults;
    providerChangeSupport.fireProviderRefresh("searchResults");
}

public Employee[] getSearchResults() {
    return searchResults;
}

public void searchForEmployees(String emplid, String name,
                               String lastName) {
    String uri = UriUtil.searchURI(emplid, name, lastName);
    Trace.log(Utility.APP_LOGNAME, Level.INFO, this.getClass(),
            "searchForEmployees",
            "Searching for employees matching emplid[ " +
            emplid + "], name[" + name + "], lastName[" +
            lastName + "] from uri " + uri);
    String response = invokeRestRequest(uri);

    Trace.log(Utility.APP_LOGNAME, Level.INFO, this.getClass(),
            "searchForEmployees", "JSON string: " + response);

    if (response != null) {
        try {
            setSearchResults((Employee[])
                JSONBeanSerializationHelper.fromJSON(
                    JsonArrayToEmployeeArray.class,
                    response));
        } catch (Exception e) {
            Trace.log(Utility.APP_LOGNAME, Level.SEVERE,
                    this.getClass(), "searchForEmployees",
                    "JSON => Search Results object conversion " +
                    "failed for JSON string: " + response);
            Trace.log(Utility.APP_LOGNAME, Level.SEVERE,
                    this.getClass(), "searchForEmployees",
```

```
                                e.getLocalizedMessage());
        }
    }
}

public void selectEmployee(String emplid) {
    String uri = UriUtil.employeeURI(emplid);
    Trace.log(Utility.APP_LOGNAME, Level.INFO, this.getClass(),
            "selectEmployee",
            "Selecting employee " + emplid + " from uri " + uri);
    String response = invokeRestRequest(uri);
    Trace.log(Utility.APP_LOGNAME, Level.INFO, this.getClass(),
            "selectEmployee", "JSON string: " + response);

    if (response != null) {
        try {
            setSelectedEmployee((Employee)
                    JSONBeanSerializationHelper.fromJSON(
                            JsonObjectToEmployee.class,
                            response));

            getSelectedEmployee().setPhototDataUrl(
                    invokeRestRequest(UriUtil.photoURI(emplid)));
        } catch (Exception e) {
            Trace.log(Utility.APP_LOGNAME, Level.SEVERE,
                    this.getClass(), "selectEmployee",
                    "JSON => Employee object conversion " +
                    "failed for JSON string: " + response);
            Trace.log(Utility.APP_LOGNAME, Level.SEVERE,
                    this.getClass(), "selectEmployee",
                    e.getLocalizedMessage());
        }
    }
}

private String invokeRestRequest(String requestURI) {

    RestServiceAdapter restServiceAdapter =
            Model.createRestServiceAdapter();
    restServiceAdapter.clearRequestProperties();
    restServiceAdapter.setConnectionName(
            "PersonnelDirectoryRestConn");

    restServiceAdapter.setRequestType(
            RestServiceAdapter.REQUEST_TYPE_GET);

    restServiceAdapter.addRequestProperty("Content-Type",
            "application/json");
```

```
    restServiceAdapter.addRequestProperty("Accept",
            "application/json; charset=UTF-8");
    restServiceAdapter.setRequestURI(requestURI);
    restServiceAdapter.setRetryLimit(0);

    //variable holding the response
    String response = null;

    try {
        response = restServiceAdapter.send("");
    } catch (Exception e) {
        //log error
        Trace.log(Utility.APP_LOGNAME, Level.SEVERE,
                    this.getClass(), "invokeRestRequest",
                    "Invoke of REST Resource failed to " +
                    requestURI);
        Trace.log(Utility.APP_LOGNAME, Level.SEVERE,
                    this.getClass(), "invokeRestRequest",
                    e.getLocalizedMessage());
    }
    return response;
};


//***** provider change support *****//
//Enable provider change support

protected transient ProviderChangeSupport providerChangeSupport =
        new ProviderChangeSupport(this);

public void addProviderChangeListener(ProviderChangeListener l) {
    providerChangeSupport.addProviderChangeListener(l);
}

public void removeProviderChangeListener(
        ProviderChangeListener l) {
    providerChangeSupport.removeProviderChangeListener(l);
}
}
```

Creating the Data Control   Find the PersonnelDirectoryDC.java file in the project
explorer. It is inside the folder ViewController/Application Sources/com.example.ps
/hcm/mobile/datacontrol. Right-click the PersonnelDirectoryDC.java node and
choose Create Data Control from the popup menu. When the Create Bean Data
Control wizard appears, accept the default values assigned in each step of the
wizard by clicking Next and then click Finish. After the wizard finishes, expand
the Data Controls palette. If it is empty, then click the refresh button (the button
beside the words "Data Control" with two arrows forming a circle). You should now
see the PersonnelDirectoryDC data control as depicted in Figure 11-8

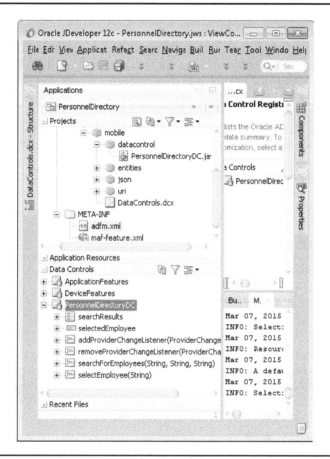

FIGURE 11-8. *PersonnelDirectoryDC data control*

NOTE
When you create a Data Control, JDeveloper opens the DataControls.dcx file. This file contains metadata describing data controls. From this file, you can edit data-control UI display hints, validation rules, and so on. If you plan to use the same data control on many views, then you can set display hints, such as the display label and default control type, in the control metadata rather than on each page that uses the data control.

User Interface

MAF displays application functionality to users through artifacts called *features*. Features become springboard icons. Locate the maf-feature.xml file in the JDeveloper project explorer (ViewController/Application Sources/META-INF/maf-feature.xml) and open the file. Click the add feature button (green plus icon) within the feature grid to create a new feature named DirectorySearch. Figure 11-9 is a screenshot of the Create MAF Feature dialog.

The maf-feature.xml file contains a significant amount of metadata for configuring the appearance of each feature, including how (icons) and when (constraints) to display the feature. To keep this example as simple as possible, we will just focus on feature content. With the new DirectorySearch feature selected in the Features grid, select the Content tab. You will see that the content grid already has one item with a default type of MAF AMX Page. MAF feature content can come from the following:

- MAF AMX Page

- MAF AMX Task Flow

- Local HTML

- Remote URL

We are going to build our solution as a single MAF AMX Task Flow. Change the Type value for the com.example.ps.hcm.DirectorySearch.1 content row to MAF AMX Task Flow. JDeveloper will immediately highlight the File field telling you that an MAF AMX Task Flow requires a file. Click the green plus sign to the left of that field to create a new AMX Task Flow. Name the new Task Flow DirectorySearch-task-flow.xml as shown in Figure 11-10.

Figure 11-11 is a screenshot of the maf-feature.xml file after adding the DirectorySearch Task Flow.

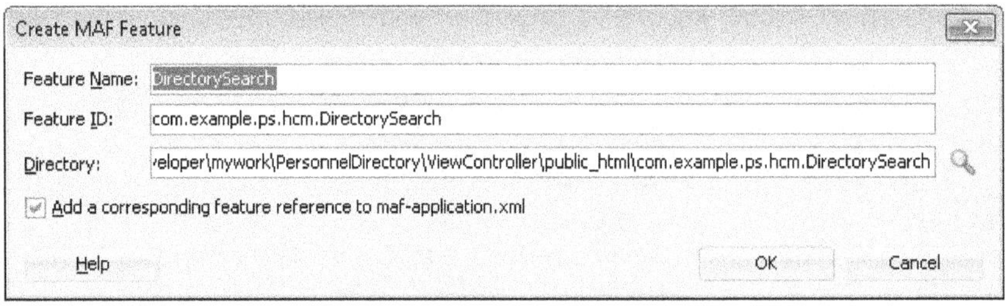

FIGURE 11-9. *Create MAF Feature dialog*

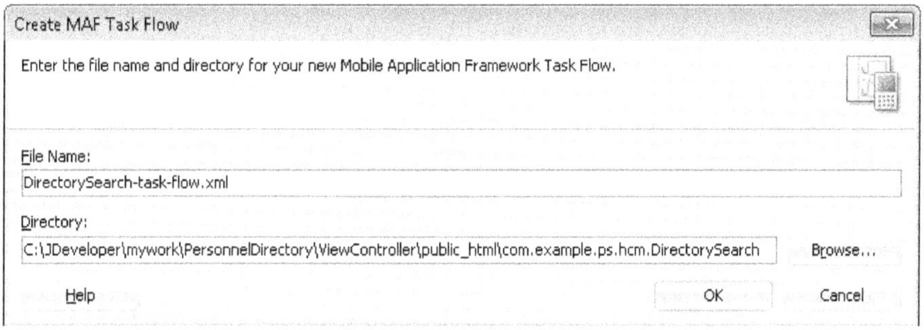

FIGURE 11-10. *New MAF AMX Task Flow*

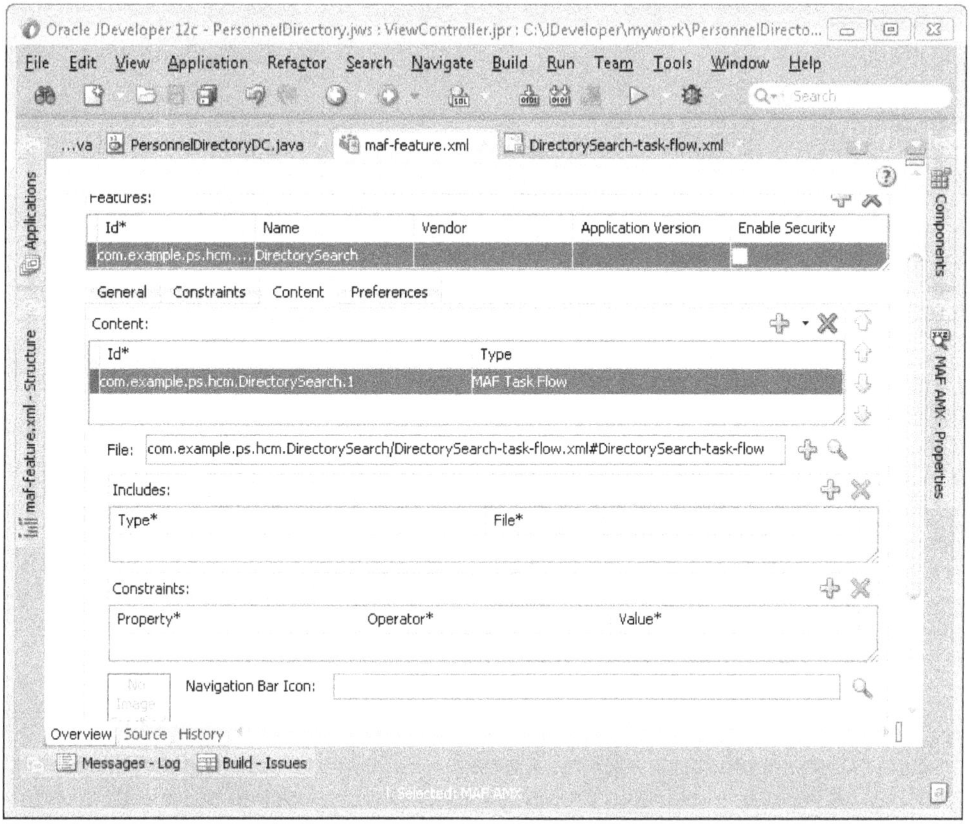

FIGURE 11-11. *maf-feature.xml file*

JDeveloper will automatically open the DirectorySearch-task-flow.xml file.

NOTE
You can reopen a closed Task Flow by searching for it under the ViewController/Web Content node within the project explorer.

Designing a TaskFlow

The Task Flow designer looks like a flow chart designer... kind of like Microsoft Visio. We will drag Views and data control Methods onto the task flow and connect them with Control Flow arrows.

From our experience with prior chapters, we already know that our Personnel Directory will have a search page, a search results page, and a details page. We also know that these three pages are linked together by two Service Operations:

- A search operation

- A details operation

Let's build a flow chart describing this use case. From the palette on the right side of JDeveloper, drag a view component into the upper left corner of the new Task Flow and name the view `search`. Drag another view to the right of the first but down a little ways and name it `results`. Drag a final view component to the right of the results view and parallel to the search view. Name this final view `details`. Align the three so that they make two eyes and a nose as if you were trying to create a smiley face instead of a flow chart. The search view represents the eye on the left (I believe that would be smiley's right eye, which is your left). The details view is the other eye. Move the results view down in the middle between the two eyes. This is smiley's nose.

The search form will gather parameters for the `searchForEmployees` data control method. The searchForEmployees data control method fetches data for the results page. Let's model the invocation of this method by dragging searchForEmployees from the Data Controls palette onto the Task Flow designer. Dragging a data control operation onto a Task Flow causes JDeveloper to display the Edit Action Binding dialog. JDeveloper noticed that the searchForEmployees method requires parameters and it wants you to specify values for those parameters. The values for the searchForEmployees method will come from data entered into the search page. What we need is a container for values that we can pass between the search page and the searchForEmployees operation. MAF satisfies this requirement through a runtime variable named pageFlowScope. The pageFlowScope variable is a dynamic object to which we can add custom properties. Later when we define the search page, we will transfer values from the search page data entry fields into the

Parameter Name	Parameter Value
Emplid	#{pageFlowScope.searchEmplIdVal}
Name	#{pageFlowScope.searchNameVal}
LastName	#{pageFlowScope.searchLastNameVal}

TABLE 11-1. *searchForEmployees parameter mappings*

pageFlowScope object. Right now, we need to tell JDeveloper the names of our custom pageFlowScope properties so we can continue defining our Task Flow diagram. Use the values from Table 11-1 to map searchForEmployees parameters to pageFlowScope custom attributes.

Figure 11-12 is a screenshot of the Edit Action Binding dialog.

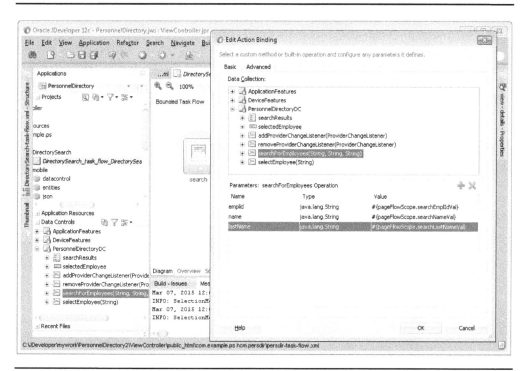

FIGURE 11-12. *Edit Action Binding dialog*

Now use the Control Flow Case component to connect the search page with the searchForEmployees method. Name the Control Flow Case `search`. Drag another Control Flow Case from searchForEmployees to the results page. Keep the default name. Your Task flow should resemble Figure 11-13. We will add a few more items to this Task Flow before we finish.

So...let's say the user performing a search enters some criteria, clicks search, and then views the results. While viewing the results, the user realizes that the desired employee is not in the list. The user decides to return to the search form and enter new criteria. Let's model this in our Task Flow. Drag a Control Flow Case between the results page and the search page and name it returnToSearch.

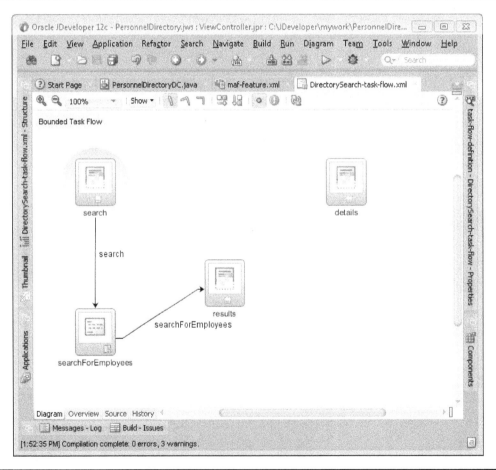

FIGURE 11-13. *DirectorySearch-task-flow intermediate state*

The Search Parameter View

We still need to connect the details view to the rest of the Task Flow components, but let's pause here and construct enough of the view definitions to test the data model. For each view within the Task Flow, double-click the view icon to create a new AMX page. Keep the default name and directory. For the Facets, select the Header and Primary Action. Figure 11-14 is a screenshot of the Create MAF AMX Page dialog for the search.amx page.

When the new AMX page designer appears, drag the searchForEmployees operation from the Data Controls palette onto the XML page just before the closing `</amx:panelPage>` tag. When the popup menu appears, select MAF Parameter Form. An Edit Form Fields dialog will appear. Enter a descriptive label for each field. For example, enter Employee ID for the emplid field and so on. Figure 11-15 is a screenshot of the Edit Form Fields dialog.

JDeveloper will insert XML into the AMX page to define the parameter form we just added. It also added a button to invoke the searchForEmployees operation. That isn't how we plan to execute the searchForEmployees method. Instead, we want to use a control flow case to route the request through the searchForEmployees operation and then to the results page. Delete the `<amx:commandButton>` XML element that should be near the end of the AMX page definition. Just to make sure you are deleting the correct button, the text for the button will be searchForEmployees. Now switch to the Bindings tab and delete the searchForEmployees binding. To delete a binding, select the binding from the Bindings list and then click the red X within the header of the list. Figure 11-16 is a screenshot of the bindings after making these changes.

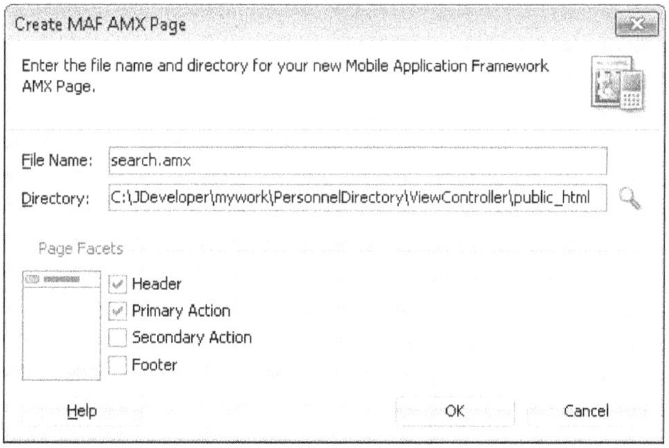

FIGURE 11-14. *Create MAF AMX Page dialog*

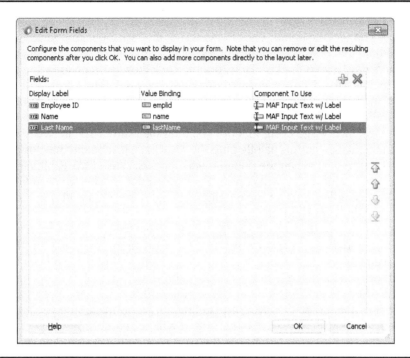

FIGURE 11-15. *Edit Form Fields dialog*

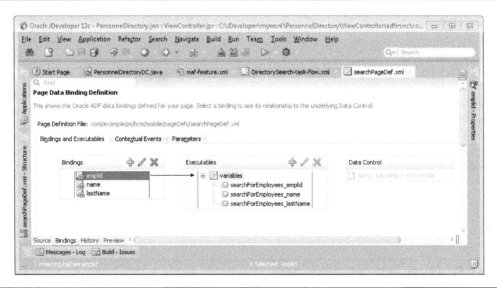

FIGURE 11-16. *Search AMX page bindings tab*

NOTE
Adding the parameter form created an extra binding we don't intend to use. Alternatively, we could have manually dragged a form and then input text elements to the page, one for each field. The add-and-then-delete approach presented here was just a little more efficient.

Switch back to Source view and locate the `amx:outputText` element within the header facet. Change the value attribute to Search. This is the text that will be displayed in the page header region. In like manner, locate the `amx:commandButton` within the primary facet and use the properties inspector to set its text attribute to `Search`. This is the text that will be displayed on the face of the button. While still editing the `amx:commandButton` within the properties inspector, set the action attribute to `search`. The action attribute identifies the Control Flow Case we configured in the Task Flow definition. From the Components palette on the right, drag three setPropertyListener components onto the `amx:commandButton` that resides in the header facet (it should be the only `amx:commandButton`). These setPropertyListeners will move values from the search parameter form into the `pageFlowScope` attributes that our searchForEmployees method expects. With your cursor inside one of the `amx:setPropertyListener` elements, you should find a Properties Inspector in the lower right corner of JDeveloper. Use the Properties Inspector to set the From and To attributes for each setPropertyListener according to values shown in Table 11-2.

NOTE
When you place your cursor inside the From or To attribute of the Properties Inspector you will see an icon appear just to the right of the field. Selecting this icon gives you access to the Expression Builder. Inside the Expression Builder, you can navigate through the bindings to select the correct binding for each `setPropertyListener`.

From	To
#{bindings.emplid.inputValue}	#{pageFlowScope.searchEmplIdVal}
#{bindings.name.inputValue}	#{pageFlowScope.searchNameVal}
#{bindings.lastName.inputValue}	#{pageFlowScope.searchLastNameVal}

TABLE 11-2. *setPropertyListener attribute mapping*

Your search.amx file should now contain the following XML:

```xml
<?xml version="1.0" encoding="UTF-8" ?>
<amx:view xmlns:xsi="http://www.w3.org/2001/XMLSchema-instance"
          xmlns:amx="http://xmlns.oracle.com/adf/mf/amx"
          xmlns:dvtm="http://xmlns.oracle.com/adf/mf/amx/dvt">
  <amx:panelPage id="pp1">
    <amx:facet name="header">
      <amx:outputText value="Search" id="ot1"/>
    </amx:facet>
    <amx:facet name="primary">
      <amx:commandButton id="cb1" text="Search" action="search">
        <amx:setPropertyListener id="spl1"
            from="#{bindings.emplid.inputValue}"
            to="#{pageFlowScope.searchEmplIdVal}"/>
        <amx:setPropertyListener id="spl2"
            from="#{bindings.name.inputValue}"
            to="#{pageFlowScope.searchNameVal}"/>
        <amx:setPropertyListener id="spl3"
            from="#{bindings.lastName.inputValue}"
            to="#{pageFlowScope.searchLastNameVal}"/>
      </amx:commandButton>
    </amx:facet>
    <amx:panelFormLayout id="pfl1">
      <amx:inputText value="#{bindings.emplid.inputValue}"
          label="Employee ID" id="it3"/>
      <amx:inputText value="#{bindings.name.inputValue}" label="Name"
          id="it1"/>
      <amx:inputText value="#{bindings.lastName.inputValue}"
          label="Last Name" id="it2"/>
    </amx:panelFormLayout>
  </amx:panelPage>
</amx:view>
```

We have now written enough code, created enough definitions, and configured enough options to test this application. But, let's make one more adjustment before testing. Our Java model classes contain Trace statements that print to the application's log file if the log level is set to INFO or higher. Since we haven't configured the results UI yet, we will have no visual feedback that our web services executed successfully. By setting the log level to INFO, however, we can view results in the log file before we finish configuring the UI. From the Application Resources palette, expand the node Descriptors/META-INF, and then open the file logging.properties. Replace all instances of the word SEVERE (the default log level) with INFO. Save and then close the logging.properties file.

Make sure your emulator is running and that you can connect to your PeopleSoft instance. When you are ready, select Application | Deploy | Android1 from the

JDeveloper menu bar. Select Deploy application to emulator when the Deployment Action dialog appears. Click Finish to begin the deployment process. You can track the deployment status from deployment log located at the bottom of the JDeveloper application window.

NOTE
Deploying to an android emulator on my laptop takes 3–5 minutes.

After deployment, look for the PersonnelDirectory app within the emulator's list of apps and then launch the PersonnelDirectory app. Enter some valid criteria into the search parameter form and then click the search button. Figure 11-17 is a screenshot of the search parameter form.

The next page you will see should be an empty results page. The page is empty because we haven't added any output controls to that page. Nevertheless, we can confirm the design of our data model by reviewing output in the MAF application log file. The log file for an Android device is a text file located in the root of the sdcard and shares the same name as the application. Therefore, we are looking for a file named sdcard/PersonnelDirectory.txt. The mount point for an sdcard varies by

FIGURE 11-17. *MAF search parameter form*

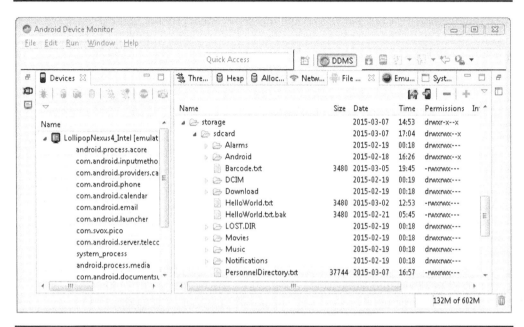

FIGURE 11-18. *Android Device Monitor File Explorer*

Android release, but is easily located by launching the monitor application from the sdk\tools folder of the Android SDK, and then using the File Explorer. Figure 11-18 is a screenshot of the log file selected in the Android Monitor File Explorer.

You can download and view the file from the File Explorer. I prefer to note the path and then use the following command line syntax:

```
c:\temp>adb shell cat /storage/sdcard/PersonnelDirectory.txt >
PersonnelDirectory.txt
```

NOTE
About my preference for the command line…it isn't that I really like typing commands. The command line just has this cool feature called command-line history. You can easily recall the last command by pressing the up arrow on the keyboard. What this means is that I type the command once and then recall it each time I want to view the log by just pressing the up arrow on my keyboard.

Download the log file and search for the text PersonnelDirectoryDC. These are the lines we printed from the `PersonnelDirectoryDC` JavaBean. You should see at least one line showing the URI that resembles:

```
[INFO - oracle.adfmf.application - PersonnelDirectoryDC -
searchForEmployees] Searching for employees matching emplid[ KU000%],
name[], lastName[] from uri /BMA_PERS_DIR_SEARCH.v1?EMPLID=KU000%
```

You should see another line containing the REST JSON response. If your search criteria did not return any results, then the log file should contain the following SEVERE warning:

```
[SEVERE - oracle.adfmf.application - PersonnelDirectoryDC -
searchForEmployees] JSON => Search Results object conversion failed
for JSON string: {"SEARCH_RESULTS": {}}
```

The Search Results View

Now that we know our data model works and our search operation executes successfully, let's move on to defining the search results view. The search results view is just a full page list of results that serves as navigation. Touching an item in the list should navigate to the details view for the selected list item.

Open the results.amx page and drag the PersonnelDirectoryDC searchResults collection from the Data Controls palette onto the results.amx page just below the primary facet. Select the MAF List View item from the popup that will appear when you drop the data control item. When the ListView Gallery appears, select the first variation of the Simple format. Figure 11-19 is a screenshot of the ListView Gallery.

Next, we need to tell the ListView wizard what data to display. In the Edit List View dialog, replace the emplid Value Binding with the name field. Figure 11-20 is a screenshot of the of the Edit List View dialog after updating the value binding.

The List View wizard added bindings for the data control and the name attribute of the searchResults collection. Since we need to pass the employee ID onto the details view, we will also need to add a binding for the emplid attribute. While still editing results.amx, switch to the Bindings tab and locate the searchResults binding. It will be in the list on the left side. Select the searchResults item and then click the edit icon (the pencil) in the Bindings list header. Note the list of available attributes and the list of display attributes. These are located at the bottom of the Edit Tree Binding dialog that will appear when you click the edit icon to edit the searchResults binding. Use the shuttle button to move the emplid attribute to the list of Display Attributes. Figure 11-21 is a screenshot of the results.amx display attributes.

Return to Source view and update the `amx:listItem` element's child `amx:outputText` element. Since we now have the employee ID available, let's

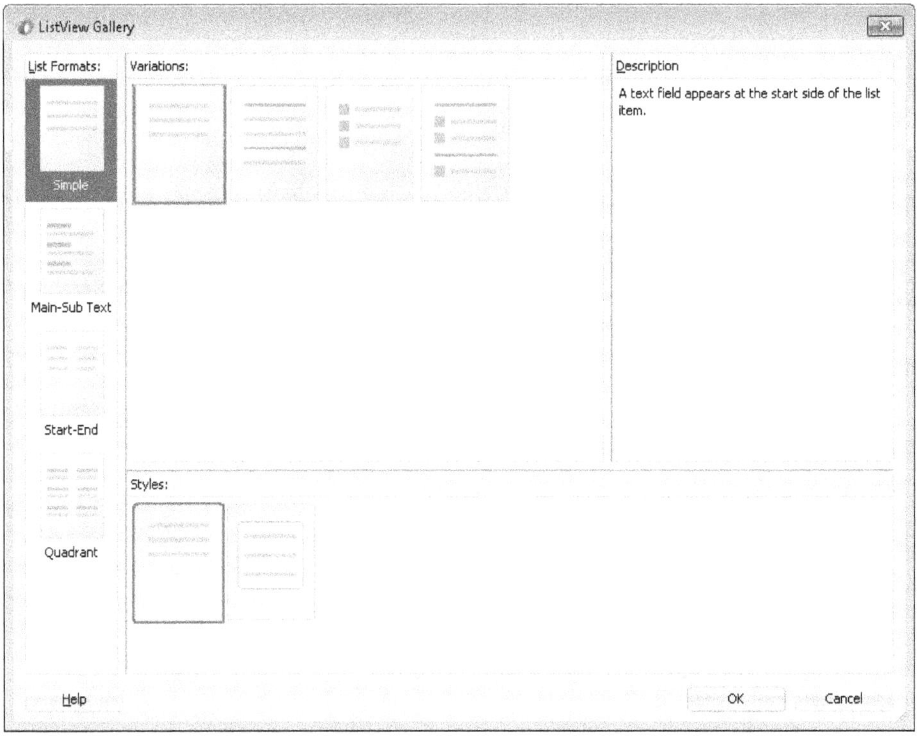

FIGURE 11-19. *ListView gallery*

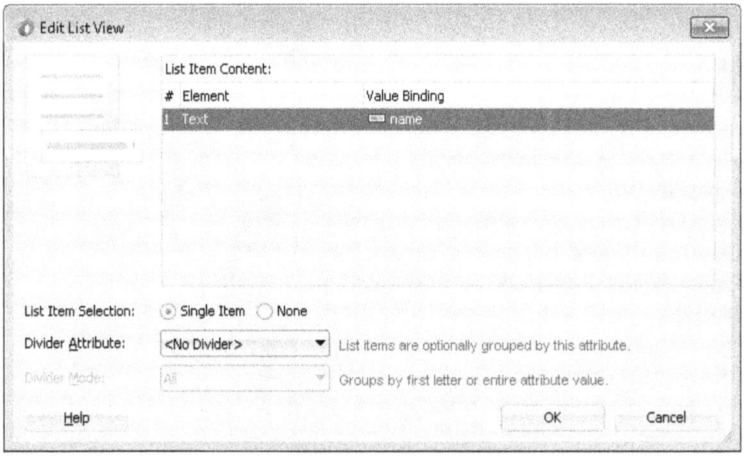

FIGURE 11-20. *Edit List View dialog*

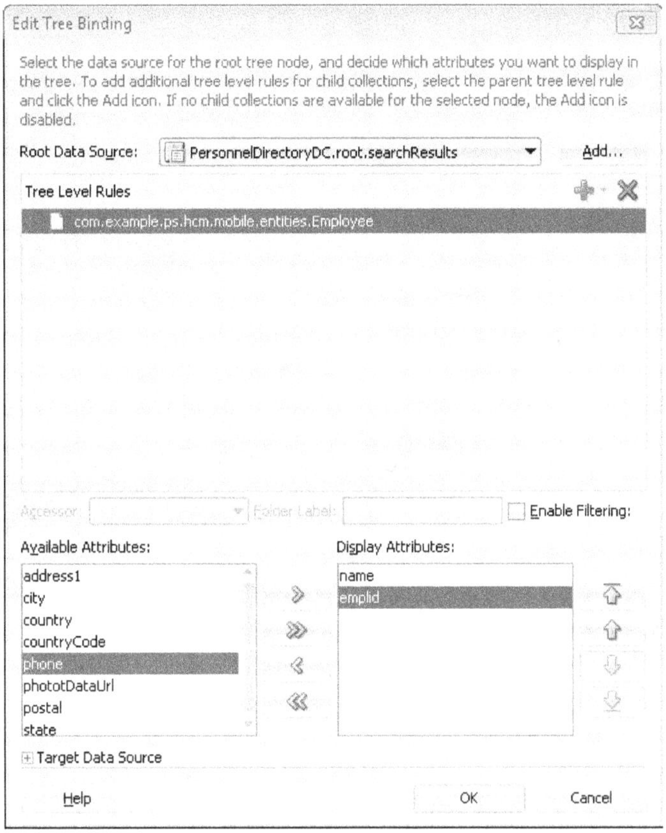

FIGURE 11-21. *Display Attributes*

add it to the list item display. Change the value attribute of the amx:outputText element to match the following:

```
<amx:outputText value="#{row.name} (#{row.emplid})" id="ot2"/>
```

Notice that we added the employee ID row attribute inside of parenthesis. When we run this we expect to see a list containing rows similar to the following:

```
Lewis,Doug (KU0001)
```

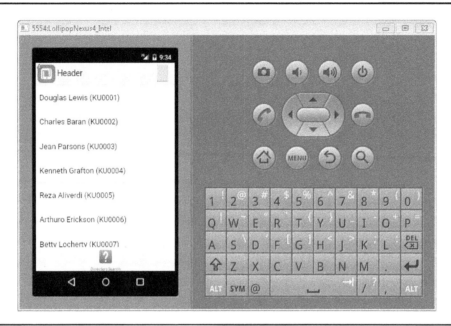

FIGURE 11-22. *Screenshot of list view in emulator*

Deploy the application to your emulator and verify that the results page appears as expected. Figure 11-22 is a screenshot of the emulator list view showing a list of search results.

Let's return to the Task Flow and finish assigning routes. As it stands, we don't have a route to take us from the results page to the details page. Drag the selectEmployee method from the PersonnelDirectoryDC data control onto the DirectorySearch task flow. When the Edit Action Binding dialog appears, set the emplid parameter to `#{pageFlowScope.selectedEmplId}`. Figure 11-23 is a screenshot of the Edit Action Binding dialog.

Drag a Control Flow case from the results view to the selectEmployee method and name it `select`. Drag another Control Flow case from the selectEmployee method to the details view. Accept the default name of selectEmployee. Now we need return routes for the details view. While viewing employee details, a user may decide to either return to the search results or perform a new search. Drag two Control Flow cases from the details view with one going to the results view and another returning to the search view. Name the results Control Flow case `returnToList` and name the search Control Flow case `returnToSearch`. Figure 11-24 is a screenshot of the completed Task Flow.

FIGURE 11-23.   *Edit Action Binding dialog*

Let's return to results.amx and finish the layout. We now have targets defined so we can invoke some action when the user selects an item in the ListView. Select amx:listItem and use the Property Inspector to set the listItem action to select. This is the name of the Control Flow case that invokes the selectEmployee data control method. Add a setPropertyListener just inside the amx:listItem; we will use this to set the ID of the employee when a user taps a list item. Select the amx:setPropertyListener and set the From attribute to #{row.emplid}. Set the To attribute to the value #{pageFlowScope.selectedEmplId}.

Let's update the header attributes of the results.amx page before moving onto the details.amx page. Locate the amx:outputText within the header facet and change the value to Search Results. Just below the header facet you should see the primary facet. Set the action of the button within the primary facet to __back.

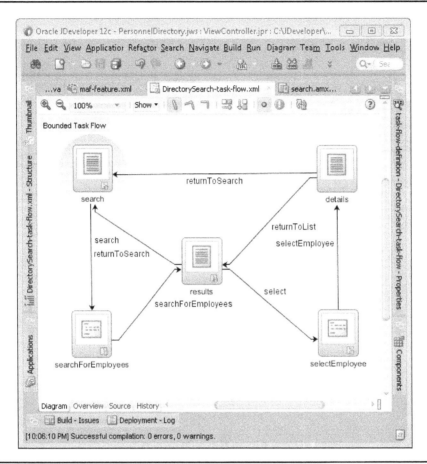

FIGURE 11-24. *DirectorySearch completed Task Flow*

This is a special MAF Control Flow case that converts the button into an operating system-specific back button. Your results.amx page should now contain the following XML:

```xml
<?xml version="1.0" encoding="UTF-8" ?>
<amx:view xmlns:xsi="http://www.w3.org/2001/XMLSchema-instance"
        xmlns:amx="http://xmlns.oracle.com/adf/mf/amx"
        xmlns:dvtm="http://xmlns.oracle.com/adf/mf/amx/dvt">
  <amx:panelPage id="pp1">
    <amx:facet name="header">
      <amx:outputText value="Search Results" id="ot1"/>
    </amx:facet>
```

```
      <amx:facet name="primary">
        <amx:commandButton id="cb1" action="__back"/>
      </amx:facet>
      <amx:listView var="row"
          value="#{bindings.searchResults.collectionModel}"
          fetchSize="#{bindings.searchResults.rangeSize}"
          selectedRowKeys=
            "#{bindings.searchResults.collectionModel.selectedRow}"
          selectionListener=
            "#{bindings.searchResults.collectionModel.makeCurrent}"
          showMoreStrategy="autoScroll" bufferStrategy="viewport"
          id="lv1">
        <amx:listItem id="li1" action="select">
          <amx:outputText value="#{row.name} (#{row.emplid})" id="ot2"/>
          <amx:setPropertyListener id="spl1" from="#{row.emplid}"
              to="#{pageFlowScope.selectedEmplId}"/>
        </amx:listItem>
      </amx:listView>
    </amx:panelPage>
</amx:view>
```

Deploy and test your application. The results.amx view should now invoke the selectEmployee operation and transfer to the details.amx page. If it weren't for the application log, we would have no way of knowing this because the details.amx page is currently empty. From the log file, we can confirm that the Task Flow is working properly because the log file contains entries similar to the following:

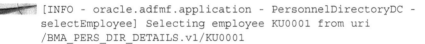

```
[INFO - oracle.adfmf.application - PersonnelDirectoryDC -
selectEmployee] Selecting employee KU0001 from uri
/BMA_PERS_DIR_DETAILS.v1/KU0001
```

The Details View

Creating the details page is a little trickier than the rest. The details view is a read-only page that exists for information and action. Not only should it provide relevant information but it should also facilitate actions such as placing a call or mapping an address. To match the mockups from Chapter 5 and provide actionable links we will need to

■ Create a layout using a mixture of AMX components and CSS.

■ Manually specify data bindings.

Open the details.amx page and update the header and primary facets just like we did for the results page. Set the header facet amx:outputText value to Details and set the action of the primary facet amx:commandButton to __back.

Details Layout Part I In this chapter so far we have used a panelFormLayout and a listView. Both of these automatically format the contents of the page according to best practices. The details page is a bit more free-formed. The layout will consist of two stacked tables. The top table will hold the photo, name, and ID. The bottom table will contain phone number and address links. Add a tableLayout just after the primary facet. Set the table width to `100%` and the margin property to `12px 16px`. To this tableLayout and a rowLayout and then add two cellFormat elements inside the rowLayout. Your XML should resemble the following (tableLayout in bold text):

```xml
<?xml version="1.0" encoding="UTF-8" ?>
<amx:view xmlns:xsi="http://www.w3.org/2001/XMLSchema-instance"
          xmlns:amx="http://xmlns.oracle.com/adf/mf/amx"
          xmlns:dvtm="http://xmlns.oracle.com/adf/mf/amx/dvt">
  <amx:panelPage id="pp1">
    <amx:facet name="header">
      <amx:outputText value="Details" id="ot1"/>
    </amx:facet>
    <amx:facet name="primary">
      <amx:commandButton id="cb1" action="__back"/>
    </amx:facet>
    <amx:tableLayout id="tl1" width="100%"
                     inlineStyle="margin:12px 16px;">
      <amx:rowLayout id="rl1">
        <amx:cellFormat id="cf1"/>
        <amx:cellFormat id="cf2"/>
      </amx:rowLayout>
    </amx:tableLayout>
  </amx:panelPage>
</amx:view>
```

The first cellFormat, which likely has an ID of `cf1`, will contain an employee photo. Drag the photoDataUrl attribute of the PersonnelDataDC.selectedEmployee data control into the first cellFormat. We don't actually want to display the photoDataUrl because it contains quite a bit of base64 encoded binary data. The reason we added it to the page in this manner is to easily create a data binding and generate the appropriate expression language selector. Into this same cellFormat, drag an image component from the component palette. Set the image source attribute to the expression language applied to the outputText. Add an `inlineStyle` attribute with a value of `width:100px;`. We don't want the image width to exceed 100 pixels. Delete the donor `amx:outputText` element. The image XML should now resemble:

```xml
<amx:image id="i1" inlineStyle="width:100px;"
           source="#{bindings.phototDataUrl.inputValue}"/>
```

Inside the second `amx:cellFormat`, which likely has the ID `cf2`, add a panelGroupLayout. The panelGroupLayout can either display its contents horizontally or vertically. We want it to display the employee name and ID in a stacked fashion so set the `amx:panelGroupLayout` element's layout attribute to `vertical`. We also want the contents aligned to the right of the layout so set the halign attribute to end. Now drag the name and emplid attributes from the PersonnelDirectoryDC .selectedEmployee data control field into the `amx:panelGroupLayout`. When prompted to select the control type, choose Text | MAF Output Text.

The city, state, postal code, and country come next, but it would be nice to add a little vertical whitespace between the name and address. Drag a spacer from the component palette and place it under the emplid outputText field. Set the height of the spacer to 20. Now drag the city, state, postal, and country fields from the selectedEmployee property of the PersonnelDirectoryDC data control and place them underneath the spacer.

We will combine these outputText bindings into just two amx:outputText elements. Dragging them onto the AMX page gives us the necessary expression language and page bindings. Cut the expression language out of the state and postal code outputText elements and add them to the city outputText value attribute so that the contents is formatted the same as an envelope. Like this:

```
<amx:outputText value="#{bindings.city.inputValue},
#{bindings.state.inputValue} #{bindings.postal.inputValue}" id="ot4"/>
```

After concatenating values, delete the donor outputText elements. For each outputText within the tableLayout, set the styleClass to `amx-text-sectiontitle`.

Identifying MAF Style Classes

MAF contains a lot of predefined CSS style classes. The trick is finding them. Since I am a visual person, my favorite way to find style classes is to first see something on the screen and then try to find its definition. The easiest way to do this is to launch Chrome remote inspector. From the Chrome hamburger button (options menu), choose More Tools | Inspect Devices. Chrome will display a list of connected Android devices including emulators. If you don't see your emulator listed, then run the command `adb start-server` from the Android SDK platform-tools directory (or anywhere if adb is available through your PATH environment variable).

NOTE
The Safari web browser has a similar feature for the Mac/iOS combination.

Alternatively, you can find every CSS definition in the deployment's CSS file. This file is generated when an application is deployed. After deploying an application, find the applications APK file within the application's deploy directory. Use a zip file program such as 7-zip to expand the file. The application archive contains another file named assets.zip. Expand assets.zip and look in the www\css folder. Here you will find skin-specific CSS files.

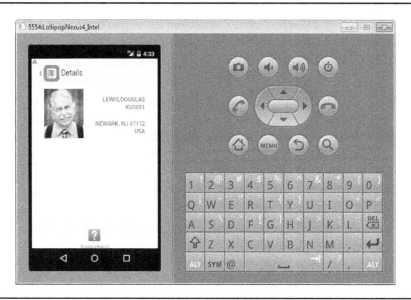

FIGURE 11-25. *Details page part I*

Now is a good time to deploy and test the details page appearance. Your details page should resemble Figure 11-25.

Details Layout Part II Drag a new tableLayout component underneath the first tableLayout. We want this table to appear similar to the first table, so set the width to 100% and the margins to 12px 16px. Later you will learn how to style AMX page content using CSS. This tableLayout is one of the items we will style. To prepare for our future styling needs, set the tableLayout element's styleClass to contactDetails.

This lower tableLayout will have two columns and two rows. The first row will contain the phone number and the second row will contain the employee address. The first column will be a textual representation of the information so a user can copy the text. The text will be two lines tall. The second column will contain a Go Link, which is a special name for a standard hyperlink that launches a task outside of the MAF application. The link in this column will use an icon that is as tall as two lines of text.

To the tableLayout, drag two rowLayout elements. Inside each rowLayout, drag two cellFormat elements. Set the halign of the first cellFormat in each row to start and set the halign of the second cellFormat to end. This will cause the contents of the left column to be left aligned and the right column to be right aligned.

Stay with me, this will get a little confusing. Drag a panelGroupLayout inside the first cellFormat of each row. Set the layout of each panelGroupLayout to vertical. Now drag an outputText element into each panelGroupLayout. Set the value of the first outputText to `Call Phone`. Set the value of the second to `Location`. If you get lost, review the full AMX XML at the end of this section.

Drag the countryCode and phone attributes into row one column one and drag address1 inside row two column one. Place them inside the panelGroupLayout for the corresponding row and choose MAF Output Text as the control type. After JDeveloper creates the appropriate `amx:outputText` elements, combine expression language in the value attributes for the countryCode and phone fields. We want these to look like a normal phone number as shown in the following listing:

```
<amx:outputText value="#{bindings.countryCode.inputValue}
#{bindings.phone.inputValue}" id="ot6"/>
```

Delete the extra amx:outputText after combining the values into a single field. Drag a Link (Go) into the empty cell in each row. Set the URL attribute of the phone row's `amx:goLink` to the same value as the phone's outputText binding with the `tel:` prefix like this: `tel:#{bindings.countryCode.inputValue}`
`#{bindings.phone.inputValue}`. This link will eventually contain an icon rather than text. Rather than using an image we will use FontAwesome, the same icon font we used in our AngularJS application. We will configure FontAwesome later. For now, set the style class to `icon phone-icon`.

The URL for the address `amx:goLink` is similar to the link we used in our AngularJS application: `https://maps.google.com/?q=#{bindings`
`.address1.inputValue}+#{bindings.city.inputValue}+#{bindings`
`.state.inputValue}+#{bindings.postal.inputValue}+#{bindings`
`.country.inputValue}`. As with the phone link, set the style class for the location link to `icon map-marker-icon`.

Deploy the application to an emulator and test your work. The layout should be functional; perhaps not pretty, but functional. Test the links to make sure the phone link opens a dialer and the location link opens a web browser. Figure 11-26 is a screenshot of our work thus far.

The following is a complete listing of the details.amx page:

```
<?xml version="1.0" encoding="UTF-8" ?>
<amx:view xmlns:xsi="http://www.w3.org/2001/XMLSchema-instance"
          xmlns:amx="http://xmlns.oracle.com/adf/mf/amx"
          xmlns:dvtm="http://xmlns.oracle.com/adf/mf/amx/dvt">
  <amx:panelPage id="pp1" inlineStyle="margin:12px 16px;">
    <amx:facet name="header">
      <amx:outputText value="Details" id="ot1"/>
    </amx:facet>
```

```
    <amx:facet name="primary">
      <amx:commandButton id="cb1" action="__back"/>
    </amx:facet>
    <amx:tableLayout id="tl1" width="100%"
                     inlineStyle="margin:12px 16px;">
      <amx:rowLayout id="rl1">
        <amx:cellFormat id="cf1">
          <amx:image id="i1" inlineStyle="width:100px;"
                     source="#{bindings.phototDataUrl.inputValue}"/>
        </amx:cellFormat>
        <amx:cellFormat id="cf2">
          <amx:panelGroupLayout id="pgl1" layout="vertical"
                                halign="end">
            <amx:outputText value="#{bindings.name.inputValue}"
                            id="ot2"
                            styleClass="amx-text-sectiontitle"/>
            <amx:outputText value="#{bindings.emplid.inputValue}"
                            id="ot3"
                            styleClass="amx-text-sectiontitle"/>
            <amx:spacer id="s1" height="20"/>
            <amx:outputText value="#{bindings.city.inputValue},
#{bindings.state.inputValue} #{bindings.postal.inputValue}" id="ot4"
                            styleClass="amx-text-sectiontitle"/>
            <amx:outputText value="#{bindings.country.inputValue}"
                            id="ot7"
                            styleClass="amx-text-sectiontitle"/>
          </amx:panelGroupLayout>
        </amx:cellFormat>
      </amx:rowLayout>
    </amx:tableLayout>
    <amx:tableLayout id="tl2" inlineStyle="margin: 12px 16px;"
                     width="100%" styleClass="contactDetails">
      <amx:rowLayout id="rl2">
        <amx:cellFormat id="cf3" halign="start">
          <amx:panelGroupLayout id="pgl2" layout="vertical">
            <amx:outputText value="Call Phone" id="ot9"/>
            <amx:outputText value="#{bindings.countryCode.inputValue}
#{bindings.phone.inputValue}" id="ot6"/>
          </amx:panelGroupLayout>
        </amx:cellFormat>
        <amx:cellFormat id="cf4" halign="end">
          <amx:goLink text="" id="gl1"
                      url="tel:#{bindings.countryCode.inputValue}
#{bindings.phone.inputValue}"
                      styleClass="icon phone-icon"/>
```

```
          </amx:cellFormat>
        </amx:rowLayout>
        <amx:rowLayout id="rl3">
          <amx:cellFormat id="cf5" halign="start">
            <amx:panelGroupLayout id="pgl3" layout="vertical">
              <amx:outputText value="Location" id="ot10"/>
              <amx:outputText value="#{bindings.address1.inputValue}"
                              id="ot5"/>
            </amx:panelGroupLayout>
          </amx:cellFormat>
          <amx:cellFormat id="cf6" halign="end">
            <amx:goLink text="" id="gl2"
                        url="https://maps.google.com/?
q=#{bindings.address1.inputValue}+#{bindings.city.inputValue}
+#{bindings.state.inputValue}+#{bindings.postal.inputValue}+
#{bindings.country.inputValue}"
                        styleClass="icon map-marker-icon"/>
          </amx:cellFormat>
        </amx:rowLayout>
      </amx:tableLayout>
    </amx:panelPage>
</amx:view>
```

FIGURE 11-26. *Details page part II*

Changing the Appearance with FontAwesome

The search button on our search page should have a magnifying glass and the details page needs icons for the two amx:goLink elements. As you learned in Chapter 6, FontAwesome is a great way to add icons to HTML elements. There are two ways to add FontAwesome to an MAF project:

- Globally, by extending the MAF skin

- Local to a feature, by adding FontAwesome CSS to an individual feature within the maf-feature.xml file

We will take the first approach and extend the default skin. Download a fresh copy of FontAwesome from http://fortawesome.github.io/Font-Awesome/ and expand the archive into your ApplicationController public_html directory. On my laptop, the public_html folder is in C:\JDeveloper\mywork\PersonnelDirectory\ApplicationController\public_html. Expanding the archive will create css and fonts subdirectories.

Return to JDeveloper and expand the Application Resources palette. Look for the Descriptors node and then expand it and the ADF META-INF child node. This will reveal the maf-config.xml file. Double-click this file to open it and look for the default skin family and version. You will need the values from these nodes to extend the default skin. My maf-config.xml file contains these values (values in bold):

```
<skin-family>mobileAlta</skin-family>
<skin-version>v1.3</skin-version>
```

From the Projects Explorer in JDeveloper, expand the ApplicationController/ Application Sources/META-INF node and open the maf-skins.xml file. Drag a skin-addition element from the components palette into the adfmf-skins element. JDeveloper will prompt for a skin-id and a style-sheet-name. The skin-id is a concatenation of the default skin-family and skin-version. My value based on my maf-config.xml file is mobileAlta-v1.3 (skin-family-skin-version). Enter the path and name of the FontAwesome CSS file into the style-sheet-name field. Since we copied the FontAwesome files to public_html, the style-sheet-name value should be css/font-awesome.min.css. MAF will now add the font-awesome.min.css file to the head element of every AMX page in our application. The following code listing contains the contents of my maf-skins.xml file:

```
<?xml version="1.0" encoding="UTF-8" ?>
<adfmf-skins xmlns="http://xmlns.oracle.com/adf/mf/skin">
  <skin-addition id="s1">
    <skin-id>mobileAlta-v1.3</skin-id>
    <style-sheet-name>css/font-awesome.min.css</style-sheet-name>
  </skin-addition>
</adfmf-skins>
```

NOTE
We won't actually be using the fa and fa-* classes directly. In fact, the only part of the font-awesome .min.css file we will actually use is the font declarations. Rather than extend the MAF skin, we could achieve the same affect by adding the FontAwesome font declarations directly to a feature-specific CSS file.

Now we need to add some custom CSS to our feature to configure the search button and details links. Back in the ViewController project, right-click on the Web Content node and choose New | CSS File. Name the new CSS file `search.css`. Delete any content JDeveloper added to search.css before continuing.

Next, we need to associate the new search.css file with the AMX Task Flow. Open the maf-feature.xml file and switch to the Content tab. Locate the Includes section and click the green plus sign to add a new resource. In the Insert Includes dialog, select Stylesheet as the type and then select the resources/css/search.css file. Figure 11-27 is a screenshot of the Task Flow after adding search.css to the Includes section.

Styling the Search Page   Let's add some CSS that will display a magnifying glass next to the search button. Open the search.css file and insert the following:

```css
.amx-commandButton.search-icon .amx-commandButton-label:before {
    content: "\f002";
    font-family: FontAwesome;
    padding-right: 1rem;
}
```

This CSS uses FontAwesome along with a Unicode sequence to display a magnifying glass icon at the beginning of any button with the class `search-icon`. The only problem is that we don't have any buttons that use the class `search-icon`. Let's remedy that now. Open the search.amx file and locate the search button within the primary facet. Set the styleClass to `search-icon`. The `amx:commandButton` will now contain the following markup:

```xml
<amx:commandButton id="cb1" text="Search" action="search"
                   styleClass="search-icon">
```

Redeploy your application and confirm that the search page search button contains a magnifying glass icon.

NOTE
If you don't see the magnifying glass or don't see it where you expect, use the Chrome's remote inspector, which was described earlier, to identify the reason.

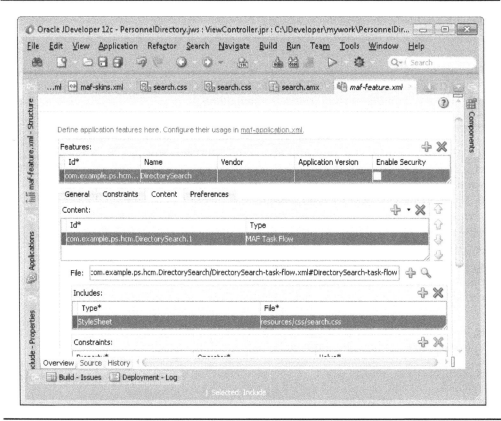

FIGURE 11-27. *Task Flow after adding search.css*

Styling the Details Page   Now let's style the lower table of the details page. This will require a little more CSS. First, let's add a border under each of the cells as well as some extra padding. Add the following CSS to search.css:

```
.amx-tableLayout.contactDetails .amx-cellFormat {
    border-bottom: 1px solid #C8D7E0 !important;
    padding: 1em 0;
}
```

NOTE
The CSS above uses `!important`. *Never use* `!important`...*unless it is the only way to override someone else's CSS.*

Next, let's style the icons within the lower table. Add the following CSS to search.css:

```
.amx-goLink.icon {
    font-size: 2.5em;
    text-decoration: none;
}

.amx-goLink.icon:after {
    content: "\f095";
    font-family: FontAwesome;
}

.amx-goLink.phone-icon:after {
    content: "\f095";
}

.amx-goLink.map-marker-icon:after {
    content: "\f041";
}
```

The first two declarations set the appearance of each icon and the second two determine the actual icon.

NOTE
Need to figure out the Unicode sequence for each FontAwesome icon? Visit the FontAwesome cheat sheet at http://fortawesome.github.io/Font-Awesome/cheatsheet/.

One last thing…we need to delete the goLink1 and goLink2 text from the details.amx page. Open the details.amx page and look for the `amx:goLink` elements. Delete the contents of the text attributes. Each goLink should now start with the following:

```
<amx:goLink text="" id="gl1"...
```

Redeploy your application. The search and details pages should now resemble Figure 11-28.

Implementing Additional Routes

Our TaskFlow defines routes on the results and details views but we haven't provided a way to invoke those routes. Our jQuery Mobile and AngularJS implementations from Chapters 5 and 6 used a panel drawer pattern and "hamburger" menu for navigation. This time we will use the AMX footer facet with FontAwesome icons and a little extra CSS.

FIGURE 11-28. *The search and details pages*

Each view has a different number of routes. The search view, for example, only has one route, search, and that route is already implemented. Remember the profile route from the prior chapters? We didn't implement it in this chapter. Let's add a profile route placeholder button to the search view. Open search.amx, identify the `amx:panelPage`, and right-click on the element. When the context menu appears, choose Facets - Panel Page | Footer. This will add a footer facet to the end of the panelPage definition. Place a tableLayout inside the footer facet and set the width to 100%. While still editing the tableLayout, set the styleClass to `footer-layout`. Add a rowLayout and a cellFormat to the tableLayout. Set the `amx:cellFormat` element's halign to `center` and valign to `middle`. Finally, add a button to the `amx:cellFormat`. Clear the button's text attribute and set the styleClass to `profile-icon`. Here is a complete listing of the footer's XML:

```
<amx:facet name="footer">
  <amx:tableLayout id="tl1" styleClass="footer-layout" width="100%">
    <amx:rowLayout id="rl1">
      <amx:cellFormat id="cf1" halign="center" valign="middle">
        <amx:commandButton text="" id="cb2" styleClass="profile-icon"/>
      </amx:cellFormat>
    </amx:rowLayout>
  </amx:tableLayout>
</amx:facet>
```

Now let's add some CSS to search.css to style the footer. Besides adding function-specific icons to buttons, this CSS rounds the corners on the footer's buttons as well applying a minor change to the background color.

```css
/* footer styles */
.footer-layout .amx-commandButton {
    border-radius: 30px;
    background-image: none;
    background-color: #cfcfcf;
}

.footer-layout .amx-commandButton.amx-selected {
    background-color: #afafaf;
}

.footer-layout .amx-commandButton .amx-commandButton-label:before {
    display: inline-block;
    font-family: FontAwesome;
    min-width: 25px;
    padding: 0;
}

.footer-layout .amx-commandButton.profile-icon
.amx-commandButton-label:before {
    content: "\f007";
}

.footer-layout .amx-commandButton.search-icon
.amx-commandButton-label:before {
    content: "\f002";
}

.footer-layout .amx-commandButton.list-icon
.amx-commandButton-label:before {
    content: "\f03a";
    padding-top: 2px;
}
```

NOTE
The CSS above contains declarations for each icon,
not just the profile icon.

Redeploy the application and confirm that the profile button appears in the footer of the search page. If it doesn't, then use Chrome's inspector tools to figure out why the CSS isn't working properly.

If all is well, copy the footer facet into the results.amx page. This page needs an icon that returns to the search page. Add an `amx:cellFormat` and `amx:commandButton` to the footer facet and configure them as before. Instead of using the `profile-icon` class, set the styleClass attribute to `search-icon`. Since we actually want this button to go somewhere, set the action attribute to `returnToSearch`.

```
<amx:facet name="footer">
  <amx:tableLayout id="tl1" styleClass="footer-layout"
                   width="100%">
    <amx:rowLayout id="rl1">
      <amx:cellFormat id="cf2" halign="center" valign="middle">
        <amx:commandButton text="" id="cb3"
                           styleClass="search-icon"
                           action="returnToSearch"/>
      </amx:cellFormat>
      <amx:cellFormat id="cf1" halign="center" valign="middle">
        <amx:commandButton text="" id="cb2"
                           styleClass="profile-icon"/>
      </amx:cellFormat>
    </amx:rowLayout>
  </amx:tableLayout>
</amx:facet>
```

NOTE
I find it easiest to copy the prior cellFormat and then use the bubble/balloon help to create unique IDs for the cloned elements.

Copy the expanded footer from the results page into the details.amx page. When the red error balloons appear in the left-hand gutter, click them and choose Generate a unique ID from the context menu. Since the details page uses a table layout, those auto-generated IDs already exist. Once again, add another button. This final button returns to the search results list so set its action to `returnToList` and its styleClass to list-icon.

Redeploy the application and verify the results. Do you see that interesting icon at the bottom of every page that is labeled PersonnelDirectory? That is a navigation bar that contains a link to each feature within an application. MAF displays this by default. Since we only have one feature within this application, let's turn it off. From the Application Resources palette, identify the Descriptors/ADF META-INF node and open the maf-application.xml file. Scroll to the Navigation section at the bottom of the file and uncheck the Show Navigation Bar on Application Launch checkbox. Figure 11-29 is a final screenshot of the details page.

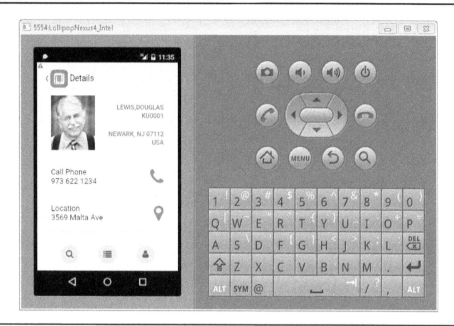

FIGURE 11-29.   *Final screenshot of the details page*

Conclusion

In this chapter, you learned how to build hybrid mobile applications using Oracle's declarative, multidevice Mobile Application Framework. This platform is extremely powerful, flexible, and efficient. Unlike the other approaches described in Parts II and III of this book, most of our work with MAF was declarative.

For extra credit, I encourage you to continue the work started in this chapter by creating a profile Task Flow for editing personal profiles. The tutorial at http://docs .oracle.com/cd/E53569_01/tutorials/tut_jdev_maf_app/tut_jdev_maf_app_2.html contains a great example of using the device camera in MAF.

If you are new to MAF and would like more information, then I highly encourage you to visit Oracle Mobile Platform YouTube channel located at https://www.youtube .com/user/OracleMobilePlatform. MAF contains a significant amount of features including enterprise specific security features that you may find of interest.

Now go build something meaningful!

Index

D

N

O

Join the Largest Tech Community in the World

 Download the latest software, tools, and developer templates

 Get exclusive access to hands-on trainings and workshops

 Grow your professional network through the Oracle ACE Program

 Publish your technical articles – and get paid to share your expertise

Join the Oracle Technology Network
Membership is free. Visit oracle.com/technetwork

@OracleOTN   facebook.com/OracleTechnologyNetwork

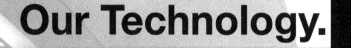

Beta Test Oracle Software

Get a first look at our newest products—and help perfect them. You must meet the following criteria:

- ✔ Licensed Oracle customer or Oracle PartnerNetwork member

- ✔ Oracle software expert

- ✔ Early adopter of Oracle products

Please apply at: pdpm.oracle.com/BPO/userprofile

If your interests match upcoming activities, we'll contact you. Profiles are kept on file for 12 months.